General William E. DePuy

American Warriors

Throughout the nation's history, numerous men and women of all ranks and branches of the United States military have served their country with honor and distinction. During times of war and peace, there are individuals whose exemplary achievements embody the highest standards of the U.S. armed forces. The aim of the American Warriors series is to examine the unique historical contributions of these individuals, whose legacies serve as enduring examples for soldiers and citizens alike. The series will promote a deeper and more comprehensive understanding of the U.S. armed forces.

Series editor: Roger A. Cirillo

An AUSA Book

GENERAL WILLIAM E. DePUY

Preparing the Army for Modern War

HENRY G. GOLE

With a foreword by
Major General William A. Stofft,
U.S. Army (Ret.)

THE UNIVERSITY PRESS OF KENTUCKY

Scholarly publisher for the Commonwealth,
serving Bellarmine University, Berea College, Centre College of Kentucky,
Eastern Kentucky University, The Filson Historical Society, Georgetown
College, Kentucky Historical Society, Kentucky State University,
Morehead State University, Murray State University, Northern Kentucky
University, Transylvania University, University of Kentucky, University
of Louisville, and Western Kentucky University.
All rights reserved.

Editorial and Sales Offices: The University Press of Kentucky
663 South Limestone Street, Lexington, Kentucky 40508-4008
www.kentuckypress.com

Photos, unless otherwise stated, from the DePuy Family Collection
Maps by Donna Gilbreath

12 11 10 09 08   5 4 3 2 1

Library of Congress Cataloging-in-Publication Data

Gole, Henry G., 1933-
  General William E. Depuy : preparing the Army for modern war / Henry G.
Gole ; with a foreword by William A. Stofft.
     p. cm. — (American warriors)
  "An AUSA book."
  Includes bibliographical references and index.
  ISBN 978-0-8131-2500-8 (hbk. : alk. paper)
  1. DePuy, William E. (William Eugene), 1919-1992 2. United States. Army—
Officers—Biography. 3. United States. Army—History—20th century.
4. Generals—United States—Biography. 5. Military education—United
States—History—20th century. 6. United States. Army Training and Doctrine
Command—History—20th century. I. Title.
  U53.D46G65 2008
  355.0092--dc22
  [B]   2008028002

This book is printed on acid-free recycled paper meeting
the requirements of the American National Standard
for Permanence in Paper for Printed Library Materials.

Manufactured in the United States of America.

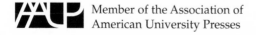

Member of the Association of
American University Presses

To the professional American soldiers
whose loyalty and dedication carried them
through the bad times and enabled them
to fix our severely troubled post-Vietnam Army.

Contents

Illustrations follow page 142

Foreword

Everyone likes a good story. And this is a really good story, about a young man from the Dakotas named Bill DePuy, who graduates from South Dakota State College in 1941 with an ROTC commission, just in time for the "good war."

Before the war ended, he had been an integral part of the transformation of a U.S. Army fighting division—the 90th—from one of the worst in the European Theater to perhaps its best. He trained with the division for over two years and helped take it to England and then Normandy as a young officer, where he watched it struggle in the hedgerows and waste hundreds of its soldiers at the hands of poor leaders. He then spent the rest of the 308 days the division fought ensuring that his part of the team fought well and no soldier was ever wasted. He started the war as a green lieutenant and finished it as the division G-3 and a lieutenant colonel, having commanded a battalion and earned the Distinguished Service Cross and three Silver Stars, all before his twenty-sixth birthday.

DePuy mastered his profession first at the "sharp end of the spear," where the killing and the dying takes place. He learned that squads, platoons, and companies make war on enemy squads, platoons, and companies. If an army can do that well, it stands a chance of winning. If not—well, in the vernacular, "Don't go there." This became his "first principle," and he spent the rest of his life building on that certain truth: war is about battle and knowing how to fight means knowing how to wage war successfully.

A number of terrific leaders surfaced in the 90th Division, starting with MG Ray McClain at the top. But DePuy made an immediate and important contribution from the first day wherever he served in the division. His experiences—especially in the first battles—seared his soul and changed his life.

There would be no second-generation DePuy in the bank back home in Brookings, South Dakota. Bill DePuy would be a soldier in America's Army until his last day. How lucky for the Army and the country.

When Henry Gole was thinking about doing this biography, he asked: Do we need it and is there sufficient evidence? Getting a yes to both those questions was the easy part. The real art of good biography comes in getting it right and telling it well. He has done both.

This is a wonderful biography of an important soldier, set in America in the context of the world in which America and its army found itself in the last half of the twentieth century. This story is about how one man in a large, complex, and conservative institution, the United States Army, became the leader almost universally seen as the one who fixed a broken army after Vietnam and set it on a path to being the best on the planet, the "gold standard" army, the model for excellence in the profession of arms.

The final chapters of the history of America's army in the twentieth century were written in the Gulf War and the Balkans. Both operations were conducted by an army that had evolved according to DePuy's plan—in doctrine, organization, training, leader development, and equipment—and they bear his personal stamp, as do the hundreds of Army leaders he trained, taught, developed, encouraged, led, and inspired. The story of his capstone tour as Commander of the newly formed Training and Doctrine Command (TRADOC) is appropriately near the end of the book. In that job, the one DePuy seemed preordained to hold, the path is set for the post-Vietnam Army to right itself and organize for victory.

Gole weaves a superb story out of the years between the war of DePuy's youth and the heady days of four-star command. DePuy's complex nature, the constant challenges of his times, and the demands of his Army developed, shaped, and prepared him for each succeeding opportunity. A list of the places he served and soldiered in the middle part of his career is remarkable for the breadth and the achievement it reflects. Consider the schools:

U.S. Army Command and General Staff College at Leavenworth
Armed Forces Staff College at Norfolk
Imperial Defence College in London
Language school at Monterey learning Russian

and the positions:

Assistant Military Attaché in Hungary
Enlisted Personnel Management directorate on the Army Staff

Two years with the CIA with duties highly classified
Two years evaluating battalion level training in Germany
Command of a second battalion and later a Battle Group in
     Germany
Three years in the Office of the Army Chief of Staff
Director of Special Warfare, ODCSOPS
Director of Plans and Programs on the Army Staff
J-3 (operations officer) of the Military Assistance Command,
     Vietnam
Command of the 1st Infantry Division in Vietnam
Special Assistant for Counterinsurgency and Special Activities
     in the Office of the Secretary of Defense
Assistant Vice Chief of Staff on the Army Staff

These read like a litany of important assignments, sought after
and prized—and they were. But it was DePuy's relentlessness in the
pursuit of excellence that caused his contributions to be consistently
recognized as unique and important in every assignment from the
start of his career. He got things done everywhere he went, in part
because he was smart, dedicated, and able to focus like a laser on
what was important in the issue at hand. He was an organizer and a
finisher who thrived on complexity, simultaneity, and sorting things
out, a man of ideas and a man of action. DePuy recognized talent in
others, sought and demanded excellence in peers and subordinates,
and was a consummate teacher in every assignment. So it wasn't
getting these posts that mattered, it was the quality of the performance once in them that propelled him along and prepared him for
the next key job.
   Highfield was and remains the family retreat in the splendor of
Marjory DePuy's native Virginia countryside. It is a beautiful place,
the family home that the DePuys all loved, individually and together. The grapes grown nearby make pleasant wine. The DePuys'
neighbors were and are their friends. The wildflowers are perfect
and too appealing not to study carefully, if you were Bill DePuy. It is
a happy place for a loving family, like everywhere they lived along
the way. Moreover, it is central and important to each member of
the family, as was their love and affection for one another throughout their lives. This is as important a part of the story of this Army
leader as any other, and is consistent from beginning to end.
   Here is a great story told by a master storyteller who is also a

superb historian. Bill DePuy, his Army, and the country they served come alive in this book. As DePuy sought to bring clarity and precision to the features on the face of future battle, Henry Gole has done the same for him.

William A. Stofft
Major General (Ret.), U.S. Army;
former Chief of Military History
and former Commandant, U.S. Army War College

Preface

When I was invited to write the biography of General William E. DePuy, I asked myself two questions. Do we need a DePuy biography? Is there sufficient evidence to do a proper job? The answers are yes and yes.

DePuy is the central figure in the transformation of the United States Army after the American war in Vietnam. As a soldier I saw the Army change from a demoralized institution in the early 1970s to a force that was prepared to fight and win the next war. But that was only a general impression. The research and analysis I would need to do in order to write the biography of a man at the center of that change would help me understand what and how such change had happened. As a historian, I knew that most individuals at any time are so focused on doing their jobs and living their lives that they lack the perspective to note that the trees in their view comprise a large forest. For example, though I lived through the 1960s, I confess that, nearly fifty years later, I'm still puzzling out what the events of that time mean. The prospect of examining how events from World War II through the first Gulf War shaped "my" Army and learning how DePuy was both formed by and shaped his Army attracted me.

Documentary and living sources are available, though the ranks of the latter thin with each passing day. At least two of the people I interviewed, Ed Hamilton (LTC, USA, Ret.), a World War II and CIA colleague of DePuy's, and Jeannie Mattison Rotz, a high-school classmate and friend, have died since I began this project. The Military History Institute (MHI) in Carlisle, Pennsylvania, is the mother lode for documents bearing on my subject. The DePuy Papers and DePuy Oral History are found at MHI, as are oral histories and papers of many senior officers who knew and interacted with General DePuy. Surveys of veterans, documents from World War II to the twenty-first century, and expert guidance by the staff made MHI my base camp in this effort.

MHI holdings were supplemented by the DePuy Family Papers; the holdings at the U.S. Army Center of Military History at Fort Lesley J. McNair, Washington, D.C.; and the archives maintained at the Military History Office, Training and Doctrine Command (TRADOC) at Fort Monroe, Virginia. Peers, contemporaries, aides, former subordinates, close observers, and DePuy's children, William, Joslin, and Daphne, made themselves available to me. A surprising number of military friends and colleagues came out of the woodwork with firsthand knowledge of General DePuy as they learned what I was doing.

So I took on the challenge of this biography, deliberately setting aside a question posed by German army captain Adolf von Schell in his little classic, *Battle Leadership,* "How shall we speak about the souls of others when we do not even know our own?" as well as Sigmund Freud's dismal pronouncement, "Whoever undertakes to write a biography binds himself to lying, to concealment, to flummery. . . . Truth is not accessible."[1]

From the beginning, I was keenly aware that biographers risk loss of objectivity. It is easy to become defensive as one's subject, once a stranger, becomes a friend or a caricature of unblemished virtue. There is an inclination to explain away faults, to flatter. Conversely, one could come to despise the subject or, worse, take on the project intending to do a hatchet job. I hope the reader finds that I did neither, that this biography is a balanced portrayal. DePuy was a man of rare intelligence, lucid expression, intense focus, and exemplary dedication to his Army and to his country. His career, particularly its culmination as Commanding General, TRADOC, benefited both. Yet DePuy was not without flaws. The very qualities that produced results also made him, by his own admission, a very impatient man. Making important decisions almost certainly guarantees that one will also make enemies. Leading is not for the squeamish. DePuy did not suffer fools gladly.

Historian Russell F. Weigley described the time of World War II and the Cold War as a period "when, personal doubts and much controversy notwithstanding, the world really did depend on that country [the United States] and those armed forces for the preservation of freedom."[2] DePuy came to maturity and played an important role in "those armed forces."

The book is chronological, describing DePuy's life from youth to death with emphasis on his military career. Strict chronology is interrupted by brief excursions into events that shaped him as a young man and influenced his later thinking. A life, like a graph of economic performance, has a long-term trend line that includes peaks and valleys of events along that trend line. My excursions are a way to connect or amplify some of the peaks and valleys in DePuy's life, a way to manage simultaneity. Many things take place at the same time in a person's life, but a written chronicle must describe and analyze them one at a time.

The purpose of these excursions is to shed light on DePuy's thinking, actions, and development, not to resolve the professional issues he addressed, many of which were contentious at the time and are still debated. For example, DePuy's account of combat in Europe from June 1944 to May 1945 derives directly from his personal experiences in the 90th Infantry Division, an organization that was transformed in the course of the war from "a problem division" to a very good one. Whether the 90th was unique or fairly representative of the learning curve of American infantry divisions in Europe is the subject of analysis by a new generation of military historians. But the focus of this biography is how DePuy's experience in World War II shaped him, not to settle this larger issue.

Similarly, DePuy's detail to the Central Intelligence Agency (CIA) during the Korean War raises doubts about the competence and effectiveness of that Agency. But DePuy, not the CIA, is our subject.

In the late 1950s, as a new colonel assigned to a cell working political-military issues for the Office, Chief of Staff, Army (OCSA), DePuy found himself in the midst of acrimonious confrontations among the services regarding role and mission, massive retaliation and flexible response. These larger issues deserve serious study, but our aim in raising them is to show how his experience of the late 1950s prepared Colonel DePuy to address Army issues of the 1970s.

DePuy was deeply engaged in Vietnam from 1962 to 1969 and in improving the post-Vietnam U.S. Army from 1969 until he retired in 1977. In these last two assignments and later, he was in the middle of what has been called a revolution in military affairs. He saw the task of the professional soldier as a never-ending process, a kind of permanent revolution: preparing for the next war. The major issues DePuy was concerned with in getting the Army ready to fight the next war—management, training, doctrine, combat developments—have produced a considerable literature. So have other issues in the post-Vietnam Army: the end of conscription, the need to recruit and retain an all-volunteer force, NCO education, the opening of many new fields to women soldiers, and the problem of a demoralized Army shrinking in size. Events in American society during those years were equally momentous: social disorder, a failed presidency, and the ignominious end of the Vietnam War. Moreover, the lethality of the 1973 Yom Kippur War, fought largely with American and Soviet weapons systems and begun from a standing start, returned the attention of American planners to preparation for war in Europe.

A biography of reasonable length for a general audience can allude to such larger issues, but it cannot discuss in great detail the many events that touched DePuy's life. Endnotes and a selected bibliography are provided to assist readers who wish to pursue issues in greater depth.

In retrospect, DePuy's life (1919–1992) and military career (1941–1977) seem foreordained to take him to the top ranks of the Army, as though his life was designed to be precisely what it was. But General DePuy, like the rest of us, did not know how his life would play out nor how it would end. He did his best; he made great contributions to his Army; and he derived deep satisfaction in knowing what he had accomplished.

Acknowledgments

For each person named here, there were two or three anonymous angels who floated through archival stacks, strained their eyes, and taxed their knowledge while running down answers to my questions.

I turned first to John F. Votaw, executive director of the Cantigny First Division Foundation, for his knowledge of the Big Red One, commanded by General DePuy in Vietnam. Financial assistance for some travel for interviews, copying, and mailing was a happy by-product. Paul H. Herbert succeeded John as executive director, continued support, and read a rough draft of my manuscript. His comments were particularly useful in improving the World War II portion of the book. My Cantigny connections put me in contact with an old friend from our teaching days at West Point, James Scott Wheeler, who was well along with his *The Big Red One*, published in 2007 by the University Press of Kansas. Scott permitted me to read and cite from his manuscript before it was published.

Frank Shirer, branch chief of the Historical Resources Branch, Center of Military History, United States Army, spared me several trips to Washington by responding to my requests for materials and sending them to me.

The DePuy family was generous in lending me several boxes of General DePuy's papers, many of which were not to be found elsewhere. The general's children, William E. DePuy Jr., Daphne DePuy, and Joslin DePuy Gallatin, made themselves available for detailed interviews, providing unique insights into family life and the personal side of General DePuy that is generally not revealed outside of the small circle of family and friends. The interviews with Joslin and Daphne were at Highfield, the family retreat where General DePuy lived from 1977 to 1992. Some of the interviews were conducted at the round kitchen table where General DePuy often drafted ideas, letters, articles, and instructions on legal pads.

I am grateful for the institution, holdings, and admirable professional staff of the United States Military History Institute, particularly for the knowledge and constant support and encouragement of Dave Keough, Dick Sommers, and Louise Arnold-Friend in this latest effort and over the years. Tom Hendrix solved almost all of my problems in recording and transcribing the interviews I conducted. At the risk of overlooking other anonymous angels, I thank Marty Andreson, Rich Baker, Art Bergeron, Tom Buffenbarger, Steve Bye, Pam Cheney, Jack Giblin, Vicki Johnson, Shaun Kirkpatrick, Diana Leonard, Mike Lynch, Jim McNally, Randy Rakers, and Pam Wiwel, all of whom assisted me with my DePuy project. Reference librarian Ginny Shope of the U.S. Army War College Library helped me in this project and in many others.

Special thanks to Reg Shrader, who listened to my scheming and false starts from beginning to end, and to Ken Robertson, Bill Gole, and Lydia Gole, who gave advice when I sought it and read some ugly early drafting. Thanks to sharp-eyed editor Tom Bowers and reliable cornerman Roger Cirillo, both of whom have had a hand in shaping *The Road to Rainbow* (2003), *Soldiering* (2005), and the current DePuy biography.

Tony Nadal facilitated access to valuable human sources. Bob Sorley was generous in his general support and in sharing with me specific sources he uncovered in his always scrupulous research. Mac Coffman, Allan Millett, Roger Spiller, and Rick Swain—historians I admire—took time from their own work to read and comment on my work, and they improved it.

In interviews and discussions, Paul Gorman, Paul Miles, Lloyd Matthews, Rick Brown, Rick Swain, John Stewart, and Bill DePuy Jr. did more than provide essential information; they also asked questions that I needed to answer to put raw information in perspective. I am grateful for the willing cooperation and support of the busy people named.

Steve Wrinn and the staff of the University Press of Kentucky were orderly, efficient, and kind, making the experience of addressing a series of little issues pleasant rather than overwhelming. I acknowledge my respect for and gratitude to Donna Bouvier, my first-rate copyeditor. Her love of our language and her ability to represent the general reader made my book better.

1

Dakota Days

He came, he saw, he conquered.
—Caption to William E. DePuy's high school
graduation photo

"Happy Days Are Here Again" and "A Pretty Girl Is Like a Melody" were first sung in 1919, the latter in the Ziegfeld Follies of that year. But they were sung without the stimulation of legal booze, for the Nineteenth Amendment to the U.S. Constitution began the Prohibition Era that same year. Also in 1919, the Treaty of Versailles was signed, reshaping the map of Europe and insuring Germany's becoming a dissatisfied power; the League of Nations was established without the United States; and *Ten Days That Shook the World,* John Reed's ecstatic account of the 1917 Bolshevik Revolution, was published.

William E. DePuy was born that year, in Jamestown, North Dakota, on 1 October 1919. Later, when he was a teenager, he moved with his family to Brookings, South Dakota, where he was graduated from high school in 1937 and college in 1941.

DePuy was probably taking his first steps in 1920 when Japan received the Caroline, Marshall, and Mariana Islands, formerly German colonies, as mandates from the League of Nations. They sat astride the sea route between Hawaii and the Philippines. If fortified and used for sea and air bases, these islands would pose a threat to a fleet steaming from Hawaii or California to relieve or reinforce the U.S. garrison in the Philippines. Between 1919 and 1941, German and Japanese influence in Europe and in the Pacific and Far East grew as the United States learned that it could not remain uninvolved in international politics.

The degree to which events in faraway places affected the thinking of American youth in high schools and colleges on the high plains in the 1930s is difficult to ascertain. We know that American interest in world politics faded after the Great War and President Woodrow

Wilson's triumphal trip to Paris. The great adventure "over there" was done. Wilson, the architect of the League of Nations, could not persuade his own countrymen to join it. The critical issue was sovereignty, a concern that League membership might allow foreigners to take Americans to war. To many Americans observing the results of peacemaking in 1919, it seemed that the Europeans were behaving in their bad old grasping ways. They divided the spoils. Realpolitik was alive and well. The general inclination of Americans was to revert to form: to avoid entangling alliances, to live in happy isolation on a continent that was rich, secure, and American. Doubts arose about the wisdom of American involvement in the Great War. Questions regarding war profiteering convinced some that the war had been fought for the profit of munitions makers.

The Great War had exhausted Europe. There was a general sense that there would not be another major war for a long time. In any event, there was a tradition in the United States of generally avoiding the maintenance of a large standing army in peacetime. That predisposition, along with the feeling that participation in the Great War might have been a mistake, created a political climate conducive to slashing the military budget. There was another reason as well: no enemy threatened the United States.

War Department expenditures from 1922 through 1935 remained below $500 million per year. From 1936, when Bill DePuy was a high school junior and tensions were rising in Europe, to 1940, expenditures climbed from $600 million to about $900 million, reaching almost $4 billion in 1941, the year Bill DePuy graduated from college, and $50 billion in 1945.

Army personnel strength paralleled expenditures. From an active duty strength of 2.5 million in 1918, the numbers from the early 1920s to 1935 hovered at about 140,000. From 1936 until 1940, these numbers climbed steadily, from 168,000 to 270,000. War clouds brought peacetime conscription to America for the first time, and the National Guard and Army Reserve were mobilized for a year of training. In 1941, almost 1.5 million men wore army uniforms.

The drop in the funding and manning of the Navy and Marine Corps after the Great War roughly paralleled those of the Army. In the 1920s and 1930s, the Navy bottomed out at 80,000 men and the Marine Corps at 17,000.

The American military was second- or even third-rate, and its leaders knew it. In 1932, former Army Chief of Staff Peyton C. March called the army "impotent." In 1933, Chief of Staff Douglas MacArthur said that the U.S. Army ranked seventeenth in the world in strength, adding that his tanks were useless for combat with a modern foe. In his message to Congress on 28 January 1938, President Franklin D. Roosevelt described our national defense as inadequate for purposes of national security, requiring increase. Almost a year later, the General Staff concurred in a War Plans Division study stating that the United States didn't have a single complete division in its army, while Germany had ninety and Italy forty-five. Japan had fifty divisions actively employed *on the China mainland.* Outgoing Army Chief of Staff Malin Craig lamented in 1939 that time is the only thing that may be irrevocably lost, because sums appropriated in 1939 would not be fully transformed into military power for two years. Finally, Army Chief of Staff George C. Marshall, appointed to that position on 1 September 1939, the day the Germans invaded Poland to begin the shooting war, said in his annual report that the army was "ineffective," a damning word in the military lexicon.[1]

Rapid transformation of the military from a small peacetime establishment to a larger force ready for war was in the American tradition of expansion in time of need. Broad oceans and weak neighbors provided the United States with a buffer and time to prepare for emergencies. Rapid expansion, however, necessarily resulted in inefficiencies and waste. The accomplishments of American industry in the production and distribution of war supplies for the Second World War was nothing less than astounding. Ships, aircraft, guns, and tanks poured from American factories, to be shipped to American forces and allies in every corner of the globe.

But there was a hitch. There was a shortage of competent military leaders for the rapidly and vastly expanded military establishment. There were leaders to herd millions of civilians to war, but there were not enough skilled leaders to train them to become effective soldiers and to show them initial success in battle with reasonable losses. Bill DePuy would be directly involved in an expensive learning curve.

Family lore has it that Bill DePuy's grandfather, a medical doctor, was on a train en route to the west coast with his brother when he was asked to get off to treat victims of a cholera epidemic in Bismarck, North Dakota. He never got back on the train. It is also claimed that DePuy's grandfather was Sitting Bull's personal physician.

DePuy's father, from French Huguenot roots, and his mother, from Scots-Irish origins via Canada, get high marks from their son as good parents. Bill, like his father, was an only child. He called his living grandfather "a Victorian romantic, golfer, and hunter" and "my closest friend." He adds, "My other companions were books." But, he said, "I was never particularly fond of school," a remark that gives one pause.[2] What and how one learns would become central to his work as schoolmaster of the Army. Despite success in school and the high opinion of others regarding his academic skills and high intelligence, DePuy preferred to come up with questions of interest to himself and puzzle them out on his own. This autonomy fully emerged later, in his professional life.

Looking back seventy years, Wayne Waltz recalled precisely when he first came into direct contact with Bill DePuy. Bill, a new kid, walked into a high school study hall at the beginning of their junior year in 1935. From then on, Waltz said, they were "fast friends" for life.

Many years later Waltz, who remained in South Dakota, brought his family east to meet Bill's family, and Bill took his family back to Brookings, where his widowed mother resided. These visits gave the two old friends the opportunity to reminisce about high school and college days and do some pheasant hunting. It enabled the DePuy children to get to know South Dakota, where they have returned for fishing and family holidays over the years.[3] The DePuy-Waltz connection continued until Bill's terminal illness in the late 1980s.[4]

Waltz remembers that Bill DePuy blended into the social life of the high school crowd as though he were born in Brookings. Bill spent a lot of time with Wayne and his two brothers, making the Waltz house their base of operations. The Waltz boys had a car, so Bill would chip in with the Waltz boys and some other friends to pay a princely sum of fifteen cents for a gallon of gas for cruising. Kerosene could be found in someone's basement or kitchen when funds were low. Instead of a grand tour in Europe, upon their 1937 graduation from high school Wayne and Bill set out by car for Canada via Jamestown, North Dakota, Bill's birthplace and a pit stop where cousins fed and put a roof over the heads of the financially strapped adventurers. Wayne had gotten permission to use the new family Ford V-8, but paying for gas was a problem that resulted in a curtailed graduation trip.

Bill DePuy's high school career had been a success by any standard. He was a good student, was a member of the debate team, performed in a play in his junior year, was senior class president, and played football. "I had the unusual job of quarterbacking my high school football team even though I only weighed 128 pounds," DePuy recalled. "I would run the ball—I could call the signals that let me run. That's hard to beat."

Cracking the small town cliques as a football player of less-than–Bronko Nagurski proportions, becoming editor of the yearbook, and winning election as class president after just a year with his classmates indicates impressive social skills. Waltz called Bill "a nervous, jumpy type." Modern jargon would probably describe him as "active" or "slightly hyper." Later, "intense" or "focused" were the words most often used to describe him. He plunged into the teenage social circuit with an unusual blend of confidence and modesty.

Waltz recalled that their crowd liked to dance, no one more than Bill, an activity he continued to enjoy for the rest of his life. Some eight or nine miles from Brookings was a lakeside food and drink hangout with a tolerant proprietor, where a circle of boys and girls would stoke the jukebox with nickels and dance. Others noted that Bill and Jeannie Mattison were an excellent pair of dancers. Musing on those days, Jeannie said, "Our little group used to bring our favorite records to one of our homes and dance through the evening. That was the swing time of Glenn Miller, Benny Goodman, Tommy Dorsey, et al. When Bill said that he had never learned to dance, I decided to make him my next project. We worked on it for several weeks and he finally passed our tests. And it did create a great friendship. Never a romance—just soul-searching talk."

Jeannie Mattison Rotz reveals a sensitivity in Bill—even wisdom, if that isn't too powerful a word to describe an adolescent—when she writes, "Bill quickly made friends with the boys in our class, but didn't get involved in the limited social life [by which she means "dating"]. I met him when school started, and admired him—so did the others. He soon became part of the activities—and we could see that he would be a leader. He told me later that he didn't make a fuss over any of the girls because he didn't want the boys to resent him. That was so typical of his life—He thought in detail *before* he acted."

She also recalled his parents. "His father reopened a bank that had been closed in the beginning of the great Depression. . . . Bill's parents soon became part of the top social group and fit in easily.

His dad . . . had a great personality. His mother was an absolute lady. I feel their home life was congenial. Bill never complained (as most teens did) of tension over any subject." DePuy himself, however, observed much later that "it was a time of depression . . . so nobody had a lot of money."

Rotz stresses DePuy's "great control over his life. He would have been a great politician! . . . And, of course, he was a great student—brains before brawn—and we all enjoyed and looked up to him." She concludes with "He will always have a warm spot in my heart."[5]

Another young lady of their social circle of the late 1930s provided another description of DePuy in accord with that of Rotz. She says that Bill fit right in, indeed that he was a leader from day one. She adds that he was a good friend, and kind; that he was articulate and very forthright but said what he thought graciously. She dug out her high school yearbook, *The Bobcat,* and pointed to the caption next to the graduate's picture that was intended to capture his or her essence. It says of Bill, "He came, he saw, he conquered."

There was little in DePuy's background to suggest a military career. His father had served as a lieutenant in the Army during World War I but did not get to France. Neither of his grandfathers had served in the military, but a great-grandfather, a captain of the Michigan Infantry, was killed in First Cold Harbor, Virginia, in the Civil War. Later, when asked specifically what prompted him to consider a military career, DePuy mentioned his father's service, his great-grandfather's death in the Civil War, and his own interest in World War I. He said that as a boy he had read some twenty volumes of *The Literary Digest History of the World War* compiled by Francis W. Halsey in 1919. Taken together, all of this hardly reflected a burning desire for a military career.

Perhaps the earliest and most direct military influence on Bill DePuy was Company H of the 165th Infantry, a National Guard organization in Jamestown, North Dakota. He was too young to join then, but he recalled joining the National Guard when he came of age in South Dakota—for the money, he said, "as did all my friends in those days." That's also Wayne Waltz's recollection. The boys in their crowd all joined the National Guard. Waltz said, "The pay was like money from home every few months." Bill recalled, "We needed the money. It wasn't much money by today's standards, but any money was important in those days." The wolf, however, was not at the DePuy door. By the standards of the time and place, the family was both well off and socially prominent.

After high school, DePuy was off to college, conveniently located in Brookings, his home town. When he entered South Dakota State College, a land grant college, in 1937, Reserve Officer Training Corps (ROTC) was mandatory for the first two years for those fit to serve. The last two years were voluntary. So, for two college years, Bill was in both the National Guard, where he became a corporal and squad leader in Company B, 109th Engineers, 34th Infantry Division; and in ROTC as a cadet. In his junior year he had to make a choice between the Guard and ROTC, a choice he found easy. He liked ROTC very much and preferred being a lieutenant to being a corporal.

At that stage of his life DePuy hadn't yet decided on a military career. "I was going to be a banker and follow in the steps of my father, which is, I guess, not an unusual thing to do. If it hadn't been for the war, I'd probably have ended up in the banking business." He enjoyed playing semi-pro hockey in southern Minnesota and eastern South Dakota to earn "a little pocket money" while an undergraduate. The closest thing in his college curriculum to banking was economics, so he graduated with a BS in economics, saying, "I didn't distinguish myself academically in any way." That is technically true, but examination of both his high school and his college transcripts reveals consistently good grades in solid academic programs.[6]

Not visible in DePuy's academic transcripts is his involvement in the social and political life of his college. He was a member of Blue Key, a senior service fraternity whose membership required "personality, character, and scholarship"; he was Social Chairman of the Student Association; he served on the Union Board (an organization that apparently regulated student activities); he was elected Captain of Scabbard and Blade, an ROTC honor; and he was regimental adjutant in his senior year. All of this suggests a kind of midwestern do-goodism and joining that may have gone the way of the buggy whip. It conjures images of bonhomie on a 1930s college campus where meanness is unknown, "Aw, shucks" is cussing, kids show good teeth as they smile a lot, and the Music Man has just left town. Nevertheless, DePuy's college activities suggest social grace and a desire to seek out responsibility.

However idyllic campus life was in isolationist America, news of the outside world must have intruded. Though we have no way of knowing precisely what DePuy and his undergraduate friends thought about the increasingly ominous activity in Asia and Europe, they likely felt uneasy, with a growing sense that American involvement was inevitable. The Japanese occupation of Manchuria in 1931–1932 may have been a matter of indifference to a boy of twelve or thirteen, but the Japanese bombing of the American gunboat *Panay* in China on 12 December 1937, halfway through DePuy's freshman year in college, could hardly have passed unnoticed. His next year in college was marked by the German annexation of Austria, followed by the Czech crisis that resulted in the Munich Conference, whose mention became shorthand for appeasement. Swift German victory in Poland in September of 1939 brought Britain and France into World War II. In the spring and early summer of 1940, Germany defeated France and occupied Western Europe from the Arctic Circle in Norway to the Mediterranean Sea. While Bill DePuy was in the senior phase of his ROTC program leading to commissioning, the Battle of Britain and the Balkan campaigns were fought. Then Germany invaded the Soviet Union.

Military service edged to the top of DePuy's priorities as admired leaders stimulated his interest in a military career. As he put it, "I was very enthusiastic by that time. I really had been swept up with enthusiasm for the military."

He speaks warmly of several Regular Army officers at South Dakota State College. Among them were Major Ed Piburn, "at least half-Indian," who would later serve as a brigadier general and assistant division commander of the 10th Armored Division; and Ray Harris—portly, ferocious, and inspiring, who turned red in the face demonstrating the low crawl on an auditorium floor—of whom DePuy kindly remarks, "he really was beyond that."

One man, recalled DePuy, "inspired everybody." This was Colonel James P. Murphy, a professor of military science and tactics (PMS&T). DePuy remembered him as "a fatherly kind of a fellow with a very entertaining and wide-ranging vocabulary with all sorts of figures of speech that made him amusing to all of us simple chaps out there on the reservation. We loved him, and he inspired us all toward the Army. There's no question that he was a great recruiter and wanted us all to be in the Army."

DePuy's high regard for Murphy was reciprocated. When his application for a commission in the Marine Corps was denied by telegram to Murphy, in his position as PMS&T, on 26 August 1941, it said that DePuy was qualified but there was no vacancy.[7] By that time, DePuy was already an Army reserve second lieutenant on active duty. Upon graduation from South Dakota State College he had been appointed to the rank of Second Lieutenant in the Army of the United States. That made him a Reserve Officer on 9 June 1941 with a date of rank of 25 June 1941.[8] Murphy immediately went to bat for DePuy by responding to the telegram in a letter to USMC Headquarters. Securing three appointments to the Marine Corps in each of the previous two years, he wrote, "has made us a bit overconfident. However, I assure you that since my detail as PMS&T I have given the Marine Corps our best officer material and am happy to say that all have made good." For reasons not clear, only one Marine Corps commission was available to Bill's college in 1941, and it did not go to him. Murphy went on to point out that "this young man declined to take the examination for Honor Graduate appointment for the Army in order to qualify for what then seemed to be an almost certain USMC appointment (as we had but two candidates this year who could qualify, grades, age, physical, etc.) and his heart has been set on this appointment from the day that I first selected him to compete." Murphy concluded by asking for reconsideration, to no avail.[9]

DePuy was "heartbroken," as he later recalled. The Marine Corps recruited very heavily in the upper midwest, and the recent experience of his college led him and Murphy to believe that he'd get one of two commissions. Having not taken the examination for the Regular Army commission, DePuy had to settle for the reserve commission. Murphy could later take consolation in the knowledge that his "boys" from 1941 did well. At least one of them besides DePuy, Chuck Wilson, retired as a general officer.

Murphy must have taken enormous satisfaction from DePuy's impressive combat record in Europe and his later successes. He maintained contact with the younger man, encouraging him and offering initial guidance as DePuy worked his way through the bureaucratic intricacies of the Regular Army after the war—all offered in the paternal tone typical of an old mentor.[10]

That Lieutenant Colonel Murphy of Brookings days was a colonel at the University of Nebraska in 1945, by which time his protégé, the former Cadet DePuy of 1941, was a lieutenant colonel, is worth mentioning. Many older soldiers served a support function in the rear, enabling the young tigers to adapt to the rapidly changing situations and stress of protracted modern war and to lead in combat. The more successful older icons, Marshall, Eisenhower, Bradley, and Patton, etc. are famous, as are the younger generals who rapidly advanced in wartime, such as James M. Gavin, Maxwell D. Taylor, and Matthew B. Ridgway. But DePuy would encounter a number of older men who, conditioned by the leisurely pace of peacetime service, failed the test of leadership in combat.

DePuy later acknowledged that he had no way of comparing the quality of schools in South Dakota to those around the country, but he believed that the schools from his home state "were rather good. The literacy rate in the Upper Plains States is perennially the highest in the nation." He added, "There was a lot more European-type atmosphere compared to other parts of the country."

William Stofft (MG, USA, Ret.), former Commandant of the Army War College, former Chief of Military History, and proud native son of South Dakota, was asked what it is about his state that has produced so many influential and decent Americans from a sparse population, including Medal of Honor recipient and governor Joe Foss; senator, bomber pilot, and presidential candidate George McGovern; newsman and author Tom Brokaw; former Senate Minority and Majority Leader Tom Daschle; and so many generals that Army Chief of Staff Carl E. Vuono once remarked to General Stofft in the 1980s that South Dakota was "way overrepresented."

Stofft's response sounds like Garrison Keillor's description of Lake Wobegone, Minnesota, just down the road: "All the women are strong, all the men are good-looking, and all the children are above average." Stofft credits a feeling of security taken for granted—no locked doors, the ability to walk anywhere day or night, keys left in the car. The general acceptance of social norms made an adventure of sneaking a smoke behind the barn or drinking a beer at the lake in one's senior year of high school. Everyone worked, demonstrated great curiosity, tried everything. Natural tolerance and congenital optimism reigned. Treatment of American Indians, Stofft admitted, was "quite another matter." They live in "awful places," in "dead ends," and enlist in the Armed Forces at a high rate to join the majority "escapees."

Except for the blot in the copybook regarding Native Americans, General Stofft's response is a song of praise to South Dakota.[11] One may smile indulgently at his proud trip down Memory Lane, but close study of the mature DePuy causes one to consider seriously the importance of the early formation of his character and world-view. So does Tom Brokaw's memoir of growing up in South Dakota as a member of Stofft's generation, the one following DePuy's. Brokaw says his "current life continues to be shaped by the currents of my formative years four decades after I left South Dakota."[12]

The overwhelming bulk of mankind may be happily oblivious to O. E. Rolvaag's *Giants in the Earth,* but, according to Brokaw, it was read by everyone in the plains states. It describes tough, determined northern European settlers persevering in a demanding place in the late nineteenth century. Stofft tells of tramping through the hills of Virginia with DePuy in the 1980s as they discussed reading and being inspired by *Giants in the Earth* in high school *and* in college.[13]

One infers from Stofft's and Brokaw's descriptions, and from DePuy's life, the benefits of growing up at a time and place clearly shaped by homogeneity and trust. DePuy's personal qualities flourished in a community confident in its shared values and clear knowledge of right and wrong. A sense of propriety came from a community of social cohesion that encouraged the individual to fit into the whole even while helping to shape it. Contemporaries described Bill DePuy as a young man who fit in while standing out.[14] Talent was to be employed in service, not flaunted. DePuy's success as a boy and young man in all aspects of his life in Brookings provided him with a quiet confidence that enabled him to lead in a world that was "a long way from home," to borrow from a Brokaw book title.

2

Apprentice to Journeyman

By any objective standard, we were untrained.
—Bill DePuy, Oral History, 1979

On 25 June 1941, Second Lieutenant William E. DePuy reported to the 20th Infantry at Fort Leonard Wood, Missouri.[1] His training was rudimentary, and he knew it. He and his fellow cadets learned some American military history and tradition; the organization of the U.S. Army; how to wear the uniform; how to march troops about in groups; a bit about the characteristics and capabilities of weapons; how to read a map and navigate, with perhaps a little field work in land navigation; and whatever gems and tricks of the trade were passed on to cadets by the Regular Army soldiers of the ROTC detachment. Training was notional and devoid of what it meant in application.

Bill DePuy was no greener than the typical product of the commissioning process. In fact, his experience as a National Guard enlisted soldier, combined with his training as a cadet and his positive attitude, probably gave him a leg up on his peers. Nevertheless, when years later he was asked his opinion of the training he'd gotten before reporting for his initial assignment, he said, "It was assumed that we were trained in ROTC, and relative to everybody else in the World War II Army, I guess we were. But, by any objective standard, we were untrained."[2]

Along with most new lieutenants, DePuy became a platoon leader. After three months he became headquarters company commander for another three months. Those were the positions he held as the 20th Infantry marched five hundred miles to Louisiana for maneuvers in the fall of 1941. And then they marched the five hundred miles back.

His retrospective evaluation of the Army he joined is a balance sheet of good and bad marks. "I'd say that I learned more about just plain soldiering from six months in the 20th Infantry than I learned in the rest of my service." Not given to hyperbole, DePuy was reporting the difference between saying and doing as they applied to soldiering. When laymen think about soldiers, they probably picture uniforms, marching, banners, and martial music; but infantry soldiering—in the doing—is mostly hard physical work.

He later spoke well of his regimental commander and later corps commander, Lieutenant General Frank W. "Shrimp" Milburn. He credits the battalion commanders of his own early experience with being "tough and hazing kinds of men." They demanded much of their troops, but "they made you do things that are good, like taking care of the men and demanding that 'nobody drops out,' and so nobody did. The soldiers were sufficiently terrified so that nobody dropped out of that 1,000-mile march unless he went to the hospital." The plainsman took to soldiering. He brought a penetrating critical faculty to his calling.

On the liabilities side of the ledger was an anachronism guaranteed to produce American cadavers. As DePuy recalled, "Tactics consisted of getting on line and advancing in rushes—it was called extended-order drill." Such tactics were recognized as a bad idea as far back as the American Civil War. Napoleonic massing of assault troops gave way to increased dispersion as defenders burrowed in holes in the ground and fired weapons ever deadlier in rapidity and accuracy. That practice continued in the Balkan wars in the last decades of the nineteenth century and in the Russo-Japanese War of 1904–1905, which was a preview of the Great War in demonstrating the temporary ascendancy of defense. Audacity, offensive élan, and the spirit of the bayonet made for big butcher bills in an industrial war characterized by the vastly increased firepower of infantry and artillery weapons. Massed troops in the open made it an even worse idea in 1914–1918. It was an idea verging on criminal folly, exercised as it was in Bill DePuy's training in 1942 and 1943 and in close combat in 1944.

Upon his return from the Louisiana Maneuvers, which had exercised large bodies of troops for modern war for the first time in twenty years, DePuy was sent to Fort Benning, Georgia, where he attended a thirteen-week communications course that began in January 1942, the month after the Japanese attack on Pearl Harbor. It is indicative of the time that only one of the thirty-three officers in the course with DePuy was a Regular.[3]

In 1942, the strength of the U.S. Army grew to 3 million, on its way to over 8 million by May 1945.[4] But Regular Army officers and NCOs were spread thin. As DePuy recalled in 1979, "the regimental commander, one of the battalion commanders, and maybe two, three, or four others out of some 135 officers" were Regulars. One of the consequences of rapid growth and the attendant shortage of professionals was that responsibilities were piled on those who had the aptitude and capacity to handle them, regardless of pedigree. That's where men like Bill DePuy came in. He and others quick to adapt to the demands of combat would eventually command battalions and, in a few cases, regiments. The sprinkling of trained pros was augmented by the gifted amateurs who rose to the top in a kind of Darwinian process.

Senior leadership was keenly aware of what that meant. General Lesley James McNair, commander of Army Ground Forces (AGF), the man responsible for training the expanding Army, after visiting a new division said of its G-3 and chief of staff, "The blind leading the blind." He noted caustically, "We have rediscovered that untrained officers can't train troops." But what was the option? His own work he assessed realistically: "It was a little wobbly when it first got going. The men knew it. The officers knew it, [but] we had to get together *something* of an Army pretty darn fast."[5]

Assigned to the 357th Infantry of the 90th Infantry Division in Camp Barkley, Texas, DePuy remained with the 357th in various capacities from the spring of 1942 until June 1945. As of 4 April 1942, DePuy became battalion communications officer, but his duties included the S-1 job, command of the headquarters company, and pioneer (engineer) officer. Effectively, the commander, executive officer, and Bill DePuy were the command and staff group. He observed that none of the Regulars had experience in war, and "there was no apparent expertise on tactics anywhere in the regiment." DePuy was particularly critical of the notion of "rank hath its privileges" (RHIP). He considered it synonymous with hazing. In DePuy's opinion, "RHIP was an excuse for mediocre officers to take advantage of those of junior rank." As a result, "there was a lot of hazing."

DePuy regarded hazing as abuse of authority, a petty practice that substitutes the superficial for the essential. It was a remnant of peacetime routine when officers stuck their heads in the Orderly Room to sign the Morning Report en route to a bit of polo before drinks on the terrace, leaving supervision of undermanned companies to the First Sergeant. The NCO-officer relationship in the film *From Here to Eternity* comes to mind, as does the remark of George S. Patton's son, himself a major general, who said that his old man never worked a full day in his life. In the small Regular Army supervised by NCOs, routine, drill, ceremony, and appearance had high priority.

The American GI of World War II gave new meaning to the word "chickenshit." By that he meant the nonessential in army life, the unnecessary annoyances dreamed up by "the brass" to torment the little guy at the bottom of the hierarchical heap who was in uniform "for the duration" of the war to do his bit and to go home just as soon as he could. In a more sophisticated way, DePuy's comments on RHIP and hazing suggest that he agreed with the GIs' observation that war is about battle. DePuy learned that to the professional soldier, peace is another word for preparation for battle. DePuy's superiors and the Regulars also learned what was essential in combat as they rapidly transformed a mass of civilians into an army while reorganizing that army.

The World War I "square division" was an unwieldy formation of well over 20,000 men. The "triangular division" of World War II, adopted by the Regular Army in 1940, was designed to be lean and agile. It had about 15,000 men, 25 percent fewer than the square division. The rationale for the smaller division was that motorized, mechanized, and armored forces had to be more nimble than the infantry-centered divisions of World War I. Trial and error marked interwar evolution as soldiers in the various nations at first saw the tank as a mobile machine gun or cannon affording the crew protection in the attack. Then the tank was seen in different roles: as cavalry, replacing the horse; or dispersed among, and in support of, infantry; or massed as an independent arm. German, British, French, and Soviet soldiers took the lead in conceptualizing the place of the tank on the battlefield.

German successes in Poland in 1939 and in France in 1940 restored mobility to the battlefield. Simply expressed, penetration of the enemy's defensive shell and exploitation in his vulnerable rear became the ideal. Most of the German Army still moved as fast as a horse or a man on foot could travel; only the cutting edge of the Wehrmacht was made up of armor formations. But the flair and dash of the old horse cavalry became the "haul ass and bypass" preached by American armored force commanders in World War II and after.

When DePuy donned his uniform in 1941, senior leadership of the professional U.S. Army was still chewing on and digesting these lessons of mobility and combined arms, even while purporting to know what kind of training was required for mobile warfare. He was a quick read; many of his seniors were not.

He recalled that his commander "didn't talk to us about tactics, he talked about movements." DePuy said he had "a theory about that. We were motorized by that time, and all the energy and imagination in the division was totally absorbed in how we could get a regiment mounted up in trucks, move down the road, not get lost, and get there on time. We spent months just learning how to do that, whereas we should have spent months learning how to fight. Perhaps the reason for that was that the division commander, the regimental commander, and the battalion commander were comfortable with a truck movement, but they weren't comfortable with training for combat . . . training was procedural-mechanical."

When asked how good he thought his outfit was when it was deployed, DePuy confessed, "I had no way of knowing how good it was." His peers, he said, "were wonderfully young, bright, eager fellows trying to do their best. They were wonderful material from which to make an army. But, for some reason, we didn't take full advantage of that." It seemed to him that the leaders always emphasized what they knew how to do. They made a lot of twenty-five-mile marches, he said, "because everybody knew how to make a twenty-five-mile march. There were truck movements, written orders, written communications—all of those things that take place above the fighting. It was the blind leading the blind," he said, echoing the words General McNair had used from his perspective at the top of the military heap.

Part of the problem was turnover. Personnel turbulence was unavoidable. As they went through the inflexible and largely pro forma training process two or three times, DePuy's division and the others had to cadre newly forming organizations coming on line as the Army expanded. People who had at least some training in one division were sent to form the nucleus of a new division. DePuy's observations on the 90th Infantry Division as it was activated and trained fairly describe what happened in the thirty-eight divisions activated in 1942, twenty-seven of them infantry divisions. Turbulence was the rule; it robbed soldiers of a sense of belonging to a family.

Every type of U.S. division was reorganized at least once, with the Regular Army divisions going from square to triangular in 1940, but the National Guard divisions were not made triangular until 1942. This added to the general turmoil of turning millions of civilians into soldiers, fitting them into units, and getting them to ports for shipment overseas. But at least the divisions activated in 1942, including the 90th, had the advantage of forming around Regular Army cadres. As the expansion of the Army to eighty-nine divisions continued into 1943, there simply weren't enough Regular officers and NCOs to cadre the newer divisions.[6]

As bad as it was in 1942, it got worse, much worse, in 1943 and 1944. When the 90th was activated in March 1942, the personnel turbulence caused by pulling partially trained men to cadre newer divisions was compounded by the loss of quality men to Officer Candidate Schools (OCS), to the Army Specialist Training Program (ASTP), to the more selective Army Air Forces (AAF), and to various technical or support jobs. Those losses represented manpower and talent taken from the infantry. Later-forming divisions similarly lost people, even as combat in the Pacific, North Africa, Sicily, and Italy added greatly to the demand for infantry replacements. After the Normandy assault in June 1944, the numbers of riflemen pulled from divisions in training and sent to divisions in combat was staggering. The 94th Division, from activation (September 1942) to departure from the port of embarkation (July 1944), lost 8,890 enlisted men; the 65th Division lost 11,782; the 106th Division, 12,442; the 100th Division, 14,787; and the 69th Division, an astounding 22,235.[7]

A high price would be paid for underestimating the demand for infantry replacements. The losing organizations were also adversely affected as shortages were made up at the last minute, during Preparation for Overseas Movement. Units were brought up to strength with a "considerable slice of men and equipment" after the division reached its port of embarkation.[8]

The Army's replacement system met its numerical goals, but the replacements were generally treated like spare parts for a machine. Being treated impersonally and finding oneself among strangers in an extremely stressful situation was invariably unnerving and often fatal. Indeed, some men died before their names were known to others in their platoon. Platoon leader James B. Giles (USMA, 1944), said, "I didn't know the non-coms . . . we were a bunch of strangers, not just in my company but all over the 106th Division."[9]

DePuy recalled that before the training cycle was complete, the 90th gave up over 1,300 officers and men to form the 104th Infantry Division in September 1942. Compared to other divisions, that was not extraordinary. At about the same time (15 September), the 90th was designated "motorized," which accounts for DePuy's observations about all the training energy being invested in mounting trucks and not getting lost. Then the 90th converted back to being a standard infantry division in March 1943.

The evaluation of the 90th in Army Ground Force tests in December 1942 and January 1943 confirms DePuy's opinion of the state of training. The 90th got a very bad report card. Soldiers were unaware of the tactical situation; tactics were terrible; division headquarters failed to supervise; there was a lack of aggressiveness; soldiers bunched up, failed to conceal themselves, failed to take cover, and failed to scout before advancing; the Second and Third Battalions of the 359th Infantry shot at one another.[10]

The process of creating new divisions was rational and in general worked when it wasn't interrupted by personnel turbulence, but the turbulence problem was never solved. And the training problem was not fixed.

What DePuy meant by "procedural-mechanical" training was the strict adherence to the *time-oriented* Army Training Program (ATP) that characterized training in World War II and lasted into the 1970s. A soldier or unit spent so many hours or days on a subject. The object was to get the training done in order to put a mark on a checklist, not to teach. Thus, complained DePuy, "the process completely obscured the product." Formal *performance-oriented* training was not introduced to the U.S. Army until the mid-1970s. Until that happened, many who passed through the Army in the bad old days will recall sitting or standing behind a large group of men as a sergeant way up front took small parts from a piece of equipment barely visible to those in the back while muttering an incantation consisting of the names of the parts. At the end of that "block of instruction," all present were "trained"—whether or not they even saw what was taking place up front. "The learning function was obscured and secondary to the scheduling function. Few took training seriously," said DePuy.

The "M-1 pencil" is a term familiar to soldiers trained between 1942 and about 1972 (and not unheard of since). Scores recording rifle qualification were adjusted by the stroke of a pencil. The klutz who couldn't hit the side of a barn—and there were several in every training company—was qualified via the magic of the M-1 pencil. There would be no blots in the company's books. Trainers recorded 100 percent successful training on the rifle range (and they didn't have to go back to the range on Saturday to properly qualify the klutzes). In other words, shortcuts were taken.

The varied locations of the 90th Division before deployment suggest a deliberate effort to confront the division with the challenge of different landscapes. The division "trained" around Fort Barkley, Texas, in Louisiana Maneuvers, in the desert at Camp Granite, near Blythe, California, briefly at Fort Dix, New Jersey, and then in England. But, says DePuy, to assume that they took advantage of the varying terrain would be misleading. "When we were in England, before the Normandy invasion, we were in terrain not unlike that of Normandy, certainly more like Normandy than the desert. . . . But for some reason or other, we did not take advantage of that. It never seemed to occur to us that we were going to be confronted in Normandy with very poor visibility, and that this would create a control problem and a firepower problem. I don't remember any of that being discussed at all. My guess is that that was not really unusual in the expansion army of World War II."

Preparation for the invasion of Normandy focused entirely on the complex amphibious aspects of assault from the sea. The planning and preparation that participants recalled was all about getting ashore in the right place, getting off the beach quickly, and getting inland to link up with the lightly armed airborne troops dropped hours earlier. The hedgerows encountered in the Bocage region had been there for centuries, but planning was silent about those features of the terrain that increased the deadliness of German defensive positions, which were prepared meticulously and manned bravely and skillfully.

Reflecting on training and the general pre-invasion condition of his division, DePuy mused on American artillery. Whatever the shortcomings of the World War II U.S. Army, American artillery and logistics have been praised by friend and foe. German soldiers of the Bundeswehr would later joke with American soldiers by asking why the American infantry always advances. The answer: if it pauses it will be buried in logistics. The Germans also admired the effectiveness of American artillery.

DePuy was profuse in his praise of American artillery in Europe in World War II, asserting, "When we went to war that part of the division that was really well-trained on the combat side was the artillery." He went on to hypothesize why that was so, concluding that it was easier to train artillery "because it's very mechanical and mathematical," meaning that effectiveness is relatively easy to measure and improve. (He might have added that American artillery weapons systems and techniques for massing fires were excellent.) Infantry, he believed, is more of an art form.

DePuy was critical of infantry training. "Although [the 90th] was an infantry division," he said, "it was the infantry battalions, companies, platoons, and squads that I thought were poorly trained." He was asked if there was much feedback from the field to guide training. After all, by 1944 the British, French, and Russians had a lot of experience in fighting Germans, and Americans had fought in North Africa, Sicily, Italy, and in the Pacific. Wasn't combat data available to DePuy and the 90th Division in Britain? The short answer was no.

DePuy recalled that after-action reports and lessons learned were compiled, but they were not emphasized—except for one negative lesson. That was "marching fire." It became, according to DePuy, a fad. The purpose was to teach soldiers and commanders to maintain fire superiority in the final assault, a fine idea. But, he said, marching fire was used "as a method of attack, as the sole method of attack. What they should have done, of course, was position the heavy machine guns and light machine guns and even rifle companies, so as to *gain total fire superiority* with small arms as well as mortars and artillery, *and then, during the assault, use marching fire, which would have maintained the fire superiority.*" He added, "The problem with infantry is that while you may get fire superiority through suppression, just at the time when you need it most, during the assault, when the troops all rise up out of their foxholes or from behind a hedgerow and move forward, you lose it. So the enemy then comes up out of his foxholes and starts to fire at you."

Marching fire in the assault, *without suppression,* was dumb. Yet that is precisely what was done. "If the enemy was professional, as the Germans usually were," said DePuy, he "was well-hidden and in very good positions. . . . Marching fire as often as not just wasn't sufficient. We marched into their killing zones." Extended-order drill had become the suicidal norm, despite general awareness of the ever-increasing lethality of modern weapons. Two decades of peace meant that the U.S. Army had officers and NCOs who were inexperienced in war and senior officers who had never maneuvered large organizations in the field, even in peacetime.

When DePuy was asked about the use of live fire to prepare soldiers for combat before Normandy, probably a reference to the infiltration course, he said it was used, but "the enemy doesn't shoot back, so you don't learn a whole lot." In fact, he was dubious about a number of techniques, some of which he found counterproductive. For example, the M-1 rifle was highly regarded for its accuracy, reliability, durability, rate of fire, and improvement over the bolt-action rifle it replaced. But DePuy opined that the rifle and the rifle marksmanship program "worked to discourage active firing in combat by the average soldier. He was trained to shoot at and hit a target, but in combat the soldier seldom saw a distinct target. So, he was indisposed to shoot. The Germans, on the other hand, used machine pistols, which were area weapons. That is, they sprayed the area ahead of them and achieved fire superiority, which we now call suppression."

By the time the 90th Division got to England, every officer in the regiment knew the other officers. In DePuy's opinion, senior officers lacked confidence in their own war fighting ability. Ineffective commanders were retained. It was generally recognized "that there was a lot of deadwood in the unit, including two out of three battalion commanders." He regretted that "there was no tough thinning out of the officers who should have been eliminated before they got a lot of people killed. And that can only happen, I guess, if you have experienced officers who have standards and who know what it is they expect. Unfortunately, we didn't have such people."

DePuy described his division and regimental commanders, both regulars, as being "clearly unqualified for command in battle." The commander who took the regiment into Normandy was "as close to being totally incompetent as it is possible to be." He "knew nothing about an infantry regiment" and was "erratic to the extreme." He ordered the regiment straight ahead into repeated performances of failed attacks three or four times. Two division commanders were relieved of command in combat before a good one was found. One of DePuy's regimental commanders was relieved in England and another in Normandy. The one who had been relieved in England was—incredibly—returned to command the regiment in Normandy. He was killed while seemingly dazed and disoriented. Two battalion commanders were relieved, one for running away. Others included a regular, a man who, according to DePuy, while brave, had an unspecified "personal problem"; a reserve officer with "insufficient inner strength" to lead troops and face battle; a "despicable punk" who had given sufficient evidence of his flawed character during the two years before Normandy. "Upon issuing his order for the first attack of the war, he went to the aid station, turned himself in, and was evacuated." He was pursued and reduced to enlisted rank.

DePuy underlines this sad account of deficient leadership with startling statistics. "In the first six weeks of the battle in Normandy, the 90th lost 100 percent of its soldiers and 150 percent of its officers. In the rifle companies that translates to losses of between 200 and 400 percent. Those losses compare with the worst of World War I." The peacetime value system in the 90th Division failed to identify and eliminate these officers "before they had done their grisly work."

It would have been no consolation to DePuy had he known that there was grisly work aplenty among the sixty-one U.S. divisions—forty-six infantry and fifteen armored—in the European Theater of Operations (ETO) between 6 June 1944 and 8 May 1945. Twenty of them had a personnel turnover rate of 100 percent or higher. The 90th, with 196 percent, was sixth on the list of U.S. Infantry Divisions. That amounted to 27,617 casualties. And the 90th had the most days in combat, 308.[11]

Victory in war, especially in a great "crusade," can allow the victor to hide, overlook, or forget the consequences of putting amateurs and incompetents into positions of combat leadership, or to write it off as the cost of doing business. But the professional soldier knows that the price of incompetence is paid at the cutting edge. Infantrymen represented 14 percent of the Army's overseas strength but suffered 70 percent of the total battle casualties. Riflemen were 68 percent of infantry division strength and almost 95 percent of infantry division casualties.[12]

Bill DePuy never forgot the squandered training opportunities and bad leadership that killed American soldiers.

3

The 90th Division Goes to School

> The consequences of all this leadership failure could have
> been predicted. My regiment simply did not perform,
> notwithstanding the heroic effort and tragic losses among
> lower ranking officers and the bewildered troops.
>> —DePuy on the 357th Infantry in June–July 1944

> By the end of the Normandy Campaign the U.S. military had
> developed an all around military proficiency.
>> —Russell A. Hart, military historian

The 90th Division was so ill prepared for combat and so badly led that it came close to being disbanded. Division and regimental commanders were assigned and fired until competent, indeed outstanding, leaders were found. At company and battalion levels leadership came from below as those tested passed or failed the unforgiving test of leading soldiers in combat. The bloody fighting in Normandy and the war of movement after the breakout from the beaches would produce two positive outcomes in DePuy's division: effective leadership and confidence in that leadership among the troops. The 90th would become one of the most reliable of the American divisions in Europe. The transformation from "problem division" to a very good one, however, took place by degrees. Bill DePuy saw that transformation and would never forget it. He called the 90th Division of June and July 1944 the greatest killing machine in Europe—of Americans.

Activated in March 1942 at Camp Barkley, Texas, the division continued individual and unit training until it boarded ships in New York bound for England in March 1944. Two years would seem to be sufficient time to train troops. In later wars, draftees were trained, fought in Korea and Vietnam, and returned to the United States for demobilization within two years.

The unofficial history of the Division says, "The Division had been well trained, *by the standard of its day.*"[1] That claim fails to make a distinction between individual training and the effectiveness of commanders in blending the combined arms: infantry, armor, and artillery. The former is much simpler than the latter. Military competence at squad, platoon, company, and battalion was rudimentary, but commanders and staffs at regiment and higher echelons were untested. Newly commissioned officers, Bill DePuy and thousands like him, were amateurs. Regular Army officers were few and lacking experience in war. "The standard of the day" was not the gold standard.

DePuy would learn his trade in war. He would later describe the race junior combat leaders ran between combat experience and death. The attrition rate among leaders at squad, platoon, and company levels was shockingly high. Mistakes were literally fatal. Leaders came from the ranks of those who survived combat, who learned their violent new trade in the process. They were young. DePuy was a veteran battalion commander at the age of twenty-five when the war ended and he was made division G-3. Those who took to combat brushed aside the less martial men, the older men, and deadwood. It was a brutal, elemental way to learn. The better young officers died or commanded battalions. Some did both. To put the age of these World War II leaders in perspective, in 1961, when DePuy commanded a battle group in Schweinfurt, his twenty-five-year-old officers were lieutenants.

The 90th Division got off to a terrible start. Poor performance in combat should have been anticipated, because the preparation for combat was a bad show. Neither leaders nor soldiers knew enough to know how bad they were. They would find out.

DePuy later described what passed for planning as late as 1944 in England. He was "borrowed" by the division staff to go to Headquarters, European Theater of Operations, U.S. Army, in London. His mission was to coordinate the shipping that would take the 90th to Utah Beach as the follow-up division behind the 4th Division. His bosses from the 90th found more interesting things to do in London, leaving the young captain to sort things out. He called it "sheer pandemonium."

DePuy found "an elderly major" of the transportation section of the Quartermaster Corps who "seemed to be the only one who knew where all the ships were." When the major asked which ships

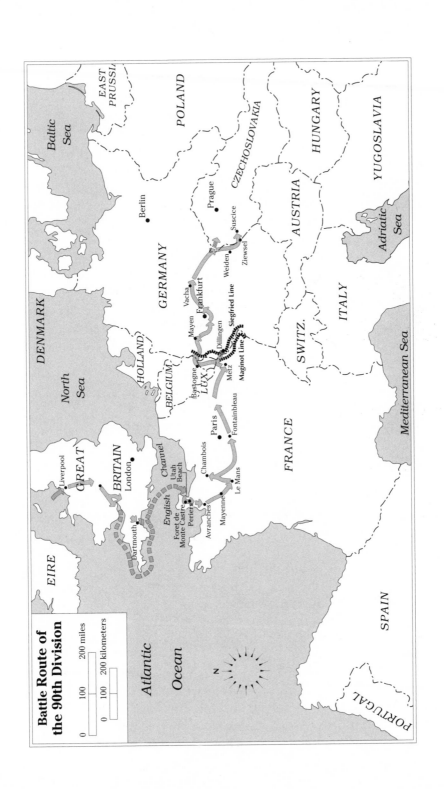

**Battle Route of
the 90th Division**

0   100   200 miles

0   100   200 kilometers

EIRE

GREAT
BRITAIN

Liverpool

London •

Dartmouth

DENMARK

North
Sea

Baltic
Sea

EAST
PRUSSIA

POLAND

Berlin •

GERMANY

Prague •

CZECHOSLOVAKIA

Suscice

Ziewsel

Weiden

Frankfurt

Vacha

Mayen

Dillingen

Siegfried line

Maginot Line

Metz

Bastogne

LUX.

BELGIUM

HOLLAND

Fontainbleau

Paris

Chambois

Le Mans

Mayenne

Avranches

Perier

Foret de
Monte Castre

Utah
Beach

English
Channel

FRANCE

SWITZ.

AUSTRIA

HUNGARY

ITALY

Adriatic
Sea

YUGOSLAVIA

Mediterranean Sea

SPAIN

PORTUGAL

Atlantic
Ocean

N

he wanted, DePuy confessed he didn't have a clue and asked for recommendations. Advised that some were larger and better, DePuy picked the larger and better ships, noting: "The 90th had about nine ships in all. The poor old 2d Division had about thirty because all the big ships had been taken by the 90th—by me. What a system!"[2]

Next he worked with a group of "old sea dogs" tasked by the British Army to prepare loading plans. They had previously planned the loading of ships for the landings in North Africa, Sicily, and Italy, so he was in good hands. One pictures the grizzled British sea dogs and the lad from South Dakota, who, at this stage of his life, was more altar boy than gladiator.

DePuy's job was to check the sequence of off-loading at destination, to consider such details as having a vehicle handily positioned to move heavy gear when the time came to land. He had to do all of this with "only the most general knowledge about the division's plans at the Normandy end." He concludes, "After all the grand plans are drawn and the generals have had their say, it devolves upon some half-trained, half-baked captain to 'do it.' It's a small miracle that anything works."

The lack of a division combat loading plan for the long-anticipated amphibious operation is yet another indication of the lack of professionalism that DePuy never forgot. New officers simply made it up as they went along as the world watched the Allies enter the continent of Europe to defeat Germany. They would continue to make it up until they got good at it.

Of course, some setbacks can be attributed to the fortunes of war. Two battalions of the 359th Infantry (1/359 and 3/359) attached to the 4th Division for the landing were aboard the ship *Susan B. Anthony,* which hit a mine and sank on 7 June 1944 (D+1). All the troops were saved, but the bulk of their equipment and weapons went down with the ship. Destroyer escorts took troops from the ship that went down, transferring some of them to landing craft. Some of the troops thus arrived alive, if shaken, on the busy Utah beach. Others were taken back to England before eventually linking up with their parent organization.[3]

Orwin C. Talbott, a company commander, was aboard the *Anthony* when it struck the mine. He would retire as a lieutenant general as DePuy's deputy at Fort Monroe some thirty years later. Retired in Annapolis, he tells his Navy friends that the U.S. Navy got him "halfway across the Channel, but it took His Majesty's

Royal Navy to get me the rest of the way, because I got off on a British destroyer."[4]

Some disorientation as a result of the shock at the newness of it all was unavoidable. DePuy's 357th Infantry landed at Normandy on Utah Beach at noon on 8 June. His observations take us from neat generalities and abstractions, the sweeping arrows and symbols on maps, to the confusion and discomfort of infantry in combat. Troops fired on imaginary snipers. The soldiers' clothing, impregnated against chemical attack did not breathe, so "they were really awful hot and, God, after a few days you could smell soldiers a mile away." When chemical attack was deemed unlikely, "we got out of the impregnated clothing—it was the greatest relief. It was almost the greatest relief in the war." DePuy talked about the load the soldiers carried—infantry soldiers always talk about the things they are made to carry—which, "of course, nobody used."

The tactics used in the first attack by DePuy's regiment were those practiced in Texas, Louisiana, California, and New Jersey. In

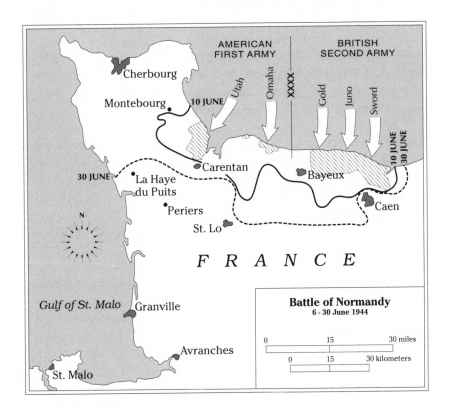

Normandy American troops were caught in open fields by Germans who knew how to use the terrain and how to fight. Extended order and marching fire failed. Casualties were heavy. "We had walked into their killing ground," DePuy recalled. "All in all, a dismal affair . . . a great bloodletting without much to show in return."[5] American troops fought the way they had trained—and paid the price.

DePuy fixes the responsibility for these casualties on poor leadership. The idea that "failure could have been predicted" remained with him and conditioned his later actions. So did the memory of the young men who took up the slack.

Demonstration of courage and skill in combat gave Ed Hamilton the First Battalion, until he was seriously wounded in September. "A good man named Ward" commanded the Second until he was wounded and replaced by another good man, Ben Rossow. John Mason took the Third Battalion and later commanded the 357th Regiment when its respected commander, George Bittman Barth, was seriously wounded. "So, we went from three disasters [as battalion commanders] to three good, but relatively untrained men. They learned on the job."

Colonel George Bittman Barth (MG, USA, Ret.) took command of the 357th after having served as the 9th Division chief of staff in North Africa and Sicily. On his first day commanding the 357th Infantry, he saw a column of some 800 men and asked DePuy which battalion they were. "Those are our replacements," said DePuy. The replacements were as large as a battalion. How could that number of men be integrated into squads and platoons without creating the impression in the minds of the replacements that they were in a very bad place and were being used pretty much as spare parts? At every turn there was more bad news. Barth correctly concluded that his new command had "zero morale."[6]

DePuy became regimental S-3 on 14 June, and Barth became commander on 16 June. They operated optimally as commander and key staff officer. The younger man's great respect and affection for his commander lasted a lifetime. DePuy called Barth "a lifesaver." Barth admired DePuy's infantry skills, reliability, and loyalty.[7]

As regimental S-3, DePuy enjoyed the confidence of his new commander. Barth, an artilleryman now commanding an infantry regiment in combat, acknowledged his lack of infantry background. Essentially he told DePuy, I command, you keep me straight. His trust was well placed in DePuy, who said, "I had . . . a very marvelous opportunity to be an operations officer for a man who wasn't an operations officer." This frank assessment of their relationship explains the free hand the young Reserve Officer enjoyed while working for the older Regular, who was already a veteran of combat in North Africa. Barth, out with his troops in the companies, knew that his S-3 had control of planning and operations. No one ever accused DePuy of being lazy, dull, or inattentive. He ran with the ball. Barth's confidence empowered him. Moreover, DePuy had served in the division for over two years by then and knew where the skeletons were buried, while Barth, however talented, was the new guy and an artilleryman. But he was not new to fighting Germans.

Like DePuy, Barth respected the enemy's skills and admired their courage. In July 1944, Barth sought and found good ideas from the Germans and discovered American mistakes by walking the recent battlefield with his battalion commanders and his S-3. He traced the course of the battle, taking special care to examine both friendly and enemy positions. Then Barth wrote a "Narrative of the operations of the 357th Infantry for the period 5–13 July 1944." It is an objective analysis by a professional that provides a feel for the intensity of the fighting, what he learned about his enemy, and his own actions.[8]

On 8 July Barth formed a company comprised of cooks, mechanics, and clerks from the Field Train (a term used for support troops). He called it Jig Company, an ad hoc improvisation that "performed excellent service." His "I" and "L" Companies consisted of twenty men each, 10 percent of normal strength. On 10 July, four of his companies lost all of their officers and many NCOs. At one point Major Ed Hamilton commanded two battalions, because another battalion commander had collapsed from sheer exhaustion.

Barth noted a German tactical technique that would be useful in future fights. The Germans fired a heavy volume of artillery on the night of 12–13 July and were gone by the morning of the 13th. DePuy and Barth learned that as the Germans broke contact, they would either conduct a counterattack or employ artillery and crew-served weapons to cover their vulnerability during the action as they thinned their troops in contact.

Appended to Barth's narrative is a three-page document, "Training Memorandum 1," dated 16 July 1944 and signed by DePuy. Barth had made his observations in his Narrative; DePuy took some of his commander's observations and turned them into specific points to be applied by subordinates, putting them in directive form, "for the commander."

This memo is a seminal document in DePuy's evolution as a professional. Several of the tactical issues he engages with here re-emerged throughout his career, as he commanded battalions, a battle group, and a division, and finally in his position as schoolmaster of the Army. Throughout, he draws heavily on what he and Barth had observed of the Germans' performance.

The first issue DePuy addressed was the placement of antitank weapons in a concealed position covering likely avenues of approach. He then emphasized the use of all weapons in all-around defense, stressing the importance of defense in-depth and mutual support. He noted that German fighting positions always provided good fields of fire, while "too often our men dig into positions for self preservation only and do not attempt to secure a firing position." To illustrate the point, he said that Germans always dug in on the far side of a raised road, providing visibility and fields of fire reaching out some distance. American troops, by contrast, dug in on the near side of a raised road, providing protection but extremely restricted fields of fire. Further, German foxholes always had firing steps, a practice he felt the Americans should imitate.

DePuy also had ideas about communications security. He believed that it must be assumed that the enemy was listening to radio communications. But that did not mean that all communications needed to be in code. Most communications, he noted, could be sent in the clear without fear of compromise, and messages that did need to be encoded could use simple methods (these were later called "brevity codes"). In brief, DePuy believed that a happy medium could be found between communications security and the need for speedy communications on the battlefield. Companies and battalions must use "ingenuity in this matter in order to prevent uniformity." He reminded them to keep regimental headquarters informed about the codes used.

These last two points become a permanent part of DePuy's leadership style. First, subordinates must use their heads, their ingenuity; adherence to rules, just because it was standard operating procedure (or "SOP"), was not enough. Second, higher headquarters can't help you if it doesn't know what you are doing and where you are.

DePuy's training memo also has something to say about maps: regiment headquarters will issue overlays designating reference points for use in reporting location. That is, headquarters should provide checkpoints on maps, thus enabling subordinate commanders to give locations to higher headquarters in a clear, concise, and complete manner while denying the enemy awareness of the system. Again, DePuy's teaching point is clear: if we are to help you with supporting fire, we must know where you are.

Artillery suppresses the enemy (keeps his head down). But, wrote DePuy, beware of bringing artillery too close when tall trees are near you. Tree bursts are an equal opportunity killer: they kill in every direction. Coordinate the time and location of fire carefully. Make your location known to friendly aircraft by the use of fluorescent panels on line and pyrotechnics (flares, rockets, smoke) on the flanks of your position.

DePuy's admonition to use both heavy and light machine guns to support an advance is an early indication of his advocacy of direct fire support with organic weapons to augment indirect fire by artillery and fire support from friendly air.

American soldiers, DePuy noted, must be taught to fire their weapons "even though no visible target presents itself." Suppression of the enemy—rather than accurate fire—and getting soldiers to fire their weapons at suspected targets become part of his combat catechism early on.

Intelligent movement to contact and defense were also among his early lessons learned. "The use of a covering party and an advancing party moving forward under cover of fire by the former is necessary," he asserted. This notion, that one soldier shoots while the other one moves, comes up in every one of DePuy's later commands. Terms changed over time as DePuy refined and improved the idea, eventually becoming the three kinds of "overwatch" DePuy taught. In essence, the challenge is to keep friendly soldiers alive as they approach a defending enemy, fix his location, and destroy him with massive firepower. Later variations on the same theme he applied in the dense vegetation of Vietnam.

The Germans taught DePuy to enhance defense in depth with a reserve. Regardless of size, each unit must have a reserve. He also noted that the Germans avoided a strictly linear defense by staggering fighting positions so that the enemy couldn't be sure of the defender's location. GIs learned the hard way that when they believed they had penetrated the German "line," they hadn't. More Germans were waiting in staggered positions.

DePuy concluded his 16 July 1944 training memo with specific directives on the details of camouflage, right down to hiding fresh dirt from foxholes and avoiding the showing of white underwear. And he urged all soldiers to share successful combat techniques with one another, particularly with regard to preparing defensive positions, minimizing the number of their fellow soldiers in the killing zone as they advance, and using massive amounts of organic and supporting firepower to suppress the enemy and to kill him.

On 23 July, one week after DePuy's training memo was published and one week before Brigadier General Raymond S. McLain took command of the 90th Division, one of the most crippling blows to division pride and confidence struck. A battalion of the 358th Infantry surrendered 11 officers and 254 men to a German force of 50 men and two tanks. Of course there were mitigating circumstances; there always are. For one thing, the Germans were very good. For another, American leadership wasn't.

After thirteen days of continuous battle, the troops of the 358th had had little rest or sleep. On 23 July, the men of the regiment were demoralized by an unnecessary and near-suicidal daylight attack across open fields dominated by heavy, accurate German fire. The butcher bill for the 358th was 1 officer and 68 men killed, 5 officers and 99 men wounded, and the 11 officers and 254 men who were captured.

Alexander Uhlig, the sergeant of the 6th Parachute Regiment who led the fifty Germans that captured the Americans, later confirmed what was in American records and added an ironic note. He had tried probes to the left and to the right. Failing to find the American flanks, he realized that American artillery was creeping up on him from his rear. Uhlig decided to press the attack, since the greater danger to him and his men was the artillery. The Germans initiated a bold night assault out of fear of dying.[9]

DePuy, at a regimental level two echelons above the company battles, said that he was "not personally a part of the endless, bitter, grinding combat at the fighting edge." But, he added, "Had I been, I would surely not be reporting as I am today." He was not exaggerating. On 22 July, the day before the 358th reported the losses listed above, the 359th suffered 2 officers and 7 men killed and 10 officers and 180 men wounded.

These were not isolated incidents. Earlier, on 10 July, the 3/358 started the day with 19 officers and 563 men; 8 officers and 220 men survived the day. K Company was particularly hard hit, starting the day with 3 officers and 139 men; 1 officer and 31 men walked away. Even the bravest men reached the limits of human endurance. The battalion commander, Lieutenant Colonel Jacob W. Bealke, "was incoherent and babbling. 'I killed K Company, I killed K Company, I killed K Company,' he said over and over." Major Gaylord Andre, a doctor, took Bealke to a rear area for a few days of rest. Then Bealke returned to the front to take over his battalion. "He was one of the bravest and the best battalion commanders in the whole Army, but even he could not stand the terrible death and destruction of such a battle."[10]

To keep the 90th Division's extremely high casualty rates in perspective, the 79th Division in five days of battle at Mont Castre, where the 90th was battered, lost 2,000 casualties, just about the same as the 90th. The elite 82d Airborne Division, also fighting at Mont Castre, was reduced by half from the early morning drop on 6 June. After four days at Mont Castre, the rifle companies of the 325th Glider Infantry ranged in size from 57 to 12 men. The regiment was down from 135 officers and 2,838 men to 41 officers and 956 men. But Russell Weigley notes an important difference: "The 82d gained its objectives."[11]

It may be too neat to say that the 90th hit rock bottom in late July and the new division commander personally turned it around, but that's the way it seemed to the veterans who were there, DePuy among them. He credits General Raymond D. McLain with saving the division. McLain told the officers that the soldiers of the 90th were as good as the soldiers of any other division, but they had been poorly led. He visited the most forward battalions and was seen by his troops. He announced that the XO, the second in command of a regiment, would be selected on the basis of readiness to command, and not on other criteria, such as seniority. All those things his two predecessors had failed to do.

The first commander, Brigadier General Jay W. MacKelvie, was simply ineffective. Corps commander J. Lawton Collins relieved MacKelvie on 13 June, along with two regimental commanders. The second commander, Major General Eugene M. Landrum, apparently attempted to control events from safe command posts, where he was out of touch with units that were in contact with the enemy. DePuy called him "a map general . . . not a good leader." The unofficial division history says he was "short, fat, uninspiring" and commanded from an armchair in a cellar. And DePuy called his relieved regimental commander, Colonel P. D. Ginder, "a horse's ass of the worst order. Goddamned fool . . . he was a disaster."[12] Landrum, the second commander of the 90th in Normandy, may simply not have been given sufficient time to address the many weaknesses in the division (he was given just a month), but higher headquarters was impatient and wanted results.

Omar Bradley called the 90th Division "one of the worst trained" and "disappointing," but was later pleased that he had not broken up the problem division. Instead, he was very pleased with McLain, later making him XIX Corps commander, and he called the 90th "one of the finest divisions in combat on the Allied front."[13] Eisenhower concurred, listing it among the "great divisions" under his command during the war.[14] When George S. Patton was told late in the war to designate one division for a Presidential Unit Citation, he chose the 90th.[15]

Barth gives McLain high marks as a division commander, but he has reservations about Bradley's assertion that the change from poor to outstanding took place overnight. "I took issue with this concept because I knew that it took several months after General McLain joined before the division could be counted as a really firm combat unit."[16] He credits McLain with giving the division "back its soul by supporting those under him," for his courage in always going forward and never sacrificing his men "for his personal ambition or gain," and for giving the division "success." Barth praised the 90th Division staff, especially Richard G. Stilwell, the G-3 who later served as a corps G-3 and became DePuy's lifelong friend and confidant. Barth said:

> General McLain was the only division commander I ever served under who used without modification the staff procedures taught at Leavenworth in running his division . . . [He] freed himself of staff details and spent most of his time with his combat units. This had a profound effect on the morale and efficiency of all units, particularly the infantry. Due to his proper delegation of authority within his staff, his constant presence was not necessary at his headquarters. It was the finest functioning staff I encountered in World War II. . . . McLain inspired leaders of major units with a spirit of dash and aggressiveness that could not be stopped . . . he

was idolized by officers and men alike . . . the climate created by General McLain's leadership caused many subordinate leaders to act aggressively without orders, knowing
that their General stood behind them.

That last remark hints at what the U.S. Army and DePuy would
later identify and admire in *Auftragstaktik*, a German concept that is
roughly translated as "mission-type orders." But it has more to do
with carrying out the commander's intent, not just specific orders.
DePuy saw this kind of initiative in his German enemies that he
would later demand of his own subordinate commanders. As division commander he would, like McLain, spend his time with his
combat units, expecting his staff to pick up the pieces. And DePuy
saw in Barth the qualities that Barth saw in McLain.

Barth is profuse in his praise of the young tigers commanding
his battalions, all majors who proved themselves in combat: Ed
Hamilton, John Mason (who would command the regiment after
Barth was seriously wounded), and Jack Ward, who had the Second Battalion. "I was very fortunate," Barth said, "in having two
very fine staff officers at regimental headquarters, Captain William
DePuy as S-3 and First Lieutenant Charles W. Ryder, Jr. as S-2, who
were able to give me honest opinions on the sort of performance I
could expect of the commanders."

Jacob Bealke, the man who wept for his K Company and later
commanded the 358th, wrote a letter dated 14 September 1944 from
France to his brother-in-law, LTC Paul Burge, the G-4 of the 10th
Mountain Division in the United States, about to deploy. He told
his brother-in-law, "There are two things that cannot be stressed
enough. Those are discipline and field sanitation . . . Then there is
the matter of how to win your battles. Paul, all that has to be done
is for our troops to *shoot and move*. That sounds like a simple solution to a damn hard problem." He says most troops will lie down,
at which point the Germans use artillery and mortars to kill. He
advised his brother-in-law to get fire superiority and get out of the
kill zone.[17] That advice could have come from DePuy, but it would
have been more detailed.

DePuy was in a good position from which to observe the meta-
morphosis of the 90th Division and his 357th Infantry as leaders
learned how to get the job done and keep their people alive. Two
decades of peace had caused training to ossify and administrative

details, like time in grade and rank, to take precedence over the real purpose of an army: to win wars. Combat tends to brush aside the administrivia of peacetime "soldiering." Distractions vanished as purposeful men rose to command the divisions, regiments, and battalions. The troops in companies who managed to survive early poor training and leadership learned the essence of soldiering: be aware of the situation, take care of your buddy, destroy your enemy. The bad June days of Normandy were costly for the U.S. Army. The bad days of July were even worse for the 90th on the Cotentin Peninsula. But the skilled German troops who killed Americans in great numbers also taught the survivors how to fight.

Years later, when asked to explain how the 90th got its units "back on their feet," DePuy said that soldiers simply learned what worked, and leaders were selected in response to a simple question: Who can get the job done?

Historian Michael D. Doubler, pondering "the differences between peacetime training and actual combat," quotes engineer battalion commander LTC Dave Pergrin, on seeing his first battlefield on 23 June 1944 after training his unit for eleven months: "Only when I first set foot on Omaha did it dawn on me that I might not have known enough, might not have done enough."[18]

DePuy's World War II experience can be divided into two phases, Normandy and after. In the first phase, the 90th learned through bloody lessons how to fight. It also learned the primacy of leadership. It is not enough for leaders to know what to do, to be technically and tactically sound. They must also demand that soldiers do the right thing when they seem too tired to do so. Infantry soldiers are routinely on the verge of exhaustion. That is their normal state. Soldiers will take life-endangering shortcuts, such as crossing open areas rather then going around them and failing to dig and camouflage when it is prudent to do so, because they are tired. As football coach Vince Lombardi famously put it, "Fatigue makes cowards of us all." The good combat leader is the unpopular SOB who demands that his soldiers do the hard, right things necessary to keep them alive so that they can close with and destroy the enemy.

When asked how the 90th Division was transformed from "problem division" to one of the best in the European Theater of Operations, DePuy began his response by describing the breakout of the allied forces from Normandy, the ensuing collapse of the German defenses in France, and the war of movement that followed. Colonel Barth captured the mood following the breakout. On 5 August 1944 he said, "It seemed very strange to be rolling down the road at 20 miles an hour into enemy territory where before we marched and fought for every gain. . . . An undercurrent of excitement seemed to go down the column, and you could almost see the men's spirit rise—morale was on the way up."[19]

DePuy also described how optimism replaced the earlier mood of fatalism as the "problem division," now part of George S. Patton's Third Army, saw the Germans to their front collapse. The division was on the move, advancing and taking prisoners. According to DePuy, "We didn't have to fight much." That "much" is relative. There were fights during the rapid advance, almost always at river crossings, but compared to earlier fighting they were brief and—most important—successful. DePuy called them "easy successes," just what the doctor ordered for a division now in the advanced stages of learning. "Sure, they were easy successes," he said, "but everybody needs success." And success feeds on itself. "It breeds confidence, and confidence breeds more success, until by the time we got to Le Mans and turned and started toward the Falaise Gap, toward Argentan and Alencon, we were beginning to feel that we were soldiers."

There was a special sweetness for DePuy in knowing "that we somehow had stuck it out . . . we took a perverse pride in the fact that we were still there." He heaps praise on General McLain for his constant presence, for being seen by the troops, for absolving them of guilt and doubt by telling them that they had been badly led, that early errors and bad decisions weren't their fault. Above all, McLain led his men well. He knew what his troops could do, and they in return had confidence in their division commander. He knew what he was doing, something new at the top of the 90th. He also had a reputation for relieving officers not suited to command in combat. In any event, DePuy credits McLain with leading his division to victories that provided confidence, "and the confidence made for a good division."

DePuy's confidence in McLain became profound respect and affection for the unassuming general. McLain was promoted to major general in August 1944 and to lieutenant general in June 1945 and commanded XIX Corps. He was made a brigadier general in the Regular Army, a most unusual appointment for a National Guard officer. Clearly the men at the top agreed with DePuy.

Colonel Barth, who was working his magic at the 357th Infantry before McLain took command of the division, was another pivotal figure in the turnaround. Barth created a climate in which success bred success, as a stream of officers in their twenties mastered battalion command while DePuy was the regiment's operations officer. Some officers continued to be relieved at company and battalion levels, and some simply opted out of the responsibility of combat command. In December 1944, DePuy literally took a battalion away from an officer who seemed to have lost his will to command. Fear and exhaustion took their toll. Others were wounded and evacuated, like Ed Hamilton, one of the division's star battalion commanders. John Mason survived hard combat from Normandy onward as a battalion commander and eventually became the 357th's commander. DePuy called Mason "the best commander in the regiment during the war."

DePuy's direct observations and later commentary about the 90th appear to mirror most of the American infantry divisions at Normandy. As a participant, he lacked the perspective enjoyed by a new generation of scholars who are now reexamining and questioning some of the accepted wisdom about the war in Europe in 1944 and 1945. One of them, having compared the militaries of Great Britain, Canada, the United States, and Germany, examined prewar preparation, and studied execution in Normandy from June to August 1944, takes issue with the conventional wisdom that "Americans prevailed through overwhelming superiority rather than skill." Instead, he concurs with recent scholarship, which has found "that the U.S. Army became increasingly skilled and perfected its mastery of both combined-arms warfare and the air-land battle during the Normandy Campaign."[20]

These conclusions are consistent with DePuy's impression. The 90th went to school in Normandy. After the breakout, under McLain at division, Barth at the 357th regiment with DePuy his right-hand man, and the young tigers leading the battalions, the 90th was ready for graduation. DePuy put it simply: "The division eventually pulled itself together through on-the-job training and the slow emergence of fighters and leaders through a process of seasoning and natural selection."

The best was still to come.

4

The 90th Breaks Out

> Each time they had one of those experiences, they gained a
> little more confidence, lost some of their awe of the Germans,
> and became better soldiers.
> —DePuy on the war after the breakout from Normandy

The Allies' European strategy called for the expansion of the Normandy lodgment and a breakout to get on with the defeat of Germany. But July found the invaders still bogged down in the Bocage region with its hedgerows that favored defense. Omar Bradley called it "the damndest country I've seen."[1]

To facilitate the breakout, Operation COBRA used thousands of aircraft to "carpet bomb" a path through the German defenses. The plan for 24 July 1944 called for bombardment by 350 fighter bombers, 396 mediums, and 1,800 heavies previously reserved for strategic bombing. Poor visibility in the target area and poor coordination between air and ground commanders regarding the axis of the flight of the aircraft resulted in 25 men killed and 131 wounded in the U.S. 30th Division on 24 July. Incredibly, the toll of the bombing error on 25 July, "a bright, clear day," was 111 American dead and 490 wounded. Lesley McNair, the commander of Army Ground Forces who was in Europe to observe the fruits of his training of the mobilized force, was among those killed.

Despite this traumatic and costly incident of friendly fire, the enemy was pulverized in some places, allowing the aggressive J. Lawton Collins to break out through an inferno of twisted German equipment, animals, and dead men. Eisenhower later called the Falaise Gap, the attempt to bag and destroy the German Army, "one of the greatest killing grounds of any war area, [scenes] that could be described only by Dante. It was possible to walk for hundreds of yards . . . stepping on nothing but dead and decaying flesh."[2] The plan was for the Allies to dash across France as additional forces and logistics continued to pour inland while the Germans were stunned and off balance.[3]

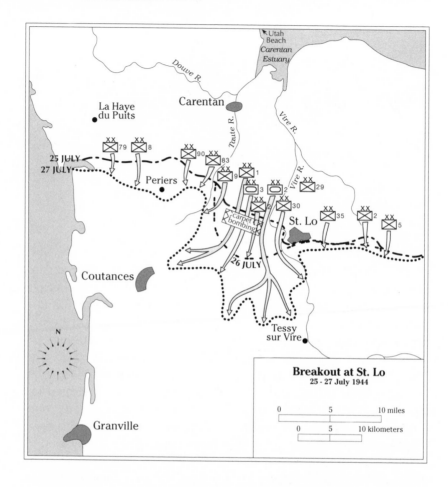

The German counterattack, designed to cut the Allied offensive at its root, separate the fighting forces from their logistical base on the beaches and at sea, and drive the Allies back into the sea, had failed. German forces were in danger of being surrounded. The Allies intended to put the German forces in a bag. Their efforts were partially successful, but an opportunity to close the bag completely at Falaise was missed. Various accusations of blame and finger-pointing immediately followed; later, lack of aggressiveness and military incompetence were charged.

Historian Martin Blumenson is particularly sharp in his criticism of senior Allied leadership. German weapons and equipment were captured and destroyed and prisoners of war (POWs) were taken, but thousands of German soldiers—Blumenson estimates as many as 100,000—infiltrated from the Falaise Gap to the rear to be reorganized. They would fight another day in the Netherlands and in the Ardennes as the struggle continued until May 1945. Blumenson argues that the Allies' respect for the Germans may have resulted in undue caution. He believes that, with the failure of Falaise, the Allies missed an opportunity to destroy the German Army and end the war in 1944.[4]

Ignorant of the big picture, the 90th began to successfully fight a war of movement. Colonel Barth discovered talent, courage, and imagination in his subordinate leaders, men who were capable of rapid decision-making and personal risk-taking. Among his admiring remarks about his battalion commanders, he described Edward Smith Hamilton (USMA, 1939) as having "the dash of a Stonewall Jackson."

Ed Hamilton was one of the few Regulars in the 357th. By the time he joined the 90th at Fort Dix in January 1944, he had been a platoon leader and had commanded a heavy weapons company under a battalion commander "who knew enough to know that he didn't know much about it." His boss relied upon Hamilton for advice. Because his company supported the whole battalion, Hamilton says, "I learned a lot about commanding a battalion from these maneuvers."[5] He had also deployed to Iceland before going to Fort Benning in November 1942 to take the Battalion Command and Staff Officer Course. He remained at Benning to design tactical problems and teach officers at the Infantry School. Thus, when he reported to the 90th Hamilton was already a well-grounded young professional. That's why the division G-3, LTC Richard Stilwell (USMA 1938), took Hamilton as his assistant G-3. Regulars, even those with just a few years of experience, were regarded as very valuable assets.

While DePuy suffered from an experience of the blind leading the blind early in his career, Hamilton and Stilwell had received substantial professional preparation for war. Some of the best among the reservists—DePuy among them—managed to avoid being killed early on, and became the battalion commanders of World War II and the generals of the 1960s and 1970s. Stilwell recognized talent. He told Hamilton, "You know, it is possible that some day I could be serving under DePuy." Talented young men—regular or reservist—moved up rapidly. Stilwell was a lieutenant colonel and division G-3 in 1943 with five years of service; DePuy would be division G-3 with four years of service. These rapid advancements in rank and responsibility contrasted sharply with prewar practices: Ed Hamilton's company commander in 1940, a captain, was West Point, class of 1923.

Major Hamilton went ashore at Normandy an unhappy staff officer, but Stilwell soon sent him to Colonel Barth to command a battalion. Hamilton quickly established his credentials as a commander in the June–July bloodbath and in the dash across France in August and September. Like DePuy, he would not forget the waste of American life. In a single week of combat (5–12 July), Hamilton later recalled, " I lost five company commanders . . . two killed and three wounded." According to him, July 1944 was by far the worst month of the war for the 90th.

August was much better. However flawed the closing of the Falaise Gap, the 90th enjoyed success. A cross-country sprint took the 357th to the Mayenne River on 5 August. Major John Mason, commanding 3/357, with S-3 DePuy and Colonel Barth present, assessed the situation at the river. The far side seemed to be lightly defended. Opportunity knocked.

DePuy later recalled that they "found a skiff and a larger old boat—very leaky," tore down a board fence, and used the slats as oars. Because his soldiers looked dubious about the Huck Finn improvisation and the possibly inhospitable welcome awaiting them, Barth crossed in the first boat. Engineer-provided rubber boats arrived later to transport two more battalions, who joined their comrades on the far side of the river.[6]

Meanwhile, Ed Hamilton, with his infantrymen and a squad of engineers, risked being blown up on the single remaining bridge in Mayenne by personally dashing onto the bridge to rip out the wires to the demolitions that had been prepared by the Germans. DePuy called Hamilton's actions on the bridge "the bravest thing he ever saw anybody ever do during World War II, bar none."[7]

Another reason for the success of the 90th during this phase of combat, according to DePuy, was air support. This "was the *only* time in World War II when we had close air support. We had Air Force officers with radios at the head of each column."[8]

The regiment pressed on to Ste. Suzanne on 6 August, where American and German forces collided in confusing mobile combat. Then they moved on to Le Mans, where Germans and Americans surprised each other. "So we had a big melee there," DePuy remarks laconically. The easy victories made the troops feel "competent and

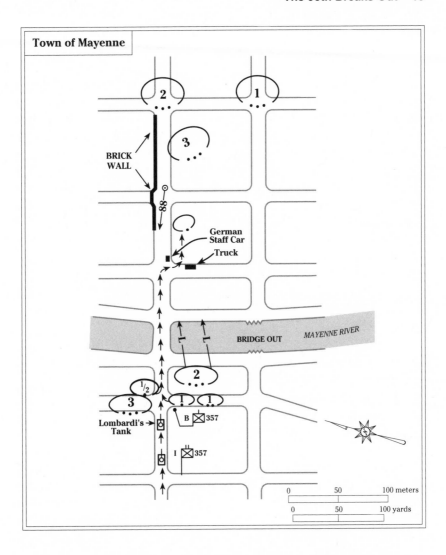

Town of Mayenne

brave." As DePuy put it, "Each time they had one of those experiences they gained a little more confidence, lost their awe of the Germans and became better soldiers."

They turned north in Le Mans to attack into the southern flank
of the Germans who were trying to get out of the Falaise Pocket.
DePuy describes friendly "observers on the high ground shooting
into a bowl."

A bottleneck in the Falaise Pocket was a town called Chambois.

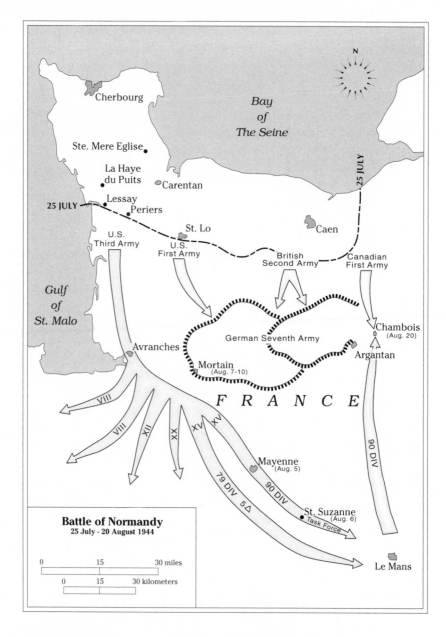

Battle of Normandy
25 July - 20 August 1944

The 358th Infantry, said DePuy, put a battalion "right in there" and absolutely stopped the escape of the German forces:

Our tanks and tank destroyers knocked out some tanks at

the head of the columns, but the real slaughter, and it was an incredible inferno, was done by the artillery. Oh, and by the fighters. I guess it's wrong to say that it was all done by the artillery. P-47s and the British rocket-firing Typhoons were also in there all of the time.

There was a main east-west road that was blocked at Chambois. There were two or three parallel [German] columns all headed to the east, right on the road where they tried to pass one another. Then on each side of the road, in the fields, were clearly discernible additional columns, about ten on each side of the road, so there were about twenty to twenty-five parallel columns as far as the eye could see. By that I mean miles of destroyed vehicles, horses, tanks, and trucks. It was just an incredible sight. And, indeed, if we fight again, and if the Seventh Army and V Corps can hold and prevent a breakthrough, and the Russians get jammed up coming in, and if the Air Force can get at them, there is no doubt in my mind that that's where the killing will occur. Killing comes from heavy firepower.

Here DePuy was responding to a question put to him in 1979 about World War II, but his segue from Chambois to a possible future war with the Soviet Army reveals how strongly his earlier experience in the war affected him. DePuy would use terrain and mobile forces so that "the Russians get jammed up," just as the Germans were at Chambois. Then artillery and aerial firepower would kill them. To make his mental image reality one day, he would need a concept, a doctrine, that would allow him to "fight outnumbered and win the first battle," a phrase that became the mantra of the U.S. Army from the mid-1970s to the end of the Cold War. He would also need rehearsed, mechanized infantry that could keep pace with armor and close cooperation and coordination between ground and air forces. Ironically, DePuy much later would work closely with the new German Army in planning to defeat the Soviet Army.

The official account of what happened at Chambois corroborates DePuy's observations. The Division's great success was particularly gratifying because of its poor showing in June and July in Normandy and at Mont Castre. The 90th passed to the control of V Corps and First Army on 17 August and attacked on 18 August to secure the high ground northeast of Chambois as part of the effort to close the Falaise Pocket completely. V Corps employed the U.S. 90th and 80th and the 2d French Armored Division to close escape routes. The official report says that 20 August was "one of the most momentous in the Division's history." Describing "a last desperate attempt to break out to safety on the part of the Boche," Stilwell, the Division G-3, called it "the greatest ambush of the war." He praised aggressive leadership, but the artillery was singled out for delivering "murderous fire upon the pocket area causing untold destruction and lowering the German morale to and below the breaking point."

Enemy losses were striking: 13,000 prisoners; 8,000 killed or wounded; 220 tanks; 160 artillery pieces; 130 AA artillery pieces; 130 half-track vehicles; 5,000 motor vehicles—and more. "All of this the Division accomplished at the cost of 600 friendly casualties."

V Corps Commander Leonard T. Gerow commended the division in a letter to the CG, 90th Division, dated 30 August, for "the excellent manner in which they functioned while under my command . . . in closing the trap around the enemy. . . . It is without reservation that I say that you have a good fighting division."[9]

The 90th Infantry Division was vindicated. But from a theater or campaign standpoint, an opportunity had been missed.

DePuy was not alone in his admiration of the German soldier. One of the volumes from the Army's official history of World War II provides an example of the steel DePuy admired in the German Army under tremendous pressure at Chambois: "Units that were under the firm control of their commanders fought to the limit of their physical and moral endurance and thereby made the escape of a sizable part of the encircled troops possible. One such unit, a parachute outfit, made quite an impression on men of an SS panzer division when, emerging from the pocket, the paratroopers passed through the tankers smartly in road formation, singing. Behind the men who had fought their way out of the pocket lay an inferno of destruction."[10]

Sixty years after the war, in a review of Max Hastings' *Armageddon: The Battle for Germany, 1944–1945*, Freeman Dyson validates DePuy's conviction that there was something special about German soldiers. According to Dyson, "German soldiers consistently fought better than Britons or Americans. Whenever they were fighting against equal numbers, the Germans always won, a fact recognized by the Allied generals, who always planned to achieve numerical superiority before attacking. This is the main reason why the Allied advance into Germany was slow. If the Allied soldiers had been able to fight like Germans, the war would probably have been over in 1944 and millions of lives would have been saved."[11]

DePuy said that even in times of pursuit "we just ran into little groups that were pretty much incoherent insofar as a general defense was concerned. But, being good German soldiers, they fought well. So, we would run into a company here, a Kampfgruppe there, a couple of tanks here, an assault gun or two there . . . the thing that impressed everybody at the time was how a handful of Germans could hold up a regiment by [siting] their weapons properly."

How does one explain what DePuy, Blumenson, Hastings, and others describe? Science fails us. Ultimately one falls back on an old notion: that the Germans glorified war. *Soldatentum*, the pursuit of soldiering as a spiritual vocation, seems about as close as we can get to an answer.

In his frequent praise of both the old and new German Armies, DePuy was convinced that German soldiers had it, whatever "it" is. Tacitus, a Roman patrician, took a stab at describing this quality in *The Germania* in AD 98: "On the field of battle it is a disgrace to a chief to be surpassed in courage by his followers, and to the followers not to equal the courage of their chief. . . . A German is not so easily prevailed upon to plow the land and wait patiently for harvest as to challenge a foe and earn wounds for his reward."[12] DePuy believed that this quality was found in only about 10 percent of the American soldiers he led in World War II.

From Chambois the 357th led the 90th, crossing the Seine near Fontainebleau on 26 August and the Marne on 29 August before holding up in Reims 1–5 September, due to a general shortage of fuel. Then it was on to the vicinity of Verdun for a two-day fight before the division advanced to the near side of the Moselle at Uckange, where the 1/357th held up again on 12 September.

There was some hope that the war might be concluded in 1944, but it was about to take on a new character. Interruption of the fuel resupply caused some stop-and-go in September; and, notes Martin Blumenson, "Pursuit had been wearing on men and equipment. Casualties had not been heavy at any one place, but their cumulative effect reduced the strength of all combat units."[13] To these problems must be added the grinding effects of sickness, noncombat injuries, and exhaustion. Additionally, vehicles had gone without proper maintenance. In one armored division less than a third of the authorized medium tanks were fit for combat. Two months of hard combat followed by two months of pursuit and intermittent fighting allowed only catnapping and irregular rest. The troops were bone tired.

Some of the logistical problems went back to June. Cherbourg, planned to be in Allied hands by D+8 (14 June), wasn't captured until 27 June. And when it was taken, it wasn't usable. The Germans had done such a thorough job of destroying the port facilities, it took the Allies months to repair them. Mulberry A, the artificial port, was destroyed on 18 June in the worst Channel storm in fifty years, requiring a slower over-the-beach operation. Therefore, as the petrol-consuming mobile forces charged away from their source of fuel, petrol-consuming trucks chased them across France. Russell Weigley wryly noted, "The Allies had come to Normandy to get ports, but they didn't have ports." The problem was compounded when resources—a heavy corps consisting of two infantry and two armored divisions that might have been added to the breakout and attack in the other direction—were diverted to the Brittany peninsula, whose "critical disadvantage is obvious: its distance from the invasion's eventual objectives in Germany."[14] Blumenson criticizes the "less than adequate abilities of the leaders at the top," particularly their failure to concentrate on the destruction of the German Army, thus ending the war sooner.[15]

Nevertheless, a general optimism in September pervades the accounts of the actual participants. The rapid advance across France and the liberation of Paris were heady stuff. And the Russians were about to enter Germany. Romania, Bulgaria, and Finland were negotiating for peace. The German troops in Italy were retreating to the North. In the Pacific, the Allies were advancing to the Philippines. The tide in the China-Burma-India Theater had turned in favor of the Allies under Field Marshal William Joseph Slim, who had been operating on a shoestring. The end of the war in Europe seemed just around the corner. But it would be March 1945 before the Allies crossed the Rhine River. A cycle similar to that of June and July 1944 was about to begin in December 1944. Relatively static and very hard combat in midwinter would be followed by another breakout and pursuit.

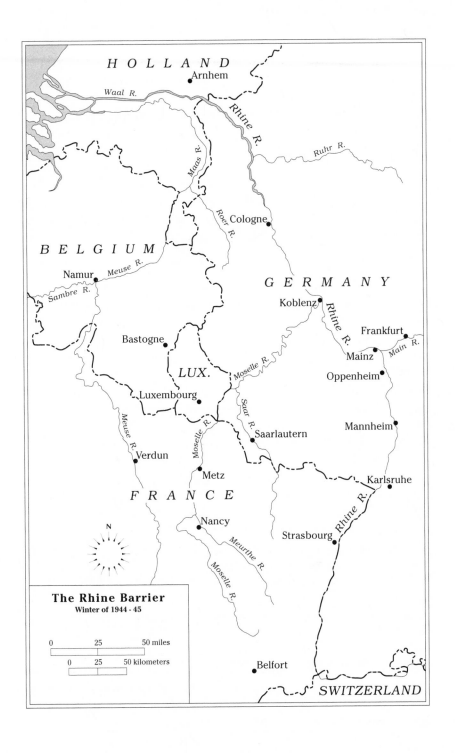

The Rhine Barrier
Winter of 1944 - 45

HOLLAND

Arnhem

Waal R.

Rhine R.

Ruhr R.

Maas R.

Roer R.

Cologne

BELGIUM

Namur

Meuse R.

Sambre R.

GERMANY

Koblenz

Rhine R.

Frankfurt

Main R.

Mainz

Bastogne

Moselle R.

Oppenheim

LUX.

Luxembourg

Saar R.

Mannheim

Meuse R.

Moselle R.

Saarlautern

Verdun

Metz

Karlsruhe

FRANCE

Nancy

Strasbourg

Rhine R.

Meurthe R.

Moselle R.

N

Belfort

SWITZERLAND

0	25	50 miles

0	25	50 kilometers

The pause in the general advance in September 1944 is described by DePuy: "The Third Army had to stop for awhile and let things catch up. . . . We bellied up to the Moselle and stopped." Later, the 5th Division and the 90th met behind Metz. "That was in November," DePuy recalled, "but we first came up to the Moselle in early September." After a pause, the next major event for DePuy's 357th was the hard fighting in Mazieres-les-Metz from early October until 29 October. As was long feared by his subordinates, who were concerned about his practice of leading from the front, Colonel Barth was seriously wounded and evacuated. The regiment had 51 men killed in action (KIA) and 552 total casualties in the biggest and bloodiest fights since July. (House-to-house street fighting takes a heavy toll on infantry. It is characterized by direct close combat, and the use of indirect fires often provide rubble useful to infantry defending against attacking enemy infantry.) After sixty days on line, the 357th went into reserve on 1 November. The 358th and 359th established a Moselle bridgehead, crossed the river, and pressed on to penetrate the Maginot line and attack the Siegfried Line, setting foot in Germany on 24 November.

DePuy was particularly affected by two events from the fighting at Mazieres-les-Metz: the loss of the universally admired Colonel Barth and John Mason's tactical brilliance. Barth was replaced by Colonel Julian H. George, described in the unofficial history of the 90th as "a zero commander" and incompetent.[16] DePuy refers to him as "Colonel X . . . a strange case. The regiment barely noticed his presence." Colonel George was soon replaced by John Mason, whose infiltration technique while commanding a battalion made a deep impression on DePuy.

Where there had been much bloody fighting without success, Mason pulled off a coup that DePuy admired and imitated. Mason assigned a house to each squad and gave them a day to figure out how they were going to get to their assigned house and what they were going to do once they got there. DePuy explained how detailed the planning and rehearsal was. "Mullen is going to throw a hand grenade in that window, then Brownlee is going to jump in that window." The men also used a little sand table or mockup in their planning. "Well," said DePuy, "this attack jumped off at three o'clock in the morning. In five or ten minutes the battle was over. In five minutes the whole thing was finished. We had, oh, I don't know, 200 prisoners—a small battalion. We lost maybe two or three men."

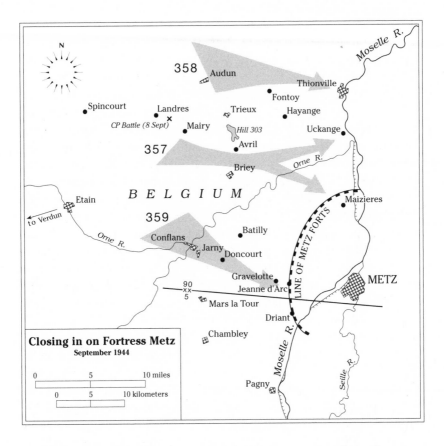

Closing in on Fortress Metz
September 1944

0   5   10 miles

0   5   10 kilometers

DePuy could barely control his enthusiasm in telling the story thirty-five years after the event. "We fought in there for weeks and had all sorts of casualties trying to get that damn city hall . . . or whatever it was. And we just fiddled and fiddled and took casualties. John Mason, the Third Battalion commander, later the regimental commander, was the genius who figured it all out. . . . it was the instructions at the squad level that made the difference. *It was totally decentralized in execution and totally centralized in planning.* Now, there has got to be a lesson in that somewhere, right?"

The commander of 1/357 told his regimental commander that he couldn't take it any more. DePuy was sent to the First Battalion by Colonel George without specific instructions. Once there, DePuy assessed the situation and told the completely dejected commander that he was taking command of the battalion. He gathered the company commanders. Aware that they were good men who had been badly led, he let them know that he was fully aware of that fact. Then he told them, "You know that everybody is going to get killed if we pussyfoot around like that. So, now we are going to go ahead and get to work."

The 1/357 had a new commander as of 5 December 1944.

Colonel Ken Reimers, commander of the 343d Field Artillery Battalion in direct support of the 357th since the June fighting in the hedgerows, knew exactly what was going on in the regiment and in the immediate situation. He had observed DePuy in combat for six months. "DePuy will make an excellent battalion commander," he said, adding, "If this crossing [of the Saar] is a success, it will be because of good leadership, not good planning."

Reimers recalled that DePuy sent a patrol to cross the river to get information about German preparations on the far side. A couple of hours later the patrol returned, saying they couldn't get across due to enemy machine-gun fire. "DePuy blew his top. He loaded them in a jeep and took them back to the river. He determined that the shooting was ineffective fire and ordered the patrol, 'By God! Get across now!'" Reimers said that the patrol brought back information essential to the success of the operation in the following days.[17]

PFC Boyd R. Burlingame captures the essence of DePuy as battalion commander. "Major DePuy single-handedly stopped the whole company from galloping to the rear when we entered the Siegfried Line."[18]

DePuy recalls the incident this way: "I walked along and went to every boat and every squad. A few of them we had to put into the boats at pistol point. I suppose that is not an approved leadership technique." No wonder that Burlingame remembered DePuy and that night.

The mission was to get a foothold across the Saar. DePuy identified a hill that dominated a road junction on the other side that had to be blocked to prevent a successful German counterattack. His concept of the operation was to infiltrate by squads to that hill. Avoiding contact with the enemy, decentralizing down to squads as he had seen John Mason do so successfully in October, he departed from the usual manner of passing orders down the chain of command. "In the day and a half I had," he recalled, "I personally talked to every company commander. Then I had the company commanders bring in every platoon leader and squad leader, and I gave them all the same orders." There was no misunderstanding the commander's intent.

They crossed the Saar near Rehlingen. To avoid assaulting a carefully prepared German defensive system of three bands of mutually supporting pillboxes, DePuy gave his squads simple instructions: Cross the river. Avoid contact. Go to the road at the hill. Set up a defense. Wait for me.

When DePuy joined the fifty or sixty men so assembled, he put them in position to control the road junction, improving his position as more men arrived. His left flank was open. That is, there were no friendlies to his left. He had each man carry a mine, and he placed them to defeat enemy armor. German tanks would attack "on five or ten occasions." But they hesitated to sweep over the light infantrymen, because DePuy deliberately left some of the mines exposed to deter the tank commanders. Reimers said, "Major DePuy had the First Battalion through the Siegfried Line and on its objective before daylight."[19]

The 1/357 was alone. On a map, Bill DePuy and his men were at the very point of the arrow showing General Patton's Third Army's deepest penetration into Germany. It wasn't cozy on 6 December 1944.

They hung tough. According to DePuy, "We used a lot of artillery. We could get three or four battalions of artillery [to support us] through our direct support battalion. The Air Corps XIX Tactical Air Command (TAC) dropped us some ammo and medical supplies in wing tanks. One pilot couldn't get his tank to drop, so when he came in for the third time he brushed it off on a tall pine tree. He flew his P-47 out of Etain, and we sent him a Silver Star."

Deplorable weather conditions caused foot injuries and pneumonia. "It was dark and raining," recalled DePuy years later; "just awful weather. You know, typical German November and December weather. Just as ugly as you can imagine." Sharp engagements every day forced soldiers into foxholes filled with water. He rotated soldiers to warm up and dry out in a couple of German storage bunkers. The doctor who was with the men ran an aid station right in the middle of the perimeter that "got loaded with wounded, people with immersion foot, and other people who were sick. We had several pneumonia cases."

PFC Jack E. Ammons, Co. C, 357th, recalled being sent with another soldier by his company commander to DePuy to present a list

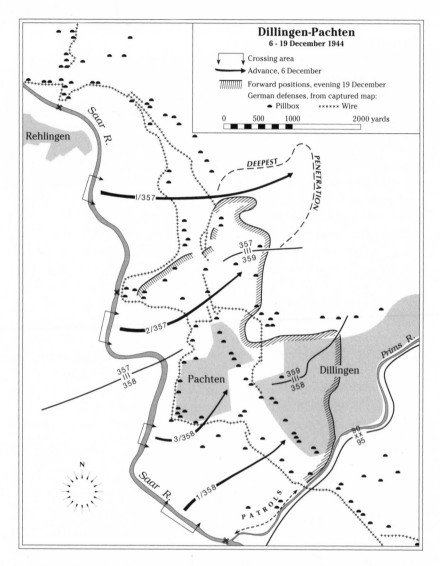

Dillingen-Pachten
6 - 19 December 1944

Crossing area
Advance, 6 December
Forward positions, evening 19 December
German defenses, from captured map:
● Pillbox   ××××× Wire
0   500   1000   2000 yards

of what the company required: men, K-rations, "ammo, oil and rags for our guns, they're going to pieces. We're down to one-third the strength we had when we came across this river and we've got men right now who need medical attention, especially for trench foot." Ammons said that "the Major listened intently as we unfolded the sad story . . . He knew we wouldn't have risked our lives coming here just for the joy of it." When Ammons had finished, DePuy said, "I'm sorry, fellas, that I can't send you the things you are asking for. . . . We haven't got a thing to offer." Ammons, timidly, replied, "Major, I wonder if you've got a K ration for me and Allison. We haven't had anything to eat for two days." DePuy got Allison and his companion two rations. "The one with the cheese," said Allison. "Even that was good."[20]

DePuy recalled getting hundreds of replacements after the events described. The newcomers had shoe packs, a thick, feltlike insert that improved the insulation of boots. Apparently that was the first time DePuy saw the shoe pack. DePuy recalled years later the many "disastrous losses" due to foot injuries, mostly immersion foot. He said he "got some of those men back, but not many. A lot of them lost toes, and others probably had trouble for the rest of their lives. By the time I brought our B Company back across the Saar and put in a rest camp, I think there were only about ten men left in it. All the rest were either wounded or killed, or had immersion foot. That's why I got hundreds of replacements in one day."

DePuy's problem was theaterwide. In a memorandum of 21 November 1944 sent to all Third Army corps and division commanders, General Patton said, "The most serious menace confronting us today is not the German Army . . . but the weather which, if we do not exert ourselves, may well destroy us through the incidence of trench foot. . . . To win the war we must conquer trench foot."

In all of World War II, American air and ground forces suffered 91,000 cold-weather casualties. Between November 1944 and April 1945, hospitals in Europe admitted 45,283 cold-weather casualties. The only uniform regulation in those days was "Wear anything that will keep you warm."

In addition, combat exhaustion, often ignored during combat, took a toll *after* combat. It has gone by various names: shell shock, battle fatigue, combat fatigue—GIs in Korea called it "battle-rattle"—and the war in Vietnam introduced PTSD, Post Traumatic Stress Disorder. The Third Army reported that 11 percent of hospital admissions in the period September–November 1944 were for combat exhaustion.[21]

The American decision to fight the war with 89 divisions meant that instead of rotating large units, a pipeline provided individual replacements. Intense combat in the European Theater of Operations (ETO) produced casualties overwhelmingly among riflemen in squads and platoons. One veteran said, "There was no way out except KIA [killed in action], WIA [wounded in action], or war over."[22]

When crossing the Moselle, six of the infantry battalions of the 90th were at 50 percent strength after four days. It was about the same in other divisions. From 1 July to 31 October 1944, the 9th Infantry Division lost 17,974 men, 3,235 of whom returned to duty within thirty days, for a net loss of 14,739, more than 100 percent of organic strength. Regiments represented one-half of division strength but sustained 85 percent of division casualties.[23]

DePuy was ordered to recross the Saar in December 1944, but not because of his losses. The theater operational situation required adjustments, so the 90th Division got a new mission. DePuy didn't know the reason. Something was brewing to the north.

He exfiltrated the same way he infiltrated, by squads. Each squad was given a sick, injured, or wounded soldier to take to the rear. The battalion got out without further loss. "We got every wounded man and every man with trench foot out," DePuy recalled with pride. "Never lost a single soul and didn't have a single casualty [in the extraction]. And all these fellows, this gaggle of soldiers, went down in the dark and did exactly what they were told to do. *It was a central idea and totally decentralized execution.*" Thus he learned another principle that became a part of his permanent repertoire: "be very specific as to what you want them to do, and if you are, they'll do it. Keep it simple!" In other words: Decide. Give clear orders. Insure these orders are executed.

Reunited with the regiment on the western side of the Saar, the 357th completed its withdrawal smoothly in the wee hours of 22 December. In fifteen days of close combat in nasty weather, the history of the 357th boasts that every man in the regiment had taken part, either in the line or by serving in carrying parties. The regiment had been steadily reduced by the constant enemy shelling and the effects of cold weather.

What followed was not a walk in the park. The 90th again went to the sound of the guns: the Second Battle of the Ardennes was raging in a bulge caused by a German offensive aimed at Antwerp. They trucked north over seventy miles of icy roads and then immediately engaged the Germans in bitter fighting.

A sense of DePuy's style may be gleaned from his attack on Berle, a small town south of the middle of a line drawn from Bastogne to Wiltz. On 8 January 1945, he made his commander's reconnaissance (see position 1 on map) and put his 500-man battalion in an attack position in deep snow after dark on a reverse slope. At 0700 hours on 9 January, using darkness and fog to conceal his movements, he led A Company, followed by B Company, into a deep ravine (position 2 on map). His position was with the A Company commander behind the lead platoon. Each company had a heavy machine-gun platoon attached. His plan was to take Berle, just beyond the head of the ravine and to his left, with this infantry force. He put his C Company plus a tank platoon and a tank destroyer (TD) platoon on the road that ran parallel to and above the ravine to Berle, about 500

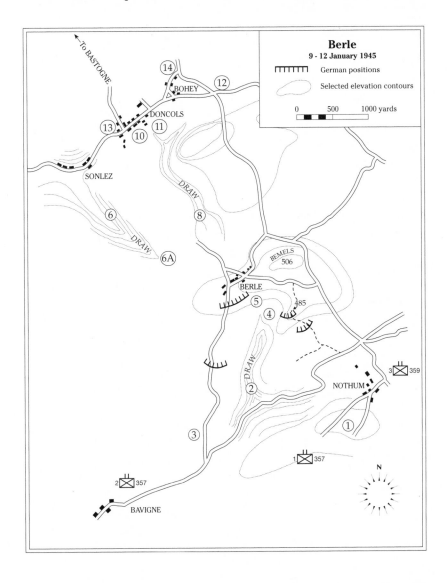

Berle
9 - 12 January 1945
German positions
Selected elevation contours
0   500   1000 yards

yards to his left (position 3). On his order, by use of a red star cluster, the men on the road would attack in coordination with the infantry in the ravine. Moving with stealth, the American infantry was invisible to the Germans on the high ground on both sides. DePuy's force in the ravine did not return fire in response to the ineffective fire by the Germans over their heads.

His plan was to use B Company as a base of fire on Berle while A Company assaulted, as C Company with tanks and tank destroyers moved simultaneously on the road to Berle. Taking machine-gun fire from his right rear, DePuy dispatched elements from B Company "to shut down the machine guns." (He had to grab a group of soldiers at this point and tell them sharply, "Go there and do that now." They did, and succeeded in silencing the machine guns.) DePuy had coordinated artillery fire and did not want to shut it off. This is in keeping with the KISS rule: Keep It Simple, Stupid. Unnecessary changes in the midst of an attack generally lead to confusion, and confusion can be deadly.

DePuy fired "a substantial artillery preparation" (position 4 on map). A Company assaulted, B Company supported with fires, and he fired the signal for C Company with tanks and guns to "go." At that point, recalled DePuy years later, "C Co. barreled up the road without any losses, picking up a few prisoners on the way, and arrived at the edge of Berle simultaneously with A Company, just like it was supposed to happen (a rare occurrence). We took about eighty-one prisoners, including the Battalion Commander and his staff." He consolidated his defense of Berle, holding B Company in an overwatch position and as reserve in case of German counterattack. "It was a good day's work," said DePuy. But it was another cold night.

On 10 January, the attached TD platoon alerted DePuy to "an astounding sight." Coming up the valley from the northwest (position 6) was a large German column moving in two files, one on either side of the road, fat, dumb, and happy. "They obviously did not know we were in Berle with armor." When they were ready, "the TDs opened fire on the left side of the road, the tanks opened fire on the right, and the artillery walked up and down the valley. It was a massacre." On 11 and 12 January, DePuy continued the attack, taking many prisoners.[24]

DePuy said that having all the pieces fall in place in the hurly-burly of battle is rare, but the assault on Berle and what followed is the way it's supposed to unfold: conduct leader's recon; use limited visibility and terrain to advantage; disregard ineffective enemy fire; coordinate infantry and supporting weapons; issue simple and direct orders; be generous in using artillery to do the killing; maintain constant overwatch; consolidate rapidly; prepare for counterattack; continue the mission. These were the methods that he would focus on for the rest of his life.

There is a broader significance to DePuy's actions at Berle in January: American soldiers and their leaders had learned a great deal from June 1944 to the beginning of 1945, in particular about the skillful use of combined arms. As mentioned earlier, recent scholarship is revising some previously accepted interpretations of the 1944–1945 war in Europe. A few examples of this recent work suggest that DePuy's experience in the 90th may have been the general pattern of many American infantry divisions.

Peter R. Mansoor is frankly revisionist. Even at Normandy, he notes that while "the campaign was not pretty" it succeeded, adding that most American divisions eventually developed into lethal fighting organizations. The U.S. Army excelled in the war of movement after the breakout and learned combined arms coordination. Michael D. Doubler debunks the notion that the American army achieved victory only because it had overwhelming numbers of lavishly supplied troops that fought an exhausted Wehrmacht. In less than three years, he points out, American soldiers learned sophisticated combined arms tactics with deadly efficiency. They learned from their mistakes and adapted.[25] Perhaps the 90th was particularly unfortunate with early commanders, but its learning curve seems fairly representative of American infantry divisions. A cautionary note, however, may be in order here: the revisionists may not be attentive enough to the difference between the German Army of 1939–1942, which was an efficient offensive force, and the battered German Army of 1944–1945.

Terms like "mopping up" and "pockets of resistance" have been used to describe the pursuit phase of battle, almost suggesting a hostess tidying up after a pleasant dinner party. Following the failed German offensive in the winter of 1944–1945 to the early days of May 1945, the Allied war in Germany was essentially one of pursuit. But American soldiers endorse DePuy's observation regarding the German soldier: even when he was incapable of organized defense, he persisted in behaving "like a good German soldier." He fought. Small groups, single gun crews, the odd tank or machine gun, hard-core elite troops, SS men fearing capture, a still combat-effective artillery unit—this motley residue of a great army continued to fight in the days, even hours, before surrender. Innocents, like the boy armed with a Panzerfaust in the famous photograph with Hitler patting his cheek, were sent to kill and die in combat without purpose. Old men beyond the age for military service joined the boys in futile efforts to defend *die Heimat*. It was like using a teaspoon to hold back the tide, but just hours before the end of the war with Germany, soldiers of the 90th Division were still being killed in combat in Czechoslovakia.[26]

On 7 May the 90th Division command post was set up in Susice, Czechoslovakia. Several men of the 357th who had been captured at Beau Coudray in July 1944 were liberated. Patrols from the 357th and 359th were sent out to contact the Russians. It appeared that German and White Russian troops might try to force an exit into the American Zone to avoid capture by the Red Army, but, on orders from higher headquarters, the trapped German soldiers became Russian prisoners.

On 8 May 1945 an armistice was officially announced, but there was no celebrating in the 90th Division. The officers of the 357th assembled in Cejkovy, Czechoslovakia, on a hill where a flagpole had been erected and the American flag raised. The Division Commander spoke. Robert Moore, the Field Artillery battalion commander and diarist who was present, doesn't remember precisely what was said, but he clearly recalls that Colonel Mason thanked everyone. There had been some 250 percent casualties in the infantry, and Moore noted that this was the first time since their days in England that all the officers were assembled in one group at one time: "Of course there weren't many of us from the other meeting who were now present. Colonel Mason started out as a major, Lt. Col. DePuy was a 1st Lieut. and Lt. Col. [Benjamin] Rossow was a captain. There wasn't one single [infantry] company commander who left England who was present. Only the Service Companies commanders hadn't changed. There isn't any more than a half dozen present today [8 May 1945] that landed on Utah Beach in June."[27]

On 14 May the 90th Division was ordered to the vicinity of Weiden, Germany.

Bill DePuy had found his calling in war. Privates, sergeants, and superiors praised his guts and his brains. He was lucky to have been only slightly wounded, considering the numerous recorded references to his being where the action was hot and heavy and where he could influence the action, eyeball to eyeball with both the enemy and with his soldiers in squads, platoons, and companies. DePuy was good at war.

The visible signs of a soldier's success are the medals on his chest and the rank he wears on his collar or sleeve. Bill DePuy said what old sweats know: acts of heroism at the cutting edge are invisible and frequent. Squad members lay it on the line on a daily basis, risking life and limb for their friends. No one sees the sharing of a cup of hot coffee in winter or shared water in summer's heat. Or: I'll go on patrol 'cause Smitty's got a cold.

DePuy was well aware of this. He minimized the many awards and decorations that most of us revere. When asked directly about them, he said, "Decorations go to the wrong people. The privates, the sergeants, and the lieutenants who do the real fighting normally perform where there is nobody around to observe it, or they observe one another; but they are not the people who write up the citations. So, the colonels and the generals get more decorations than they should."

Nevertheless, the fact is that DePuy was awarded a Distinguished Service Cross (DSC) in World War II, the valor award just below the Medal of Honor. He would get another DSC in Vietnam. He also got three Silver Stars in World War II, a Bronze Star, and two Purple Hearts. He, and all combat infantrymen, got the Combat Infantryman's Badge (CIB) which was initiated in World War II. All soldiers respect the valor awards, but a better sense of DePuy's professional competence is found in the words of his wartime superiors.

Major General Herbert L. Earnest, who commanded the 90th at the end of the war, used the military superlative "outstanding" to describe DePuy's work as battalion commander, regimental executive officer, and division G-3.[28] (Commanding generals typically select their best battalion commander to be the division's G-3.)

Major General Lowell W. Rooks, who commanded the 90th before Earnest, wrote, "I visited Lt. Col. DePuy's battalion on several occasions when it was engaged and can testify personally to his courage, leadership, and skill as a combat commander. Moreover, I observed his strong, pleasing personality, which, combined with his other high attributes of character, made him one of the outstanding battalion commanders of the war."[29]

Major General James A. Van Fleet commanded the 90th from 16 October 1944 to 1 February 1945. He called DePuy's staff work "brilliant" and added that DePuy's "inspiring and courageous leadership" of his battalion in many actions, including the Ardennes, provides "some of the finest examples of infantry operations in this war." Having mentioned DePuy's love of service, professional pride, intelligence, and "capacity for any staff or command position," Van Fleet concluded, "Colonel DePuy is one of the finest officers I know and one of the most skilled and successful battalion commanders produced by this war."[30]

Richard G. Stilwell, then a colonel and G-3 at XXII Corps, was lavish in his praise of DePuy, calling him "one of the most brilliant and courageous combat leaders developed during the war. I consider that this man represented 20–25 percent of the regiment's overall battle efficiency." DePuy's actions in his first hours of battalion command and the infiltration method he used to cross the Saar were described earlier in this chapter, but here is Stilwell's brief account from the perspective of someone up the chain of command at the time of the action: "Thirty-six hours after assumption of command, he attacked across the Saar River . . . In the furious ten-day fight that followed, DePuy's battalion displayed an aggressiveness, a tenacious spirit, and a coordination not heretofore approached." He also described DePuy's methods: "He achieved his objectives by attacks which were models of small unit maneuver, surprise, and deception, as well as of planning and consequently kept casualties at the irreducible minimum. For my money, he represents the ideal battalion commander among that group of battle leaders whose combat job was the most difficult of all." Stilwell concluded, "I am convinced—completely—that this officer would have a meteoric career in the Regular establishment."[31] (DePuy said of Stilwell, who would become a lifelong friend, "He came up and pinned on my lieutenant colonel's leaves in the little town of Binsfeld, Luxembourg, in the middle of the Battle of the Bulge. . . . Dick Stilwell really ran the 90th Division during the whole time he was there, certainly during McKelvie and Landrum's time. McLain was a fine, great leader, a wise man, and just. But under the first two generals, Dick ran the division.")

John H. Mason, DePuy's regimental commander, a former battalion commander in the 357th, and a man DePuy held in highest regard, says that DePuy "was by far the best combat Battalion Commander and natural leader of man [*sic*] that I have known." Mason and the others also refer admiringly to DePuy's personality.[32] Cheerful, generous, invigorating, direct, intelligent, compassionate, exacting, decisive, skillful, and courageous are words often used to describe him.

George Bittman Barth, DePuy's former regimental commander, wrote in a letter on 25 July 1945, while still a patient at Walter Reed Hospital: "His performance of duty was so superior that it is hard to do justice to it on paper. He combined great professional ability with untiring effort and complete loyalty. . . . I was able to turn over to him all details of operation that so often weigh on the mind of a commander." Barth concludes, "I know of few officers of his age and service who are his equal and none who are superior to him."[33]

These kudos should be placed in perspective, of course. After all, they were all composed by men who were enormously relieved: the war was over; they would not die today. The triumphal atmosphere at war's end was replete with bonhomie and praise all around. Moreover, in the U.S. Army all stops are pulled when it comes to recommendations and efficiency reports for worthies. Prose reaches for poetry in the recommendation to appoint a skilled Reserve Officer to the Regular Army. Nevertheless, Bill DePuy had indeed compiled one hell of a war record.

5

Regular Army

Patton asked me if I would like to be his aide. I was
astounded.

—Bill DePuy in his Oral History

High praise from superiors contrasts sharply with Bill DePuy's sober self-analysis. Asked what led him to stay in the Army after the war to make it a career, he responded, "Well, I assumed I would get out. I didn't realize that there would be an option to stay in." Turning to the practical matter of income, the child of the Great Depression reckoned his army pay and allowances to be $535 a month. His likely alternative at the time, to be a bank teller back home, would pay about $150 per month. In addition, he had explored the world beyond the horizons of the Dakotas and liked it. "So, number one, I enjoyed the Army and felt comfortable with it, and secondly, I really didn't want to go back to South Dakota. I found Washington to be an exciting place for a young fellow right off the reservation, so I decided to stay. That's about how complicated my decision was."[1]

Before the war, DePuy had failed to obtain a commission in the Marine Corps, and while on active duty as a Reservist, he had applied for a Regular Army (RA) commission, only to be rejected again.[2] He thereupon went off to war "for the duration," and was pleased to be encouraged to apply again after the war. His demonstration of skills and courage on the battlefield made all the difference.

His RA date of rank as a first lieutenant was adjusted to 7 December 1944. His Army of the United States (AUS) rank, the rank he wore on his collar and for which he was paid, was lieutenant colonel with a date of rank of 18 January 1945.[3] An officer's RA rank, permanent rank, typically lags a grade or two behind his serving rank.

DePuy retained his rank as lieutenant colonel after the war, while others, such as his friend Dick Stilwell, for example, did not retain theirs. This was the luck of the draw, the numbers game of fitting individual officers into the total personnel picture of the downsized Army. Estimates were made of the size of the Army and the numbers of officers required at the various ranks. This was the norm in the U.S. Army as demobilization followed mobilization. After World War I many officers were forced to take two and even three grade reductions. Patton dropped from colonel to major and had to wait until the eve of World War II to become a colonel again. Eisenhower went from lieutenant colonel to captain. The officers in the Army War College class of 1920, the first class after the war, included four major generals who became colonels, six brigadier generals who became lieutenant colonels, and three who became majors.[4] This was the consequence of serving in a force that was reduced from well over two million in 1918 to about 200,000 in 1920 and leveled off to about 140,000 men for more than a dozen years in the period between the world wars.

The size of the Army fluctuated significantly during DePuy's career, with deleterious consequences. The Army was about 180,000 men strong when he graduated from high school, about 1.5 million when bombs fell on Pearl Harbor, and some 8.4 million in May 1945. In 1950 U.S. Army strength was 590,000 men, climbing to almost 1.6 million for the Korean War. Then, from 1957 to 1961, it was between 860,000 and 900,000 before its numbers climbed again to almost one million during the war in Vietnam.

The accordion effect of increases and decreases in size is usually caused by war, but there are other causes. The increase from about half a million before the Korean War to over a million and a half during that war has two causes, as two armies were raised. Signing on as a member state in the North Atlantic Treaty Organization (NATO) in 1949 meant that the United States had to fill the Seventh Army in Europe, requiring it to be considerably expanded to meet treaty obligations after the severe post–World War II reductions. Then, because of the surprise attack from North Korea in 1950, the Eighth U.S. Army was raised to fight in Korea.

Unpreparedness in numbers and training and neglect of Army modernization meant that U.S. armed forces went to the Korean War with World War II hand-me-downs. This partially explains their bad performance in Korea, particularly early in that war. For example, the World War II shoulder-fired 2.36-inch rocket launcher known as the bazooka was ineffective against the Soviet T-34 tanks employed by the North Koreans in the summer of 1950. (In fact it was ineffective in 1944 against the German Mark V tank.) A new and effective 3.5-inch launcher existed, but it was not in the hands of the first U.S. troops sent to Korea to stop the attack from North Korea. The effects of rapid contraction and expansion of the Army early in his soldiering made a deep and permanent impression on Bill DePuy. Nevertheless, in 1945 he was optimistic as he embarked on his career as a new Regular.

There is a progression of schooling for Regular Officers in more settled times. It has varied over time, but generally entry training for lieutenants and troop duty is followed in five or eight years by a course for captains with emphasis on branch skills, such as infantry, artillery, armor, and the like. At the grade of major, one learns at the Command and General Staff College (C&GSC) at Fort Leavenworth, Kansas, how to fight a division by knowing its capabilities and limitations and by practicing staff skills. Finally, the successful colonel or lieutenant colonel in about the twentieth year of service is selected to attend a senior service college—a sort of prep school for those who might be promoted to flag rank (generals and admirals) and for those who will function in key slots at high-level staffs as colonels.

DePuy missed the first two steps of normal career progression. He was given credit for the courses normally taken by lieutenants and captains and was selected to attend an abbreviated Command and General Staff College course at Fort Leavenworth in 1945. Normally an academic year in length, his course was four months long. Later, when asked about his impressions of the Staff College in light of his experience as a battalion and operations officer, DePuy observed that it was a peculiar atmosphere, "since everybody there considered himself an expert." The instructors had a very hard time managing classes of five hundred men, most of them experienced combat veterans. But, he said, he learned quite a bit. He learned the technical vocabulary, the right words and terms for many of the operations he had conducted in combat as an operations officer or commander—rather like learning the grammar for one's native language.

Most of his learning was in those staff areas in which DePuy had little or no previous training or experience: G-1, Personnel; G-2, Intelligence; and G-4, Logistics. Instruction was primarily at the regimental and division levels with a little at corps level. Discussions with peers and faculty and reflection allowed DePuy to consider and compare theory and practice. By 1946 he had two formal Army courses under his belt, the ten-week communications course at Fort Benning in 1941 and the curtailed staff course at Leavenworth after the war, as he looked forward to his first assignment as a Regular.

His Brookings ROTC mentor, Colonel James Murphy, was Professor of Military Science and Tactics (PMS&T) at the University of Nebraska in 1945, proud of his "boys" who had made good. In a letter to DePuy at Fort Leavenworth, Murphy congratulated DePuy for selection to C&GSC and proposed that he consider requesting a position in the ROTC system. And, he asked, "How is the young lady? Give her our best and we hope that she is becoming used to army life and procedure." And later, "I fully appreciate your desire to settle down on some assignment that will offer you an opportunity to resume normal home life and I know of no better solution than ROTC."[5]

Bill DePuy and Barbara Whiplery were married on 25 July 1942 in Abilene, Texas, while he was regimental communications officer in the 357th Infantry at Camp Barkeley. Their divorce was made final on 7 October 1949 in Nevada. Not much is known about DePuy's wartime marriage. He listed his father-in-law, H. E. Whiplery, Lake Preston, South Dakota, as "emergency addressee" on his application for language and area training dated 24 September 1947, suggesting that Barbara lived at home with her parents in South Dakota while Bill was overseas and even later.[6]

Bill DePuy Jr. hypothesizes that Barbara rejected the nomadic life that promised to be hers as the wife of a career soldier, but that is pure speculation.[7] Still, after waiting for her "temporary soldier" to come marching home from the wars to resume an orderly life as a banker in South Dakota, Barbara was faced with a husband who was soon off to Kansas for four months, then on to Washington, and then talking about language school in California and probable assignment to the Soviet Union.

Wayne Waltz, DePuy's lifelong friend, reported hosting Bill and Barbara DePuy at their first get-together after the war, a dinner at the Waltzes' in South Dakota. He doesn't know why the marriage failed, but he said that Bill "finished Barbara's sentences," implying that Bill's quick mind and wartime responsibilities were not matched by Barbara's personal evolution. It was, in the vernacular of the day, a bad wartime marriage.[8]

DePuy's job in 1946 and 1947 was to fill the All Volunteer Army "at the time we went off the draft." There were three officers involved in enlisted procurement in the whole Pentagon, and DePuy *was* the enlisted volunteer program. "The only one!" he said. But the Army couldn't buy enough volunteers in 1946. As he recalled, the army needed about 15,000 men a month to meet requirements, but the chart DePuy kept behind his desk revealed a shortfall of "a couple of thousand men" per month. "So, by the time the Korean War came along and Congress reinstituted the draft, we were very much understrength." Apparently the prospect of military discipline and low pay was singularly unappealing in the years after the Big War.

DePuy liked the city of Washington, but one suspects that he didn't like the routine and discouraging work he was doing there in 1947. After less than two years on the General Staff, he applied for Russian language training at the Army Language School in Monterey, California, where he spent the entire year from January to December 1948. Asked why he volunteered for language school and area specialization, he responded, "Because I thought that Russia was important. I was a little bit tired of the tactical side of things at the moment, and I thought that that would be a good thing to do. It was, and I learned it [Russian]."

The euphoria of victory in 1945 evolved to the sobering realization that Europe was broken and the Soviet Union might pick up the pieces. Churchill remarked that the only thing between the white cliffs of Dover and the white snows of the Urals was the Red Army. The post–World War II devolution of European empires around the world created opportunities to be exploited, and the civil war in China suggested that communism might be the wave of the future. DePuy was doing his G-1 job in Washington when the Marshall Plan was announced and the Soviet Union and its satellites refused to participate in a program of European reconstruction. California beckoned, and Russia was an exotic place where an adventurous and imaginative young man might find purpose as Soviet–U.S. tensions increased.

While DePuy studied Russian in 1948, the Brussels Treaty, a step toward collective European defense that would lead to the establishment of NATO, was signed by Britain, France, Belgium, the Netherlands, and Luxembourg in March. In July the Soviets blockaded Berlin, to which the Allies responded with the Berlin Airlift. NATO was founded in 1949; the United States became a member; the Cold War was on.

In Hungary, Josef Cardinal Mindszenty was charged with conspiracy to overthrow the Communist government. On 8 February 1948, he was found guilty and sentenced to life imprisonment. He sought and received asylum in the American Legation in Budapest. In retaliation, the Hungarian government declared the American military attachés persona non grata, affecting the plans of a certain young army officer.

Upon completion of his language training, where he ranked fifth in a class of twenty-seven, DePuy returned to Washington in January 1949, still in student status, to prepare to be the Assistant Military Attaché in Moscow.[9] While attending the attaché course, DePuy's orders were changed. He would go to Hungary. "So," he said, "all of my Russian went for naught, and Hungarian is an impossible language. I never did learn it. It was rather an exciting time in that the Communists were in the process of consolidating their power."

His tour in Hungary was brief, but exciting. The high point began as a routine task that cascaded into an adventure with equal parts of drama and comedy. As DePuy told the story, "It almost turned me into the intelligence game permanently, something that I did not want."

A message from Washington directed a report on the condition of a bridge over the Danube which the Germans had dropped late in 1944 to delay the Russian envelopment of Budapest during the war. Intelligence analysts in Washington were compiling books for each of the countries that had come under the sway of the Soviets. Road and rail networks were of interest to the intelligence community. Lieutenant Colonel DePuy got the task: report on the condition of the bridge. So, as he recalled, "One sunny autumn day in 1949, I put on my Air Force fur-collared flight jacket, no hat, civilian trousers and shirt, and stirred up my Hungarian jeep driver, a blond crew-cut chap in a field jacket with no hat . . ."

The drive to the bridge at Mohacs, some seventy-fives south of Budapest, was uneventful, and DePuy saw that the bridge was not being rebuilt. Reconnaissance complete, it remained only to drive back to the office and to write and transmit his report to Washington.

As DePuy and his driver were on their way back to Budapest, they encountered a Russian military convoy headed in the direction they were traveling. "It consisted of U.S. jeeps, two-and-a-half-ton trucks, stake and platform ten-ton trucks, plus artillery and towed tank guns." In other words, the seemingly endless convoy included U.S. materials and vehicles, including jeeps like the one in which he was riding. Good soldier DePuy sat at a road junction reflexively counting vehicles and recording bumper numbers. After an hour, growing impatient, he directed his driver to pull into a gap in the long column of vehicles. "The only identification on our jeep was a small six-by-eight-inch enamel U.S. flag on the right base of the windshield. Fortunately, we looked like all of the Russian jeeps in the convoy." After some thirty miles the column pulled into a huge forested area off to the right. DePuy and his driver spotted a large group of officers and military police ahead, but they had no choice but to pull up snugly to the big truck in front of them and "scooted in with the convoy." They got some hard looks along the way, but they were not stopped. The issue was simple: how the hell to get out of the mess and away from the Russians. The most nervous moments were when DePuy found himself alone on the road. Fortunately, a Budapest municipal water sprinkler was wetting down the road. Following the sprinkler—and madly scribbling the bumper numbers in his notebook, counting tanks and artillery, locating the positions of command posts, and drawing antennas—DePuy, miraculously, found himself back on the main highway where they had entered the woods. Alas, a Soviet checkpoint had been set up right there! So they made another circuit, feeling like a small fish in a school of sharks. DePuy kept counting and identifying military impedimenta until he and his driver found a firebreak in the forest leading to back roads and eventually to the main highway, Budapest, the embassy, and safety.

Once back in Budapest, DePuy worked through the night to get out "a very voluminous and detailed report." Integrating what he had observed with reference books on hand that identified Russian divisions and regiments by bumper markings, he scored a significant intelligence coup. It turned out, he said later, that "we had seen ninety percent of the 17th Guards Mechanized Division moving from the USSR to Hungary in preparation for the invasion of Yugoslavia from the north." Since satellite photography was not yet available to the intelligence community, his report was the most comprehensive, timely, and unimpeachable report available on the subject.

The Washington intelligence community had a superhero in the enemy's lair. But their hero of the moment didn't want to be a professional spy. "For a short time I became the darling of the U.S.

intelligence community," DePuy recalled. "It nearly did me in professionally. It nearly sucked me into the intelligence business permanently. But after one tour with the Central Intelligence Agency, I was able to squirm out of an assignment to G-2, U.S. Army, Europe (USAREUR), in 1952 and resume my career as a tactical officer with infantry units and staffs." (DePuy's memory failed him here: it was in September 1953 that he "squirmed out" of the G-2 job in Germany.)[10]

Not very long after this incident, DePuy broke his leg while skiing. He was treated in a Hungarian hospital, "but they did such a bad job on my leg that I had to come back to Munich, where the Americans redid it." He had only been a military attaché for eight months when the leg injury required his evacuation to Germany and back to the United States. Still gimping about and unfit to ply his trade as a combat infantry officer in Korea when war broke out in June 1950, DePuy's career—and his personal life—took an interesting turn.

6

CIA Detail

At times, the mighty power of the U.S. government resembles the marriage of Aladdin's genie with the Three Stooges.
—Frank Holober

Frank Wisner [founding director of OPC] called CIA analysts "a bunch of old washerwomen exchanging gossip while they rinse through the dirty linen." CIA reciprocated by calling OPC "a bunch of amateurs who didn't exercise good tradecraft."
—William E. Colby

DePuy's skiing accident in Europe laid him up for a long while in 1950. "My leg was really banged up very badly," he recalled. "They had to operate on it and put in a lot of screws, wrap wire around it, and so on. So, I was at Walter Reed in June, when the Korean War started, and about September I was able to get around a little bit on a half-shell cast."[1] In fact, the doctors had made a mess of it in Hungary. The medics in Germany took a look at DePuy's leg and packed him off to Walter Reed, where he was listed as a patient for 115 days as the botched work was fixed.[2]

Like the old fire-horse responding to a fire alarm by champing at the bit, DePuy reacted to the sound of the guns. "I really wanted to do something," he said. "Dick Stilwell was just starting up an element in the CIA which had to do with functions such as guerrilla warfare and things like that . . . so, as my leg slowly got better, and without any experience of any kind, I was placed in charge of China [paramilitary] operations, believe it or not."

It was improbable. The United States entrusted a thirty-year-old lieutenant colonel without experience or expertise in China—or anywhere in the Far East—with, in the words of CIA Director Allen Dulles, the "formulation of plans and high level operational policies and [duties] as director of operations in a functional area in which there were few precedents."[3] He was made responsible for a politically sensitive covert paramilitary operation in China. Why? Moreover, why was Colonel Richard Stilwell responsible for clandestine CIA operations in the Far East and in a position to hire DePuy for the China job?

Stilwell was "present at the creation," to borrow Dean Acheson's book title describing the early days of the Cold War. In January 1946, Stilwell was appointed Assistant Military Advisor to the Secretary of State in the latter's role as the U.S. member of the Council of Foreign Ministers, the organization established to deal with postwar issues. As an outgrowth of this assignment, in 1947 he was named Special Military Advisor to the U.S. Ambassador in Italy. Over the next two years, Stilwell's staff responsibilities encompassed the politico-military problems of Trieste, the finalization of the Italo-Yugoslav boundary, and Italian rearmament. Then, from 1949 to 1952, he held important posts in the CIA.[4] Stilwell knew who had the guts, brains, and initiative to get the job done, so he recruited heavily among his comrades of the 90th Infantry Division.

Despite Ed Hamilton's strenuous efforts to remain on active duty, after a long series of operations he was mustered out of the Army he loved with a medical discharge in 1946. (The demobilizing Army didn't want a one-eyed officer.) The call from Stilwell came in 1949 as Hamilton was running his own insurance company in Oregon, his home state, ten years after his graduation from West Point.

Hamilton was sent to Germany in 1950, where he trained Albanians with the help of a collection of unlikely characters, including Office of Strategic Services (OSS) veterans, old soldiers, and young adventurers. He infiltrated his teams from Greece into Albania. The operation was compromised. Some got out, and some didn't. Hamilton, the "One-Eyed Colonel Schmidt" in this operation, was the very same "One-Eyed Dragon" who later planned and directed raids from offshore islands on the Chinese mainland during the Korean War with equally unlikely characters.[5]

Dick Stilwell's "old boys" from the 90th soon included Bill DePuy, Gilbert Strickler, Lon Redman, and John Mason. In Hong Kong, Mason ran Civil Air Transport (CAT), an airline owned by Whiting Willauer and Claire L. Chennault of Flying Tigers fame, which was purchased by the CIA in 1950. In addition to owning an airline, the CIA acquired a small fleet of boats under the cover of Western Enterprises Incorporated (WEI), whose address was in Pittsburgh, Pennsylvania. Hamilton planned and directed raiding operations from the islands in the South China Sea, Stilwell ran the Far East Division from Washington, and DePuy ran the China Branch from Washington and various places in the Far East.[6]

Assignment of bold amateurs to sensitive and powerful positions—many of them neither experienced, nor educated, nor trained in the social and political complexities in the Far East—can only be understood in the context of the evolving American intelligence community. Neither the recently established CIA nor the United States was prepared for conflict in the gray area between peace and conventional war. The confrontation of the United States and the Soviet Union was classic Great Power politics among nations, but the Cold War also presented the United States with unfamiliar challenges and opportunities, to which it responded with a pick-up team that made things up as they went along.

President Harry S. Truman disestablished the OSS on 20 September 1945, just a month after World War II ended, but the need for strategic intelligence soon became evident. By 15 February 1946, a Central Intelligence Group (CIG) was established to collect information and to present intelligence to the president in a "Daily Summary." An arena of activity that was not clearly diplomatic or military emerged as competition with the Soviet Union intensified. By 25 October 1946, an Office of Special Operations (OSO) was created to conduct espionage and counterespionage operations outside the United States and to collect intelligence. The Central Intelligence Agency (CIA) was established and placed under the National Security Council (NSC) by the National Security Act of 26 July 1947. In the bureaucratic chaos that followed, intelligence functions were scattered among the State Department, the Defense Department, and the White House "with only loose coordination by the CIA's new head, the Director of Central Intelligence." In addition, the NSC created the Office of Policy Coordination (OPC) to develop "a covert political action capability."[7] At the time, there was concern that Italy and/or France might vote their Communist parties to power. Covert political action to affect elections by bribery and propaganda over time became the "dirty tricks" and paramilitary operations used around the world.

The OPC took on a life of its own. According to Alfred McCoy, "Paid through CIA but housed in the State and Defense Departments, OPC flourished in this anomalous situation—freed from normal bureaucratic controls and funded far more liberally than even CIA itself."[8]

The perceived need for intelligence resulted in the Central Intelligence Act of 20 June 1949, which contains this sentence: "The sums made available to the Agency may be expended without regard to the provisions of law and regulations relating to the expenditure of Government funds, and for objects of a confidential, extraordinary, or emergency nature, such expenditures to be accounted for solely on the certificate of the Director and every such certificate shall be deemed a sufficient voucher for the amount therein certified."[9] Much of the CIA's clout came from this money tree and the Director's extraordinary authority in its use. The combination of authority to classify secrets (and embarrassing information) and to spend mounds of money made the CIA a powerful bureaucracy. And the OPC was "far more liberally" funded.

Just as the disestablishment of the OSS punctuated the end of World War II, the step-by-step accretion of power by the CIA reflected the recognition of a need to wage war with means other than traditional armed forces. The international situation was characterized by two superpowers, both capable of using nuclear weapons. Constant competition in a zero-sum game, while avoiding direct confrontation, led to the use of surrogates in a post–World War II period of devolution of European empires that created a "Third World" of newly established and usually poor and politically immature states. Clandestine operations and a perceived need for plausible denial of involvement characterized the behavior of the Soviet Union and the United States. In the American intelligence community, the internecine competition was almost as keen as that between the two superpowers, particularly between the collectors and analysts of the CIA and the clandestine direct-action operators of the OPC. OPC was the loose cannon on the CIA deck.

CIA Director Bedell Smith, within a week of his appointment in October 1950, "demanded and won nominal control over OPC," but its autonomous bureaucracy remained intact for another two years. The U.S. intelligence community was still a "vague coalition of independent baronies."[10]

Frank Wisner, a former OSS operative and head of OPC, was one of those barons. He attracted OSS veterans, including William Colby, a future CIA Director. Colby recalled that OPC was "operating in the atmosphere of an order of Knights Templar, to save Western freedom from Communist darkness." Colby, who himself reveled in the thrill of parachuting into occupied France or Burma in direct action, called Wisner a "messianic cold warrior" who recruited promising agents with lavish salaries. Wisner called CIA analysts "a bunch of old washerwomen exchanging gossip while they rinse through the dirty linen." CIA agents reciprocated by calling OPC "a bunch of amateurs who didn't exercise good tradecraft."

The OSS spirit and memories of direct action in wartime pervaded the OPC. Colby joined the OPC's Far East Division, calling it "a rich stable of immensely colorful characters . . . from swashbucklers accustomed to danger to quiet students steeped in the culture of the Orient." Richard Stilwell headed up "the rich stable" that included his old boys from the 90th Division and a collection of World War II China and Burma hands. One authority described the CIA of 1949 as "a forest of cliques."[11]

With the sudden collapse of Chiang Kai-shek's Kuomintang (KMT) regime in January 1949, U.S. government agencies scrambled to devise policies "to block further Communist expansion in Asia."[12] The scramble was accelerated when North Korean forces crossed the 38th parallel into South Korea in June 1950. By early September, North Korea held the Korean peninsula, except for the U.S.-led United Nations (UN) forces around Pusan. The UN amphibious landing at Inchon (15 September 1950) was coordinated with a counteroffensive from the south that returned UN forces to the starting point of the war, the 38th Parallel. UN forces attacked into North Korea. As they approached the Yalu River and the Manchurian border in November 1950, troops of the People's Republic of China crossed the Yalu into Korea, thus entering into direct combat with the U.S. forces and increasing the already heightened sense of urgency in Washington.

President Harry S. Truman approved an OPC plan to use KMT "remnants in Burma" to invade southern China. Those remnants, under the command of General Li Mi, had earlier been driven out of China by the armies of Mao Tse-tung. The hope was that by invading South China the KMT force from Burma would attract 600,000 to one million guerrillas ready to overthrow the Communist regime. But Li Mi's troops were neither an effective fighting organization nor local heroes. They were masterful at bullying peasants in Burma and Thailand, creative in getting cash, weapons, and logistical support from the United States, and highly successful in stimulating an enormous opium trade for decades to come. Li Mi was more Mafia or war lord than Chinese Nationalist. Relying on his troops to bring down Mao was an OPC pipe dream. CIA Director Walter Bedell Smith opposed the plan, but President Truman approved it, overruled the Director, and ordered the strictest secrecy about it.[13]

In the months after the outbreak of the Korean War, the OPC grew from 302 people with a budget of $4.7 million to a worldwide covert action apparatus of 5,954 employees funded at $82 million per year. A congressional analyst later said that in this expansion OPC was achieving an "institutional independence that was unimaginable at the time of its inception."[14]

That was the state of the intelligence community when Bill DePuy joined the CIA—or, more specifically, the OPC—in 1950. His assignment proved to be personally gratifying. By this time, his future wife had been with OSS and its successor organizations since 1944.[15]

In September 1950, DePuy reported for duty to a division of the CIA located in the temporary buildings that were put up during World War II on the Mall between the Capitol and the Lincoln Monument as a result of the space shortage caused by the wartime influx of people to Washington. There he met a veteran of the OSS and its successor organizations who would become his wife on 8 June 1951. All evidence indicates that they had a good marriage. Being reunited with Dick Stilwell, joining a still evolving CIA, marrying Marjory, and beginning a family were some of the major results of DePuy's thirty-month detail from the Army to the CIA.

Marjory Wysor Walker was born in Virginia on 19 September 1914, making her five years older than Bill. CIA personnel records show that she retained her married name, Marjory Walker Kennedy, until she married Bill DePuy. (Her first marriage, to Logan Lithgow Kennedy on 19 October 1934, ended in divorce on 13 August 1941.)

When Marjory's father died in 1925, her widowed mother took the family from Virginia to Boston, where there were relatives. In 1929, Marj returned south to Washington, was graduated from Western High School in 1933, and married Kennedy. During her marriage she lived in New Jersey. Afterward, she returned to Washington, attended the Temple Secretarial School for typing and shorthand, applied for the OSS on 6 November 1944, and was hired as a clerk-stenographer "for duty outside the United States."

Her son later said that Marj had been a member of the upscale social set while living in rural New Jersey. "She got good exposure to the bright, well-bred, wealthy lawyers, bankers, and industrialists of the New York social scene. When she came down to Washington she had relationships with very well-connected people. She was having tea with Mrs. Roosevelt in the White House and things like that. OSS was recruited through the New York banking and lawyering business. . . . It was a social connection that resulted in her application and assignment to OSS."[16]

After attending the OSS Assessment School in February 1945, Marj was trained as a Japanese Order of Battle analyst. On 18 April 1945, she departed on a literally slow boat to China with stops in Florida, Bermuda, the Azores, Casablanca, Tripoli, Cairo, Iran, Karachi, Delhi, and Calcutta before arriving at her destination, Kunming, China, on 31 May 1945. The war with Japan ended in August, the OSS went out of business in September, and Marj was assigned to the War Department with duties in the Strategic Services Unit (SSU). She was assigned to various organizations as the American intelligence community was reorganized after World War II.

Marj broke her leg in Kunming and was evacuated from China to Calcutta, India, on 5 November 1945. She then sailed on the USS *A. W. Greely* on 7 November, arriving in New York City on 6 December. She was brought to the Marine Hospital at Staten Island on a litter.

At the beginning of 1946, Marj attended an orientation course for those reassigned from the OSS to the newly designated SSU organization, and then she took a three-month course in Russian from June to August. By October 1946 she was an Administrative Assistant in the Office of Special Operations (OSO), Central Intelligence Group (CIG). From 11 October 1946 until April 1948 her focus was on Korea, Siberia, and Mongolia and on Russian, Japanese, and Korean activities in China and Mongolia. A supervisor wrote, "It will be observed that the subjects assigned to Mrs. Kennedy include most of the top priority targets in the Far East." Her performance evaluations were consistently "excellent."

On 8 September 1947, the CIG became the CIA. In the period April 1948 to October 1949 her duties in OSO shifted to an "emphasis on the development of long-range deep cover operations" in China and projects in, among other regions, Manchuria. She moved up to Deputy Branch Chief and was promoted to GS-9 on 30 October 1949. From October 1949 to July 1950 her job description included "dealing with anti-Communist minority ethnic groups in China" and joint OSO (her office) and OPC operations, where Stilwell and DePuy were active.

Having been promoted to GS-11 on 14 July 1950, Marj married Bill DePuy in June 1951. In August that year she was promoted to GS-12, and she was promoted again, to GS-13, on 3 January 1954.

The DePuys' son, William, was born on 2 July 1952. A daughter, Joslin, followed on 24 July 1953; another daughter, Daphne, was born on 22 November 1954. When Bill was assigned to Germany, Marj was assigned to the G-3 Section, V Corps, in Germany, a cover for her continued CIA work. The Agency tried to accommodate two professional careers by sending Marj to Europe with her husband, but she encountered some kind of problem with William Harvey, the CIA Chief of Station in Berlin, and Marj refused to work for him. The near simultaneity of Marj's swift promotions and the birth of her three children suggests that she faced a classic family-or-career choice. She chose family. After a period of leave without pay, she resigned from the CIA on 27 October 1954. Daphne was born a month later.

Some years later W. Lloyd George, Marj's former boss as Chief, Far East Division, in a letter dated 31 December 1963, expressed interest in having her rejoin the CIA, and he included the necessary paperwork to make that happen. A letter from her dated 6 February 1964 indicates receipt of the letter and papers, but apparently she did not follow through. (At the beginning of 1964, Bill expected to go to Vietnam as General Westmoreland's J-3; the children were nine, ten, and eleven years old.)

Clearly, Marj was intimately familiar with China and Korea before she met Bill DePuy. She had worked her way up from clerical to professional and supervisory levels in the CIA and had served in China, Washington, and Germany. She was an independent woman and a successful professional with a promising future in intelligence when she married him, and then she opted for family over career. Theirs was a marriage of equals.

She refused to discuss what she had done in her career when asked just that by her adult son many years later. "Long-range deep cover" meant just that. Marj knew people who continued to be at risk even decades after her active years in the intelligence community.

Bill DePuy was as circumspect as Marj about what he did in his CIA service. In 1979, DePuy gave the interviewers for his oral history only brief, generic, and opaque remarks, except for his reference to "very active covert operations against China." After that interview he did not reveal much more, but books published more recently did.[17]

The CIA opened Cold War records pertaining to the founding of the CIA and to China during the Korean War and published some of them in 1994 in *The CIA under Harry Truman,* a book written by the History Staff, CIA.[18] But the CIA slammed the door shut from about 1999 onward, even reclassifying formerly declassified documents and pulling them from the National Archives. This is very much akin to trying to put the genie back in the bottle. While these documents were declassified, scholars from around the world copied, filed, discussed, and analyzed them.[19]

In 1979, DePuy said, "For a couple of years, I busied myself with those kinds of things which took me to the Far East on many, many trips. I guess that's really all I want to say. I was to spend a lot of time around the periphery of China, and in Thailand, Taiwan, Japan, and Okinawa. It was a very active life and rather exciting. I have to say in retrospect that it was not all that productive, but everybody was working hard. At that time, you see, China was clearly the enemy. Remember, it wasn't long after the Korean War began when China intervened. So, I'll go this far: we were involved in very active covert operations against China. You asked how I felt about sitting out the war in Korea. Well, I'll have to say that I was actively employed in government service."

DePuy's language is deliberately vague. It would, however, have been uncharacteristic for him to describe his own derring-do. Reference to the Communist Chinese intervention in the Korean War at the end of 1950 goes right to the point of the American-supported Nationalist Chinese raiding operations from the offshore islands between Formosa and the Chinese mainland. These operations were conducted specifically to deflect the military efforts of the Chinese Communists from operations in Korea to defense of the Chinese homeland. As we have seen in the case of General Li Mi's Burma remnants, pockets of resistance continued to exist for some time after Mao's victory and Chiang Kai-shek's retreat to Formosa in 1949.

A CIA estimate regarding intervention in Korea dated 12 October 1950 concluded that "barring a Soviet decision to precipitate a global war . . . the Chinese Communists probably will not in 1950 attempt to invade Korea, Formosa, or Indochina."[20] A National Intelligence Estimate (NIE) of 27 December 1950 considered and rejected recommending the use of Chinese Nationalist troops in Korea.[21] Could it be that CIA analysts writing the December NIE were unaware of OPC's plan for the "remnants in Burma" to invade South China and that President Truman had approved? The United States certainly preferred to limit the war to Korea, but clandestine coastal raiding by Chinese Nationalists with U.S. advisers was approved and conducted by DePuy's outfit.

In short, during this period bold and patriotic characters right out of a comic strip or a particularly outrageous adventure film were deeply engaged in hazardous operations that might have been fun when they weren't terrifying. Among the players were Allen Dulles, Claire Chennault, Madame and Generalissimo Chiang Kai-shek, William E. Colby, World War II China and Burma hands, Ivy Leaguers, and veterans of the 90th Division, including Bill DePuy.

Major Robert H. Barrow, a future Commandant of the U.S. Marine Corps, is an alumnus of the China Raiders. He valued the experience, but he joins others in a net assessment saying that "any contribution to the Korean War was modest at best. Any real success was local, mixed with failure, and of short duration. Early on, lofty expectations gave way to the lure of adventure."[22] Frank Holober is less generous, saying the involvement was akin to a marriage of Aladdin's genie with the Three Stooges. He concludes that the operation "may eventually have been in vain, but not for lack of effort."[23] Still, another analyst notes, although these operations were not crowned with great success, "to dismiss these operations as a total failure is too smug . . . the first generation of CIA operations officers was learning its trade by doing, by developing know-how, both in what to do and what not to do."[24]

But on-the-job-training came at a price. In a synopsis given to President Eisenhower in May 1959, intelligence officers said that the Chinese Nationalists in Burma—who were then still bullying peasants and still engaged in heroin production and sales—"make trouble for our friends but do not have sufficient capability to tie down significant ChiCom forces."[25]

Another assessment calls CIA operations in Manchuria and Yunnan almost totally ineffective, adding, "As in the Burma project, some CIA efforts proved positively detrimental to larger U.S. foreign policy interests, and those along the China coast contributed to the inception of the series of crises in the Taiwan Straits that repeatedly brought America near war with China during the 1950s. Covert action irritated the Chinese without producing any American advantage in the Cold War."[26]

Bill DePuy would chalk up his China adventure as another part of his professional education that would serve him well in future assignments. Appreciation of strategic intelligence and direct collaboration with foreign military and civilian officials in Europe and Asia broadened his understanding of the world. His career got a boost from the evaluation written for his CIA service from 8 September 1950 to 6 February 1953 by Allen W. Dulles, Director of the CIA. Dulles praised him "for the selection, training, and deployment of civilian and military personnel who, in many instances, were senior to him in both age and rank." The letter is complimentary and, in the best tradition of the Agency, opaque. One learns that DePuy is a helluva guy, but the lack of specificity regarding places and activities leaves readers with an indistinct impression: for all they know, he might have performed magnificently on Mars or in Iceland. In any event, Dulles also refers to what would later be called "interagency skills" for DePuy's liaison with the State Department and the Department of Defense (DOD) and his adroitness in dealing with "cabinet officials of a foreign power."[27]

Qualities that surface throughout DePuy's professional life are singled out for praise in the Dulles letter. "His forceful presentations of facts and his thorough understanding of the security mission made him an impressive and successful advocate for this Agency." Mastery of facts, logic, lucidity, forceful presentation, and successful advocacy characterized his style as a staff officer, just as verbs like "decide," "order," and "check" capture his style of command.

7

Armed Forces Staff College and a Second Battalion Command

It was a very relaxed kind of course . . . I didn't get much out of that course; I don't think anybody did.
—DePuy on his Armed Forces Staff College experience in 1953

As I looked at the training of the battalion, which was as good as any of the battalions over there, I found that at the squad level it was a shambles, just like my battalion had been in World War II.
—DePuy as he assumed command in 1954

Beginning 5 February 1953, Bill DePuy attended the five-month Armed Forces Staff College (AFSC) course in Norfolk, Virginia, before returning to Europe for his third of four tours there.[1] Among his classmates and on the faculty were a number of officers who later served as three- or four-star generals. Over the following twenty-five years, their career paths crossed and recrossed.

Frederick C. Weyand would serve as Chief of Staff of the Army (1974–1975) when DePuy commanded the Training and Doctrine Command (TRADOC). Weyand commanded the 25th Infantry Division in Hawaii and took it to Vietnam when DePuy commanded the neighboring 1st Infantry Division.

Jack Norton, who had commanded a battalion in World War II, went on to lead the 1st Cavalry Division in Vietnam as well as the Combat Developments Command (1970–1973), which was absorbed by TRADOC.

George Forsythe served in both the Pacific and the European theaters in World War II, commanded the 1st Cavalry Division in Vietnam, and as a lieutenant general was General William C. Westmoreland's Special Assistant, Modern Volunteer Army (SAMVA) from 1970 to 1972, when DePuy was also a three-star general in the Pentagon and Assistant Vice Chief of Staff (AVICE). Forsythe shepherded the process as conscription ended and the army learned again to rely entirely upon volunteers.

Harry Kinnard, airborne veteran of World War II, commanded the 11th Air Assault Division, Test, (1963–1965), the 1st Cavalry Division in combat (1965–1966), and the Combat Developments Command (1967–1969).

Walter T. "Dutch" Kerwin ended his career as the Vice Chief of Staff of the Army (1974–1978) after commanding Forces Command (1973–1974) when DePuy was the TRADOC Commander. He and DePuy would also serve together on the Army Staff as three-star generals under General Westmoreland.

Ferdinand Chesarek commanded an artillery battalion in Europe in World War II, was the Army's first AVICE, and went on to command the Army Materiel Command (1969–1970), a four-star billet.

The careers of these successful men intersected often over the years. They shared the World War II experience, mostly as battalion commanders, commanded in Vietnam at the division level, and would shape the post-Vietnam Army as senior leaders. And something inconsequential to the world at large was going on, something that mattered personally to DePuy and his contemporaries who were not West Point graduates. That is, the distinction between West Point officers and "others" was becoming less important as men commissioned in ROTC and Officer Candidate Schools (OCS) demonstrated that they were good at war. In 1939–1945 it was noteworthy that George C. Marshall, a graduate of the Virginia Military Institute, was the U.S. Army's Chief of Staff. By 1974 it was not particularly noteworthy that ROTC graduate Frederick C. Weyand was the Army's Chief of Staff. West Point had produced enough leaders for the smaller army of the 1920s and 1930s, but the expanded U.S. Army of World War II allowed men like DePuy to show that they had what it took to lead in combat and even to run the Army. DePuy and contemporaries Weyand, Forsythe, William B. Rosson, and Melvin Zais got four stars without the benefit of being West Pointers.[2]

DePuy had not attended professional schools before the abbreviated course he took at Leavenworth in 1945–1946. The communications course at Fort Benning and the Russian language course in Monterey were skill courses. He was unimpressed by the Armed

Forces Staff College course. In fact, he found army professional schools mediocre or poor. Since he would one day, as TRADOC Commander, be the schoolmaster of the army, his attitude regarding military schools is worth noting.

While attending the AFSC, DePuy lived in Washington, commuted to Norfolk, and, he said, "played golf every day." He added, "I did not hold the Armed Forces Staff College in very high regard. The Navy held it in such low regard that they sent mostly supply officers and people like that, although they did send Admiral Nimitz's son, who very shortly thereafter left the Navy. But, by and large, they sent the second team, and so did the Air Force." Notwithstanding the Army all-star cast that attended the AFSC course with him, DePuy dismissed the school as "one of the 'brownie points' that you were supposed to get."

The apparent intent was to polish promising officers by familiarizing them with the other services and preparing them to work with allies. The AFSC was established after World War II because Dwight D. Eisenhower was convinced that purely service-oriented schooling hadn't prepared him and his colleagues sufficiently for joint (multiservice) and combined (multinational) operations. Eisenhower was also responsible for the establishment of the National War College, for the same reasons: to train officers to work with other services and with allies. Officers who attended both Leavenworth and AFSC generally regarded the former as rigorous and the latter as "a gentleman's course." The fact is that despite Eisenhower's concern for "jointness" and for the development of the skills required for working with allies, until the 1980s jointness got little more than lip service in the U.S. Army. Career advancement was based clearly upon how well an officer did in his service. That's why Bill DePuy saw AFSC as nothing more than "one of the brownie points you're supposed to get."

Young Bill was an infant when his father began the course, and Joslin was born as DePuy completed it. The long daily commute, two to three hours each way, was necessitated by his domestic situation. He knew that the short course in Norfolk would be followed by another move to Europe. Uprooting the family twice in a six-month period was clearly undesirable. Marj at the time was juggling her career in the CIA and new motherhood. So in the first half of 1953, Bill spent five hours a day in an automobile, played a round of golf, and attended a course that apparently neither taught nor demanded much.

His later attendance at the Imperial Defence College (1960) was a pleasurable experience for the entire family, but his recollections of his year at the British college have more to do with the social and cultural experiences than anything he learned from his course work. It, too, was a gentlemen's course, but with interesting professional travel, good colleagues, and sweeping geopolitical analysis from a British perspective. So, when DePuy later assumed responsibility for army schools, he had to have recalled his personal experiences as a student and his courses' lack of substance. The true value of Leavenworth to DePuy was that he could be stamped "Regular Army." Norfolk allowed him to decompress from his CIA adventures and tend to his young family.

DePuy's appetite for learning how things work and his skill in explaining complex matters to others derived from the pleasure of private study and define him as an autodidact. His children later commented on his curiosity and the fact that he read constantly and widely. His concept of military professionalism evolved over the years until his ideal became one who searches for knowledge, not one who waits passively for information to be presented in a formal setting. Rigorous private study was his habit and style. It was supported by a high intelligence, boundless energy that thrived on intellectual challenge, and a degree of concentration best described as intense focus on the issue at hand. His compulsion to know and his striving for excellence were private traits that would become public as he rose in rank and responsibility. In the vernacular of a later day, he was a self-starter. When DePuy later controlled the army's school system, he would identify subordinate self-starters and give them great latitude. Those deserving to lead large and complex organizations would teach themselves by study and by watching masters at work. Most Army schools, by contrast, teach hands-on skills, practical subjects. In DePuy's scheme of things, ideas per se are individual accomplishments of the very capable. Self-starters, by definition, are few. Schools were useful for the less driven, the less talented.

The degree to which DePuy was aware that he held such convictions is not absolutely clear, nor is it clear when the various bits and pieces came together in a coherent philosophy, but his later behavior reveals his belief that some people learn fast and should lead, while others simply cannot keep up. The DePuy style was taking form; it would become visible in his senior duty positions.

But all that was in the future. After DePuy's own experience at the AFSC in 1953, he was sent back to Germany.

His first task upon arriving on 22 September 1953 at the Head-quarters, U.S. Army, Europe (USAREUR) was to try to squirm out of his assignment, which was a legacy of his Hungarian and CIA experiences. He was, he said, "horrified" to find himself the executive officer of the counterintelligence branch of the USAREUR G-2. DePuy marched in to tell the general that he didn't want the job. The general didn't like that very much, but DePuy got lucky, again. One of the old boys put in a good word, again. And he landed on his feet, again. What could have been a complete redirection of his career was nipped in the bud. Had he passively accepted the intelligence staff job, he probably would have found himself pegged as an intel type, making his later assignments in Vietnam and Washington very different.

He used some strong language with the unnamed general in Heidelberg to get out of the G-2 job. That course of action is not usually the best way for a lieutenant colonel to treat a general, but it worked for DePuy. He spent just one week in the intelligence staff job. A vacancy was created when the officer conducting infantry battalion Army Training Tests (ATT) was relieved. Colonel George Forsythe, DePuy's AFSC classmate, recommended DePuy to the V Corps Commander for the training job—another important break for DePuy.

For more than a year he was the Assistant G-3 for Training. He personally tested and evaluated twenty battalions each year from the 1st and 4th Divisions in Germany and from the 350th Infantry Regiment in Austria. In his words, "I learned a lot doing that." He said he watched people do it right, and he watched them do it wrong. And he saw a lot more do it wrong than right. He was struck by the fact that "those who had commanded battalions in war were something like five times as good as those who hadn't."

He blamed some of that on Leavenworth, saying that those who had not commanded in war were more passive, waiting for "voluminous recommendations from their staff." While trying to get all the information necessary to write a perfect plan, company commanders and their subordinate leaders didn't have enough lead time to move troops, allow them to dig in, and do the many things that needed to be done at the individual and squad levels. Battalion commanders who waited too long for more information denied subordinate leaders the time *they* needed to make *their* plans. According to DePuy, they were always late, lost, or screwed up one way or another. By contrast, he said, "The guys who previously had commanded battalions more or less made up their own minds, and the staff ran around behind them and made it work." That's precisely what DePuy had done for Colonel Barth in 1944. The veteran commanders insured that the troops had time to do the many little things that make a tactical unit skilled and successful.

DePuy was satisfied with the time he spent as the Assistant G-3 for Training. He said later, "After two years of testing battalions, there was very little I didn't know about the infantry in Europe, including the personalities as well as the good things and the bad things." That job was his finishing school as a battalion commander.

Distinct personal characteristics were emerging and becoming increasingly evident in Bill DePuy. He trusted his intuition in combat, what the Germans call *Fingerspitzengeuehl*, a gift of situational awareness. His confidence in his sense of the tactical situation allowed him to conceptualize rapidly, which in turn allowed him to issue orders quickly. He would not be steered by his staff. He made tactical decisions and expected his staff to pick up the pieces. Those who could not keep up would be fired. His mantra was decide, order, check. To him, the process was crystal clear.

His self-confidence came from intuition and experience, things not taught in schools. Those around him invariably remarked that he knew exactly what he was doing and how to go about getting things done. In addition, the creativity in his thinking shaped both his leadership and his views regarding the training of soldiers and leaders. His reservations about the training at Leavenworth increased with the passage of time. The staff course at Leavenworth attended by the majors who would become battalion commanders and staff officers emphasized thoroughness and what DePuy regarded as voluminous written orders that arrived late. DePuy's style was closer to what George C. Marshall as Infantry School Commander had taught at Fort Benning in the 1920s.

Marshall emphasized the need to recognize that battle situations are constantly changing and that this requires new estimates of the situation and oral fragmentary orders. Speed was essential. Plans had to be modified on the run. In brief, DePuy was convinced that Marshall's methods, which emphasized flexibility and speed of decision, were more appropriate to the training of combat leaders at battalion than the thorough, complete, and slow methods of Leavenworth.

Of course, a distinction must made between the volume and detail necessary for a division or corps operations order and the orders of a battalion commander in direct contact with the enemy. DePuy was convinced that the Leavenworth experience was designed for the former but unfortunately inclined tactical leaders at battalion level to wait for more information, when speed was essential to success. Generations of American soldiers are familiar with the Fort Benning formula that was reduced to the acronym KISS: Keep It Simple, Stupid! That captures the essence of clear orders, usually oral and fragmentary, that derive from the rapid personal reaction of the leader to changing situations. In addition, the leader must follow up to see that the orders are executed. Personal control was DePuy's style.

DePuy emphasized the importance of field work in training. Commanders had to learn to move large groups of real people in real time in real geography by doing it. His experience in war taught him that arrows and military symbols on maps, friendly and enemy order of battle, and learned theory invoking Clausewitz, Sun Tzu, and Jomini may be useful, but the acid test for commanders is in the doing. Many American errors in the early stages of combat in World War II would have been less costly if senior American commanders had had more practical experience in maneuvering large formations of troops before encountering skilled enemies.

The need for a National Training Center to prepare battalions and brigades for combat was taking shape in DePuy's fertile mind long before it became a reality. The best way to train commanders in maneuvering troops in real time, he felt, was to have them do it, measure results, study them, and make corrections. General Paul Gorman had similar views and provided the ideas and tools that would bring innovative experimentation and measurement to realistic training after the war in Vietnam. DePuy gave Gorman full credit for the rationalization of training, but others close to the two men said that they thought so much alike that they finished each other's sentences.[3] Capable as he was of conceptualizing complex abstractions and managing large organizations, a part of DePuy remained strongly attracted to the details of tactics at the lowest level. This pragmatic inclination may have been a matter of personality and his having grown up on the Great Plains during the Depression, but certainly experience in war left a deep impression. DePuy had witnessed the price of getting it wrong.

The time DePuy spent testing infantry battalions in 1953–1954 could hardly have been better preparation for his next assignment, as infantry battalion commander in 1954–1955. Since the early 1970s, battalion commanders have been selected by boards convened in Washington, much the way selection for promotion is done. Potential commanders of a specified seniority and branch, such as infantry, are considered by a board of officers that reviews the records of potential commanders, most particularly Officer Efficiency Reports (OER). This centralized system results in a published list of those selected for command. But in 1954, DePuy did it the old-fashioned way: he simply asked the Commanding General of the 4th Division for a battalion of the 8th Infantry "stationed all alone in Budingen." Most battalions shared a Kaserne with other units, or worse, with a higher headquarters. In this battalion, DePuy would be what the Germans call *Koenig und Kaiser,* king and emperor. His superiors were somewhere beyond the horizon (and not in his hair). He took command on 18 October 1954.

He recalled that when he arrived, "it was just as if it was the day after World War II. Nothing had changed." The weapons were the same. (The infantry weapons of World War II found in a battalion—the M-1 rifle, the Browning automatic rifle, machine guns, mortars, and so on—were not replaced with a new family of weapons—the M-14 rifle, M-79 grenade launcher, M-60 machine gun, and the like—until the early 1960s.) DePuy was familiar with the terrain. He was very much at home. As he observed the training of his battalion, he concluded that it "was as good as any of the battalions over there." That is, "at the squad level it was a shambles, just like my battalion had been in World War II. At the platoon level, it was a little better. The company commanders were better. They had good potential. So, I decided to spend my time at the bottom."

DePuy's decision to spend his time "at the bottom" specifically addressed what he found in 1954, but he made the same decision in his battle group in 1961, in his division in 1966, and as the TRA-DOC Commander in 1973. His lifelong conviction was that if you get it right at the squad and platoon levels, the rest would fall into place. Considering the key part he played in the upper echelons of national and military strategy, dealing with top military and civilian officials, including the President of the United States, it is noteworthy that the nitty-gritty of soldiering comes instantly to mind when those who knew him best describe him. He never tired of teaching at the squad and platoon level.

DePuy contended that it was as battalion commander in Budingen that he used the term "overwatch" for the first time in teaching tactics to his troops and junior leaders. He had used the technique of fire and maneuver as battalion commander in combat, long a part of U.S. Army doctrine. But he credits the tank training conducted by General Hamilton Howze in the 2d Armored Division with being a personal revelation. While at V Corps he took the opportunity to watch tank training, concluding that everything Howze wrote about how to train a tank platoon "struck me as precisely the way to train a rifle squad, since each of them has two operating sections or teams."

DePuy wrote and reproduced booklets for his leaders as guides to training. They are in simple language and provide sketches of the various kinds of overwatch, all based on two elements, fire and maneuver, whether at squad or platoon level. First, in relative safety, one advancing element trails the other, prepared to support the lead element by maneuvering left or right to flank the enemy. Second, when contact was imminent, one element took a position from which immediate fire was available to support the moving element—for example, from a hill with a view of both the friendly partner and where the enemy was likely to be found. Third, when in contact with the enemy, pull out all stops in providing fire support from all organic and supporting weapons in order to suppress the enemy. DePuy's inclination to make maximum use of firepower, already evident in World War II and in his later peacetime commands in Germany, became most widely associated with his name when he commanded the 1st Infantry Division in Vietnam. He expressed it in unambiguous terms: Since the United States is a rich country, he'd spend that wealth with steel on the target to get the job done with minimal risk to infantry soldiers.

But before DePuy was known throughout the Army, he wrote his little booklets.[4] One was designed for squad leaders and another for platoon leaders. Then he rehearsed them. "I trained all of the squads and platoons uniformly," he said. "I personally tested them all. I tested every squad three or four times." He clearly had a good time with this, spending days and weeks in the field with squads until "I knew every squad leader well—both his good points and his bad points. They got very, very good."

There were, and are, officers who later expressed reservations about a general seemingly obsessed with minor tactics and fundamental combat techniques. According to DePuy's critics, those concerns—digging foxholes and the like—are the business of sergeants and junior officers. Generals have other, grander issues to ponder. But DePuy regarded no single aspect of soldiering more important than how to fight at the squad and platoon level. That was his conviction as a battalion commander and as TRADOC Commander.

Consider, for example, DePuy's thoughts on foxholes. It is perfectly normal for a soldier at risk to look in the direction of his personal menace. That means that the infantry soldier hiding in a hole in the ground has to lean forward in his foxhole and raise his head to get a glimpse of the enemy threatening to overrun him. Then he aims his weapon at the enemy. Wrong, said DePuy. And what he taught, indeed insisted upon, was absolutely counterintuitive.

A foxhole would, in the first place, be hidden in the natural terrain so that it could not be seen from the front. Second, a parapet of earth and rocks would be built at the front of the hole, and the dirt used for this purpose would be camouflaged. The soldiers, usually two per hole, would focus their attention and shooting in a 45-degree angle—one to the left front, the other to the right front—protected by the mound of camouflaged dirt, or a small hill, or a rock, to the front. This is, of course, unnatural. The natural reaction of someone threatened from the front is to look and to shoot in that direction. However, the DePuy technique meant that the men in the hole would fire across the front of their neighbor's foxholes, left and right. Their neighbors would fire in the same manner, so that the fires were mutually supporting, and no one would be exposed to the front.

That was the basic (and unnatural) idea. It was enhanced by staggering the holes in some depth, the way the Germans had, not in a straight line, which would be easier for the enemy to locate. Overhead cover would be added if the unit remained for more than a few hours. Bunkers followed the same principle: orient outgoing fires at a 45-degree angle to the front. That way, no apertures or firing ports were presented to the direct front.

Soldiers conditioned to sandbag castles with firing ports to the front—the way it was routinely done by the U.S. Army in Korea—would find a DePuy battalion in a defensive position unusual, even anathema. And so it was. Knowing that his tactics and techniques would be regarded as odd, DePuy taught them to his battalion any-way. Delighted in his command, he derived enormous satisfaction from teaching. He passed on lessons from his war experience to his soldiers, even when they seemed odd or idiosyncratic to others. His insistence that battalions be dug in and invisible from the front would become his trademark. Generals are entitled to trademarks, but DePuy wasn't always a general. He encountered many doubters along the way.

The Army had learned some bad habits in the Korean War. Large bunkers—DePuy called them "big forts"—were often built on the skyline, making them visible from the front. This foolishness was compounded by the placement of apertures and firing ports to the front. Not only did the big forts say, "Here I am," but the aper-tures to the front announced, "Aim here." DePuy recalled that the umpires who tested his battalion "thought I was crazy. They didn't understand why I hadn't built Korean pillboxes on the military crest [just below the top of a hill] or at the bottom of the hill. Instead, I had my guys behind rocks, trees, and bushes. I wouldn't let them dis-turb the bushes, but made them dig in behind them, so you couldn't see a thing from the front."

DePuy's techniques and tactics of 1954–1955 can be traced to what he adopted from the German use of natural cover and correct concealment as documented in his 357th Infantry Training Memo-randum in July 1944. But the umpires grading DePuy's battalion in his first annual training test had no idea what they were looking at nor why he did what he did. "All of the company and platoon umpires ran back to the battalion umpire and said, 'This battalion is totally unsatisfactory. They don't know how to dig in.'" DePuy had to call for a conference of the senior umpires to explain what he was doing. Eventually everything was sorted out for this phase of the test, the battalion in the defense, but he also had to explain his overwatch techniques in other phases of the test.

DePuy's experience with the umpires here illustrates two points.

First, he was innovative. Soldiers have exercised certain opera-tions for as long as there have been armies. They conduct reconnais-sance, move to contact, attack, defend, and withdraw. It isn't brain surgery. But DePuy added creative fillips and twists drawn from personal experience to his repertoire that puzzled those evaluating his battalion's performance. He knew what "they" wanted and ex-pected—he had been "they" just months earlier when he was testing battalions—but his self-confidence and conviction drove him to do it his way. And his ability to communicate allowed him to convince others that his way was the right way.

Second, resistance to sound ideas and workable tactics is a by-product of a larger issue in the history of the U.S. Army: the frequent lack of professionalism. DePuy's Army—the Army that went to war in 1941—was a force overwhelmingly manned by amateurs, a force that was demobilized even faster than it had been mobilized. Shortly after that demobilization, the army quickly expanded again for the war in Korea with shortages of skilled leaders and with barely trained soldiers, most of them conscripts. The early poor performance by American troops in Korea must have reminded DePuy of the poor performance he had experienced at Normandy. Later he would fix the Army. At this stage of his career he would fix his battalion.

Reflecting on his battalion years later, DePuy said, "The battalion ran like a clock. The problem was that it was about a decade or two ahead of its time. That sounds a little egotistical, but that's exactly right, because if you went out and looked at a rifle squad today, you would see exactly that. If you looked at defensive positions, you would see what you knew in Vietnam as the DePuy foxhole, where they all had frontal cover and were camouflaged. So, that's what happened to the Second Battalion, 8th Infantry."

When asked to compare the quality of his mid-1950s and mid-1940s soldiers, he said that his soldiers in the 1950s were "fine," perhaps better than those of the 1940s. (He thought that the soldiers he had in his battle group in 1961 were the best he ever commanded.) He thought his company commanders of the mid-1950s were "superb," adding, "Only one was a Regular. The others were products of Korea—enlisted men promoted to officer." And he pointed out that because the war in Korea had just come to an end, "there was a wartime mentality in the Army. A wartime mentality means that you get a lot of soldiers furnished to you who do what they are told."

His only Regular Officer was First Lieutenant George Psihas (USMA 1951), Korea veteran, F Company Commander, and unabashed admirer of his battalion commander. He remembered DePuy as "a soldier's soldier who could do everything better than his troops and officers," describing how DePuy commanded each unit—squad, platoon, company—to demonstrate "how to." Crediting DePuy as his mentor, Psihas proudly recalls that F Company won the best squad in V Corps competition for two years running as well as platoon and company awards in offense and defense. He said that DePuy trained his battalion in "battle run formations" and later published them as Army doctrine. (This is what DePuy called Overwatch.)[5]

Black soldiers were new to DePuy in 1954, since there were no black soldiers in his World War II regiment. He thought they were "fine." His comment may seem gratuitous, but President Truman's Executive Order no. 9981 of 26 July 1948, integrating the races in the Armed Forces, wasn't fully implemented until the early 1950s.

In addition to DePuy's conviction that small unit training is the key to success in combat, there was another powerful incentive to emphasize squad and platoon training in 1954: the Bundeswehr (Federal Armed Forces of Germany) had not yet been fielded. From its defeat in 1945 until its rearmament in 1955, Germany was disarmed. "In those days," recalled DePuy, the United States and NATO "were very thin on the ground." His battalion had to get into defensive positions toward the inner German border and then delay. DePuy had enough combat power to assign a platoon for each paved road. There were only two 106mm recoilless rifles in a company, and the platoon's antitank weapon was one 3.5-inch rocket launcher. That's not much capability when the enemy is known to be heavy in armor and artillery and the battlefield has many roads and trails, as was the case in Germany. DePuy estimated that there would be a mile or two between his platoons. "That's one of the reasons why I concentrated on squad and platoon training," he recalled, "because it was going to be a squad and platoon war."

On 15 July 1955, DePuy was promoted to colonel, "promoted out of the battalion," as he put it.[6]

8

Clever Chaps

The View from the Chief's Office

> Eisenhower was the President, and massive retaliation was
> the strategy. The Air Force was riding high. The Army was
> feeling sorry for itself.
> > —DePuy's description of the climate
> > in Washington, 1956–1959

Throughout his career Bill DePuy alternated between muddy-boots
assignments overseas and high-level staff jobs in Washington. Upon
his return from Germany in May 1956, where his focus for three
years had been hands-on training, he joined the clever chaps in
Washington who were at the top of the Army hierarchy. The ease
with which he excelled in both capacities caused one who knew him
well to describe him as "thinker and doer," a man equally able to
lead soldiers and wrestle with complex concepts.[1]

In May 1956 DePuy joined the Coordination Group in the Office of
the Chief of Staff, Army (OCSA), and served there until October 1959, a
particularly interesting time in the formulation of military strategy. As a
member of a small cell of sophisticated officers working directly for the
Chief of Staff, DePuy both observed and participated in the strategic
debates that had begun in the last year of the Korean War and continued through both Eisenhower administrations and into the Kennedy
years. The debates came close to being fistfights as partisans, pushing
for a piece of the action, often blurred national interests with those of
their own branch of the armed services, as they struggled over roles
and missions in the face of the availability of atomic and nuclear weapons to both sides in the Cold War. DePuy was at a place where politics
and strategy intersect; his job required him to consider the interaction
of national policy, national strategy, and military strategy. What he
learned here would serve him well a decade later.

DePuy believes he got the job because George Forsythe, who

had recommended him for the G-3 training job in Germany, now recommended him as Forsythe's successor in the Coordination Group, as Forsythe went off to command a battle group in the recently reactivated 101st Airborne Division. DePuy described what he found in 1956 as an "amazing situation." The military services were at war—with one another. Rancor among soldiers, sailors, and airmen pervaded the Department of Defense. It started among the chiefs of the Services who met together as the Joint Chiefs of Staff (JCS), and it percolated down the respective Service staffs.

Historians, nuclear theologians, game theorists, revisionists, and revisionists of the revisionists have produced a vast literature on the Cold War of the mid-1950s. In brief, Eisenhower succeeded Truman as President and brought a "new look" to military strategy, which was designed to provide the United States with both solvency and security. It was popularly understood as the doctrine of "massive retaliation," a strategy that would yield a bigger bang for the buck. By contrast, Maxwell D. Taylor, Army Chief of Staff under President Eisenhower and later a special assistant to President John F. Kennedy and Ambassador to Vietnam, was a strong advocate of "flexible response," a strategy that would give the Army a larger role than it would under that of massive retaliation.

The Air Force, particularly the Strategic Air Command (SAC) under General Curtis LeMay, was riding high. This is the Air Force satirized in the Stanley Kubrick film *Dr. Strangelove,* in which one true believer gleefully rides a nuclear bomb like a bucking bronco to its Soviet target while waving his white Stetson. In addition, the Chairman of the JCS, Admiral Arthur Radford, said DePuy, "despised the Army even more than most admirals." Discretion, decorum, diplomacy, and polite language seemed not to characterize relations among the comrades in arms of that day.

Compared to the sleek bombers and missiles of SAC, and next to the majestic and potent carrier battle groups of the U.S. Navy, the grubby infantryman of the recent war in Korea was a plebeian figure. It was evident to all but the benighted Army that, with his rifle, bayonet, and muddy fatigue uniform, GI Joe had no place in future wars, which would be fought (or deterred) with nuclear-tipped intercontinental missiles, Jules Verne–style submarines, and aircraft capable of delivering massive retaliation to every corner of the earth. The U.S. Navy and Air Force were the best in the world, while the Army was so . . . World War II.

DePuy remembered, "The Army was feeling sorry for itself," thinking "it was getting short shrift." He and others attributed much of that sorry state of affairs to President Eisenhower, who put too much credence in the idea of massive retaliation. The mission of the Army Chief's Coordination Group, "without it ever being put into a charter," said DePuy, "was to assist the Army in surviving the regime of Eisenhower and Radford, and the era of massive retaliation." DePuy's predecessors in the group—and their allies in other key positions in the office of the Secretary of the Army and Legislative Liaison—apparently took on that mission as aggressively as they fought World War II. Brigadier General Lyle Metheny, "a marvelously leathery former cavalry sergeant" who was both "brilliant and combative," surrounded himself with bright young colonels ready to take on the Navy and Air Force.[2]

Later generations of military officers will marvel less at the inter-Service competition for finite Department of Defense resources (nothing new there) than at the intensity of the competition and the bitterness that accompanied it. In proponents' efforts to do right for their beloved Army, "they went a bit too far," in DePuy's understated language. Still, both George Forsythe and James F. Hollingsworth later wore the three stars of a lieutenant general, indicating that their part in what the latter called the "colonels' revolt" did not hurt their careers. Someone, it appears, had made the decision to get these two Army loyalists out of town for their own well-being, one to command a battle group, and the other to attend war college. It is not clear who made that decision. In any event, theirs was an orderly withdrawal, not the flight of defeated troops in disarray.

DePuy believed he was brought in because Forsythe and others in OCSA and elsewhere on the Army staff, "to put it kindly, were dispersed." Hollingsworth, who would later serve as DePuy's Assistant Division Commander in Vietnam, never minced words. He described what the Coordination Group did and how "George [Forsythe] and I ran the colonel's revolt together. . . . They disbanded us."[3] He said that he was sent to the Army War College a year early. Forsythe went to battle group command. Asked when all of this happened, Hollingsworth, without hesitation, replied, "April 26, 1956." The speed of his response fifty years after the event suggests that to him it was a day not to be forgotten. DePuy took up his duties in the Coordination Group in early May to replace one of the several officers sent away from Washington, apparently because they were too heavy-handed in protecting Army turf from the other Services in the fight for resources.

Hollingsworth recalled that his position while he was in Washington was in Legislative Liaison. It was his job to make the Army's case to members of the House and the Senate and to deal with the major players in what Eisenhower dubbed "the military-industrial complex." Holly, as he is called by all who know him, briefed and lobbied the Washington power brokers of the day, including General James M. Gavin; Secretary of Defense Charles E. Wilson; Senators John Stennis, Sam Nunn, and Carl Vinson; and "a little kid called Jack Kennedy," the senator from Massachusetts. "I was calling people in General Motors to see if they could build this and that . . . airplanes and all that, and then I would go to Congress to brief [selected people] there" in order to get the funding for the Army's wish list and to influence key players to see national strategy the Army's way. Hollingsworth's world was divided into two parts: right-thinking Americans, who were pro-Army; and everyone else.

In essence, Hollingsworth saw the future Secretary of Defense in action. He was impressed with Robert S. McNamara's memory for facts and details. "You know I didn't like him," he said, "but that's besides the point, liking or not liking. But he was a smart son of a bitch."

DePuy's language is less salty, but the message is the same. In describing what his predecessors had wrought, he said, "This little office became very active in trying to influence members of Congress and members of the press. They became a little overactive and went a bit too far at one point, and some of the papers they had written were exposed to the full daylight. Anyway, there was some slight embarrassment, and I arrived at just that time."

After the housecleaning, the office continued to be staffed with bright guys. For two years, one of DePuy's office mates was Bernard W. Rogers, later Chief of Staff, Army, and Supreme Allied Commander, Europe. DePuy's best Army friend, Jimmy Collins, later Brigadier General and Chief of Military History, was also with him in the office. So was Trevor Dupuy, whose name was pronounced *da-PWEE,* and a constant source of confusion with DePuy (*da-PEW*). Secretaries gave up on the names and referred to "the tall one," Dupuy, or "the short one," DePuy.[4]

DePuy said that at first he "wrote learned papers." The buzzwords of the day were "massive retaliation" and "flexible response."

After the "dispersal" of DePuy's predecessors at the Coordination Group, the successors to the dispersed must at least initially have felt that they were tiptoeing through a minefield, but the task remained the same. It was to determine what should be the mission of the Army in a nuclear age, and then to organize and equip the Army to execute that mission.

A brief excursion into strategy is required at this point for the reader to understand the Army's search for its role in the context of national strategy and Bill DePuy's role in the middle of it. World War II leaders Matthew B. Ridgway, James M. Gavin, and Maxwell D. Taylor, all airborne generals known to the American public, wrote popular books in the late 1950s in which they outlined the basic issues.[5]

Ridgway made the case for "a properly proportioned force of all arms" kept in being to put out big fires and little ones, wherever the Communists might set them. He endorsed tactical nuclear weapons for the Army and mobile battle groups of combined arms dispersed on the battlefield. He regretted the overemphasis on the use of long-range bombers, the notion of massive retaliation, and all-weather fighter planes, the cost of which denied the Army strategic lift and close air support. Ridgway concluded his book with an appendix: a ten-page letter to the Secretary of Defense dated 27 June 1955. It lays out what he saw as threats to the United States and, pointedly, the proper role of the Army Chief of Staff as a military advisor to civilian authority.[6]

Gavin was concerned with the issue of "national survival" in the period 1955 to 1965. As he prepared his book, which was published in 1958, the Soviet Union shook the United States to its roots by launching a space vehicle called *Sputnik* on 4 October 1957. Until then, it had been assumed that the United States was far ahead of the Russians in technology, including space research. The shock resulted in a new emphasis on academic rigor in American schools, with a particular focus on science, math, and languages. Gavin concludes his book with a two-page summary entitled "A Strategy for Peace," in which he asserted, "we are in second place militarily and in the exploration of space." His wanted to "restore to us the strategic initiative," including an Army with a sky cavalry, drone surveillance, tactical nuclear weapons, and psychological operations forces. His major point was that reliance upon massive retaliation alone is a mistake.[7]

The most influential of the three generals was Maxwell D. Taylor, Chief of Staff and intellectual point man in defining the Army's reason for being. He advocated the concept of flexible response as a national and military strategy. DePuy explained, "This was his response to the fact that the Army seemed to have been left out of the atomic age and needed to sound and appear very modern." That statement could have been applied to Ridgway and Gavin as well, but the most comprehensive and clearest expression of the Army's position is found in Taylor's book *The Uncertain Trumpet*, published in 1959.

His thesis was simple. Since the United States had lost its atomic monopoly, lacked an antiballistic missile defense, and was unwilling to match the Communists on the ground, "We are playing a losing game and should change it." The game to be changed was massive retaliation. Its premise, said Taylor, was not credible. No one believed the United States would risk a nuclear exchange with the Soviet Union over a relatively small issue or a remote and unimportant place. The United States had demonstrated that already, having declined to use atomic weapons in Korea and at Dien Bien Phu in 1954. (At the time of these events, however, the enemy could not be sure that Eisenhower would not use them.) The question was, did the enemy believe that the United States would use nuclear weapons to deny the Communists a peripheral piece of real estate in the so-called Third World—for example, to keep the Communist Chinese from the offshore islands between the Chinese mainland and Formosa?

Taylor's answer was, no. The prospect of mutual destruction ruled out American use of "special weapons" for contingencies short of survival. So, Taylor concluded, "we may be forced to rely again on conventional means." Presidential candidate Dwight D. Eisenhower had promised a New Look strategy in 1952, but Taylor said the New Look was "the old air power dogma," massive retaliation with Madison Avenue trappings. Taylor's book was published as the Eisenhower Administration came to its end, but from 1955, when Taylor became the Army's Chief of Staff, he had expressed his views in internal papers and in "the tank," where the JCS meets. The United States required a flexible response.

Taylor cited George F. Kennan ("limited military operations are the only ones which could serve any coherent purpose")[8] and invoked the wise men of the period, Liddell Hart, Vannevar Bush, and Bernard Brodie. But to no avail. He wrote that the Army was in "Babylonian captivity," isolated from 1954 to 1960 as the Army came up on the short end, four to one, when the Joint Chiefs voted. He referred to "the deep schism in the JCS." The Air Force was pleased with the idea of massive retaliation, as it required bombers and high-performance fighter aircraft. The Navy also had no complaint. It had ships, its own air force, and its own army. According to Taylor, the Army position couldn't get a serious hearing among the Joint Chiefs. He said that on more than one occasion the Army position was "politely studied" by the other Service chiefs and quietly put aside.

The Army was a dissatisfied customer of the Navy and the Air Force. Focused on the Strategic Air Command's primacy in defense and deterrence, and possessing the best high-performance aircraft and pilots in the world, the Air Force was not particularly interested in the Army's need for close air support of ground operations, nor in the Army's reliance on the Navy and Air Force to get to the war. Taylor wrote, "A major effort of this book has been to expose the Great Fallacy [of massive retaliation] as an all-purpose strategy."[9] For some time Taylor's was a voice crying in the wilderness, but the Kennedy Administration would eventually respond to Taylor's logic.

In his position with the Coordination Group in the Office of the Chief of Staff, DePuy learned that on any chart of a complex organization, one is well advised to view with suspicion blocks labeled "special assistant," particularly if they are connected with a solid line to the block labeled "CEO." DePuy said: "We generally watched over the interservice battles that went on. Now, this was a rather awkward thing to do, because General [Clyde] Eddleman, for example, was the DCSOPS [Deputy Chief of Staff, Operations], and if you asked him who was responsible for all these [operations] matters, he would have said that he was. So, it was not always a comfortable place to be. It was one of those little groups that is often resented, sometimes does some good, sometimes doesn't do much at all, but often does some things that need to be done which the large formal staffs either don't want to do, can't do, or don't do." The lesson was not lost on DePuy: a small cell can move a large bureaucracy.

A decade later, when DePuy wore three stars and served as the Assistant Vice Chief of Staff (AVICE) when General William Westmoreland was Chief of Staff, Army, his position was similar, but with far greater clout. Establishing "little groups" of bright, hard-driving officers—who were sometimes resented by the barons of "the large formal staffs"—became a part of his leadership style.

In 1956–1959, DePuy's job was to spread the word of the Army wherever it might do the most good. He enjoyed considerable latitude across a very broad band of activities and was in contact with leaders all over the American landscape. His correspondence with Richard G. Stilwell, Plans and Policy Officer, Supreme Headquarters Allied Expeditionary Forces (SHAPE), reveals that the two men shared a warm personal relationship as they discussed professional issues and tested out their ideas on each other. In an exchange of letters in October and November of 1956, DePuy tells Stilwell that he "contributed to one of the chapters" that would appear in Taylor's book *The Uncertain Trumpet,* published after Taylor retired; but DePuy doesn't elaborate. DePuy's analysis of Army affairs at the time revolved around atomic and conventional war, with terms such as "small wars," and "limited," "peripheral," and "brush fire" wars. These topics, and even the terminology, were the stuff of Taylor's book.[10]

DePuy asked Stilwell about Europe, and Stilwell referred him to Gordon A. Craig of Princeton (and later Stanford University), a distinguished historian particularly well informed about modern Germany and with ties to German academics and universities, particularly in Berlin. As a Rhodes Scholar in the late 1930s, Craig had traveled in Hitler's Germany before the war, knew German history, and spoke the language. During World War II he had served in the OSS as a Marine Corps captain. Craig's book *The Politics of the Prussian Army, 1640–1945* was published in 1955, the year that Germany regained sovereignty as the Federal Republic of Germany, joined NATO, and began to rearm after a ten-year period without an army. DePuy tapped Craig's expertise to inform himself about a country that was literally central to the defense of Western Europe in the Cold War.

DePuy's study of doctrine and strategy and its practical application also brought him into contact with Henry Kissinger, then a professor of history conducting a national security seminar at Harvard. The publication of Kissinger's 1957 book, *Nuclear Weapons and Foreign Policy,* earned him a reputation beyond the academy and set him on course to a stage much larger than Harvard Yard. In 1958,

Kissinger and DePuy corresponded on issues of mutual interest, as DePuy focused on nuclear weapons and the future of his Army.[11]

DePuy also exchanged letters with Samuel Huntington, another Harvard scholar, in 1957, the year in which Huntington published *The Soldier and the State: The Theory and Politics of Civil-Military Relations,* in which Huntington states that from early in the nineteenth century to the 1940s, "Americans had little cause to worry about their security . . . a given fact of nature and circumstance." Changes in technology and international politics combined "to make security now [in the midst of the Cold War] the final goal of policy rather than its starting assumption." In other words, the question that had earlier concerned Americans—What pattern of civil-military relations is most compatible with American liberal democratic values?—was supplanted in the present age by the question: What pattern of civil-military relations will best maintain the security of the American nation? Huntington wrote, "The principal focus of civil-military relations is the relation of the officer corps to the state." He asked, "What sort of man is the military officer?" The distinguished civilian academic at Harvard then startled his readers with this question and answer: "Is it possible to deny that the military values—loyalty, duty, restraint, dedication—are the ones America most needs today? America can learn more from West Point than West Point from America."[12]

Bill DePuy personified Huntington's yearning for a bit of Sparta in the midst of Babylon. His conduct exemplified the very values Huntington praises in his book: loyalty, duty, and dedication. DePuy consulted with Craig, Kissinger, and Huntington while a colonel in the Pentagon, demonstrating the initiative he expected later of those who worked closely with him, regardless of rank. Intelligence and the courage of one's convictions complement initiative, and all are attributes that DePuy respected and sought in subordinates.

In a period characterized by degree-chasing and admiration for the soldier-scholar, given his frequent tours in Washington, where several fine universities are located, and given his demonstrated intellectual curiosity, it seems odd that Bill DePuy never earned a graduate degree. Part of the explanation may be that his professional duties allowed little time for formal study. On 20 January 1958 DePuy wrote a letter to Georgetown professor James D. Atkinson opting out of a program that he had either considered or begun: "I am pained to admit that the press of other business has prevented me from pursuing my studies under your able tutelage with the vigor and care which they deserve. I think it best to face facts and discontinue them at this time."[13] Perhaps as relevant as "the press of other business" was DePuy's confidence that he could educate himself more efficiently in private study, and he did so. His bold thinking and lucid prose were noticed by his superiors.

An internal memorandum DePuy wrote on 25 June 1957 for Secretary of the Army Staff Major General William C. Westmoreland, "The Likelihood of Limited War," was important for two reasons, one having to do with the future of limited war and the other DePuy's personal future. In the memorandum, DePuy wrote that emerging nations outside of the NATO area pressing for independence from colonial powers would be encouraged to violence by the Soviet Union. Should the United States wish to intervene, massive retaliation would not be feasible, because the risk to the United States was simply too high. Nothing less than a vital interest of the United States would make the use of nuclear weapons credible to friend and foe. He went on to say that although the time and location of limited wars are not entirely predictable, limited wars are more likely to happen than general war. Therefore, DePuy concluded, the United States absolutely required capabilities for limited wars.[14]

Westmoreland praised the paper and in so doing "discovered" DePuy, thus beginning a rewarding association for both men. DePuy would work for Westmoreland in Vietnam and later as his right-hand man when Westmoreland was Army Chief of Staff.

But it wasn't enough for the Army to make its case in inter-Service debates in the Pentagon. Public relations also required attention. DePuy called himself "the Chief of Staff's man" for the Association of the United States Army (AUSA). "We helped organize and put on the first annual meeting and the initial symposiums," he recalled. The "we" included George Forsythe and General James Gavin. They were well aware that the Navy had the Navy League, the Marine Corps had influential boosters, and the Air Force had captured American fancy with high technology, but the Army had Bill Mauldin's Willie and Joe, the "dogface sojers" of World War II who carried over to Korea and after. The Army was in need of image shining and effective PR.

With his usual intensity, the Chief of Staff's man threw himself into the task. DePuy's managerial and organizational skills and his personal contacts were instrumental in getting AUSA off the ground. So was his increasing understanding of how to use the military bureaucracy. He killed two birds with one stone by being an early contributor to *Army*, AUSA's monthly publication. *Army* needed good copy, and DePuy found an audience for his thinking about tactics at the squad level.

In 1958, he contributed what became his first published article, "11 Men 1 Mind," a refined expression of battle drills that he had been improving and teaching since 1944.[15] The *Army* article documented DePuy's practical lessons, but it added an almost mystical element: the concept of the squad as the binding of individual men into a selfless whole. DePuy's piece elevated a discussion of the mechanics of moving, shooting, and communicating to the realm of poetry and philosophy, evoking a powerful reaction from the field.[16]

This effort to understand leadership and why soldiers fight was DePuy's first published piece on issues that deeply concerned him. The squad as an idea morphed into his later speculations about large and complex organizations as ideas. The 1958 article is a hint of DePuy's habitual search for first causes, a preoccupation noted by those who worked closely with him. (He would, for example, at the start of every project ask, "What's the concept?") He mastered the bits and pieces, the details of many complex projects, but his cast of mind impelled him to fit those pieces into a whole. He would not allow the trees to block his view of the forest.

For the rest of his life DePuy maintained close ties to AUSA, and he was loyal to *Army* as a contributor—to the distress of editors of other publications. In later years, when editors of other publications asked the now-famous military man for an article, DePuy usually declined, saying that the *Army* audience was just the readership he wanted.[17]

The seamless mingling of personal and professional ties that DePuy enjoyed in his correspondence with Dick Stilwell also characterized his relationship with George Forsythe. DePuy and Forsythe gave each other professional tips, provided a leg up in various matters, and aided each other's career. They also recommended promising officers to each other. Forsythe told DePuy that then-Major John H. Cushman (LTG, USA, Ret.) was bright and broad-gauged, the kind of fellow DePuy might want in the Coordination Group. DePuy recruited Cushman and then wrote Forsythe, saying, "You will be happy to know that Jack Cushman is joining us in the Coordination Group around the first of the year."[18]

In time, Cushman's "Dear Colonel" salutation becomes "Dear Bill." Many of their letters in 1957 concerned the new draft of the key Army Operations Field Manual, FM 100-5, Cushman writing from the Command and General Staff College (C&GSC), Fort Leavenworth, and DePuy from Washington. They were both keenly aware that they were leaving the Continental Army Command (CONARC), the echelon between C&GSC and the Pentagon, out of the loop in their discussion of the new Field Manual. Interestingly, the major Army reorganization of 1973 put CONARC out of business as DePuy assumed command of the newly established TRADOC. The FM 100-5 of 1957 brought Cushman and DePuy together; the 1976 version caused their falling-out.[19]

Uppermost in DePuy's mind from 1956 to 1959 was the need to have an army ready to fight anywhere along a spectrum of conflict that stretched from atomic war and its deterrence at one end to small wars at the other. The Korean War demonstrated America's unwillingness to use atomic weapons—at least not in Korea over Korea—even when things went very badly for the friendly forces, as they had both in the summer of 1950 and in the winter of 1950–1951. Future wars were likely in which the United States had interests requiring military involvement, but whose outcome was not worth the risk of using weapons of mass destruction. Risk assessment also had to consider the atomic capability the Soviet Union acquired in 1949. The Army would be paramount in limited wars.

And what about a general war in Europe in which the United States and NATO faced a numerically superior Red Army? Perhaps the U.S. Army should have tactical atomic weapons that could be directed at enemy soldiers, fortifications, and tanks instead of enemy cities.

From the 1960s, American and German artillery units in Europe (with U.S. officers holding the key) had artillery capable of firing atomic projectiles. Dr. Strangelove had joined the U.S. Army—including the infantry. While DePuy was in the Coordination Group, questions arose regarding both the configuration and the arming of the Army. One response was the Pentomic Division. The creation of Maxwell Taylor, its purpose was to get the Army back in the game in the atomic age. The Pentomic Division was, as its name suggests, organized around five maneuver elements called "battle groups," rather than three regiments, which had been the norm for the infantry divisions of World War II and Korea. In terms of numbers of men, a battle group, which consisted of roughly 1,500 men, fell between the size of a battalion (around 800) and a regiment (around 3,000) as they were constituted in World War II and the Korean War. Commanded by a colonel, the battle group was armed with an atomic weapon (called "Davy Crockett"), which was more frightening to its own troops than to the soldiers of the Soviet Army. The mordant joke among infantrymen in the early 1960s was that the bursting radius of Davy Crockett exceeded its range; Americans and Russians would all be blown to smithereens, presumably leaving God to sort out the mess.

Bill DePuy would command a battle group of his own in Germany a little over a year after leaving the Coordination Group, allowing him to practice theories he himself had helped develop. His stint in the Pentagon, close to the power centers, taught him political infighting, ways to get things done in a bureaucracy, and the challenge of managing a large organization.[20]

9

School in London; Command in Schweinfurt

It was the most relaxing year of my life; it was a very nice sabbatical.

—DePuy on his Imperial Defence College experience

The most striking feature of the test operations from start to finish was the unquestioned ability of Colonel DePuy, the battle group commander.

—BG Andrew Goodpaster, Chief Umpire, 1961

Late one night in the early 1970s, Lieutenant Colonel Colin Powell found himself alone with his boss, Lieutenant General DePuy, in a small executive aircraft as they returned to Washington from a field visit. During that late-night flight, DePuy proffered some advice to the promising young officer: "Never become so consumed by your career that nothing is left that belongs only to you and your family. Don't allow your profession to become the whole of your existence." At that moment, Powell later wrote, he understood why he and the others on the staff had never seen the inside of DePuy's home. DePuy's advice was given just at the time when Powell was sorting out his personal and professional sense of self.[1]

Bill DePuy practiced what he preached. A year-long sojourn in England permitted him, Marj, and the children to spend a lot of time together, a closeness that each family member recalled with fondness.

Bill, Marj, and their children all felt their stay in England in 1960 was special for them as a family and for the lasting friends they made there.[2] DePuy's lifelong love affair with things British, as well as his reticence to discuss his family in a work setting, is captured in his understated response to an interviewer's invitation in 1979 to "tell us about your experiences" at the Imperial Defence College.

DePuy replied, "I'll just say that it was a very pleasant interlude for me and the family. I happen to enjoy the British. The course lasted for a year and was a very high-level type of thing. We were concerned about things like the Commonwealth and the world, and we traveled around a lot, including a trip to the Middle East. Also, I met a lot of people who are still friends. It was the most relaxing year of my life; it was a very nice sabbatical."[3]

This crisp response reveals DePuy's capacity to compartmentalize and his brevity, precision, and understatement in his professional speech and writing. Invited to be expansive on a subject dear to his heart, he nevertheless was brief. DePuy scrupulously separated the professional from the personal, and the question was posed by two military officers in the course of an interview with a retired four-star general for the edification of fellow soldiers and historians. This probably goes a long way toward explaining why DePuy was so brief. Despite his reputation as a brilliant briefer and lecturer, his notoriously intense demeanor in pressing for answers to his own questions, and the fact that intimates knew him to be witty, funny, and a wonderful storyteller, he would have seen this interview as the place for professional commentary, not personal matters. His self-effacement at such moments conforms to two stereotypes: that of the understated English gentleman and that of the laconic American plainsman. Fortunately, his children were more expansive in describing their year in England.

Bill DePuy moved his family to London in December 1959. He placed his children in British schools and found a flat in London before beginning his one-year course at the Imperial Defence College. Daphne, born 22 November 1954 in Frankfurt, Germany, was the youngest and might fairly be characterized as "daddy's little girl" from her birth to her father's death. One of her earliest recollections of her father was his announcement that they were going to England at the end of 1959. Her first sight of New York City was followed by the grand adventure of crossing the Atlantic by ship and the special treat of watching films and eating in restaurants. "My parents were not moviegoers or restaurant frequenters," Daphne recalled. "Our life was very much home-centered." DePuy showed his children around the ship and "played with us the whole time." He took enormous pleasure from all aspects of family life, then and later.

Having arrived in England, brother Bill was packed off to boarding school, the first time the three children had been separated. This was a "horrific experience," said Daphne, because the children, born in 1952 (Bill), 1953 (Joslin), and 1954 (Daphne), had up till then been inseparable. Young Bill's school was called Highfield, the name the family later gave to their house and fourteen acres purchased in 1971 in bucolic Fauquier County, Virginia. While young Bill attended English public school (a private boarding school to Americans), Joslin and Daphne lived with their parents in a London flat for a couple of months before the family moved to a house just off Kensington High Street. The girls attended "a very proper English day school run by a high-society headmistress named Lady Eden."

Daphne said that her mother was "at her happiest" that year, thoroughly enjoying British society and her life in London. "She loved the Brits and she made lots of friends that lasted through the rest of her life." Weekends were spent traveling to Wales and Scotland, to castles and military tattoos, and when not touring they visited the country homes of friends. Daphne also has fond memories of going to Hyde Park with her father, who would paint—he was, in her estimation, "a talented artist"—while she and Muffin, their terrier, ran around the park. Muffin was the English replacement for their beloved Snuffy, a victim of British quarantine laws, who had been given to trusted dog-loving friends in the United States before they left. Relinquishing Snuffy was painful, since the dog had grown up with the children. The DePuy family always had dogs.

Marj, recalled Daphne, was "tickled telling stories about how gentle Muffin was going after the Queen's ducklings. Mother had an interesting way of painting a pretty picture of life as she saw it should be." Bill is described by the mature Daphne as "one of the warmest, dearest, gentle and loving people. He was one of my dearest friends and advocates for my whole life." Her recollections of England evoked a general assessment of her childhood and growing up in the DePuy household: "Our life was so wonderful."[4]

Joslin, born 24 July 1953, repeated Daphne's adjective: "The British experience," she said, "was wonderful!" Like her sister, Joslin recalls her attentive father taking the girls in their little blue pinafores, red Mary Janes, and white socks to Lady Eden's. "Dad would take us into the cloak room and make sure that we had our raincoats and winter coats or whatever hung on the proper hooks and that we were all squared away for the day." The affection and coaching of their father was lovingly described forty-five years later; memories of him are fond.

The girls also remembered "Mrs. Hamburger," a babysitter described as "horrible" by Joslin, mainly because she made "the most God-awful hamburgers." Happier was their memory of dancing for the Queen. "Daddy came out and watched all of our practices. Mother not so much." Daphne danced well, as a perfect bunny; Joslin did a bit less well as a pig. Joslin also learned to dislike milk after drinking hot milk direct from a cow. Despite dancing less well as a pig and her unpleasant memory of hot cow's milk, in 2000 Joslin returned to the DePuy London digs of 1960 for a sentimental journey down Memory Lane. Her visit was punctuated by a kindness that reinforced her good feelings for the British as the occupant invited Joslin into the apartment. Despite slight renovations and repainting, Joslin found the flat very familiar. Seeing the place again released a flood of happy memories.[5]

Thinking about the year in England evoked a characteristically far-ranging and analytical response from DePuy's son, Bill Jr. Begun as a recollection about England, his comments became a general reflection on his parents, their relationship with one another, family dynamics, and the cohesion of the family over time.

Bill DePuy and Marjory Walker were in many ways polar opposites who were attracted to each other. The son described his father as "a quintessential high plains populist" formed by the rugged place and the "very practical and sturdy people" who live in that part of the world. DePuy was the third generation of his family to live in the Dakotas. Young Bill traced his family's history, starting with two DePuy brothers, who left France in the late 1680s after the revocation of the Edict of Nantes set Catholics and Protestants against each other yet again. The trip to North America is lost in Atlantic fog, but the trek over time from the east coast to the west coast spread DePuys—with several spellings of the family name—along the way. The senior DePuy's correspondence reveals various Depews and Depuys who, on seeing stories or photos of General DePuy in the press when he became famous, wrote letters, inquiring into the possibility of kinship. In any event, the plains populist of the twentieth century married a lady with ties to Old Virginia.

Marjory Walker DePuy was proud that her ancestors had been given a 10,000-acre land grant by George II in what later became Albemarle County, specifically in the region known today as Brown's

Cove, where Bill and Marj are buried in a family plot. The Browns of Brown's Cove were Marj's ancestors. The land was divided at some point into 1,000-acre plantations with slaves, a memory of former family status that made Marj proud of her old Virginia roots.[6]

She was toughened early in life. Her father died in 1924, when she was nine or ten, and her mother took four children from Virginia to Boston, where Marj's maternal grandmother and friends helped the young widow and her brood to scrape by. The loss of father and breadwinner was compounded by dependence on others and the Great Depression. Marj's children remarked on her frugality, even when the bad old days were well behind them. The psychological impact of being "the poor relations" cannot be measured with any precision, but, Bill Jr. said, "My mother was like a mother grizzly bear that defends her family and children with ferocity." She was "a modern woman" in the 1930s, independent and professional decades before feminism became "a movement."[7]

Marj was High Church, another link to England, as well as to Old Virginia tradition and status. Later family attendance at Christ Church in Georgetown put the DePuys in contact with smart people—"smart in the fashionable sense," added Bill Jr.[8] A close observer of the DePuys and a longtime associate of Bill's believes that Marj was High Church for the social status it conferred rather than for reasons of faith or theology.[9] The point was to see and be seen in the right church, in the right schools, and in the right neighborhood.

Marj reveled in her year in London, pursuing cultural activities both for her own pleasure and for her children's edification, and spending weekends in the country houses of British friends. For Bill, an unselfconscious and frequent use of British colloquialisms—"chaps," "winkle-out"—became a permanent part of his everyday speech. Their year in England was memorable for them both.

On 14 February 1961, Colonel William DePuy assumed command of the 1st Battle Group, 30th Infantry, in Schweinfurt, Germany, where he remained until 28 February 1962. DePuy enjoyed all of his commands very much, including the battle group, despite his reservations about the way the Army had organized the infantry division. In the Pentomic setup there were no command jobs for infantry lieutenant colonels, meaning that when a captain relinquished command of a company, he had no prospect of troop command until he became a colonel twelve or fifteen years later. The principal staff positions in the battle group called for majors, jobs that captains filled in battalions. So "there wasn't any career progression." In DePuy's estimation, "You can't train an Army that way. You need a lieutenant colonel level command for sure, in order to keep them current and give them command experience."

He also considered the companies too large and unwieldy, a conviction rooted in his combat experience as a commander and operations officer and confirmed by his command of the battalion in Schweinfurt. DePuy favored smaller units and a higher density of NCOs and junior officers controlling the men directly fighting the enemy. Later association with Israelis would confirm his preference for a high ratio of leaders to troops.

Many veterans of the period between the wars in Korea and Vietnam agreed with DePuy on another point: the span of control in a battle group was simply too much for the average commander to handle. Before and after the Pentomic experiment, commanders from platoon leader to division commander controlled three maneuver elements and a fire support element. This was the triangular organization dating from the early 1940s. The battle group commander had five organic maneuver elements; rifle companies; a large combat support element with mortars, tanks, assault guns, and reconnaissance gun jeeps; plus communications and medical platoons. To that already large package, nonorganic elements were attached, typically a tank company or cavalry troop and often a combat engineer company. Span of control was one of the reasons the Army returned to battalions under brigades. The battle group experiment ended rather quickly.

The novelty of the battle group, the Pentomic Division, and the arrival of new armored personnel carriers gave DePuy an opportunity to experiment and improvise. The fact is that no one really knew what they were doing in this new game. Many of DePuy's fellow battle-group commanders came from staff jobs after having spent a long time away from troops. But the situation was perfect for the self-assured, experienced, and imaginative DePuy. He clearly had a great time in command, and he was very successful at it.

He thrived on complexity and challenge. "I had fun with it," he said, "because commanding a battle group was really like commanding my third battalion. It was just a great big battalion." In his view, those who found it cumbersome simply lacked experience commanding battalions. They tried to run the command through the staff "like a brigade or regiment rather than command it directly like a battalion."

DePuy's point was that officers who had grown up in the regimental system were conditioned to battalion commanders (lieutenant colonels) directing companies and regimental commanders (colonels) directing battalions. The battle group, with so many moving parts, overwhelmed many commanders. It was neither fish nor fowl, neither battalion nor regiment. Moreover, infantry colonels accustomed to the pace of foot infantry were unprepared for the speed at which things happened in the tank-mechanized infantry team as it prepared to fight a Red Army heavy with tanks and artillery. Not all men in their forties can learn new tricks; DePuy could and did. And he applied the lessons he had learned in the mobile phases of World War II.

His was one of the first formations in Europe to get the new Armored Personnel Carrier (APC), the M-113. Like a kid who gets a new bike for Christmas, Bill DePuy took his new toy to the field to try it out. He took his soldiers to the field with him, and kept them there until they learned to ride the new bike. He taught soldiers and leaders how to fight as mechanized infantry.

DePuy had experienced a war of movement. Except for the static warfare before the breakout from Normandy in July and the initial Allied defensive response to the German offensive in the winter of 1944–1945, DePuy had fought on the move from the English Channel to Middle Europe in eleven months. Movement to contact, meeting engagements, and pursuit characterized much of his experience as regimental S-3 and as battalion commander. When not walking, his troops had moved in the back of the reliable, bumpy, and too often open "deuce-and-a-half" truck familiar to infantry veterans of World War II and Korea. But they moved. Typically the two-and-a-half-ton trucks delivered their human cargo and then disappeared as the infantry resumed walking. The trucks did not belong to the infantry. Neither did the tracked M-59 personnel carriers that belonged to Transportation Corps companies, an interim solution between the "deuce-and-a-half" and the "one-one-three." Colonel DePuy and the new M-113 arrived in Schweinfurt almost simultaneously. At about the same time, the World War II family of infantry weapons—the M-1 rifle, carbine, Browning Automatic Rifle, and Browning .30 caliber machine guns—was replaced by the M-14 rifle, the M-60 machine gun, and the M-79 grenade launcher.

The M-113 is found in many armies around the world even to-day. It is a tracked vehicle capable of carrying a squad on roads or cross-country while affording a limited degree of protection from bits of metal flying about the battlefield, but not from direct hits. Hasty preparation permits the M-113 to swim across water obstacles. Each of the four APCs of the mechanized infantry platoon mounts a .50-caliber machine gun. The firepower of these four heavy machine guns exceeds the firepower of all of the other weapons of the pla-toon combined. And the M-113 was organic, meaning it belonged to the infantry commander. DePuy's reaction to the mechanization of his battle group was simple. He could move like an armored force, "which I liked."

DePuy divided the training of his battle group into two parts. First, he did just what he had done with his battalion in 1954–1955. He trained his soldiers from the bottom up and conducted "all sorts of testing of squads, platoon, and companies," the kinds of things all infantry must be able to do. Then, about a month after the M-113s arrived, he put his mechanized organization in the field in February, when the ground was frozen, and stayed in the field until April, training tactically, teaching his troops and leaders battle drills suit-able to rapid movement.

DePuy trained his companies to be ready to move in five min-utes and to operate after simple orders. For example, he would say, "Charlie Six. Move to Checkpoint 55." The commander of Charlie Company responded within a few minutes with, "On the way." SOPs (standard operating procedures) would inform the company commander what to do when he got there. Without orders, the com-pany commander knew that he would occupy a battle position, look around to assess the situation, contact friendlies in the area, face the company in the direction of the enemy, and prepare to move again. A brevity code, of the kind that DePuy described in his 357th Infantry Training Memo No. 1 in July 1944, told the commander just what to do. A word on the radio meant "dig in" or "conduct local patrols." The orders were brief because the battle drills had been rehearsed often. Commanders and troops knew what they were do-ing. That's why their commander kept them in the field: to mas-ter their new equipment with techniques appropriate to them. "We could go anywhere," DePuy recalled. "We went down [to Bamberg] and played games with the 2d Cavalry, the 4th Infantry, and the 15th Infantry." In fact, he took his command from that training directly into his Army Training Test at Hohenfels. "The wives didn't like that, but it was absolutely super training. It was the kind of training that you would do if you knew that you were going to war." The troops were dirty, the vehicles were dirty, clothing was torn, but they had learned to maintain themselves in the field. "They were not eating candy bars anymore. They were eating Army food. The replacement system, the maintenance system, the supply system, and the tactical system were all working in the field." His battle group experience was sweetened by the fact that as senior colonel in Schweinfurt DePuy was also task force commander. He had his own 30th Infantry plus the 38th Infantry (another battle group), a tank battalion, and a cavalry squadron. It was exhilarating.

The added dimension of mechanization did not alter his practice of training rifle squads and platoons personally and leading directly with clear, terse commands. He knew what he wanted to do, and he had a plan to do it. Experience gave him knowledge, knowledge gave him confidence, and his confidence permeated his battle group. Soldiers read those signs and follow the man who knows what he's doing. Outsiders, observing DePuy's intense personal style from the sidelines, unaware of context, might see his confidence and briskness as arrogance. His juniors reacted with the highest form of praise, emulation.

George Joulwan, who earned four stars and served as Supreme Allied Commander, Europe (SACEUR), spoke of DePuy with admiration and affection long after his assignment to Colonel DePuy's Battle Group in 1961. A Pennsylvania All-State football player, Joulwan was recruited to West Point by the legendary Earl "Red" Blaik in 1957. As a cadet he spent the summer before his senior year with an infantry unit in Germany, an experience that decided him on his branch and on Germany for his first assignment. Directly out of Fort Benning's Basic Infantry, Ranger, and Airborne courses, Second Lieutenant Joulwan was the optimal young tiger, aggressive and eager. He needed only to be trained by a master craftsman.[10]

Joulwan savors his recollection of the time he spent in DePuy's outfit. He valued the tactical lessons he learned and had enormous respect for his colonel, known by the troops to be a decorated battalion commander of World War II.

Six or seven replacement Second Lieutenants, newly arrived in Schweinfurt, stood in front of Colonel DePuy's desk as he queried them about their expectations and hopes in his battle group. Joulwan regretted that the interview began with the man on the other end of the row, making Joulawn the last to respond. When his turn came, Joulwan burst out with, "I want to be a platoon commander. That's all I want. That's why I came here."

Later, as the new lieutenants left the commander's office, the adjutant put his arm around Joulwan's shoulder, saying, "The Colonel wants to see you." The young man returned to face his commander. DePuy recalled Joulwan's firmness in requesting a platoon and told him to get his gear together to join his platoon in the field in the morning. The introduction to his commander made a deep impression on the new officer. So did his first day in the field.

After just a few hours with his men, a helicopter descended. DePuy emerged, fit and trim, and sharply turned out in starched fatigues, glistening eagles, and shining boots to check the defensive positions being prepared. He asked various soldiers who was on their left and who was on their right as he made a beeline for a machine gun position, jumped in, sighted along the gun, and asked the gunner for his final protective line. "Good," said DePuy, nodding. He asked for a range card. Then he asked how much grazing fire the gunner had on a certain azimuth. When the young man responded, DePuy got out of the hole and walked away on that azimuth saying, "Watch me." He fell out of sight not far from the hole. He asked the soldier if he had lost sight of DePuy. The soldier said he had. Then DePuy returned to explain what dead space is, how an enemy could throw a hand grenade from that dead space uncovered by the gun into the machine gun position, and how important the machine gun was, not only to the platoon but also to the company and the entire defensive position. He said that the enemy seeks seams between companies through which to infiltrate. The young machine gunner learned that his machine gun interlocked with a gun of the neighboring company. That soldier was one of the key men to the position. Something could be done about that dead space, by using barbed wire or mines, by registering artillery on it, or by moving the foxhole.

Joulwan, his platoon sergeant, and his squad leaders were all watching from behind and around the hole where the group commander was holding forth. Joulwan later realized that the colonel was teaching a class to the entire platoon leadership by speaking to the soldier in conversational tones. Then DePuy asked, "Who's in charge here?"

"I am, sir," said Joulwan.

"Come with me," said the colonel.

DePuy walked ahead of Joulwan to a point several hundred meters from the defensive positions being prepared. Then he turned, facing the positions. DePuy looked at his lieutenant and said, "You are the Soviet regimental commander. You are to attack that position. What are your actions to accomplish that mission?" Joulwan said he'd direct artillery fire on the objective. DePuy approved, noting that the Soviet style was to use artillery pieces hub to hub, making massive use of indirect fires.

"Where's your aim point?"

Joulwan spotted a big tree and made that his aim point, an easily recognizable terrain feature. Then DePuy asked related questions about the attacker's likely avenue of approach, considering the terrain, the enemy, and friendly forces. Lessons DePuy had learned from the Germans in June and July of 1944 he passed on to the novice officer: defensive positions must be hidden from the enemy by the use of natural concealment and natural cover. Rocks, folds in the earth, and depressions were to be used to supplement digging in and using overhead cover.

Still, the tutorial was not finished.

Joulwan and DePuy returned to their original positions to review the situation. DePuy asked again about the aim point for enemy artillery. Joulwan noticed that one of his machine gun positions was right under the big tree that was the enemy aim point. He would move that machine gun and make other adjustments based upon what he had learned. But he had learned something else. Time and the situation permitting, don't settle for inspecting your line only from your own perspective. Get out and see it from the enemy's perspective. Use the terrain. Get in the enemy's head.

Describing that first day in the field under DePuy's command, Joulwan recalled another flood of thoughts he experienced at the time. The colonel had spent hours tutoring a single platoon leader in the field. The colonel knew the nuts and bolts of the trade. And he knew how to talk to soldiers, how to teach both smart men and dumb men. He knew and passed on techniques he had learned in the 1940s to those who would lead in the 1980s and 1990s.

Joulwan was impressed and grateful, and he never forgot the lessons of that first day. Years later, as the four-star SACEUR in 1996, when visiting a Russian position in Bosnia, Joulwan repeated with a Russian lieutenant precisely what DePuy had done with him in 1961, including a check of his range cards and the positioning of his machine guns. The young Russian platoon leader was mightily impressed that the American general knew what he was doing—and *that he bothered to do it.* Joulwan was conscious of being fundamentally formed by DePuy in the German countryside thirty-five years before his encounter with the young Russian.

Teaching did not stop in the field. Joulwan learned other leadership techniques: to use Fridays at the Officers' Club to review lessons, to wrap up the week, to look forward to the coming week, to talk tactics with fellow officers, to recognize that they could outfight the enemy, to love what they were doing and one another, and to laugh and enjoy life after business. The Army was a way of life, a calling.

Joulwan credits DePuy with creating a bond among the officers of his battle group that lasted their entire lives. Certainly that was the case with Joulwan. He recalled the fun that followed the "official" part of the Friday routine in the club in Schweinfurt. DePuy would challenge the biggest young officers in the battle group to a pool game—but not because he was a great pool player. The point was to get all of the officers yelling and cheering, pleased to be in the company of brothers. It didn't matter if the cheering was for the little colonel or the big lieutenants. The point was that they belonged to one another. DePuy's outfit was "a happy ship."

The barroom game of wits called "Liars' Dice" is mentioned in almost any extended interview with those who knew DePuy well. He used the game throughout his career when on the road with his aides and key men. He played to win, but more important was the cohesion his playing built among fellow professionals winding down after intense concentration. Few senior officials might be comfortable with head-on-head competition with subordinates at a bar, but DePuy's self-confidence allowed him to fit in socially while standing out professionally. There was absolutely no doubt regarding who was boss. But soldiers, particularly the promising officers who often surrounded him, also needed to understand the human dimension of soldiering.

Joulwan confessed to imitating DePuy's style, techniques, and methods shamelessly both in the field and in social activities. He was happy to give DePuy full credit for teaching Joulwan the tactics, techniques, and procedures that took him to the very top of his profession. DePuy lived the Army adage: work hard; play hard. Unspoken was a corollary: develop professional leaders.

DePuy said that the Schweinfurt period described by Joulwan "was the time when the Army had the best people it has ever had." He backed up this opinion with statistics: in the early 1970s, DePuy said in his 1979 interview, the Selective Service System was rejecting about 35 percent compared to a 78 percent rejection rate at the Armed Forces Examination and Entrance Station in 1960 and 1961. The statistics he cited indicated that the Army was far more selective while DePuy commanded his battle group and had to dip deeper into the manpower barrel late in the war in Vietnam. DePuy was satisfied that he got "roughly the top 20 percent of the physical and mental specimens in the country. In short, the troops were super. Of course, they [most of the young soldiers] were not volunteers."

But the officers were. "I had some marvelous young fellows there," DePuy recalled. "George Joulwan and Jim Madden were both there, as was Charlie Getz and a number of other chaps who have done rather well." He had not recruited them. They arrived in the battle group via the normal personnel replacement system. When DePuy commanded his division in Vietnam, the situation was quite different. Officers queued up for command of his companies, battalions, and brigades. Combat officers go to the sound of the guns, and his division was in the thick of combat. Great careers are boosted by successful performance, particularly command in combat. By 1966, DePuy's reputation in the Army was that he knew what he was doing and that he was going places. A great number of his subordinates would go on to great things, but he was also quick to relieve officers in combat when the need arose. Feared by some, he was also a magnet for talent.

Those "marvelous young fellows" were joined by solid NCOs, for whom DePuy had a special place in his heart. He attached enormous value to the fighting NCO tank commander, squad leader, and platoon sergeant who led by the Fort Benning dictum "Follow Me!" But DePuy was critical of the bad habits too many of the captains and middle-grade officers had picked up. He was especially critical of the "sandbag castles" commonly used in the Korean War: in DePuy's concept of defense, they were the very antithesis of intelligent use of natural concealment and cover. In addition, in the period between the Korean and Vietnam Wars, a pervasive conservatism had developed among officers who had survived the post–Korean

War reduction in forces that said: don't take chances. Too many of these pretend-leaders imitated the turtle who plods slowly and pulls its head into its shell when confronted by the unfamiliar. The plodding and unimaginative would not get on with Colonel DePuy in Germany nor with General DePuy in Vietnam; nor would those seeking "command time" simply for career enhancement.

In his retirement years, DePuy looked back on his battle group command as a thoroughly gratifying professional experience. "I would say that the 30th was the practical culmination of my experience as an infantry unit commander," he said. "I felt I was able to put it all together, make it work, and really move it around tactically."

A junior member of the sister 38th Infantry said that DePuy "was already known as a star because the 30th outshone every battle group in the division. He basically ran the 3rd Division in Schweinfurt. Everybody thought very highly of DePuy."[11]

BG Andrew Goodpaster (General, USA, Ret.) agreed. As Chief Umpire, he said in his evaluation of the annual training test of the 1st Battle Group, 30th Infantry, on 10 May 1961, "The most striking feature of the test operations from start to finish was the unquestioned ability of Colonel DePuy, the battle group commander, with the assistance of his staff, to control and command effectively a battle group task force. . . . Many of the highly competent umpires stated that they would be proud to be members of this well-trained unit."[12] A report like this on a colonel in command is a big step toward a star, particularly when the rater is himself "a comer" like Goodpaster, later Commander in Chief, Europe (CINCEUR) and Supreme Allied Commander, Europe (SACEUR) as a four-star general.

A chaplain in a sister battle group in Schweinfurt used several adjectives to describe DePuy, including "brilliant"; "organized"; "focused"; "intense"; "controlling"; "demanding"; even "feared." This last may have been prompted by the report that DePuy relieved two company commanders shortly after assuming command, something that "had not been done" in Schweinfurt.[13]

Jim Holland (COL, USA, Ret.) served under DePuy in Vietnam; his father commanded DePuy's sister battle group in Schweinfurt. His father told him a story about DePuy that made an impression on the younger Holland. At one point in Schweinfurt, commo wire was in short supply, and the elder Holland discovered that one of DePuy's communications sergeants was rolling up commo wire belonging to Holland's battle group. "Dad assured me," said Jim, "that Bill DePuy had not ordered the young man to salvage dad's wire." DePuy "had made it absolutely clear that [his] battle group would not be short wire. People got things done for Bill DePuy."[14]

DePuy could be feisty in dealing with powerful seniors who could damage his career. At the end of one training phase, DePuy's boss, the Assistant Division Commander, made remarks that DePuy considered thoughtless. DePuy felt the commander's words had "discouraged" his troops. "Expecting praise, they had cold water tossed on them." Despite the fact that his battle group earned an award for excellence in training, DePuy was not mollified.

The general presented the award before a dinner at the Hohen-fels Officers' Club attended by DePuy's officers, invited guests, and the commanders of other major units. In the words of the general's aide, William J. Mullen III (BG, USA, Ret.), "I anticipated that the colonel was going to invite his boss to the dinner . . . [But] we stood around for a few more minutes. It seemed clear to me that the general had just been invited in for a cameo performance [not dinner]. After a short while, [the general] and I ate our dinner in the Generals' Mess by ourselves." DePuy let it be known that his soldiers were not to be "discouraged" by an outsider, not even if the outsider was his boss.[15]

DePuy's reputation as a smart and skilled—some would add ruthless—officer was growing. Recognition of his intelligence, skill, and diligence were universal. His reputed ruthlessness and arrogance would make him a contentious figure. In any event, the observation that "people got things done for Bill DePuy" was correct.

DePuy saw himself as a commander. While he was serving as battle group commander, the Army personnel system offered him assignment as the Army Attaché at the American Embassy in London.[16] He declined forcefully, emphasizing that he was asked to *volunteer* for that position. He chose not to. He did not say why, but it is safe to assume that despite his affection for Britain and Marj's strong attraction to life in England, he chose not to be sidetracked from his own idea of a military career. His intelligence assignments in Hungary and with the CIA were enough time away from the mainstream for him. The London plum, however attractive, would stamp him "intel." So he turned it down.

10

Back to Washington

If I were to pick one word to describe my father and what he
was about, he was a teacher. He turned every opportunity
into a teaching and learning experience.

—Daphne DePuy

We were trying to do force planning at the department level
so that weapons development, organization, training, tactics,
and resources were all synchronized.

—DePuy on his Plans and Programs job in 1963–1964

As the family said good-bye to British friends and relocated to Germany, President John F. Kennedy delivered his Inaugural Address on 20 January 1961, asserting that a new generation of Americans was ready to bear any burden and pay any price in accepting leadership. Robert S. McNamara, who would serve Kennedy and Lyndon B. Johnson as Secretary of Defense, writes, "I first confronted the Indochina problem in a relatively brief meeting between President Eisenhower and President-elect Kennedy. It was 19 January 1961, President Eisenhower's last full day in office." McNamara recalls that an "immense number of subjects" were covered on that afternoon before Inauguration Day, "but the emphasis was on Indochina."[1]

While DePuy commanded his battle group in Germany, dramatic international events succeeded one another with disconcerting regularity. Crises in Berlin, Cuba, and Vietnam competed for the attention of policy makers in Washington. Provocation by the Soviet Union regarding access to Berlin resulted in heightened American military readiness in Germany followed in turn by the Soviet response: construction of the Berlin Wall in 1961. The phrase "Iron Curtain" was more than a rhetorical flourish: walls and minefields fragmented Germany, creating an atmosphere of hair-trigger readiness for war.

The Bay of Pigs operation in Cuba in 1961 failed, a great embarrassment to President Kennedy early in his administration. By late 1961, the United States had some 16,000 military advisers in South Vietnam to train the South Vietnamese to defend themselves against pressure from North Vietnam and insurgency in South Vietnam. In October 1962, the Cuban missile crisis took consideration of a nuclear exchange between the superpowers from the realm of the unthinkable to the stark reality of a clear and present danger. At home, black Americans were demanding the civil rights guaranteed to all. Resistance to the civil rights movement resulted in violence, including the burning of American cities.

Policy for Vietnam was, therefore, only one of several major issues confronting American decision makers as the DePuys returned to Washington in 1962. In fact, concern for Vietnam, a small country 10,000 miles from the United States that few Americans could find on a map, was dwarfed by the frightening crises in Berlin, where the United States directly confronted the Soviet Union, and in Cuba, where enemy missiles were in easy striking distance to the American mainland.

In his 1995 confessional, McNamara, reflecting on U.S. policy in Vietnam from Kennedy's inauguration to his assassination on 22 November 1963, cites Montaigne's *Essays:* "We must be clear-sighted in beginning, for as in their budding we discern not the danger, so in their full growth we perceive not the remedy."[2]

McNamara, who was at the center of the evolving story of the war in Vietnam from 1961 until he left the office of the Secretary of Defense on 29 February 1968, says in the preface to his book, "we were wrong, terribly wrong. We owe it to future generations to explain why." He spells out in considerable detail the small steps that led to policy failure and ignominious defeat, and he accepts responsibility for two assumptions that were wrong, assumptions he inexplicably failed to challenge early on: the domino theory, and the capacity of South Vietnam to govern itself effectively and responsibly. In his words, "We both overestimated the effect of South Vietnam's loss on the security of the West and failed to adhere to the fundamental principle that, in the final analysis, if the South Vietnamese were to be saved, they had to win the war themselves."[3]

As Bill DePuy went to work in the Pentagon in May 1962, his government was taking the small steps "in beginnings" while failing to discern the danger "in their budding." It was believed, or hoped, or assumed that South Vietnam was making progress with the training of soldiers and police forces and was close to self-reliance. But the assassinations of both President Ngo Dinh Diem and President Kennedy in November 1963 were followed by the political disintegration of South Vietnam in the first year of President Lyndon Johnson's administration.

DePuy would be totally engaged in the Vietnam War from 1964 to 1969. But both before and after those dates, his duties included actions related to Vietnam, particularly his first job on the Army Staff in counterinsurgency in 1962, and certainly after 1969, when his broad responsibilities as a three- and four-star general included fighting the war and dealing with the consequences of that war. In addition, Vietnam affected his personal as well as his professional life.

Marj DePuy had strong views about keeping the family's private and social life apart from her husband's job. As her son put it, she "treasured" her space and distance from the Army. When it became possible to buy a country retreat in 1971, the DePuys did so. They bought it "for a song," her son recalled, because it was dilapidated. They fixed it up themselves—a labor of love for the entire family— and they called it Highfield.

Before they moved to Highfield, Marj took Bill away from the Army on weekends and holidays to insure that they enjoyed time together as a family. She held the Army at arm's length, and the Army knew it. When Bill DePuy was TRADOC Commander at Fort Monroe, the word among the staff was: hold up General DePuy on a Friday afternoon at your own risk![4]

Of the many joys of the professional soldier, the details entailed in what the Army calls PCS, Permanent Change of Station, are not among them. A long move, interruption of a school year, finding a place to live—with the attendant questions of proximity to work, good schools, affordability, and quality of life—all these problems are a part of the PCS. Fortunately for the DePuys, they were already familiar with Washington.

Upon their return in the spring of 1962, they lived in an apartment in Arlington, Virginia, before Marj found the house she wanted on 35th Street, a block from the National Cathedral off Garfield Street. The family would live there for much of the 1960s, but DePuy would be off to the wars for three of those years. Daphne recalls those years as she grew from little girl to young lady. "Our life was so wonderful. It was back in the days when parents would send children out and say, Go play and come back at such-and-such time."[5] Bill, Joslin, and Daphne were so close in age that they played together and had the same friends. And Joslin used the present tense in 2005, saying, "We kind of go as a unit." As if to underline that point, to this day young Bill continues to manage Highfield for himself and his sisters as a family retreat.

The two sisters recall that when they were children, their brother Bill was the general while they were the privates in his organization, the United States Secret Intelligence Service. They were joined by other neighborhood children, including the son of the Norwegian ambassador. Spy skills included codes, passwords, and clandestine activities. The command post, the DePuy basement and garage, was replete with maps and Christmas lights poking through holes drilled in walls to represent Moscow, Paris, London, Washington, and other places of interest to the USSIS.

Neighborhood children "flocked to our house," said Joslin. "Mother loved the children, and she loved having neighborhood children over, playing actively. She adored all of that as long as we were well-behaved. She had no tolerance for any nonsense, like being too loud. And we had to be tidy."[6]

A television set entered the DePuy household when General Bill Rosson, Bill DePuy's friend and the man who brought DePuy to his job on the Army Staff in 1962, was, the sisters recalled, "so horrified that my parents didn't have a television that he bought one and brought it over so the children could have TV."[7] Now young Bill's secret agents could watch *Mission Impossible, The Man from UNCLE,* and *Get Smart* as advanced training to enhance their intelligence expertise. Daphne recalls that her father particularly loved *Get Smart.* "He thought that was one of the funniest shows." One imagines General DePuy chortling as Maxwell Smart demonstrated his finely tuned ineptness.

Daphne, at eight or nine years of age, was unaware of what her father did as Deputy, then Director, Counterinsurgency, in the Special Warfare section of DCSOPS. But she recalls the installation of a mysterious red telephone in the DePuy residence. *That* was impressive! She was keenly aware of the interesting people in the neighborhood and the memorable guests in her parents' active social life. Many of the guests were intelligence officials from foreign as well as American agencies. Marj enjoyed the company of bright and sophisticated people who had interesting stories and knew how to tell them. So did Bill.

Young Bill put the DePuy guests into three groups. The first was the old China hands, specialists including veteran collectors and analysts from the Korean War and "chiefs of station from all over Southwest Asia." There was a "constant movement of people like that through our house." The second group consisted of military friends, including Dick Stilwell, John Mason, and Ed Hamilton. Since the latter two and DePuy were recruited by Stilwell to the CIA during the Korean War, there was considerable overlap of World War II and CIA colleagues. A "third bucket" was "people from the foreign military, political, and intelligence establishments." Theirs was a cosmopolitan circle.

"The children were very much a part of those things," said Bill Jr. They were expected to be polite, engaging, and able to converse intelligently. Even the fun aspects of their lives were used as teaching opportunities by Bill and Marj to civilize and refine their children. Reference books were at hand to settle matters of fact that arose in dinner conversations. The DePuy children learned early in life that they were entitled to their opinions, but no one was entitled to his or her own "facts."

The children attended public schools into their junior high years, and then Marj decided to put all three in private schools while Bill was in Vietnam. She was determined that her children would get first-rate educations. A military officer, even one enjoying a fine career, could barely afford living in a good Washington neighborhood with three kids in good schools, but those were the choices that Bill and Marj DePuy made. The girls attended National Cathedral School, and the son went to Landon. The family attended Christ Church in Georgetown, where young Bill's communion instructors included Rowland Evans, of the syndicated column team Evans and Novak; George Herman, of CBS news; and the head of the anthropology department at Georgetown University.

General DePuy's religious views are complex. He was a serious student of religion and philosophy for his entire life. His son believes that his father "read every word of George Santayana and his treatises on spirit and faith, among many others, such as Huxley and Lewis." He thought hard about what men believe and why; his intellectual curiosity seemed limitless. "We argued endlessly about nature versus nurture; he could see the genetic connection that I could not."[8]

A chaplain who knew DePuy from the Vietnam years to DePuy's death, was convinced that DePuy found religion.[9] That may be. But late in life, when pressed on his religious views by his grown son, DePuy said he was an Electro-Chemist. Asked what that meant, he said that chemical and electric impulses were probably embedded in genetic codes yet to be discovered. Science would continue to crack those codes. His religious musings reveal open inquiry and a clear historical and anthropological understanding of biblical times, but they do not suggest faith or belief in God. He reckoned that Hebrews, for example, developed tribal cohesion to face down enemies and enforced dietary rules for survival in the sense of nourishment and to avoid poisoning in an austere environment. He thought his way from his Presbyterian roots to the position of a tolerant if bemused agnostic, perhaps an atheist, at the end of his life. But Bill Jr. believed his father knew an enormous amount about the history of religion. One concludes that DePuy was a profoundly ethical man, but lacked faith in God.

David Halberstam called DePuy one of the Army's intellectuals, a man "considered by most civilians in the Pentagon the brightest general they had ever met." He lived "in the nice Cleveland Park area" in a "better residence from which to meet important civilians and influence them."[10] Perhaps. But perhaps he lived there to accommodate his wife's preferences, his children's needs, and his own taste. In any event, the neighborhood and the family's life style did not hurt his career.

Daphne praises her mother's management of the family during the three years that her father was in Vietnam, saying that she "rose to the occasion," that she was "completely in charge of everything around her—at all times, but particularly [when father was in Vietnam]."

Marj told her children, "You all need to be strong. This is the way life is. We all need to be strong and responsible and do what we need to do. And not get too sentimental about all of this. Just move on." And, Daphne adds, "Mom wanted life to be as normal as possible. She was a remarkable woman. During Vietnam, she was sort of our commander." Bill Jr. also describes the division of labor in the family in military terms. "If you think of the household as a theater of operations, there was absolutely no question as to who was CINC."

Joslin said that Marj "adored" her brothers, but had "strained relations" with her sister. She liked her father-in-law but had little in common with her mother-in-law. She seems to have valued the masculine directness and sense of purpose she found in the world of the OSS and the CIA.[11]

Many ambitious Washington professionals hear the siren call of power and sacrifice family for career. Such was decidedly not the case in the DePuy family. Marj gave up her career; Bill was a model father. Daphne said, "If I were to pick one word to describe my father and what he was about, he was a teacher." Figuring out how something worked pleased him, whether it involved solving a tactical problem, fixing a garage door, running a large organization, or quickly producing a field manual. Late in life he studied wildflowers. And he was gifted at explaining how things work. Daphne's description gets to something central about what made him tick: he was a teacher.

Joslin says she never had the sense that her father was too busy to pay attention to his kids. He did not go back to work after dinner or come home late from work. Reflecting on this aspect of her father when she was herself a mature and engaged professional, she said, "He was able to go and do the job and come home and have that family life. I don't know how he did it." There was never a hint that in helping his kids he was interrupting something more important. Looking back, she says, "Thinking about how much time he spent with us and what he was able to accomplish in his career kind of amazes me."

Each of the children said that their father helped with homework and enjoyed doing it. He was firm, but he was also affectionate and sensitive. He was that way for their entire upbringing—when they were tiny tots in London and he would help them put on their coats and tie their shoelaces; when they were faced with the challenges of reading, writing, and arithmetic; and when, as bright teenagers stimulated by quality schools and by the climate of protest against the war in Vietnam, they began to become more politically aware. His daughters' description is entirely compatible with that of DePuy's professional colleagues, who noted his capacity to set aside distractions to focus on the task at hand, whether it be homework, post-hole digging, determining squad tactics, or reorganizing a major command.

When their father returned from Vietnam in 1967, the children, particularly young Bill, had reservations about the war in which their father had distinguished himself. He had, in fact, appeared on the cover of a national magazine and was mentioned frequently in press accounts of the war in Vietnam.[12] Despite a period of tension between father and son stemming from differences about the war that compounded the usual problems between parents and their teenage children, young Bill gives high marks to his father for being a master teacher and a wise man. He treated his teenage son and his son's friends as intellectual peers, using logic and an Aristotelian style of question-and-answering in a joint effort to find the truth. He was not condescending in debate. Young Bill recalls with great respect and affection the way his father would join young people around the kitchen table as they sipped beer and discussed the hot-button issues of the day. In short, the DePuy kids had an affectionate father who was a master teacher of shoelace-tying when they needed it, and of geopolitics and philosophy when they were ready for that.

As of May 1962, DePuy was Deputy Director, then Director, Counterinsurgency, Special Warfare, DCSOPS in the Pentagon, though he later said he didn't know anything about "special warfare."[13] His self-assessment was accurate only in the narrowest sense; the term was relatively new. His attaché training and experience in Hungary in the late 1940s had introduced him to strategic intelligence. Infiltrating Chinese Nationalist troops into mainland China from Formosa during the Korean War familiarized him with clandestine and irregular operations. His broad responsibilities in the Chief of Staff's Coordination Group from 1956 to 1959 had required him to conceptualize the entire spectrum of conflict, from insurgency to nuclear war, in the debates about massive retaliation and flexible response. In fact, his previous assignments had prepared DePuy quite well for his new job.

The devolution of European empires after World War II had resulted in the creation of new states, many of which had been ill prepared for self-government. They were poor, lacked experienced and responsible leadership, had borders that were in dispute, and often had diverse populations not necessarily loyal to the new central government. They emerged from colonialism to find themselves in an east-west power game played by the superpowers in which the new nations were pawns.

"None of us were experts," said DePuy. He and his colleagues were feeling their way, assembling packages ready to do "whatever the President said this country was going to do anywhere in the world." President Kennedy, at the start of his administration, had announced an activist philosophy. His intent was to thwart subversion in the Third World in what the Communists called "wars of national liberation."

As statements of appealing ideas and noble intent were transformed into national policy, it became necessary to develop a national strategy and then a military strategy to support and implement the administration's foreign policy. The Army's piece of the action appeared very large indeed. It called for Army capabilities ranging from those needed to fight a general war—on the order of World War II, perhaps with nuclear weapons—to other, lower levels of conflict, for which "special warfare" was to be tailored. Bill DePuy became deeply involved first in special warfare generally, then in Vietnam.

Combat in Vietnam was at a low level of intensity in 1962, but it was becoming the stage on which the Army would play a role in what the President had made a "new and exciting high-priority endeavor." The symbol of that priority was the nonstandard Green Beret that President Kennedy gave to Special Forces. The subsets of "special warfare" included guerrilla warfare, unconventional warfare, psychological operations, political action, and civic action. DePuy said, "We were trying to organize Special Forces units around the world—a group in Okinawa, a group in Panama, a group in Europe, plus groups in reserve at Fort Bragg."

Special Forces officers and NCOs were reading the writings of Lenin, Trotsky, Mao, and (Ernesto) Che Guevara in order to better understand the guerrilla fighter. The histories and after-action reports from veterans of Tito's resistance to the Germans and of China and the Philippines' resistance to the Japanese in World War II were their texts, as were accounts of the post–World War II efforts of the communists in Greece and China. Communist terrorist efforts in Malaya, and the British counterstrokes, were also studied. The Army sought to make itself capable in both conventional and special warfare.

DePuy was open-minded about special warfare, but he continued to regard the training of the conventional Army as seriously defective. It was mechanistic and unimaginative, with progress measured in hours spent on a subject rather than by competence in doing combat tasks. At the policy level, the domino theory was accepted without much analysis. According to this theory, if Vietnam fell to the communists, Vietnam's Asian neighbors would also fall, like dominos.

DePuy first visited Vietnam in 1962 with Colonel George Morton to set up the Special Forces headquarters in Nha Trang. The CIA was running a number of Special Forces detachments in the Central Highlands around Ba Me Thuot with the Rhade tribe of Montagnards, with some success. The concept was to establish defensible camps along the border with Laos. The camps were to serve as magnets to the aboriginal Montagnards, who inhabited the remote Central Highlands and regarded the Vietnamese as oppressors, much as American Indians saw European settlers as a threat. The camps were intended to block infiltration routes used by the Hanoi Government to send people and supplies in support of the insurgency to the south. The north-south infiltration route in Laos fed into west-east entry trails to South Vietnam at several points, among them the tri-border area where Laos, Cambodia, and South Vietnam met. The hope was that the camps would expand like ink blots, stabilizing the Central Highlands. Special Forces recruited, armed, trained, paid, and led the Montagnards in the service of the Republic of Vietnam in a program called the Civilian Irregular Defense Group (CIDG). Over time, the CIDG effort became increasingly more military than paramilitary, and the Army took over the mission from the CIA in 1964. Some 10,000 indigenous irregulars led by Special Forces soldiers came under Army control under "Operation Switchback."

DePuy said, "Counterinsurgency was all the rage in Washington because the Kennedys had come into office pledged to help any friend," a reference to Kennedy's inaugural address. Maxwell Taylor was brought into Kennedy's confidence as flexible response became the buzzword to describe a balanced military capability in American forces. The Army reclaimed a big chunk of the action from the Air Force, which DePuy called "the prima donna of national defense."

While serving as Director of Special Operations during the Cuban missile crisis, Colonel DePuy got "an interesting mission" from Army Chief of Staff Earle Wheeler. He was told that President Kennedy "wants a Cuban battalion in the invasion of Cuba." DePuy was given the assignment on a Tuesday and was told to have the battalion organized, trained, and ready to board aircraft by the following Monday. DePuy told Wheeler he would need a letter from the Chief to get things done fast and to overcome resistance. Wheeler said, Write it, bring it in, and I'll sign it.

Armed with the letter, DePuy went to Fort Bragg, where General Hamilton Howze was issuing the invasion order. During a break, DePuy told General Howze what he was up to. Howze asked what kind of a battalion DePuy had. "I don't have it yet," said DePuy. Howze was furious.

DePuy quickly assembled a 300-man battalion, with 100 Cubans per company. Each company was commanded by a Special Forces A Team; the battalion was commanded by a B Team. All the Special Forces leaders were Spanish speakers. DePuy recalled, "We got them [and the aircraft], flew them to Miami from Fort Knox. They got uniforms, shots, fired weapons on ranges, threw hand grenades, and we got them to Florida." DePuy called Wheeler to say, "They are there." Wheeler said, "It's been called off."[14]

DePuy's reflections on how the United States moved to ever deeper involvement in Vietnam, a place Americans knew little about at the time, is eerily suggestive of later commitments of American troops to uncongenial, unfamiliar places.

"We thought we could bring some disadvantaged country in the image of America," he said. "Well, now, after all these years, we know better. We have a much more modest view of our capabilities. So, I look back on all of that as a period of fumbling—national fumbling. A lot of rather important people in the Administration were behind it. . . . There was a great deal of confidence in Washington, naive confidence, that we could do anything we set our minds to. What we discovered in Vietnam and are discovering in Central America is that the political dimension of an insurgency is central to the outcome. On the political side we are really amateurs. Our belief in political freedom—that is, one-man-one-vote—ties our hands in the rough and tumble politics of dictators and communists."

Specifically regarding Special Forces, DePuy wryly observed, "It had worked rather well, and the history of Vietnam is that anything that worked well with ten good men, we tried to expand to ten thousand men right away." Perhaps he was caught up in the special operations Zeitgeist of the early Kennedy years. His Officer

Qualification Record shows that he qualified as a parachutist on 30 November 1962. He was forty-three years old.

DePuy was soon promoted out of his counterinsurgency job. Upon selection for promotion to Brigadier General, he became Director, Programs and Budget in DCSOPS in April 1963, before becoming Director of Plans and Programs in ACSFOR (Assistant Chief of Staff for Force Development) in July 1963, a job he regarded as being particularly important to his understanding of how the Army worked. DePuy often said that dealing with plans, programs, and budgets was excellent preparation for his later positions of great responsibility. "Basically, we were trying to do force planning at the departmental level so that weapons development, organization, training, tactics, and resources were all synchronized." Comprehending the whole and synchronizing the many parts of a complex organization were the very skills he would later exercise as AVICE (1969–1973) and TRADOC Commander (1973–1977).

Except for those who have operated at the very top of the military hierarchy, it is easy to believe that the United States has a lot of armies. There is the sweaty-soldier-muddy-boots Army that fights, bleeds, and dies; the clever Army of MBAs, PhDs, writers, and teachers; the businessman's U.S. Army Incorporated, of logistics, procurement, and distribution; the scientists' and engineers' Army of equipment design; the headquarters Army of "four copies each" of any document; the touchy-feely army of public relations. In his programming job, DePuy learned that he had to roll all of those armies into one. He also learned that a fix was never final. It was a never-ending process that required constant adjustment. Even as one popped the corks on the champagne bottles to celebrate the victory of the moment, the old pros knew that a new season, with new demands, was just around the corner. One didn't fix Army problems; one rearranged them.

In May 1964 DePuy embarked on what became a three-year tour in Vietnam. In staff and command assignments there he would continue his professional education, enhance his reputation as a warrior, and become a contentious figure in the military subculture. He would also miss his family and be missed by Marj and the children.

DePuy with his dog, Mac. In later life, he, Marj, and their children always had a dog.

Corporal DePuy, Squad Leader, Company B, 109th Engineer Battalion, 34th Infantry Division. He had to choose between the National Guard and ROTC in his junior year of college. He chose ROTC and excelled.

Solid student, active in college service organizations, and adjutant in his ROTC detachment, DePuy was commissioned as a Reserve Officer despite his mentor's best efforts to get him a Regular Army or U.S. Marine Corps commission. He was a good dancer, a "big bands" man, and a fan of the Mills Brothers. Copied by Betsy Holdhusen from South Dakota State University yearbook, 1941.

"CAPT" BILL DEPUY

Captain Bill is wearing the 90th Infantry Division patch in 1944. The 90th was formed in 1917 with men mostly from Oklahoma and Texas, took part in the 1918 offensive in the Great War, and fought in World War II from Normandy in June 1944 to Czechoslovakia in May 1945.

A note in DePuy's handwriting on the reverse side of this sketch from 1944 says, "What a hell of a looking guy you married. Love, Bill."

Maj. DePuy near Metz, France, in October 1944, as S-3, 357th Infantry. He would take command of 1/357 in December, in miserable weather conditions, in one of the most difficult tactical operations while in contact with the enemy, a night river crossing in boats. TRADOC News Service.

LTC DePuy is awarded the Distinguished Service Cross for valor while 1/357 commander by Major General S. Leroy Irwin, XII Corps Commander, at Weiden, Germany, June 1945.

A note on the back of this photo says "Bill DePuy, Brookings, S.D., 8 May
[1945] VE [Victory in Europe] Day, WWII, in Czechoslovakia. The daughter of a Sudeten German."

From left, standing, DePuy, George Bittman Barth, John Mason, Ed Hamilton; squatting left, Richard Stilwell and unknown. DePuy adored Barth, called Mason a tactical genius, said Hamilton performed the bravest act DePuy saw in World War II. He credited Stilwell with holding the 90th Division together before good commanders replaced bad. DePuy, Mason, Hamilton, and Stilwell later served in the CIA and directed irregulars in the Korean War.

DePuy (left), Assistant Military Attaché in Hungary. DePuy had studied Russian and was preparing to go to the Soviet Union when Josef Cardinal Mindszenty was charged with conspiracy to overthrow the Hungarian government. He was given asylum in the American Legation in Budapest. The government retaliated, declaring the attachés persona non grata. DePuy was the emergency replacement.

John Mason (left) and DePuy (right) in Hong Kong, 1950. Stilwell recruited them and Ed Hamilton to organize, train, equip, and lead Chinese Nationalist raiders. The idea was to occupy Mao with security at home and so discourage the use of Chinese troops in Korea.

(*Above*) Marjory Walker Kennedy (left) outside the OSS compound in Kunming, China, in 1945. She served in the OSS in World War II and in the CIA later. She and Bill DePuy met while he was detailed to CIA, and they married. Elizabeth MacDonald (right) was later Elizabeth MacIntosh, author of *Sisterhood of Spies*. (*Below*) Marj, Billy, Daphne, Bill, and Joslin in their quarters in Budingen, Germany. Marj enjoyed the cultural opportunities in Germany and in England. She maintained close ties to British friends until her death in 2002.

DePuy (center), officers of his 2/8th Infantry, and guests in the Budingen Officers' Club, September 1955. He tested V Corps infantry battalions for a year before getting battalion command for a second time. He concentrated on squad and platoon training and perfected the DePuy foxhole and "overwatch" movement drills.

Bundeswehr LTC Krieger, commander in Hammelburg and NATO ally, with DePuy, CO 1/30th Infantry, Schweinfurt, Germany, July 1961. DePuy respected his German enemy in World War II and admired Wehrmacht skill in fighting the Soviets while outnumbered.

Colonel DePuy leans on his jeep in Hohenfels, Germany, in 1961, looking at the M-113 armored personnel carrier that enabled the U.S. infantry to keep pace with armor. The M-113 arrived about the time he assumed command of 1/30. He had his troops maneuver on the frozen German fields all winter, learning to be mechanized infantry.

Doing the Twist, the dance craze of the time, at DePuy's Auf Wiedersehen Party in Schweinfurt in early 1962, as Marj (in glasses) watches. DePuy was a good dancer and particularly liked the big band music of the 1930s and 1940s, but he was game to try the new.

Marj DePuy is in the center of this picture of a reception at Fort McNair on 24 September 1963, honoring foreign officers touring U.S. Army schools. Bill, now a Brigadier General on the Army Staff, is to her left. His next assignment was to Vietnam.

In May 1964, DePuy became Westmoreland's J-3, MACV. His note of November 1964 on the back of this photo says "Gen. Nguyen Khanh (left), Commander-in-Chief, Vietnamese Armed Forces, one time Prime Minister, short time President, and constant source of trouble and turbulence. A proud, vain, and brilliant little guy—completely and utterly untrustworthy."

This envelope from Vietnam is dated 21 July 1964. DePuy was very attentive to his family, including his mother, even when busy with coups in Saigon and major events in the field. The attached note says, "Sgt. Mullane did this for you children. He is very good, isn't he? Pops."

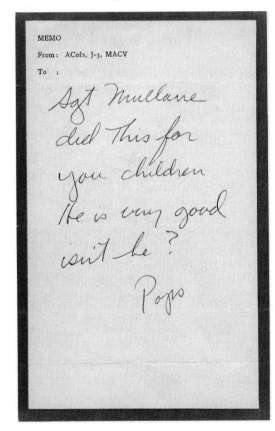

(Above) DePuy with the sergeants who lead from the front. He affectionately called them, their troops, and junior officers "the little fellers." He made the leader his radio operator, acted as platoon leader, and demonstrated combat techniques in the field. *(Below)* MG DePuy, CG, 1st Infantry Division (March 1966–February 1967), critiques an engagement of the 1st Squadron, 4th Cavalry. The 90th Division's breakout from Normandy and command of mechanized infantry in Germany in 1961 taught him how to employ tracked and armored vehicles effectively in Vietnam. PAO, TRADOC.

LTG Jonathan Seaman, who was succeeded in command of the 1st Infantry Division by DePuy. As II FF Commander, Seaman was DePuy's boss, but he seems to have been intimidated by DePuy. From George L. MacGarrigle, *Combat Operations: Taking the Offensive, October 1966 to October 1967*. United States Army in Vietnam Series. (Washington, D.C.: Center of Military History, United States Army, 1998), p. 33.

MG Frederick C. Weyand, shown here with Lt. Gen. Nguyen Van Thieu. Weyand commanded the 25th Infantry Division while DePuy commanded the Big Red One in Vietnam. Soldiers compared the lanky and easygoing Weyand to the short and intense DePuy, once called "a banty rooster." The two got along fine. From MacGarrigle, *Combat Operations: Taking the Offensive*, p. 149.

(Above) MG DePuy and BG Hollingsworth, Vietnam 1966. DePuy's inscription, "The incomparable Jimmy Hollingsworth," captures the essence of this magnificent soldier. This picture hung in DePuy's offices after his return from Vietnam through his retirement. *(Right)* General Earle G. Wheeler, Chairman, JCS (front) and Bill DePuy, Special Assistant for Counterinsurgency and Special Activities, visit leaders in Vietnam to assess the meaning of the enemy Tet Offensive, 1968. U.S. leaders in Vietnam saw the destruction of enemy infrastructure; Washington saw the enemy in the American Embassy.

TRADOC Commander (1973–1977). After Vietnam DePuy worked for Chairman, JCS, Wheeler (1967–1969), then for General Westmoreland as Assistant Vice Chief of Staff (1969–1973), where he got a third star. In a major reorganization of the Army in 1973, he got TRADOC command and a fourth star. Photo by Clyde Wilson, Fort Monroe.

Chief of Staff, Army, General Bernard Rogers (right), DePuy's Assistant Division Commander in Vietnam, presided at DePuy's retirement ceremony at Fort Monroe on 30 June 1977, honoring a thirty-six-year career begun in 1941.

BG Jimmy L. Collins Jr. (left), who served as Chief of Military History and was a longtime friend, relaxing with DePuy and young Bill DePuy's wife, Patricia L. DePuy, in April 1980 at Camp A. P. Hill, Virginia.

DePuy, showing the focus and intensity that frightened some people, with German General von Mellenthin in May 1980. DePuy learned that German methods in fighting the Russians in World War II and American war fighting methods were compatible. He was pleased that battle-tested German and American generals made strikingly similar decisions in tactical situations.

Legacy. Five TRADOC Commanders in 1987. L-R: DePuy (1973–1977), Maxwell Thurman (1987–1989), Carl Vuno (1986–1987), William Richardson (1983–1986), and Donn Starry (1977–1981). Not pictured are other DePuy protégés, Glen Otis (1981–1983) and John Foss (1989–1991).

DePuy's grandchildren tend to his burial site at the family graveyard in Brown's Cove, Albemarle County, Virginia. He died on 9 September 1992.

11

Vietnam

[We] felt the impress of his personality and his professional
performance. . . . There I am, a lowly captain at that point and
I would hear the name General DePuy. All the advisers were
familiar with his name.
    —Lloyd Matthews, reflecting the view from the field in 1964

You asked me who is in power in Vietnam. The fact is, no
one is in power, and this explains much of the trouble we are
having.
        —DePuy, letter to his son from Saigon, 18 January 1965

From 1964 to 1969, Bill DePuy was totally immersed in the Vietnam War from three perspectives: theater operations, as J-3, Military
Assistance Command, Vietnam (MACV), 1964–1966; tactics, as the
commander of the 1st Infantry Division, 1966–1967; and national
strategy, as Special Assistant for Counterinsurgency and Special Activities (SACSA), JCS, 1967–1969. His jobs in Saigon, in the field, and
in Washington shaped his personal appreciation of events at various
stages of the war. Moreover, events in Vietnam were often interpreted differently by American officials in Saigon and Washington. And
during those years American popular opinion of the war went from
ignorance to acceptance to rejection. DePuy was aware of changing
opinion, privy to policy differences that arose between the official
Americans in Vietnam and those in Washington, and keenly aware
of political and military conditions in Vietnam.

    As General Westmoreland's trusted operations officer, DePuy
was intimately involved in recommendations from the field and
policy decisions in Washington that changed the mission of American troops in Vietnam, from advising the Army of the Republic of
Vietnam (ARVN) to directly engaging the enemy in combat. A composite picture of DePuy, then in his mid-forties, can be formed from
four sources: his letters to his family; the observations of his briefing

officer, who had almost daily contact with him; the writings of a dubious but discerning American journalist; and DePuy's own recollections of events some fifteen years after his Saigon days.

DePuy's letters to his family while he was J-3 provide unguarded insights into his personality and his first impressions of historic events. Between 2 May 1964, when he sent his first letter home from Saigon, and the end of that year, DePuy sent at least fifty-six letters to his family.[1] Often he addressed Marj and the children by name within letters sent to one of them. Clearly they were intended to be shared by the family. The personal sections of the letters cited here are quoted sparingly; references to the course of the war are given in greater detail.

Frequent references to money and budgeting in DePuy's letters indicate that maintaining a house in the high-rent district of Washington, sending three children to private schools and camps, and fixing their teeth required strict financial management. In addition, DePuy had some social obligations in Saigon; he was, for example, required to provide cocktails to his staff section on New Years Day. After being a dinner guest at the homes of some of the senior officers who had wives and children in-country, he felt he should reciprocate by taking host and hostess out for dinner. But DePuy managed on less than $200 per month for his personal maintenance and obligations. This included gifts for members of his family back home, as well as cash awards to his children for good grades in school.

Many of his letters were dialogs with each of his children. Despite the physical distance from them and the demands of his job fighting a war, he remained very much in the family. He was keenly aware, in detail, of the children's school grades, moods, health, interests, and activities. He was attentive to the birth of Daphne's mice, the furnishings in Joslin's dollhouse, and Billy's military insignia and stamp collections. References to Muffin, the family dog, figure prominently. It was clear that DePuy missed his family. And he was ever the teacher. His duty trips became geography or anthropology lessons in his letters home. He encouraged the children to write. He prodded Billy regarding schoolwork, told him to "RTP" (read the problem), and encouraged him to be analytical. Teaching his children was a joy and a responsibility not relinquished due to professional duties.

He often sent his children little gifts, each carefully selected with the individual child's tastes and preferences in mind. From early on, he treated each of his children as individual personalities. His letters sometimes included pencil drawings and sketches to amuse and inform. Interspersed with personal observations for the children would be a cryptic line or two designed to keep Marj informed. Her field experience with the OSS and the CIA and their understanding of one another enabled just a few well-chosen words from him to suffice as a kind of shorthand between them. Taken together, DePuy's letters home tracked progress, or lack of it, as he saw the situation and reported it.

In a letter to Marj dated 17 May 1964, for example, he wrote, "I haven't made up my mind whether we are gaining or losing ground. It is grave indeed. Whether the 'will' exists I do not know." That same month he told her, "It is awfully difficult to tell how all this turmoil will come out. Without a miracle it will drag us further down."

In a letter to Billy dated 21 June 1964 DePuy noted a milestone: "Yesterday Gen. Westmoreland assumed command and Gen. [Paul D.] Harkins left for home." That same month, he made mention of other personnel changes. In a letter to his children dated 24 June he was anticipating the "forthcoming arrival of General Taylor as the Ambassador." Around that time, in a letter addressed to the family but clearly intended for Marj, he said that he was "happy about Gen. Johnson's appointment [to Chief of Staff, Army]. That is a great jump forward over the heads of 43 generals." His satisfaction is noteworthy in light of the differences DePuy and Johnson would have later, when DePuy was commanding a division and Johnson was Chief. In a letter addressed to the entire family around that time he mentioned that a number of top-level people were visiting headquarters and noted wryly, "Soon all the people in Washington will be in Vietnam and there won't be any room for the Vietnamese. That perhaps is one way to win the war." And in another letter to the family that was probably sent around the same time he noted, "The tempo of the war seems to be slowly increasing," and then made comment on the presidential race of that season: "The nomination of Mr. Goldwater seems assured. What a disgrace." DePuy usually voted Democrat; Goldwater was a Republican. In a 7 November 1968 letter to his mother, however, he explained "what caused me to go for the Republicans for the first time in my life. Humphrey is the better man, and I certainly preferred Muskie over Governor

Agnew," he said, but he had "little use for the extreme liberals of the Democratic party . . . and would like to see them out of Washington."

By June 1964 DePuy was pessimistic, writing to Marj, "We can't *win* [double underline] but we can *perhaps* [his emphasis] keep from losing. We can't back down now, or we're finished in this part of the world—and many other parts too." But that same month, in a letter to Marj from Kuala Lumpur, he said, "The British did a really bang up job here." British success in putting down the Communist terrorists (CTs) in Malaya was held up by some as the model for counterinsurgency operations in Vietnam early in the war. Only later was the difference between the essentially police operation there and the need for much heavier forces in Vietnam generally recognized. He added to Marj, "At best we can buy time and time may not be on the side of the communists."

While all this was happening, DePuy continued to write sweet daddy letters to his children, as this one to Daphne at the beginning of June 1964: "All the people in this part of the world, except crazy Americans, have a nap from about 1 o'clock to 2 o'clock." Here he is teaching Daphne about the Vietnamese siesta, called *pak*, while alluding to Noel Coward, probably for Marj, and his song in which only "mad dogs and Englishmen go out in the noonday sun."

On 28 July 1964, in a more serious letter to Marj, DePuy analyzed the situation, noting that "there is a great collection of brass in this area. Frankly, the poor little Vietnamese are overwhelmed and bewildered, and I am not sure they are not slightly frightened by it all." He mentioned names in a manner suggesting that Marj knew the players; he generally addressed her as a fellow professional. "The situation out here is somewhat tenuous at the moment because the Vietnamese are visibly weary of the war and apparently are unwilling to contemplate another ten years of grinding, tedious but bloody pacification. But I am sure they would like to have us attack North Vietnam for them and thus take off some pressure and provide a diversion from the difficult war they are fighting on their own soil. Obviously no new American policy will be forthcoming until after November unless some cataclysmic event interferes. [This is a reference to the LBJ-Goldwater presidential campaign.] Therefore, our relationship with the Vietnamese may be a little strained for a few months." DePuy was right. In his *In Retrospect*, Robert McNamara would lament the fact that the political campaign in the United States took LBJ's eye off the ball in Vietnam at a critical juncture.

Two weeks later DePuy was again writing to Marj: "The situation here is unbelievably complicated. We are all working like mad to make the pacification program succeed. But [General Nguyen] Khanh [who led the coup of January 1964] and his boys are not convinced it will work and anyhow they don't like to contemplate another 5 to 10 years of fratricidal war. This explains their interest in such pipe dreams as 'Marching to the North.' They have as much chance of marching north as 'Gimo' [Generalissimo Chiang Kai-shek] has of reconquering the mainland. In short it's hard to see how we can win if the leaders of the country don't think they can win. You can see that we have a dandy problem on our hands." Just a couple of weeks later, in a letter addressed to "Marj and Family" on 26 August 1964, DePuy offered this stark assessment: "In fact there is no govt. There is only the Army and the U.S. It is a dead body somehow held up by these two supporters. There is no longer any chance of winning. It is now a matter of figuring out some alternative to winning. Frankly no one has a clue as to what that could be."

Violence and uncertainty were never far away. In a letter to his son from 27 August 1964 DePuy wrote, "Saigon is a very exciting place these days. Another mob is trying to get into the radio station." He then described crowds rushing and shooting, with seven people hurt. And a month later, in a letter to his family dated 23 September, he reported, "I arrived here just in time to become completely embroiled in the Montagnard uprising which is by no means settled. The American Special Forces are in a very difficult and dangerous situation." But on 29 September, still with the Montagnards in Ba Me Thuot, he was able to tell them, "It has been fascinating and luckily all has been settled without bloodshed . . . for 3 days we didn't go to bed once. Reminiscent of war." And the next day, in a letter to Marj, after expressing some concern for Billy's sickness and the family budget, he said, "Montagnard problem seems to be well on the road to recovery."

Afterward, in a letter to Billy dated 10 October 1964, DePuy explained the conflict to his son. "Special Forces armed Montagnards to fight the Viet Cong (VC). They did so, but the constant antipathy between the Vietnamese Government and the Montagnards from time to time broke out in fire fights. The Vietnamese regarded Montagnards as savages; the Montagnards had a sense of being a nation in the Central Highlands apart from the rest of Vietnam. This is akin to an American frontier conflict of Army vs Indians within the context of a larger war." He praised the bravery of Colonel Freund, the Special Forces commander, in putting down the revolt of the Montagnards.

As 1965 began, the political situation, wrote DePuy, "continues to worsen. The impasse between Taylor and Khanh persists. The VC are now standing up to fight for longer periods and in Phuoc Province have inflicted a grave setback on the Government." A few days later, he wrote again: "The prospects for a happy solution here continue to decline. Power rests in the hands of the generals . . . arbitrary and capricious power." Then, to Billy: "I urge you to write-write-write."

On 18 January 1965, replying to a letter from his son, DePuy told him: "You asked me who is in power in Vietnam. The fact is, no one is in power, and this explains much of the trouble we are having." Then, turning attention back to his son, he admonished Billy to "work hard to get at the bottom of things—don't be superficial."

On 7 February 1965, in a letter to Marj, DePuy reported some grim news: "At 0200 this morning the VC hit Pleiku." U.S. troops suffered 8 men killed and 109 wounded in action. At eight o'clock that morning a meeting was convened, with Ambassador Taylor, Alexis Johnson, Westmoreland, McGeorge Bundy, Assistant Secretary of Defense McNaughton, Andy Goodpaster, Stilwell, DePuy, "and all the rest of us." After several calls to Washington, "the decision is to hit NVN [North Vietnam]" from the air. The weather, however, was against them; only a single target was hit. DePuy went on, "We may have opened a new dimension in war here . . . it is sure to become bloodier. We simply couldn't ignore this one. We have a hospital full of badly mangled young men. We aren't about to turn our back on that. At a minimum we must teach people around the world that we may be rich but we are also tough as hell. If we are hit, we hit back." He concludes, "I was rather proud of my country today in that there were no timid voices in evidence here or at home."

Two weeks later, on 22 February 1965, he told Marj about a change of living quarters. "Dick Stilwell and I are in the Combat Operations Center after a long night," he wrote, adding, "This is really a comic opera place. Two nights ago we were also up all night watching the most recent abortive coup. Next week Jim Collins and I are moving into Stilwell's house to share expenses." At about this time, Stilwell,

Westmoreland, and other senior officers sent their families out of Vietnam for their safety. Westmoreland asked his officers to share houses because the hotels were full.

The same day, in a letter addressed "Dear Family," DePuy said, "My letter writing has been thrown off by a steady succession of incredible developments—the worst of which was the coup of the last 24 hours." Explaining some photos he was enclosing, he said, "The pictures show the enlisted men's BEQ [Bachelor Enlisted Quarters] at Qui Nhon. You can see why so many were killed and wonder how anyone survived."

In a separate letter to Marj from around that date, DePuy had more to say about the disruption of American families who had been in country. The "families out here are in a terrible dither," he said. Families were given just ten days to leave. "Thank goodness we were wise enough to foresee this kind of thing." Apparently Marj and Bill had discussed bringing the family to Saigon and decided against it. The senior Americans were not on one-year tours in Vietnam, as was later the case for troops. Generals and key colonels remained in country as long as they were needed. Some of the wives were living in Thailand and the Philippines. DePuy himself said good-bye to the Westmoreland family that month. "The war is bound to get rough from now on out," he told Marj, adding in an aside, "Incidentally, I spent 3 hours with Mr. Charles (Chuck) Percy, the erstwhile candidate for Governor of Illinois who went down with Goldwater. He is very impressive (detests Goldwater)." Percy had been the Republican candidate for vice president on the Goldwater ticket.

Then, in a letter to Marj: "Will *see* !! you soon." General Westmoreland sent DePuy to Washington to present Westmoreland's views and recommendations in March 1965. DePuy accompanied Ambassador Taylor on the trip home and, while there, had a chance to visit Marj and the children.

In March 1965, back in Vietnam, he wrote again to his family, this time in a reflective mood. "Obviously, our country is on the edge of great decisions. Which way they will go is anyone's guess. It seems quite clear to us out here. We have embarked on a program to punish the North Vietnamese." Later that month, he told them, "Now that the war is hotting up a bit and more serious days lay ahead, I have a feeling that many officers will spend 18 months to two years in Vietnam, and I am certain that I will be here at least that long." In fact, DePuy was in Vietnam for thirty-three months. When policy for the Army became one year tours, most Regular Army officers and NCOs did more than one tour in Vietnam.

Nearly a year later, in a letter to Billy dated 21 February 1966, DePuy sounded hopeful. He wrote, "I am tolerably optimistic for the first time since I arrived here. We have the VC in an awkward position. He has organized large forces but finds it difficult to employ them without running head-on into U.S. troops. He cannot survive a stand up fight. We have too much firepower for him, artillery, air support, etc. On the 15th of next month—three weeks away—I will take command of the 1st Infantry Division—The Big Red One—I am very proud to be given this opportunity. The 1st Division is the oldest and most illustrious unit in the Army."

As seen above, DePuy's earliest letters after his arrival in Vietnam in May 1964 reflected the confused situation there. At first he was unable to determine whether his side was gaining or losing ground, saying that at best we can *perhaps* avoid losing. He questioned the willingness of the Vietnamese military junta to fight on for another five to ten years of fratricidal war. At one point he wrote, "there is no government." At another he says the generals exercise "arbitrary and capricious power." At another, "no one is in power, and that explains much of the trouble we are having." And then, "This is really a comic opera place." He was clearly skeptical about the capacity of Saigon to govern responsibly and the ability of ARVN to defeat enemy main force formations.

Still, he very much enjoyed being in the game, though he felt that he could ply his trade with more satisfaction in command. He was "tolerably optimistic" as he went off to command his division, believing that the enemy had put himself in a box. The force the enemy had assembled to whip ARVN, intimidate militia troops, and bully the population would be severely punished by American firepower and mobility. As he assumed command of the Big Red One, DePuy was, as his soldiers would put it, full of piss and vinegar.

Lloyd Matthews (Colonel, USA, Ret.) is a particularly valuable source of information about DePuy during the Vietnam years. After experience in the field as an adviser to the Vietnamese, he worked closely with DePuy in 1964 and 1965 as his briefing officer. Then he served as Westmoreland's executive officer and senior aide-de-camp while DePuy continued as J-3. Matthews, a keen observer and precise reporter, was thus able to observe DePuy from several angles.[2]

Matthews was a captain about to become a major when he met DePuy in the summer of 1964 at Bien Hoa, where Matthews was a senior adviser to the Vietnamese. His first meeting with DePuy followed "a disastrous VC attack on the air base at Bien Hoa where we lost several aircraft due to mortar attacks. He came to talk to me about that." Even before their first face-to-face meeting, Matthews recalled, "[We] felt the impress of his personality and his professional performance. . . . There I am, a lowly captain at that point and I would hear the name General DePuy. All the advisers were familiar with his name."

Shortly after their meeting at Bien Hoa, DePuy sent tactical ideas to Matthews. Everyone knew that the ambushing was one-sided: ARVN never ambushed the enemy; the enemy always ambushed ARVN. DePuy told Matthews to have his ARVN opposite number do the following. *Bait the enemy.* Send a well-armed force into an area controlled by the VC; stomp around, letting the VC know you are there; stop at a place previously selected with great care; ambush the VC.

Matthews, reflecting later on the difficulty Americans had in influencing ARVN to do anything, said, "I don't think anything ever came of it, but that illustrates that even though he was in a relatively removed position, he's doing his best to redress problems out in the boonies." DePuy would bait the enemy on a grander scale as division commander; he simply could not resist addressing tactical issues.

Another DePuy proposal to counter ambushes strikes a familiar chord. He proposed a scheme for a small company of three platoons, all armed with automatic weapons. One platoon would carry "grease guns," the M-3, a .45 caliber-firing weapon; one platoon would have BARs, Browning automatic rifles, a .30 caliber-firing weapon; and the third would carry Thompson .45 caliber submachine guns or .30 caliber M-2 automatic carbines. All these weapons are fully automatic, like the weapon the Wehrmacht had used to suppress DePuy's troops in 1944. DePuy proposed an immediate response to ambush, laying down "a withering barrage of fire" with all automatic weapons in the direction of the VC causing "momentary docility," during which two platoons would maneuver to destroy the enemy.

Several points leap out here. DePuy, although a general officer and a staff officer in Saigon, injected himself into platoon tactics, as he always did. He favored suppression over aimed firing, as he always did. Expose the minimum number of friendly troops to enemy fire, suppress the enemy, use the majority of the friendly force to finish the enemy. Suppression keeps the enemy hunkered down, allowing the maneuver platoons to kill VC with automatic fire and grenades. Unable to see very far in a jungle, one shoots at likely enemy locations, not point targets. He proposed a small company, as he always did, because he wanted a high proportion of officers and NCOs to troops, leaders to privates, to insure that troops fired their weapons.

Here, DePuy proposed using the means available in Vietnam in 1964. The United States had provided World War II hand-me-downs to ARVN. Even from DePuy's lofty position, helping his boss puzzle through theater strategy, he experimented with ways to apply what he knew of basic infantry techniques to the concrete reality of combat in difficult terrain. Veterans of the 1st Infantry Division and students of the Vietnam War will recognize the skeletal outline of an evolution in technique that became "cloverleafing," in movement to contact followed by the immediate employment of all fires, which would be available to American infantry in 1965 and after, but was not yet available to ARVN in 1964.

Matthews began his job as DePuy's J-3 briefer in September 1964. As he recalled those days, he said, "The most exciting things that happened, oddly, were not on the battlefield. They were the political coups." The coups were "enormous events" in the Command Operations Center, particularly, one assumes, to the new Major Matthews, who briefed Ambassador Taylor, Westmoreland, the CIA, and other senior officials in the presence of his attentive boss. This was heady stuff for the bright young briefer. There were ad hoc briefings as important events unfolded, and there was a daily 1700 brief for the staff and commander. From his position under the direct supervision of DePuy, Matthews received instructions from him and had the chance to see his boss in action.

He describes DePuy, who was less than 5 feet 8 inches tall and who "probably didn't weigh over 140 pounds," as "an extraordinarily forceful personality. You would have thought that he was 6 feet 5. I don't mean he was a blusterer or anything like that, but he just had a very strong personality." Matthews added, "He had a penetrating intelligence. You could not bullshit General DePuy. He went to the heart of the matter. He cut through the peripheral matters and came to the heart of the issue. He had an extraordinarily roving, active mind, and he would constantly work a problem. Sometimes even when you were talking to him you had the feeling that with his left cerebellum he was working a problem."

Matthews admired that very well-organized and analytical mind married to an impressive capacity to articulate. He was particularly in awe of DePuy's responses to General Westmoreland's nonagenda questions regarding issues as they arose at briefings and staff meetings. "What do you think of that, Bill?" Westy would ask. DePuy, recalled Matthews, "leans back and with a perfectly organized Aristotelian reply, with a beginning, a body, an end, a conclusion, and a recommendation, he would deliver this on an impromptu basis and it was better than nine out of ten officers could have sat down and written in three or four hours. Yet he did it off the cuff in a beautifully articulated, analytical manner. Then he came to the answer, he came to the recommendation, and everybody just sat there for a moment, amazed at this performance. And I saw him do that over and over and over. I was impressed, I will tell you."

Matthews, himself an articulate and serious professional, called DePuy "an all-business kind of guy and extremely professional. Sometimes you will hear the dichotomy between the guys who are time-servers and guys who are true professionals. He was not a time-server. He ate, drank, and lived professional concern, sort of Old Army in that regard."

Among the serious professionals Matthews knew over the years as an infantry officer, as an English professor at West Point, and as an editor hobnobbing with military intellectuals, Matthews sorted the good ones into two baskets. There were thinkers, and there were doers. What made DePuy special, said Matthews, is that he was both. He was comfortable and capable in a pragmatic way, a doer curious about how things work, and he loved hands-on tactics at the lowest level. He was also comfortable and capable in the world of ideas, the world of abstraction and speculation. He was pleased to take a promising concept that seemed to be on target, mull it over, and turn it into a concrete solution to a real problem.

Matthews was fascinated by his boss, finding DePuy "extraordinarily articulate, even eloquent at times, both orally and in writing. He had absolute self-confidence. Of course, when you have that kind of background in World War II, and you had all that experience, you wore a DSC, it was easier to be self-confident than you might be as a brand-new lieutenant just arriving in country for the first time. He struck me as a person with answers."

DePuy revealed a personal dimension to those who worked closely with him that others did not see. Matthews saw it in his Saigon days with DePuy. "He was very professional," said Matthews. "He usually had a very serious look on his face, but once in a while he would flash that smile and reveal a warm side, and when he did, he was absolutely irresistible. We would have gone to hell and back to give him what he wanted. So I don't want to convey any impression that he was a remorseless automaton. He had a warm side, and he could be a very attractive man and leader."

Those whose contact with DePuy was peripheral, or a one-time exposure, did not see that warmth. The perspicacious chaplain who served in a sister battle group in Schweinfurt while DePuy commanded there acknowledged DePuy's professionalism, intelligence, and communication skills, but he emphasized something else: fear. DePuy scared the hell out of many people, probably far more than he charmed.[3]

Another source, a tough and decorated combat infantry leader, also saw behavior by DePuy that made him uneasy, even as a detached observer. Captain Henrik O. Lunde was in DePuy's J-3 shop as liaison officer from an incoming brigade of the 101st Airborne Division. Invited to staff briefings, he had the opportunity to see DePuy in action for a short period and was impressed with the incisiveness of DePuy's questions. But he also remarked that DePuy pressed briefers hard, often to their embarrassment in front of an audience that included their subordinates. Lunde was never a victim of these interrogations, but he recalled them with disapproval. "He asked the right questions, but I wouldn't want to work for him."[4] That probably was, and remains, his image in the Army at large. All who knew him well agree that DePuy did not suffer fools gladly.

Matthews and DePuy, of course, were never close friends—"he never invited me to his hooch for a drink or anything"—but Matthews says that there were moments between official events when his informal conversations with DePuy took the form of professional ruminations. One of these moments provides a useful insight into DePuy's later management style.

"In a relaxed moment," recalled Matthews, "a contemplative

moment where he leaned his head back and looked up, as if to just kind of praise God a little bit, he said, you know, Lord, in the best of all possible worlds, this is the way that I ideally would build and organize a staff. I would scour the Army and come up with the twelve brightest, most intelligent, articulate majors in the entire Army. Then I'd get myself twelve cubicles, and I would put the majors in those cubicles. I would give them no particular portfolios, no S-1, S-2, S-3, S-4. Just bright majors who had a good basic education in the military profession prior to their arrival. Then, as problems came up, as I needed a staff study, as I needed a position paper, as I needed a reply for the boss, or as I needed to solve a problem, I would just distribute these problems to my stable of intelligent majors. I'd tell them, with no strings attached, here is my basic guidance. Here are my basic thoughts, tentative. Now you run with the ball and you tell me what I ought to do, in 5,000 words or less."

Later, in 1969 in the Pentagon, DePuy was able to assemble a group of brainy majors and lieutenant colonels to do precisely what he described to Matthews back in the mid-1960s in Vietnam. And as he prepared to command TRADOC in 1973, he told his subordinate, LTC Max Thurman (GEN, USA, Ret.): "Go to the Army personnel office. Get me the twenty brightest colonels you can find. I want twenty of the brightest lieutenant colonels and twenty of the brightest majors. Then we can run the other 100,000 in the command."[5] Clearly, DePuy's personal style was evolving during his time in Vietnam.[6]

Matthews described Westmoreland's MACV staff as the "crème de la crème." And the "two predominant officers on that staff" were the Chief of Staff, Major General Richard Stilwell, and Brigadier General DePuy. Matthews stood in awe of the intelligence of each man, and he makes an interesting distinction. Stilwell had "an incredible memory," a brain "like a sponge." He read everything and knew more about the various staff actions than the officers responsible for them. He was "omniscient" and rarely went to bed. Catnaps of ten or fifteen minutes sufficed to keep Stilwell at his desk almost always. DePuy, by contrast, was the active operator, "the penetrating, articulate intelligence." Matthews concludes, "They were a terrific team," always very direct with each other. Matthews added that the staff consisted almost entirely of West Point officers, with the exception of DePuy.[7]

Regarding DePuy's influence with Westmoreland, Matthews

said, "I became General Westmoreland's aide, so I saw [DePuy's] performance from two perspectives . . . General Westmoreland had enormous respect for General DePuy." DePuy was outspoken, a function of his self-confidence, which in turn stemmed from competence and experience. "He was not untactful," said Matthews, "but he was direct." The way he presented matters, few arguments ensued. "General Westmoreland was aware of his outspoken tendencies, and [reacted with] a wide grin. . . . I believe he appreciated that, because he knew where General DePuy stood. And he knew that General DePuy was not trimming his remarks for advantage or to be an apple polisher." Moreover, DePuy always made his case objectively. "I never heard him raise his voice. He always spoke in calm, deliberate, clipped terms."

That high-profile leaders have both critics and admirers is no surprise. DePuy had both. As a Pentagon staffer, as a lieutenant colonel and colonel, and as a troop commander in Germany, he enjoyed an excellent professional reputation in the relatively small circle of fellow professional soldiers. In the J-3 job, and even more so as division commander in combat, he was visible to a much larger audience, including the press. During the Vietnam War and for the rest of his career he had two reputations in the officer corps. Proximity and duration of contact with him usually resulted in admiration, even affection, the kind of reaction Matthews had. Peripheral association, one-time contact, and hearsay sometimes produced another reaction: his intelligence and logic were seen as arrogance; his decisiveness was seen as ruthlessness.

Journalist and author David Halberstam described DePuy as General Westmoreland's most trusted adviser on strategy. For Halberstam, DePuy was the brightest general, a skilled bureaucrat, an effective military politician, "extraordinarily important in the early planning of the American ground strategy," and a controversial figure. He wrote that DePuy projected a toughness that said, Don't mess with DePuy. He was, said Halberstam, "a formidable figure, tiny but cocky and imperious as if to make up for that lack of height; when he finally got a division in Vietnam, the 1st Infantry, a pick division, he made a fetish of firing his battalion commanders."[8]

John Paul Vann told Halberstam that DePuy wasn't interested in advice from old hands in Vietnam, but by the time DePuy took command of his division, he *was* an old hand in Vietnam. As noted earlier, DePuy believed that overwhelming American firepower and mobility would crush the enemy, "that the enemy simply could not stand up in the face of it." He believed in taking and maintaining the initiative. Those who experienced the war in Vietnam will recall an omnipresent caricature depicting a vulture poised on a branch over a caption that read, "Don't just sit there. Go out and kill something!" DePuy seemed to endorse that sentiment.

Neil Sheehan, another skilled author and journalist, expressed similar observations regarding DePuy in his book *A Bright Shining Lie: John Paul Vann and America in Vietnam*. His Vann is a flawed personality, self-serving, but a man with real leadership skills. DePuy, as described by Sheehan, is a smart officer who believes in "more bombs, more shells, more napalm . . . till the other side cracks and gives up."[9] These comments invite a brief digression regarding the reporting of the war and the reputations of some major players.

Halberstam, Sheehan, and Peter Arnett were young men who made their reputations in reporting from Vietnam early on. Their dubious take on military honesty was influenced by John Paul Vann, an Army officer who was well informed and mentored them. Their views were greatly influenced by a shared experience that revealed the ineptness of ARVN and what they regarded as duplicity on the part of the U.S. military command in Saigon.

On 2 January 1963, a battle began in a place called Ap Bac. Sheehan described it in a lengthy, and fascinating, section of his book.[10] In brief, "those raggedy-ass little bastards," as General Harkins and his staff in Saigon described the Viet Cong, mauled a "superior" ARVN force. The "little bastards," armed with odds and ends of World War II vintage weapons, defeated a well-armed and U.S.-supported ARVN force. ARVN had the latest and the greatest from the United States, including the M-113 armored personnel carrier, just out of the showroom. They had modern weapons, artillery, communications, and U.S. advisers. They had air support from troop-carrying helicopters, gunships, and fighter bombers. And ARVN got whipped—badly. They were "superior" in all save will.

The journalists who had witnessed the battle got back to Saigon for a headquarters briefing that they knew was a misrepresentation of what had happened. This was an early event in what became an increasingly acrimonious relationship between the Young Turk journalists, who went on operations with advisers they respected, and the military command in Saigon, whose out-of-touch press briefings became known as the "five o'clock follies."

The journalists gleaned some lessons from the Ap Bac battle. ARVN was ineffective, chiefly due to lack of leadership and will. The American advisers in the field were straight shooters who, the journalists believed, leveled with them. The headquarters in Saigon wanted happy talk, not bad news. The bad news from the men in the field was turned into happy talk at the briefings for the media representatives. The young journalists' appreciation of corrupt political leadership in Saigon and their exposure to the good-news-only briefings from the U.S. military resulted in what became almost permanent confrontation of the press and the military during the war in Vietnam. Tensions were not eased by the fact that some journalists remained in country for a long time, cultivating sources, learning the language, and in some cases marrying Vietnamese women, while most American military people spent a year in Vietnam and then returned home. By the time DePuy took command of his division, three years after the battle of Ap Bac, the Young Turk journalists had become veteran war correspondents who were inclined to think the worst of new boys from Washington or people coming out of the MACV headquarters. Even more suspect than a MACV officer was a MACV general. That's probably why Halberstam accepted Vann's uncomplimentary remarks about DePuy as truth. Public figures require thick skin, and DePuy was wise not to respond to unflattering commentary. Later, as division commander, he got good press.

DePuy's own recollections of his years in Vietnam, in his lengthy interview in 1979, are quite close to the text of his letters of 1964 and 1965.[11] When he arrived in MACV in May 1964, he recalled, Westmoreland was second in command and "being groomed to take Harkins' job" in June. It was "a deceptively quiet atmosphere. . . . People were still very much concerned about the overthrow of the Diem regime [in November 1963] and were trying to pick up the pieces . . . political turmoil continued with a series of almost comic opera coups. . . . There wasn't a Vietnamese government as such. There was a military junta that ran the country. . . . Politically, they were inept . . . corruption was rampant. There was coup after coup."

His evaluation of ARVN in the field was equally damning. ARVN motivation never did match that of the VC; they were not technically sound; they lacked the mobility required to react rapidly to a Viet Cong attack. As had been the case in the French war in Indochina, the enemy picked the time and place to fight. From the moment of the first shot, force ratios moved in favor of the enemy as casualties mounted and ARVN either could not reinforce or was ambushed while attempting to do so. The VC determined when to terminate contact, when to disappear, and when and where to repeat the process.

DePuy was well positioned to observe the enemy's escalation from low-level harassment to a willingness to stand and fight. In the fall of 1964, the enemy reinforced its "main force" elements and upgraded its weapons. In rapid succession, the enemy's 9th Division destroyed four battalions, including ARVN Rangers and Marines, the best units available to the Saigon government, recalled DePuy, sending "shock waves through GVN [the Government of Vietnam], MACV, and the U.S. government." Enemy activity intensified in 1965, when ARVN was losing battalions faster than they could be replaced. In several instances the enemy forces shifted from hit-and-run tactics to holding towns and cities and ambushing friendly forces reacting to earlier combats. Furthermore, American advisers were being killed. The price of war was going up as 1964 came in like a lamb and went out like a lion, forcing a hard policy decision in 1965. Westmoreland and DePuy believed that the United States could either walk away from an ineffective ARVN and corrupt Saigon government or prop them up with U.S. combat troops.

Differing perceptions by American officials in Saigon and Washington often caused the two parties to become out of step with each other. Part of the problem in 1964, according to former Secretary of Defense Robert McNamara, was that President Johnson's policy on Vietnam drifted during the American presidential election campaign. That was just when conditions in South Vietnam went bad—when the situation required, but did not get, careful attention and decisions to resolve "the dilemma between avoiding direct U.S. military involvement in the conflict and avoiding the loss of South Vietnam to communist control."[12]

Westmoreland and DePuy believed that ARVN was close to collapse. This estimate of the situation by the soldiers on the scene validates the later impression of McNamara that President Johnson's first year in office witnessed the disintegration of government in South Vietnam. The assassination of President Ngo Dinh Diem at the end of 1963 caused consternation in Washington, occurring as it did just weeks before the Kennedy assassination, while political ineptness crowned with corruption continued in Saigon. By 1965 Westmoreland "gave [ARVN] no more than six months unless the U.S. intervened." There it was. Walk away or introduce American combat troops. What McNamara much later called "drift" during the presidential election campaign of 1964 is echoed in DePuy's impression of how it looked from Saigon at that time. "General Westmoreland found the game changing under his feet. Washington was almost always one phase behind in its understanding."

The policy debate in Washington regarding Vietnam had been going on since 1963, when Lyndon B. Johnson succeeded John Kennedy and essentially retained JFK's foreign policy team. Guessing what Kennedy might have done had he lived has produced a cottage industry of what-ifs. A long trail of documentary evidence shows conflicting advice from civilian and uniformed advisers.[13] McNamara called the six months from 28 January to 28 July 1965 "the most crucial phase of America's thirty-year involvement in Indochina," as the United States embarked on "a course of massive intervention in Vietnam."[14]

To DePuy and Westmoreland it appeared that Hanoi had decided to reach for the big victory—a unified Vietnam—perhaps in 1965. In Mao Tse-tung's concept, this phase of the war would pit North Vietnamese Army main-force units against Saigon's best troops. The situation was going to hell in a handbasket, as the enemy was regularly defeating the best formations ARVN could put in the field. It was against this backdrop that U.S. combat units began to arrive in Vietnam in 1965.

Initially General Westmoreland and Ambassador Taylor disagreed about how and where to use U.S. troops. Westmoreland and DePuy believed that 1965 would be the decisive year, that bombing would neither bring Hanoi to its knees nor to the negotiating table, that ARVN was ineffective and that the government was tottering; ergo, U.S. troops had to engage enemy main-force units in combat. These were the views that Westmoreland dispatched DePuy to Washington to represent in March 1965.

Taylor—ambassador, confidant of President Kennedy, former Army Chief of Staff, World War II airborne hero, author, and intellectual—made this case: an open-ended commitment in Vietnam was not in the U.S. interest. Moreover, a big buildup of U.S. forces would let ARVN "sign off," that is, abdicate responsibility.

Westmoreland believed that time was running out. If the situation was to be salvaged, U.S. troops had be introduced in a combat role swiftly. Taylor floated the idea of establishing enclaves along the coast. Others advised a similar strategy. A fear of U.S. troops fighting Asian hordes on the Asian mainland was discernible; it seemed logical to put troops in where they could be supported from the sea—or gotten out quickly. Lloyd Matthews tells an amusing story from his time as Westmoreland's aide that exemplifies the Navy's general aversion to getting too far from the sea.

Admiral Ulysses S. G. Sharp, who supported the enclave concept, was nervous about the initial commitment of American ground forces. He recognized that a threshold was being crossed when the 173d Airborne Brigade arrived in the summer of 1965 and set up in Bien Hoa. "He sent Westy a back channel message," said Matthews. "It wasn't arrogant or nasty in any sense, but it was highly detailed. 'Be sure to put out security.' I seem to remember that little phrase. You know, a Navy guy telling an Army guy to put out security, make sure all of your ducks are in order, make sure they get good barracks, and on and on and on. General Westmoreland went through the ceiling. . . . He sat down immediately and wrote a message . . . and here is one line I remember. 'I would not tell you how to blow your bilge, you don't tell me how to put out local security.'"

Westmoreland then told Matthews to send the message. "I looked at that thing," said Matthews, "and even with my twelve, thirteen, or fourteen years of service, I knew that it should not go out of the headquarters, so I did not send it." Several days later, he recalled, "we were going somewhere in a car, and [Westy] asked, 'Lloyd, have you heard anything on that back channel? You did send it, didn't you?' And here I was scared to death. I knew I was going to get relieved. I said, 'Sir, I didn't send it.' He kind of looked at me, grinned, and said, 'Good decision.'"[15]

Between March and June 1965, the further deterioration of the situation in the field just about decided the issue along the lines advanced by Westmoreland and backed by the JCS and the Commander in Chief, Pacific (CINCPAC). Westmoreland was most concerned with enemy successes in the field, and he estimated that the enemy had much more as-yet unused capacity. According to DePuy, ARVN lost fifteen or sixteen battalions in six months in 1965. "That's big business," said DePuy. As American combat troops were brought in to turn it around, "we were totally preoccupied with the growing VC forces. From then on, pacification was secondary."[16] By June, Taylor and the American civil-military community had lined up behind Westmoreland.

Debates about how to fight the war and the role of pacification, counterinsurgency, psychological warfare, special warfare, and conventional warfare raged before and during the war and continue into the twenty-first century as scholars, professional soldiers, and armchair generals look back to the war in Vietnam and study newer conflicts. But the DePuy-Westmoreland appreciation of the situation in 1965, during the buildup of U.S. forces, and in 1966, when DePuy assumed command of his division, was that the task of U.S. combat formations was to destroy enemy main-force organizations.

Main-force battalions were the key. They could disrupt government efforts to "secure" populated areas and undermine the central government by dominating a district or province capital, if only for hours or days once or twice a year. They could disrupt government efforts to "clear" an area by destroying locally recruited, lightly armed, poorly trained, and hardly motivated regional or popular forces (abbreviated RF and PF and called "ruff-puffs" by American soldiers). Main-force VC units could undo government efforts to control the population by demonstrating for a short period of time that the main-force unit could inject itself at will, kill or maim those who supported the government, issue warnings, and disappear into the jungle in Vietnam, Cambodia, or Laos. They could control the tempo of the war and their losses by the simple device of fighting or not fighting. They had the initiative.[17]

The intent by 1965 was that ARVN would control populated areas, their own people, via "secure" and "clear" missions. As DePuy put it, "We didn't know how to do counterinsurgency very well, and we had white faces."[18] The American first team would defeat the enemy main-force first team and keep it off ARVN, which was to do the less combat-intensive secure and clear missions. The U.S. forces taking on well-armed, skilled, and motivated enemy main-force units would use all available means to destroy them, including overwhelming firepower and the mobility afforded by the helicopter.

"Search and destroy" was the term used to describe operations to find, fix, and finish enemy main-force units by using the best ARVN units and later U.S. forces. This originally sterile descriptive term later became emotionally loaded as the merits of the war and how it should be fought were publicly debated. DePuy put his finger on an incident that gave new meaning to the term: "Unfortunately, television coverage of a Marine putting his cigarette lighter to a thatched roof in a small hamlet turned 'Search and Destroy' into a dirty word." But that was later.

In his later musings on the strategy in Vietnam, DePuy said, "We were captives of our own emphasis on counterinsurgency, which blinded us to the escalating dimensions of the war." By "we" and "us" he meant his contemporaries who were charged with thinking about how to address revolutionary warfare. DePuy's own view was that the level of enemy activity and capability by the end of 1964 required the employment of overwhelming U.S. conventional force. He said, "At one time General Westmoreland had the brilliant idea of putting the 1st Cavalry Division into Thailand and operating across the narrow panhandle of Laos, from the west, and interdicting the Ho Chi Minh Trail." When that idea was rejected, Westmoreland proposed putting the 1st Cav in Laos astride the Trail. That was rejected for the same reason: fear of bringing in China and expanding the war. DePuy regretted that the United States did not view the war from a theater perspective that included both Vietnams, Laos, Cambodia, and Thailand. The enemy did.

DePuy's J-3 service pleased General Westmoreland. He admired DePuy's intellect, trusted him, and recommended him for division command in Vietnam. As Army Chief of Staff in 1969, Westmoreland would appoint DePuy to a position that brought with it a third star, a job that positioned him later to command TRADOC and acquire a fourth star.

To the extent that the 1965 decision to commit U.S. combat troops and to lend U.S. prestige to the support of a corrupt government can be laid at the feet of the U.S. military advisers in 1964 and 1965, Bill DePuy, as General Westmoreland's right-hand man, shares responsibility. The commander and his J-3 believed it was their duty to provide sound military advice to political authority. That advice boiled down to a go–no-go proposition: prop up the Saigon government with U.S. troops or get out of Vietnam. The decision was to prop up the Saigon government. DePuy shifted gears from theater strategy to tactical command in March 1966.

The insights of Richard Hooker (COL, USA, Ret.), from his vantage point as a captain and junior aide to General Westmoreland in Saigon, as provided four decades later, reveal two DePuys. "He was regarded by all of us as a brilliant operations officer.

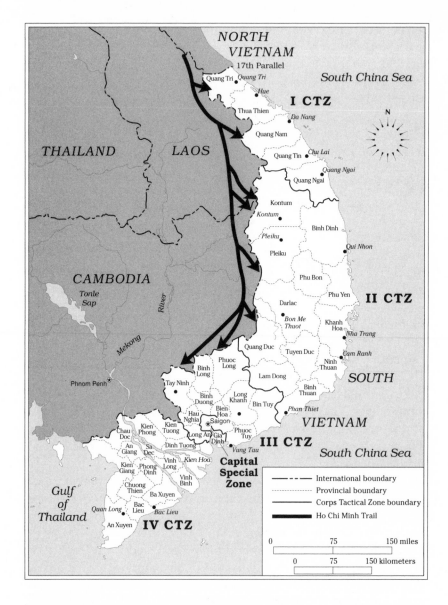

Unfailingly courteous to underlings like me, he had a reputation for impatience with briefers who did not know their stuff, and was feared by many, some senior to him, because of his close relationship with Westy, who relied on him without fail so far as I am aware."[19]

When Bill DePuy assumed command of the 1st Infantry Division in 1966, he was convinced that the mission of his instrument, the Big Red One, was to break the back of enemy main-force formations. There, he would not be "unfailingly courteous to underlings." He was impatient and was "feared by many, some senior to him."

12

The Big Red One

It was clear to me that he [General Westmoreland] wanted me
to get cracking.

—DePuy as he assumed command
of the 1st Infantry Division

Of the many commanders I have observed in combat in two
wars, General DePuy is the only one I would unhesitatingly
describe as an authentic tactical genius. . . . The soldiers under
his command knew that their general fought hard, fought
smart, and fought to win.

—General Paul Gorman

As commanding general of the 1st Infantry Division (called the Big
Red One, or BRO, for the red numeral patch the troopers wore on
their shoulders), General DePuy applied unrelenting pressure on the
enemy. From mid-March 1966 to February 1967, his personal style
and effectiveness as a fighting general won him the admiration and
loyalty of officers and individual soldiers pleased to be on his team.
To many of them, loyalty became affection. But he also acquired a
reputation as a demanding, even ruthless leader. Soldiers talked
about him in orderly rooms, mess halls, clubs, and snack bars. Division command in combat made him visible to the general public as
no previous assignment had.

The 2d Brigade of the 1st Infantry Division, under MG Jonathan
Seaman, deployed to Vietnam from Fort Riley, Kansas, in June and
July 1965. By November, the entire division was astride the main
avenues of approach to Saigon from Cambodia. This area of operations (AO) had long been under the control of the Viet Cong (VC),
who moved logistics and troops about as though the border between
Cambodia and Vietnam did not exist. General William Westmoreland had DePuy assist Seaman in positioning the division.

In February 1966, the 25th Infantry (Tropic Lightning) Division, under MG Frederick C. Weyand, established its division base camp in Cu Chi. The buildup of U.S. forces in Vietnam required adjustments to insure effective command and control. On 15 March, General Westmoreland created II Field Force, a corpslike headquarters in Long Binh. Abbreviated II FF, pronounced "Two Field Force," it was an unusual name. The Vietnamese allies had established corps areas from I Corps in the north to IV Corps in the south. To avoid confusion the Americans called their echelon above division Field Force.

General Westmoreland moved Seaman up to command II FF and sent DePuy to command the Big Red One. Seaman was promoted to lieutenant general in August and the DePuy to major general in April 1966. The 1st and the 25th Infantry Divisions were the major combat components of II FF.[1]

Fred Weyand and Bill DePuy knew each other at the Armed

III Corps Tactical Zone
December 1966

Forces Staff College, and they enjoyed a cordial personal relationship in Vietnam as well as later, when they both wore four stars. Weyand was tall, gangly, and, in the vernacular of professional soldiers, "old shoe." DePuy was small, wiry, and intense. By 1966, Army insiders recognized both as "comers" destined for great things. It was not unusual that they were compared, particularly since their divisions were side by side in the same chain of command, and because they were very different personalities with different command styles.

DePuy was champing at the bit. He respected enemy main-force organizations put in the field to defeat ARVN, but he was convinced they couldn't stand toe to toe and slug it out with American combat formations. DePuy wanted to use firepower and mobility "to go after the main forces wherever they could be found and to go after them with as many battalions as I could get into the fight—what was later called 'pile on.'"[2]

He knew that Westmoreland's intent in bringing in American troops was to turn the war around. U.S. troops in DePuy's AO were there to fight the enemy "big boys" who were "tearing up the ARVN and destroying the pacification effort." He believed that his predecessor, Seaman, hadn't been aggressive enough: "I knew the difference between what the division was doing and what was expected of it." DePuy said that after working closely with Westmoreland for almost two years, "It was clear to me that he wanted me to get cracking." The manner in which he got cracking drew attention to him and to his methods.

Historian George L. MacGarrigle has written that by October 1966 the American troop buildup begun in April 1965 had reached the point where Westmoreland could "move beyond simply defending South Vietnam." For the first time, he had enough arms and men to take the initiative from the enemy.[3]

But DePuy had not waited until October to seize the initiative. He brought a spirit of aggressiveness to his AO. From operations ABILENE in April 1966; LEXINGTON in April and May; BIRMINGHAM in April; EL PASO I in May; EL PASO II in June and July; the Minh Thanh Road Battle on 9 July; AMARILLO in August, including a big fight with the Phu Loi Battalion on 25–26 August; and TULSA and SHENANDOAH into October of 1966, DePuy relentlessly sought to find, fix, fight, and finish the enemy. When the enemy chose to fight, he risked being mauled; but there were U.S. casualties and U.S. mistakes, particularly early on.[4]

Two references to a tough fight on 11 April 1966 involving C Company 2/16 should alert the reader to exercise a high degree of skepticism *always* when reading accounts of small-unit combat actions. The official account gives the fight two bland sentences, including American losses "during close-quarters fighting, in part because effective fire could not be brought to bear . . ."[5]

The second account is far more graphic. It describes a U.S. rifle company fighting for its life, unsupported due to poor tactics and poor coordination. In brief, because of dense jungle, a supporting company was unable to move fast enough to assist C Company, despite strenuous efforts to do so. Help was simply too far away to be effective. Additionally, uncertainty regarding the location of friendly troops in contact with the enemy, and others in the vicinity beating the bush to get to them, resulted in casualties from friendly fire and then a stop-fire that denied artillery support to the U.S. troops in contact. Charlie Company went into the battle with 134 men and came out with 28. General Harold K. Johnson, Army Chief of Staff, flew from the Pentagon shortly after the battle and visited DePuy in Lai Khe. Johnson warned him, "The American people won't support this war if we keep having the kind of casualties suffered by Charlie Company."[6]

This experience, which took place in the first weeks of DePuy's command of the division, and other cases of American infantry stumbling into deadly combat led to DePuy's new tactics in the summer of 1966. But the casualties issue was added to later differences between General Johnson and DePuy regarding DePuy's use of artillery and his relief of officers. Professional differences cannot be discounted, but personality differences loomed large in DePuy's relations with the Army Chief of Staff and the II FF commander.

General Seaman was aware of uncomplimentary remarks circulating about his leadership as II FF commander. Dynamic, imaginative, and decisive, DePuy ran his division from a helicopter just above the jungle, frequently mingling with his soldiers in their squads and platoons on the ground. The more conservative and formal Seaman issued orders from his headquarters. He suffered by comparison, and knew it. The situation was particularly awkward since Seaman did not vanish from the scene when he turned the division over to DePuy. He became DePuy's boss, and he couldn't fail to see what his successor was doing with his former command.

Seaman vented (to the extent his personality permitted) in later interviews. He displayed his anger while maintaining a gentleman-ly avoidance of personal criticism of a fellow general. He said, "I didn't relieve a single combat commander. I didn't relieve a single one. Shortly before I left the division a new ADC [Assistant Division Commander] was assigned [a reference to the rough-hewn James Hollingsworth, the ultimate not-Seaman]. Later one of my former battalion commanders reported to me that the ADC in a briefing said that the reason that he and the new division commander [DePuy] had been sent there was 'to clean out the damn 1st Division and organize it.' This made me pretty unhappy, *but I never said anything*. But they did relieve a number of commanders on the spot, for what they felt was good cause."

Seaman was particularly pained that his former aide, who asked for and got command of a troop of 1/4 Cav, was relieved when he stumbled in an operation after a month in command and was told by the unnamed ADC (it was James F. Hollingsworth) to, in essence, "Find yourself a job." Seaman said sadly, "I've never seen such a broken young man in my life." His concern for the young man is ad-mirable, but the incident illustrates that the DePuy-Hollingsworth team was more concerned with combat effectiveness than with any-one's feelings or career.[7]

That Seaman "never said anything" to his successor, who was raising hell with the outfit he had just commanded, despite the fact that he was DePuy's boss, suggests that he was intimidated by DePuy. In addition to DePuy's being Westmoreland's fair-haired boy then and later, the force and intensity of DePuy's personality and the certitude he brought to combat command seem to have been daunting to this gentlemanly Old Army type.

Seaman was, in short, critical of "them." He avoided using DePuy's and Hollingsworth's names. Referring to the ADC who came in "shortly before I left the division," he said, "this particular individual [when he was selected for his permanent second star] is going to get the Army into a hell of mess one of these days." The fact is, these people did have names. The "them" was DePuy and Hollingsworth; and the "particular individual" was Hollingsworth (who did get the Army into a hell of a mess later when he served as commander in Korea by intimating that the UN forces in Korea might attack into North Korea).

Seaman provides one of several versions of a confrontation be-tween DePuy and Johnson when the latter was Army Chief of Staff visiting Vietnam. "You know, I think that General Harold K. Johnson is one of the greatest people I have ever known in the Army, and I heard him tell a division commander one time, who was complaining about the quality of some of the officers he had, many of the officers he had. I happened to be standing there, and General Johnson said, 'Well let me tell you, So-and-So, to me the mark of a real leader is doing the best with what you got.'"

The So-and-So to whom Seaman was referring, "a division commander," was DePuy. Perhaps Seaman was oblique in his 1971 reference because DePuy was by then again working for General Westmoreland, the Army Chief of Staff, and he was probably the most powerful lieutenant general in the Army. Or perhaps this is a reflection of Seaman's being "old school," incapable of speaking ill of a fellow general officer. In any event, Seaman and DePuy mixed like oil and water.

Seaman was a cautious man. In the interview with Seaman conducted in 1971, the *Study on Professionalism,* published by the Army War College in 1970, was discussed. This document was highly critical, identifying Army leadership as one of the chief causes of the Army's disarray and low morale at the time. It was particularly damning because the sources of the scathing critique were the winners in the system, students at the Army War College, the insiders, and future top leadership. General Westmoreland decided that the study should be briefed worldwide by officer-NCO teams so that leaders could restore integrity to the Army. Seaman's reaction to the study is indicative of his personality. Briefed at an Army Commanders' Conference by the study's authors, Colonels Walt Ulmer (LTG, USA, Ret.) and Mike Malone (Colonel, USA, Ret.), he was given a copy of the study. He said, "After I read that study, I locked it up in my safe and said it was to be opened only by the CG or a General Officer of the Headquarters because there are statements in there that are so damning to the Officer Corps. . . . I felt that if it ever got out into the public, it would really do the Army a lot of harm, *and no doubt it's true"* (italics added). Seaman's inclination to keep the frank study conclusions on "close hold" contrasts markedly with Westmoreland's decision to disseminate it in the belief that the truth must out. Seaman's hyper-caution contrasts sharply with DePuy's boldness.

DePuy's dual reputation as admired and ruthless stems in part from a dysfunctional command relationship among DePuy, Seaman, and Westmoreland. DePuy apparently intimidated Seaman, and Seaman disliked DePuy. The clear implication is that Westmoreland communicated to DePuy impatience with Seaman's handling of the Big Red One. Putting Seaman over DePuy invited skirting the chain of command via back-channel communications between Westmoreland and DePuy, a violation of one of the most rudimentary principles of management and leadership. Seaman's authority as II FF commander was undermined. Officers loyal to their immediate bosses were placed in awkward positions, requiring them to choose sides. The DePuy-Seaman relationship was corrosive.

DePuy's loyalty to Hollingsworth and something just short of public disrespect for Seaman require comment. DePuy was a sophisticated man whose personal conduct was characterized by propriety, correctness, good manners, and an analytical approach to professional matters. In a staff setting, say in the Pentagon, one suspects that DePuy would have had a better professional relationship with the deliberate Seaman. Moreover, he might have seen Hollingsworth in that context as a bull in a china shop. DePuy's relationships with each of them can be understood in the context of the absolute priority he attached to combat effectiveness. Hollingsworth was very effective in assisting DePuy in fighting the Big Red One exactly the way DePuy wanted to fight it: by being intimately engaged at battalion level and in frequent direct contact with soldiers on the ground in squads and platoons. Hollingsworth was good at war. What DePuy wanted from Seaman were the assets the latter owned as II FF commander; what he wanted from his subordinate commanders was skill in combat.

Richard Hooker, a junior aide to General Westmoreland in Saigon, said of DePuy, "I remember him with respect and admiration, and I believe most who operated within his expectations would say the same." But those "regarded as incompetent or simply not up to his standards" were fired. "Thus sprang up the mythical stories of the 'midnight hook'—the CH-47 that suddenly appeared in the dead of night and whisked away the unwanted, usually battalion commanders never to be heard from again."[8] Lt. James Holland, platoon leader in Captain William J. Mullen's C Company and later aide to ADC Hollingsworth, recalls the expression as being "the midnight Chinook."[9] A new verb was coined by DePuy's troops to describe being disciplined or relieved by the Commanding General, as in: "He was DePuyed."

General Weyand later commented on the quality of leaders in Vietnam. He observed that the Army was "drawing down, down, down to keep the Vietnam forces filled, and finally it broke down and they simply could not give us good battalion commanders or good squad leaders." Asked when that process began, he said, "Right at the end of our rotation period," one year after his Division arrived in Vietnam in February 1966." This opinion is confirmed by those who commanded the companies. The units that deployed to Vietnam in 1965 and 1966 arrived fresh, cohesive, and with skilled leadership from squad through battalion. A year after arrival in Vietnam, however, there was almost 100 percent turnover. Those not killed, wounded, or evacuated with various diseases and injuries simply rotated home at the end of a one-year tour. Some were transferred to other divisions in Vietnam to avoid the mass exodus of experienced troops and their replacement by new people all at the same time. This fixed one problem, but it created another, reminiscent of the Second World War personnel and replacement issue: the lack of stability in the infantry, a constant curse.[10]

But DePuy got the BRO cracking. Sometimes, he said later, he "just moved it to get it moving," because he wanted mental agility as well as physical mobility. "I visualized a division command from a helicopter in flight. And I looked for people who could do that"— and, ominously, "also people who couldn't think that way, so that I could send them on to other duties." Everything about him, and knowing Westmoreland's intent, added up to "full speed ahead!"

As did the division's operational situation. The Big Red One stood between Saigon and Cambodian sanctuaries from which the enemy was supported and to which he could retreat to refit. To protect Saigon, and to break the enemy's back, DePuy went after the enemy "big boys."

His assessment of his division was mixed. He liked the soldiers. "They were fine. They were just as good as their leaders." As he left his battle group command in Germany, he had remarked that the quality of the men in the 1960s was probably the best the Army ever had. The same quality soldiers were in Vietnam, at least initially. He was pleased with "a lot of good long-term, experienced sergeants." And he noted that the junior officers were what they always are: eager to do well and inexperienced.

He expected success and instant competence from his entire chain of command. Leadership had to measure up to the fine raw

material. Combat leadership in the 1st Division would be entrusted to the best people DePuy could find. Since success in combat
command is the shortest route to promotion and glory, ambitious
professional soldiers move to the sound of the guns. There was no
shortage of officers seeking command. DePuy could be selective.

He wanted leaders who were "flexible minded," people who
didn't need a lot of instructions, men who would do something useful on their own once they had been given a general direction. "Of
course," he said, "I was also interested, as I always have been, in the
problems down in squads and platoons, because I realized I was
seeing the same problems occur all over again. They just weren't
trained and were stumbling into battles. Mind you, they stumbled
into battles under me, too, but I wanted to try to help all I could in
that respect." So he wrote and disseminated instructions on the basic techniques that win battles and save lives.

Alexander M. Haig Jr. called DePuy's "Big Red One Battle Principles" the shortest (it was just one page) and best military directive
of the war.[11] DePuy did in Vietnam what he had done at each of his
previous commands. He taught squads and platoons. But at company and battalion command levels, and on his staff, he expected
competence. Now!

DePuy noted with scorn that the first time he ordered the division to the field, "the principal staff officers stayed back at base
camp, while all of the second team [the assistants] went out with
me. We turned that all around. The first team went out and the second team stayed back." He was changing the "division's mentality."
This can only be taken as sharp criticism of the previous management. The habits of peacetime, a headquarters mentality, hanging
around base camps and waiting for something to happen were not
DePuy's style. He was dynamic and forceful, and he knew just what
he wanted. Bill Mullen, who commanded a company and served
as a battalion S-3, said, "I believe that the esprit and aggressiveness that I found . . . were the results of MG DePuy's leadership.
He changed the division's attitude. Morale in the division was very
high. We knew we were in a well-led, aggressive, fighting outfit . . .
we were in the Army's premier unit."[12]

Upon his arrival in August 1966, Jim Holland began hearing
DePuy stories while still processing in. Next, he was interviewed by
a personnel major, who asked what he wanted to do in the division.
Holland had been told that if an incoming infantry lieutenant did

not want to lead a platoon in combat, for whatever reason, another job would be found for him. That was DePuy's policy. It recalls Lt. Joulwan's arrival interview with Colonel DePuy in Schweinfurt. DePuy wanted tigers eager to lead his platoons.

Holland reported to Captain Mullen on 22 August and took the 1st platoon, C Company 1/2. One of the first things Bill Mullen did was give Jim Holland "a little booklet on division tactics" signed by General DePuy. Holland, who had served on a Ranger committee at Fort Benning, recognized the tactics as standard U.S. infantry: in contact, put down a base of fire and maneuver to find the enemy flank and turn it. This was in accord with HQ, 1st Infantry Division Regulation 350–1, dated 15 March 1966. Holland recalled that, after heavy fighting in August, DePuy directed new tactics "almost overnight." (It may have seemed almost overnight to Holland, but the 11 April 1966 experience of C Company 2/16 and Chief of Staff Johnson's visit to DePuy at Lai Khe had already stimulated DePuy's revision of tactics, especially the use of firepower that was missing in C Company's fight at the critical moment.) Now, upon making contact with the enemy, infantry was to *avoid becoming decisively engaged*. The new tactic was to get out of the kill zone and use supporting fires. "The use of firepower became key, and only when our artillery and air had done their job did we move forward again."[13]

DePuy was adapting his bag of tricks from 1944 to the conditions of 1966. Some components were constant: know where you are; anything is better than frontal assaults; if you can infiltrate, fine, if you can't, get out of the kill zone and blow them to hell with artillery and close air support. He had been thinking through infantry combat the way a football coach draws up new plays. His SOPs and training directives in the middle 1950s, in 1961, and in 1966 are strikingly similar to his 1944 memo. They are "how to fight" tips. As important as his mulling over and doodling about fighting were to him as he worked things out, he knew that the *doing* was important. Skills had to be practiced. Fighting requires thinking, but it is really a doing thing. DePuy had thought it through. In Vietnam he was prepared both to tell men how to do it and to modify tactics as dictated by the situation.

Details were important: rehearse what you intend to do; each man should carry so many hand grenades and so much ammunition for his basic weapon; machine gun ammo is carried in boxes, not draped, "macho bandito" style, on bodies, where it would collect gunk in the links that causes malfunctions; upon return to base camp weapons and equipment are to be cleaned before we wash up and relax; foxholes are to be prepared in a prescribed manner.

As comfortable as he was with abstractions and theory, DePuy was a hands-on and graphic man. His first words upon arrival at a battalion or company were, Show me your line. With troops he would ask, Who is on you right? Who is on your left? How far out do you have grazing fire? Where is the dead space? Where is your FPL (Final Protective Line)? In Vietnam he jumped into fighting positions, just as he had in Germany, seemingly correcting an individual soldier or machine gunner, but in fact teaching the group that always assembles when a general is present. As he spoke to individual soldiers his audience included the squad or platoon leader, who was getting a lesson in the best classroom, the fighting position. Lieutenant George Joulwan of Schweinfurt days was now Captain Joulwan. He had learned his lessons well and served with distinction in DePuy's division as company commander and battalion S-3.

DePuy gets good grades even from some who were initially dubious. Paul Gorman, a brave, skilled, and proven battalion commander and a veteran of the Korean War, was pulled up to division to be DePuy's G-3. Gorman, unhappy to give up his battalion, said, "You can't do this to me!" DePuy's response was, "I just did." Later Gorman worked for DePuy again as chief trainer in TRADOC. Gorman said that DePuy would accurately assess the quality of command in a company or a battalion in minutes. He arrived, looked at positions, talked to soldiers, and knew what kind of an outfit it was. Experience and passionate interest that never diminished enabled him to evaluate the situation quickly. He knew what he was doing, and his soldiers knew that.[14]

Alexander Haig was DePuy's G-3 before commanding a battalion. In fact, he and Gorman exchanged positions upon DePuy's order as Haig took Gorman's battalion and Gorman became G-3. Haig said, "When it came to the tactics of small units, DePuy was a genius—the best squad leader, platoon commander, and company commander in the division, if not in the entire U.S. Army in Vietnam." Haig credits DePuy with inventing "cloverleafing" and designing an improved foxhole.[15]

Cloverleafing permitted what DePuy called "saturation searches" while reducing friendly casualties. Most searches were what GIs called "dry holes." After hours of hot walking while fighting vines or splashing through streams or rice paddies, soldiers became careless and sometimes literally stumbled into contact, incurring casualties from mines, booby traps, snipers, punji stakes, and surprise contact. Often the first indication of the enemy's presence was automatic weapons fire from a bunker whose aperture was low, very close to the ground. Leaders are trained to lead, so typically, squad and platoon leaders and company commanders were hit because they exposed themselves to enemy fire in an effort to observe what was happening. More soldiers would be hit as they entered the kill zone to pull out wounded buddies. Initial shock and recoil were typically followed by an attempt to flank the enemy in difficult terrain. Nothing was clear. Jungle was dense. The notion of the commander being able to see the battle from a hilltop was a relic of other wars. In Vietnam the leader on the ground often saw only his radio operator and, in more open terrain, perhaps one or two of his soldiers—and usually no enemy—while taking casualties, talking on the radio, reading the situation, and figuring out what the hell to do. He had to hear and feel the situation. Usually the enemy was skillfully dug in, concealed, and initially had the upper hand. Bad situations rapidly became worse.

These were the conditions DePuy encountered in his Area of Operations (AO) in III Corps. Similar conditions were encountered in the Central Highlands along the border with Laos in II Corps, and in I Corps, where the U.S. Marine Corps operated facing North Vietnam along the DMZ (Demilitarized Zone) to the north and the Laotian border to the west. (David Halberstam's novel *One Very Hot Day*, about an advisory team in the south very early in the war, captures the feel of heat, confusion, and close combat in Vietnam.)

Cloverleafing, a variation of overwatch, was a technique suitable to platoons, companies, and battalions. For example, a platoon moving to contact with the enemy in difficult terrain—usually familiar to the enemy and strange to friendly troops—would employ this technique. One squad moved slowly and deliberately to the front for a specified distance, say 200 meters, on a specified azimuth. Then it returned to its departure point by looping left or right, outlining one leaf of a three-leaf clover. Another squad did the same thing to the right; a third squad moved to the left. The main body, the platoon leading a company, perhaps a battalion, moved forward in the knowledge that at least the 200 meters to the front and to the left and right had been checked for enemy presence. "Stumbling around" had been reduced.

In the best case, the friendlies initiated combat. In the worst case, friendlies took enemy fire, causing American casualties. But, using the new tactics, there would be relatively few such casualties. Some American soldiers were in the kill zone, but as few as possible. Cloverleafing was derived from DePuy's formative combat experiences, when he found that the infantry's job was to grab terrain from which his artillery forward observer could direct overwhelming fires on the enemy. The squad had thus found and fixed the enemy. The next action was to get out of the kill zone and put artillery fires and air strikes on the enemy quickly. Fires were placed not only on the enemy, but on likely avenues of enemy reinforcement and routes of withdrawal. DePuy believed that the United States was a rich country that valued the lives of its soldiers. Once the enemy was found, DePuy would spend shells made in America, not sons made in America. Certain aspects of his way of fighting were questioned, but his subordinates admired the way the boss fought. They sensed that he knew what he was doing. That is a good feeling when you find yourself in a strange country among strange people who are doing their very best to kill you.

DePuy was unforgiving of those who stumbled around by walking on trails, thus inviting ambush. Leaders who failed to do what they knew was right usually had either surrendered to fatigue or were unwilling to be tough enough with their troops. Infantry soldiers in combat are generally on the edge of exhaustion. They won't dig in unless forced to. They will cross open areas instead of taking the long route around, because they are tired. Squad leaders, platoon leaders, and company commanders are human beings who want to be nice guys. Forcing men on the verge of exhaustion to do the correct but difficult things necessary to keep them alive requires moral courage. Many combat leaders opt for being a nice guy. DePuy fired nice guys for lacking the moral courage to do the right thing.

The DePuy foxhole may be what DePuy is best known for. As early as July 1944, DePuy noted that poor preparation for combat resulted in the notion among American infantrymen that a foxhole's purpose was protection. Not so! The hole or bunker was a fighting position, not just a place to hide. Initially, soldiers hastily dug holes that were uncovered. Over time, the holes were improved, mainly with overhead cover consisting of logs and filled sandbags. Helicopters delivered chain saws, sandbags, metal stakes, D-handled shovels, and picks to facilitate the improvement of night defensive positions in strict accord with DePuy's standard operating procedures. Soldiers were expected to know who was on their left and right and where the Claymore mines and outposts were, as well as their final protective line.

While positioning and caring for their troops, leaders were expected to be particularly attentive to emplacing crew-served weapons with good fields of fire. Registering artillery and mortar concentrations for fire support and illumination was a high priority. DePuy attached great importance to the ability of his ground commanders to orchestrate fire support quickly. The battalion commander had organic indirect fire weapons, his mortars, backed up by artillery and fire support from the air. One of DePuy's operating principles was that his maneuver units would always be within range of his artillery, preferably within the range of several firing units. This put pressure on his maneuver unit commanders to take maximum advantage of the fire support available. It also put pressure on artillery commanders. DePuy demanded that artillery response to a fire mission be almost instantaneous. His respect for the suppression and destruction of the enemy by artillery was matched by his demand that artillery always be available. He wanted it always, he wanted it now, and he was not tolerant when told of limitations.

A veteran artilleryman who served as operations officer in his division artillery said that DePuy was often unreasonable in his expectations of artillery. William Burns (MG, USA, Ret.) believes that DePuy was an extraordinary man who later fixed the broken U.S. Army, but he expressed severe doubts regarding DePuy's use of artillery in Vietnam.

Burns, knowing DePuy's reputation for being a hard man, nevertheless wanted to serve in his division. He recalled standing with other officers new to the division in a tent for a ten-minute welcome by DePuy. It was hard to see DePuy from where he stood in the crowd, but Burns was struck by DePuy's commanding presence as he spoke of duty, honor, and responsibility.[16]

Another account of DePuy's commanding presence tells of DePuy's spotting a sergeant dozing during his welcoming remarks. DePuy glared at him and said in a low growl, "I want you out of the division by the close of business today. Now get the hell out of here." He fired the man before he had a specific assignment in the division, saying, "I don't want worthless men like that in the division."[17]

DePuy fired three artillery battalion commanders in his first months as division commander. Burns's boss had some simple advice for Burns: watch out for DePuy.

Burns wasn't sure that DePuy fully understood some of the ripple effects of his demands for artillery. For example, in the late summer of 1966, DePuy wanted 1,000 rounds per night fired for harassment and interdiction (H&I)—that is, *unobserved* fire at places where the enemy might be. Burns said that intelligence simply could not find targets to justify firing at that rate. It only made holes in the ground; it wore out tubes; it might kill innocents in a "free fire zone" (where anyone in the zone was regarded as enemy); and it fatigued gunners, who fired H&I at night and fired *observed* fire missions by day. And, said Burns, there was another ugly statistic: each 100,000 rounds fired resulted in two friendly fire KIAs and some five or six WIA.

And there were other costs. The 175mm gun had good range, but it didn't make sense to use it for H&I fires that made splinters of the jungle as its barrel burned out after 150 rounds fired. And while it was clearly desirable to have a 360-degree firing capability for heavy artillery, allowing it to put multiple friendly units within supporting range in all directions, to get those optimal firing positions in dense jungle required engineers to build roads that enabled the big self-propelled guns to move on their tracks. And it took thirteen loads to move a battery when the division norm was some four to six Chinooks per day. Burns doubted that DePuy was aware of these second- and third-order effects of his demands on artillery.

There was near-unanimous agreement among professional soldiers with General Westmoreland's statement calling firepower "our major advantage" and General Sid Berry's calling it "the key to success." But extremely heavy use of H&I, sometimes called "blind firing," was severely criticized by artillerymen and others. General Seaman said it "was overdone in many cases because we were firing into the wild blue yonder [and] not exactly sure what was there." General Johnson called ammunition costs "astronomical, [and] we found something in the neighborhood of 85 percent of it was unobserved fire . . . I don't know what good it was doing."[18]

Burns saw DePuy about once a week at division briefings,

which Burns called more a "show" than a briefing, an observation shared by other observers of DePuy at this stage of his life. Sid Berry said that DePuy and Hollingsworth "had drinks before dinner or before the briefing [and] there was a running commentary of sly remarks. . . . They tended to sharp-shoot their staff. . . . To me it was a very unpleasant atmosphere." When their division and brigade headquarters were co-located, DePuy told Berry he was welcome to the briefings anytime. Berry said he didn't like the atmosphere, to which DePuy responded, "You know, sometimes I don't either."

Paul Gorman, as division G-3, made similar comments about the tense and unpleasant atmosphere as the staff briefed DePuy and Hollingsworth. He said that after he joined the staff he realized why he, as battalion commander, received orders late at night for the next day's operations. It had to do with the fact that the briefings at division were late. Gorman said that DePuy changed that by making the briefings earlier, in response to Gorman's recommendation.[19]

Burns knew of DePuy's opinion that General Seaman did not get the most out of the Big Red One, and said that DePuy's low regard for Seaman was not a secret. He said that word of this eventually got back to Seaman. Clearly, DePuy's incisive style and incessant pressure on subordinates alienated some officers, but his demand for perfection was admired by those who believed that his motivation was to keep American soldiers alive and fighting.

Bill Mullen (BG, USA, Ret.) first got to know DePuy in 1962, and their relationship lasted until DePuy's death in 1992. He calls DePuy "the finest officer of his and my generation to lead our Army." Mullen commanded a rifle company in Vietnam, for which he had asked DePuy. He tells the oft-repeated story of DePuy visiting each battalion to demonstrate cloverleafing by borrowing a platoon and personally leading it in the jungle with the platoon leader or company commander carrying the radio. "Sergeant X, take your squad 40 meters in that direction [pointing]. Take up a hasty defense oriented to your front. I will come to your position to tell you what to do next." Mullen adds, "In retrospect, he was teaching us two things: the cloverleaf and the technique of providing detailed instructions to subordinate leaders." Mullen could not have known that DePuy had learned the effectiveness of short, direct orders as a battalion commander in Germany in 1944 and at Berle in 1945.

Mullen said, "MG DePuy had a great affection for the 'little fellers,' as he called the privates, sergeants, lieutenants, and captains who were doing the fighting. He took care of us. Soldiers were a very real concern to him. In their turn, the little fellers had great confidence in him." Gorman said that DePuy was on fatherly speaking terms with every radio-telephone operation (RTO) in the division. (The RTO is the soldier who carries his leader's radio and sticks to his leader like glue.) And it was a point of honor that DePuy's division would leave no one behind. Gorman said, "We sent two battalions to get [Sergeant Rudolph] Nunez's body." Soldiers knew that.

Mullen offered an illustration of DePuy's soldierly concern for those who did the fighting. "One day MG DePuy monitored my [radio] report to 1st Brigade that an attached tank had been hit by a mine during a road clearing operation. He quickly came up on the battalion net and asked me, Did everyone get out OK?" Mullen then described a similar event when the division had a new CG. The question the new general asked was how the event occurred—he did not ask about the troops' welfare.

DePuy established a scholarship for the children of killed Big Red One soldiers. He was moved by a letter from the brother of KIA Sergeant Rudolph Nunez in which the brother told of how Sergeant Nunez's widow described her husband's pride in his service in the division. She also mentioned the pride her two children had in their father. Mullen said, "I believe the first contribution came from a poker game. Eventually other sources joined." DePuy maintained his commitment to the Big Red One Scholarship Fund long after he left the division.[20]

DePuy's official correspondence is generously sprinkled with notes from junior soldiers over the years. People who served with him in World War II or later in his battalion or battle group in Germany would write to find out if the now-famous general of Vietnam celebrity is the same DePuy as the major who pushed him across a river at night in December 1944, or the lieutenant colonel who taught "overwatch" in the middle 1950s, or the colonel from 1961 in Schweinfurt.

Writing as a civilian, one of his former soldiers of the 30th Infantry said in a letter of 1 September 1966, "If you are the same man . . . I knew to myself that someday that not so tall Colonel would be someone, and now you are a General." DePuy thanked him for the letter, named four men from the 30th Infantry currently with him in the Division (including Captains Madden and Joulwan), and confessed, "I am, indeed, the same not so tall Colonel."[21] There are quite a few "I saw your picture" or "I read the unusual name and wonder if you are the same fellow who . . ." letters. There are also several inquiries over the years about the name that read, more or less, my name is DePew, or Dupuy, or some other spelling, asking if there might be a connection. DePuy answered the letters in a friendly, unpretentious, and direct manner.

Sometimes supplicants wanted a recommendation for promotion, a Regular Army commission, or a change in assignment. Each response from DePuy was individual, personal, and correct. One young soldier probably wasn't pleased to get a response saying, "it has always been my practice to do the duty assigned before moving on to a new job." But if the correspondent seemed to have a case, DePuy would challenge the system to insure that the soldier received proper treatment.

John Stewart (Colonel, USA, Ret.), who is generally not kindly disposed to DePuy, tells an amusing story about one of those "little fellers" DePuy favored. Stewart was assigned to II FF and engaged in providing helicopter support for subordinate units. He was thoroughly fed up with DePuy's apparently unceasing demands. Nor did he appreciate what he regarded as DePuy's demeaning treatment and relief of officers, saying that the G-4 survived only "because I don't think DePuy was very up on logistics." Stewart saw DePuy arrive and, with his arrival, "what I consider the downward spiral of the 1st Infantry Division." That is a minority view, but DePuy was clearly unpopular with II FF staff officers, or at least suspect. DePuy wanted the assets for his division. He wasn't at all interested in how higher headquarters handled the requests of others for the same assets. Some on Seaman's staff at II FF, loyal to their boss, learned to dislike DePuy then and for decades.

On his flight to R&R in Bangkok, Stewart was seated next to a 1st Infantry Division corporal who regaled him for the entire flight with stories about a great man, his General DePuy. John Stewart, in the best tradition of the old soldier, swallowed hard and listened to the young soldier, nodding assent. Stewart thought DePuy was an arrogant tyrant, but, alas, the "little feller" had found a hero. We all need that. Stewart said, "Apparently, General DePuy had extreme rapport among the enlisted people." But Stewart disapproved of the way DePuy treated officers, and he charged DePuy with disregard for some measures used to control combat activities so that friendlies don't kill one another.

Stewart said DePuy "had a problem with boundaries," suggesting that he would poach on his neighbor's AO, in this case in General Weyand's 25th Division area. The charge is classic in illustrating how difficult it is to depict a combat action accurately, despite all of the record keeping and attempts at precision. Such actions will almost always be described differently from different perspectives. What Stewart saw as a gross impropriety appeared otherwise to another observer.

Paul Gorman described a quick reaction to combat intelligence in which his 1/26 Infantry was inserted by helicopter and conducted a successful combat operation in the AO of the 25th Division on 13 August 1966. Years later, when Gorman was in Paris with Weyand in connection with peace negotiations, Weyand, over a drink, described the very action in which Gorman was involved. Gorman believes that Weyand knew exactly who the culprit was. But the story is better when the culprit remains unnamed, particularly when the listener is the culprit.

Weyand recalled it this way. Because he had missed lunch for one reason or another, he sat down alone for a sandwich in his mess. Suddenly, in clear view, a combat assault replete with suppressing fires, darting helicopters, and storming U.S. infantry was conducted right in his back yard. He called his G-3 to ask just what the hell was going on. His G-3 did not know the answer.

Later there was finger-pointing and blaming. The 1st Division asserted that II FF had been notified of the operation to exploit hot intelligence and had given the 1st Division clearance to go to it. II FF said it notified the 25th Division. The 25th denied it had been notified. Obviously there had been a screw-up. One predisposed to suspect DePuy of being overaggressive could blame him. One inclined to question Seaman's aggressiveness—and there were also allegations that he was not well served by his staff—could make Seaman the villain of the piece. Hearsay, eyewitnesses, and rumor improve the story over the years, particularly over a drink. A journalist once said that the first victim of war is the truth.

Stewart said that Seaman had no respect for Hollingsworth, confirming Seaman's opinion of the anonymous ADC he spoke of, who was Hollingsworth. On the other hand, MG Weyand, CG of the 25th Infantry Division, was, in Stewart's words, "a great individual."[22] The personal animus between Seaman and DePuy affected attitudes and conflicted the loyalty of the staff officers of the 1st Division, the

25th Division, and II FF. The contrasting personalities of DePuy and Weyand also affected the opinions of the various staff officers.

Weyand was effective, easygoing, a pleasant man with a calming nature. DePuy made some people nervous, especially those who were sensitive to his barely contained energy. Recall that Wayne Waltz, his lifelong friend from South Dakota, called DePuy "a nervous, jumpy type" as a lad, characteristics that seemingly became the intensity that all note in the mature Bill DePuy.[23]

Weyand said that he and DePuy "were really close friends. I had the greatest admiration for Bill. He was an aggressive commander. He was also a thinker. . . . He was a great believer in artillery and interdictory fires. . . . I didn't believe in that, so of course, inevitably, back at MACV and maybe even back in Washington there were sides chosen." Weyand also said, "Bill would not accept officers that did not meet his standards from the onset," thereby, in Weyand's view, injuring some good ones.[24] Intense DePuy fired people and made extraordinary use of artillery, especially H&I. Weyand did neither. They served side by side in Vietnam, and each ended their careers with four stars. It was natural for comparisons to be made to DePuy's disadvantage. Weyand himself said as much. DePuy certainly knew how he was perceived, but he didn't need the approval of the crowd. His professional objectivity was seen as just that by some and as arrogance or ruthlessness by others. The charm and natural courtesy he showed to intimates was not on general display.

Another officer assigned to Seaman's II FF headquarters who had reservations about DePuy is Robert Gerard (COL, USA, Ret.), who recalls his initial impression: "MG William DePuy was a man of small stature, but his introduction [upon DePuy's assumption of command] to the officers was large and ominous. There were no smiles nor humor in his talk. He announced that now that he was in charge, things were going to change." Gerard says that he concluded from the way DePuy spoke that his predecessor had been relieved of command. In fact, Seaman had been elevated to II Field Force command and promoted.

As Weyand asserts, comparisons of the two divisions operating side by side under II FF were inevitable. Gerard puts it this way: "These two division commanders, Weyand and DePuy, were as different as night and day." Weyand focused on pacification, while "DePuy's approach was to overwhelm the enemy with firepower and offensive action by U.S. units. . . . Typically, General DePuy would bypass General Seaman and send messages to General Westmoreland about future operations. General Seaman would receive only an 'info copy.' Suddenly, I understood what was behind General DePuy's harsh introductory talk. . . . Apparently, General Seaman had not been aggressive enough to suit Westmoreland. DePuy was sent forward to take charge and get the division moving."

Gerard describes "a nightly occurrence" as he allocated helicopters to subordinate units, mostly to the 1st and 25th Divisions. Every night at nine or ten o'clock a call would come to him at II FF from the 1st Division saying, "General DePuy says he needs (three, four, five) more assault helicopter companies" for the following day's operations. Every night Gerard would explain that the assets had been committed, and every night his opposite number at 1st Division would say that this conversation had to be elevated to the Division G-3 and II FF G-3 level. His boss would trudge off to Seaman's trailer as Gerard waited outside for a decision. The decision was always "The old man [Seaman] says to give him [DePuy] what he wants." Gerard would then have to call the 25th Division with the bad news regarding promised assets that they would not get. Seaman would not say no to DePuy.

Gerard provides an essential insight into DePuy's concept of what soldiering is about. Seaman was in the United States for some reason, and Weyand, senior to DePuy, was acting II FF Commander when the helicopter issue was once again raised to the general officer level. DePuy made an appointment to speak with the Field Force Commander. Gerard was told to sit in as subject matter expert for the meeting between DePuy and Weyand. He briefed Weyand and was invited to take a seat while they awaited DePuy's arrival. "What happened next was one of the most interesting experiences of my Army career," wrote Gerard.

First, General DePuy politely knocked at the office door. Weyand beckoned for him to come in and said,
"Hi, Bill!"
DePuy approached Weyand's desk, stood at attention, and saluted.
"Good morning, Sir!"
Weyand motioned him to a chair, introduced me, and they proceeded with some small talk for the next five or

ten minutes. Finally, DePuy got to the central issue. He told Weyand that he was planning a large operation in War Zone C for the next day. He needed all the available helicopter support in order to get the job done. Weyand leaned back in the swivel chair and looked at the ceiling in silence for several moments. Then he said,

"The 25th Division is also planning a large operation in the Rung Sat Special Zone. They are going to need a lot of helicopter support, too."

Then he leaned forward, looked DePuy squarely in the eyes and said,

"Bill, our helicopter assets are limited. What would you do?"

Without a moment's hesitation, DePuy said,

"Sir, I would allocate the helicopter support to the highest priority mission."

Weyand nodded slowly.

"You're right, Bill. Tomorrow, the 25th Division has the highest priority."

General DePuy replied,

"Yes, Sir."

He rose, saluted, did an about face, and left the office. General Weyand turned to me and said,

"Thanks, Gerard."

What did I learn? While I was sure that General DePuy was furious in not getting his way, it reminded me that General DePuy was a soldier. He understood the chain of command. He understood the word "no." He understood the relationship between subordinates and seniors, and he did not challenge his boss, even though General Weyand was in charge temporarily, until General Seaman's return. Why couldn't Seaman just say, "No"?[25]

DePuy's reputation attracted some officers seeking command and apparently frightened others away. Richard Cavazos (GEN, USA, Ret.), a decorated veteran of Korea and charismatic commander, arrived in Vietnam in January 1967. While at the replacement center he saw a notice on the bulletin board signed by LTC Jim Pennington. It said that any newly arriving lieutenant colonel seeking battalion command should call Pennington at the telephone number provided. Cavazos expected a "huge waiting line," but, he remembered, "I was the only person within a two- to three-day period who responded to the note." He assumes that the buzz about DePuy discouraged many of his contemporaries. Cavazos served for only a short period before DePuy left the division, but he reflected warmly about 1967 and chance encounters with DePuy over the years following. He said that DePuy was "the most brilliant officer I have ever run across, and it was a pleasure to be around him. He is a teacher more than he was anything else. . . . I was never in the inner circle like Paul Gorman and some of the others, but I must say I couldn't have been treated better by anybody."[26]

But Bruce Palmer (GEN, USA, Ret.) recalls Army Chief of Staff Harold K. Johnson "calling me and Abe (Creighton Abrams) [into his Pentagon office] one day and saying, 'Goddamn it, what am I going to do with DePuy? If every division commander relieved people like DePuy, I'd soon be out of lieutenant colonels and majors. He just eats them up like peanuts.' Abe grunted and said, 'You are right, do you want me to call him?' Johnny said, 'No. Let me tell him.' So Johnny wrote him a back channel and said just that. He said, 'You've got to realize that your utilization of people is not very good at all, I can't afford division commanders like you. Point one. Point two, you are relieving people without giving them a chance. In many instances it strikes us back here as capricious. Thirdly, a part of our job is to train people and develop them and you've got to do better with your people.' Well, Bill slowed down a little bit, I guess. He has mellowed over the years, and today he is quite improved. In those days, he was just horrible on that score."[27]

DePuy may have mellowed over the years, but there is a better explanation for his behavior: the ghosts of 1944. He consistently set high standards for his combat leaders and for those who worked for him in peacetime. Palmer's reference to "those days" has less to do with an evolution in DePuy's leadership style over time—a mellowing—than with the situation. To DePuy, combat was a unique realm. It legitimized his demanding behavior. Later, in the Pentagon and at Fort Monroe, he used less draconian techniques: he assigned vital tasks to very bright people and routine tasks to those he regarded as ordinary types. But he didn't fire the ordinary types.

Those familiar with Harold K. Johnson may take exception to the "Goddamn it" quoted above. Johnson was a scrupulous Christian. It is improbable that those were his exact words, but Johnson certainly disapproved of DePuy's relief of officers. There are several accounts of what passed between Johnson and DePuy during Johnson's Christmas visit in 1966. The two generals had a confrontation regarding relief of officers that was sufficiently acrimonious to cause DePuy to think he himself might be relieved. In addition to the conversation reported by Palmer, there are at least two other accounts regarding DePuy's relief of officers while he commanded his division.

According to one, an officer recalled hearing "a heated argument" involving Johnson, DePuy, and Hollingsworth.

"I'm not here to run a training ground," General DePuy shouted. "They get people killed!"

"I can't have you be the filter for all the best officers we have in the Army to see if they meet your approval," General Johnson retorted. The listener said that they went back and forth for what seemed like half an hour.

That there was a confrontation is not in question. But neither DePuy nor Johnson were shouters. Nevertheless, DePuy was sufficiently concerned about his clash with Johnson that he told brigade commander Sid Berry that Johnson might relieve him. According to Berry, Johnson told DePuy, "I can't afford another Big Red One. . . . I need division commanders who make the best of the human material they are assigned." Berry says he never saw DePuy so dejected.[28]

There is another account of the Johnson-DePuy meeting. James F. Hollingsworth (LTG, USA, Ret.) is a character right out of Hollywood's central casting version of a fighting general. Known to all as Holly, he is profane, bombastic, brave, and the antithesis of a diplomat. Despite their very different personalities, DePuy admired Hollingsworth for his combat effectiveness. Holly had been in place since 1 March 1966 when DePuy arrived on 15 March to command the division. According to Holly, in their initial meeting DePuy asked, "How do you want to fight this division?" And "I said, well, we have got to get the division out in the field and find the enemy. We are going to kill them with firepower, artillery, and air. And he [DePuy] says, that's exactly the way we will do it."

Holly said, "We never had a cross word. We never had a disagreement. I just loved the guy, the first goddamned guy that I had seen since I got there who knew what the hell he was doing, what he wanted to do, and how to do it." Holly approvingly described DePuy's command style as "issuing orders and then getting out to see that they were done." The two of them seemed to be in complete accord in how to fight, including the need to fire people who couldn't get the job done in combat. DePuy told Holly about his experience with incompetent commanders in World War II.

About the confrontation in late 1966, when asked about it nearly forty years later, Hollingsworth said, "Well, let me give you the straight on that. Nobody knows about that except Bill DePuy, Johnson, and me. Johnson showed up on Thanksgiving Day of 1966." (Hollingsworth meant Christmas.) They went to DePuy's hootch. "Johnson looked at me and said, 'You are relieving too many battalion commanders. You are supposed to train them.' Bill DePuy was sitting within three or four feet of me, and he said, 'I'll answer that.' I said, 'No, sir, he asked me.' And I said, 'General, I had the idea that you were going to train them and we were to fight them over here and save soldiers' lives.'"

Johnson also expressed concern about the number of casualties in the 1st Division. Holly retorted by saying that that was the reason for relieving incompetent commanders and using lots of artillery. He emphasized that just the three of them were in DePuy's hootch. Asked about shouting, he said the discussion was conducted in conversational tones. Afterward, the three generals left DePuy's quarters to attend a dinner with the troops, where Johnson gave a short talk. Hollingsworth recalled, "Bill DePuy and I stressed on him that if you are going to clean up this country and get the enemy out, you have to get off your dead ass and get on with it. I will always remember that."[29]

Holly did not say, "and they lived happily forever after," but he left the distinct impression that Johnson had learned something about fighting the war in Vietnam during his visit to the division and was mollified. It must be said, however, that although Hollingsworth's account of the exchange has the advantage of being the recollection of one of the three participants, this story of the Chief's conversion to DePuy-Holly methods is inconsistent with the shouting match reported elsewhere and with Palmer's account of Johnson asking what he should do about DePuy.

Bill's letters to Marj and the family in late 1966 and 1967 illustrate that generals are as subject to disappointing decisions as the rest of the Army.

In a letter to Marj dated 9 November 1966, he gave her news

of a possible change of command. "For your information only," he wrote, "I have a strong indication that I will take command of the Infantry Center at Fort Benning [Georgia] on 1 Feb. Nothing would please me more professionally, although I know you would not be keen about moving into that area."[30] He understood Marj's preference for the stimulating cultural and social climate of Washington to the sound of guns, the smell of cordite, and the sight of very large insects and soldiers everywhere in the Chattahoochee Valley. He sounded even more sure about the change in another letter, likely written the same month: "I have been told quite definitely that I will return sometime in Feb . . . it also appears *highly* likely that my next assignment will be as Commandant of the Infantry Center at Fort Benning." And he had this to say on 18 December 1966: "General Johnson is going to spend Christmas afternoon and evening with us, staying over night. At that time, I am quite sure that my next assignment and the timing of my return will be finally decided upon."

Sure enough, two days after Christmas he was able to tell his wife, "I will depart on or about 15 Feb . . . Although you must not discuss this because it is not out in the open yet, I am to be assigned to the JCS in Washington. This will at least take some of the pressure off the house hunting and house selling business." On 10 January 1967 he had more to say: "My new job is not the one that I would have picked. I made this clear to General Johnson when he was here; however, it appears that General [Earle G.] Wheeler [Chairman, JCS] and Mr. [Cyrus] Vance [Deputy Secretary of Defense] were the ones to bring about this assignment. I will, of course, do whatever my superiors ask me. My real desire was to go to Benning to teach there what we have learned here because I am sure I could save many lives that way." Then, a week later: "I will tell you all about the reasons for the assignment to SACSA."

The reasons were simple: Johnson didn't want him; Wheeler did.

Former Secretary of State Alexander M. Haig Jr. (GEN, USA, Ret.) sheds light on DePuy's career in particular and Army internal politics in general. As a political sophisticate intimately familiar with governmental agencies and bureaucratic behavior, Haig's firsthand observations regarding hiring, firing, ambition, careerism, and protégés are particularly valuable.

Haig wrote in his book *Inner Circles* that DePuy gave him a free hand in exercising his responsibilities as division G-3 and battalion commander

> as long as I did the job right, in his eyes. If he had not been satisfied, he most certainly would have fired me. DePuy, the personification of a fighting general, was known to have little use for officers who came to Vietnam from soft billets in the Pentagon with the idea of getting their tickets punched for future promotions by spending a few months in the war zone before going back to another desk job. Before I arrived, he had fired no fewer than thirteen lieutenant colonels from the First Infantry Division. Many who left under the cloud of DePuy's stern judgment were officers straight from the Pentagon whose political skills were greater than their leadership ability. . . . Some had been the protégés of very important generals back home who believed, and openly said, that DePuy was ruthlessly destroying the reputations and careers of some of the most promising young officers in the service.[31]

Haig admires his former boss for his intelligence, decisiveness, leadership, combat skills, total dedication to Service, and for his major contributions in shaping the post-Vietnam Army. But Haig also recognized DePuy's "abrasive communications style [and] impatience."[32]

DePuy's feisty readiness to fight enemies, foreign and bureaucratic; the Seaman-DePuy mismatch; Westmoreland's confidence in DePuy and his reservations about Seaman; favorites of "very important generals back home" being canned by DePuy; the personal counseling by the Army's Chief of Staff; the Chief's concern for casualties, use of firepower, and the relief of officers—this is the stuff of fiction akin to Anton Myrer's *Once an Eagle* and James G. Cozzens' *Guard of Honor*. But all were part of DePuy's life in the Vietnam period.

On 29 December 1966, DePuy wrote a letter to General Johnson in response to the back-channel message that Johnson sent to DePuy after his meeting with Palmer and Abrams in the Pentagon. The subject is: "Personnel Relieved or Transferred During My Period of

Command, Other Than Those Through Normal Rotation and Reassignment." The officers are named in DePuy's letter. To spare unnecessary embarrassment, they are not named here. Of the eleven relieved, seven were battalion commanders. Nine of the eleven were lieutenant colonels, and two were majors. Excerpts from DePuy's letter provide quintessential examples of what Haig called DePuy's abrasive communications style.

About a G-2, DePuy wrote:

> Col. A was a fat, disheveled officer without any soldierly characteristics whatsoever who made a bad impression on all those people whom he briefed as a representative of the 1st Division.

About a Provost Marshal, he had this evaluation:

> LTC B is completely without talent of any kind whatsoever. He had no initiative, no imagination and repeatedly performed his duties in a sluggish, unintelligent manner.

Then there was a battalion commander:

> The first day I saw C, I strongly suspected that he was weak ... [he] lost complete control over his battalion and suffered a number of unnecessary casualties while inflicting none on the VC. . . . I relieved him and indicated on his Efficiency Report that he should not command troops in combat. (He was recently promoted to full colonel.)

Then there was a G-5:

> A completely inadequate officer; no initiative, imagination or drive. Valueless . . .

And an artillery battalion commander:

> He refused to admit responsibility personally or for any of his people for gross errors in artillery firing which led to civilian and friendly military casualties. He did not have the character to stand up and be counted.

Another artillery battalion commander he wrote about this way:

> .. a weak officer. He had no force, was not a commander of men. . . . In short, he was a man who easily took NO for an answer.

Then there were the infantry battalion commanders:

> D is a brave man but lacked the courage to demand high standards from his soldiers and to enforce those high standards.

And about another infantry commander:

> He is a third rate officer who should not be entrusted with command of soldiers in combat.

DePuy's vow never to allow American officers to kill American soldiers is evident here, as is his barbed prose.[33]

Johnson wasn't buying it. He said later that DePuy "took the division and proceeded to rip the command structure apart by transfers and dismissals," and he was critical of DePuy's lavish use of firepower. Johnson was almost certainly referring to DePuy in 1966 when he said, "it's very popular to say let's send a bullet instead of a boy . . . I think we overemphasize firepower."[34]

DePuy's guidance to his leaders regarding the importance of firepower is recorded in detail in a student paper written at the Army War College by then–Lieutenant Colonel Richard Cavazos, one of more than thirty of DePuy's First Division men who became generals. Writing on fire and maneuver in Vietnam, Cavazos cites extensively from 1st Infantry Division Pamphlet 350–1, 1 February 1968 (DePuy's 1966–1967 original version was retained and reprinted by his successors). Cavazos wrote:

> Aggressive instinct to flank enemy positions must be curbed. Once the enemy position is established all Commanders will bring all available fires to bear.

> The underlying purpose of Infantry [is] . . . to locate the enemy so that our fire can destroy him.

Infantry finds the enemy and with supporting fire destroys
him.

No maneuver is undertaken without covering artillery and/
or airpower for all missions.

The mastery of fire control and fire coordination is the most
important challenge faced by battalion and brigade commanders in Vietnam.[35]

The views of Johnson and DePuy regarding the use of artillery and
the relief of officers could not be reconciled.

Sid Berry provides a balanced professional evaluation of his old
boss: "Bill was an outstanding soldier," Berry said. "Like so many
'runts,' he tended to be cocky and abrasive to others. He was extremely confident and really knew his soldiering. Whenever he
spoke to soldiers he could really generate loyalty, enthusiasm, and
spirit. He was an inspiring leader. But he, like the rest of us, had
his flaws. Around his headquarters there tended to be a Byzantine
atmosphere with people jockeying for his attention and his good
favor."

Berry said that Terry de la Mesa Allen and Ted Roosevelt Jr., 1st
Infantry Division icons from World War II, come to mind when he
thinks of the DePuy-Hollingsworth team and the Big Red One in
Vietnam. Of DePuy, he said, "I guess any of us who served in his
division will always talk about him, usually admiringly, but not always uncritically. DePuy pressed his personality on that division to
a degree that few commanders can."[36]

DePuy got rave reviews in 1967 from a general whose jobs put
him in positions from which he observed and worked with all the
major commanders in Vietnam. Major General George P. Seneff Jr.
served from February 1966 as U.S. Army Vietnam (USARV) Aviation Officer and then as commander when the 1st Aviation Brigade
was established in March 1966. He called the 1st Infantry Division
"the most professional division in country" and spoke of its "degree
of technical perfection that no other division over here has got." The
reason? "I will say here that the effectiveness of the 1st Division . . .
is entirely attributable to General Bill DePuy and his assistant division commanders, Jack Deane, Jim Hollingsworth, and Bernie Rog-

ers. They're all pros; they know combat, they know the battlefield, and know their people and they take proper care of them and taught them well."

General Seneff's assessment of DePuy and his division rings true. Abrasiveness, impatience, and his methods alienated more than a few, including the Army Chief of Staff, but DePuy was effective. Soldiers in the bush and fellow generals said that he knew what he was doing. His job was to get after enemy main force formations in an area in which they moved freely, posing a threat to logistics installations around Saigon and to the South Vietnamese government itself. DePuy was successful in dominating the battlefield by mastering new mobility techniques and firepower. However, at the end of his command of the division, the enemy continued to decide when to fight and remained determined to persevere.

In this exit interview in September 1967, as he left Vietnam, Seneff also praised DePuy's earlier performance as MACV J-3. He called DePuy brilliant. "[DePuy] pretty much played the damned thing out of his hip pocket," said Seneff. "He had Westmoreland's complete confidence."[37]

But not Johnson's.

Johnson's reservations about DePuy and his methods did not result in DePuy's being relieved from division command, but Johnson did deny DePuy the job he wanted: command of the Infantry School. DePuy believed his entire career to that date pointed to that job.

Aware of Johnson's opinion of DePuy, Westmoreland informed General Wheeler, the Chairman of the Joint Chiefs of Staff, that DePuy was available for assignment. Westmoreland later told his former aide and longtime confidant, Paul Miles (Colonel, USA, Ret.), that it was at this point that he "saved Bill DePuy's career."[38] Wheeler knew of DePuy's talents from the early 1960s, when Wheeler was Army Chief and DePuy was a colonel and brigadier general on the Army Staff, and he trusted Westmoreland's judgment. DePuy would serve on the JCS Staff before returning to the Army when Westmoreland became Chief—and Johnson was gone.

13

SACSA, Tet, and Policy Review

> McCloy, speaking for the group, told Dean Rusk and me: "We are about to get our nose bloodied, but you've got to do it. You've got to go in."
> —Robert McNamara on Wise Men advice on Vietnam, July 1965

> What really surprised me when we got onto the whole question of Vietnam was that there was no political base on which to build.
> —Dean Acheson in the policy review after Tet 1968

His having spent almost three years in Vietnam and his earlier work in counterinsurgency made Major General DePuy one of the most knowledgeable officials in the U.S. government regarding Vietnam. He began his new job with the Joint Chiefs of Staff on 15 March 1967 as the Special Assistant for Counterinsurgency and Special Activities (SACSA). Within a year, the Tet offensive in 1968 became a turning point in that war.

When DePuy returned from Vietnam in 1967 he was forty-eight years old. His children had become teenagers as the United States was undergoing a social revolution, while he was away fighting a war. The transformation of his three small children into thinking and almost-independent young DePuy adults coincided with dramatic events unfolding in Vietnam and in America, including mass demonstrations not far from the DePuy home, the assassinations of Robert Kennedy and Martin Luther King Jr., and the burning of American cities. The father found himself in the middle of policy debates about the Vietnam War at the highest national level just as his children were becoming prepared to discuss serious issues. Bill DePuy proved himself a sophisticated political player and a compassionate teacher of his children in a tumultuous time in American history. His Army would advance him in rank and responsibility, and his children would love and respect him. He was never too busy to be a caring father.

Bill Jr., known to family and friends as Billy, remembers the period from his father's return from Vietnam to about time of the Watergate affair, which resulted in President Nixon's resignation, as the only rough patch in his relationship with his father. Those were the days when some generals in the Pentagon had one son in an Ivy League school protesting the Vietnam war and another at West Point preparing to fight in it. Billy says that his father treated the son's views with respect. He has positive memories of having his high-school buddies over for dinner or for a beer. "We would sit in the kitchen with my father when he got home from work, usually at seven or eight at night." He and his friends challenged the establishment in which the general was a key player. "There was a natural tension between us," says Billy, "natural" as the adolescent, bursting with ideas newly discovered, questioned authority, a universal scenario. But DePuy earned the respect of Billy and his buddies by treating them as peers and by embracing the norms of civilized discourse. He could have played the authoritarian general—as he was indeed in his professional life—but he didn't. "Even when we had periods of enormous disagreement, as I did with him over the Vietnam War, there was an encompassing love that permeated the atmosphere."[1]

Love took the edge off the father-son differences, but whether he was dealing with president, soldier, staff officer, or schoolboy, the senior Bill faced issues head-on with rigorous analysis. His son was pleased to be treated as a serious person and was proud of a dad who treated his adolescent pals as intellectual peers in their kitchen-table debates. A number of DePuy's professional subordinates made similar observations about his attentive listening, which caused them to believe that what they said mattered to the boss. He took them seriously. That quality and his effectiveness as a teacher pervade commentaries about him in both his professional and his domestic life.

Billy recalls his father being "prescriptive and disciplining" when the son would backslide. For example, his father gave him French passages to memorize and checked up on the assignment when he came home from work. You can't fake memorization!

He recalls asking his father about research projects that were historical and analytical, Billy's strengths. His father was "a serious student of history," according to Bill Jr., and was "terrific" at teaching it. Working with his father, he learned that in August 1914 the mobilization of European armies was tantamount to a declaration of war, as the timely call-up of reserves and rigid railroad schedules took on critical importance, to the ultimate pain of all European belligerents. Similarly, as he studied the fortifications of Vauban, the great French military engineer, which featured star-shaped forts providing enfilade fires and mutual support, the elder DePuy told his son of the German and French fortifications he had seen in World War II, and he explained how those observations led to the DePuy foxhole. Connecting Vauban, World War II, and Vietnam made an impression on the boy. History was more than an academic exercise. It was a living thing to both father and son.

DePuy derived great pleasure from the company of his children, perhaps none greater than teaching them. He taught practical things like post-hole digging, fence building, oil changing and checking the timing of a car engine, and the need to go beyond the superficial in thinking about historical events, religion, chemistry, and physics. He had an insatiable thirst for knowledge and for figuring out how things worked.

And the DePuy family knew how to play. When the children were in their teens, weekends often involved some work around the house with everyone pitching in, but on Saturday or Sunday, they would pile into cars with friends and pets to head for picnics, drives, and fun, often at Camp A. P. Hill for eating, drinking, poker playing, shooting, fishing, and good conversation that reached across generations. The children and their friends mingled with their parents' friends from the State Department, the CIA, and the military friends. The DePuy family all fired rifles and shotguns. (The children contend that Marj was a better shot than their father.) The father taught the children to fish.

Billy repeated the story that Colin Powell told regarding what General DePuy advised him about preserving time for family and maintaining some private space.[2] Billy thought that anyone who encountered the DePuy family would conclude, "There is a group of people who really like each other and seem to get along pretty well."

Family dinner in the DePuy household was learning time, a colloquium with a dictionary or encyclopedia readily at hand. During dinner discussions, unfounded assertions were fair game for challenge. Parents and children would track down information or check on the exact meaning of a word, theory, or concept. Both parents were thoughtful and analytical people interested in a broad array of topics and placed particular emphasis on precise language and intellectual rigor. "It was a highly enriched intellectual environment," recalled Bill Jr.

Reason and general compatibility accommodated a standing political difference between Marj and Bill DePuy. She was conservative and voted Republican. He usually voted Democrat. Watergate put father and son in the same camp, with Marj on the other side. According to Billy, "It was Watergate and President Nixon that was the reconciliation between my father and me." They "saw eye to eye" and "were joined at the hip" in their condemnation of Nixon. Marj, according to her son, took her usual position: "My President, right or wrong."[3]

Joslin's memories of DePuy family life are similar to Billy's. A year younger than her brother, she was less certain and not as intense about the big political issues of the times. She was just discovering those issues while Billy was already taking positions on them in debates with his father. Joslin felt that she "developed much more of a relationship [with her father] after he was retired." Regarding DePuy's important work and regular contact with the famous and powerful, Joslin said simply, "I had no idea." But the installation of a red telephone in her father's closet got her attention. "Aha, that is an important telephone!" And she could not fail to notice her father's picture on the cover of *Newsweek* and his name in newspapers when he commanded his division in Vietnam. Her school friends were impressed, even if she wasn't.

Looking back on those years, Joslin observed that before, during, and after Vietnam, he was always an engaged parent. "He was able to go and do the job and come home and have that family life." She remembers the fun, the parties at A. P. Hill, "these huge debates about the military-industrial complex." Still, they had "wonderful times" as the family would "fill up the house" with friends. "And we have all done this with our own children," said Joslin, "Bill with his and I with mine."

As the children went off to college, their father made a point to personally drive each of them to their schools and settle them in,

Joslin in Lynchburg College, Daphne in Roanoke College, and Billy in Boston University. That seemed perfectly normal at the time, but Joslin later noted that it was quite time-consuming for her father to take them all to college when he had pressing professional responsibilities. But to him it was clearly part of being a father. He got his children settled at their colleges the way he had settled them into their school routines in England.

The DePuy children seem not to have gone through that phase of growing up when friends are more important to them than family, perhaps because their parents routinely made a point to include their children's friends at parties and on family outings. Joslin says that as a college student she visited both Daphne and Billy at their schools and met their friends. In fact, Joslin married her brother's college roommate. They enjoyed the independence of living away at school, but they also enjoyed coming home. Sibling rivalry is not evident among the DePuys. They seem to have sorted out their roles and missions early on. Billy was the big brother, Daphne was the baby, and Joslin accepted being "the in-betweener."

While Billy challenged authority in his passage from boyhood to young manhood and Joslin did the scatter-brained teenage things one winks at as children wend their way through adolescence, Daphne was generally more subdued than her older brother and older sister, perhaps more sensitive. She was absolutely clear about her deep affection and profound respect for her father. She missed him "horribly" when he was away at war for almost three years. She saved his letters and recalled how "he would relate to my world, not his," writing of the sights and scents of flowers in season in Washington and of her hobbies and interests.

"When he came back in 1967," said Daphne, "I was twelve or thirteen. Our relationship resumed—walking dogs, teaching me how to fix things, build things, change the oil in his car." Daphne wondered where Billy and Joslin were as she recalled so much private time with her father. "I liked being with him because he was so smart, and he was full of interesting stories and information. I loved to listen to him talk. He would turn everything into some kind of learning experience. He taught me how to saw properly and use tools. We didn't hire people to fix things. We fixed them and saved money." And he taught her to sail and to ski. "Dad was a quick study," she said. If the kids expressed an interest in sailing, he would learn to sail and teach them.

Daphne and her father shared some things neither learned nor shared with the rest of the family. They were both sleepwalkers. Her father told her of waking up in a snowstorm on a rooftop in South Dakota when he was a boy, not knowing how he got there. They were both red/green color-blind. They were both very good dancers. And Daphne's father supported her in practical ways by helping her with her collections as a child, with her house repairs later in life, and in intangible ways as a confidant. Their strong bond was present from her birth to his death without interruption. It was special to each of them.

In a city of work-obsessed professionals, Bill DePuy succeeded as a father and husband. He took great pleasure in his family while enjoying a highly successful career. As adults his children wondered how he found the time and energy to do so much with them. His sensitivity and attention to their individual personalities, interests, and hobbies are clear in their recollections of him. Professionally engaged in the direction and control of great numbers of people, in a manner some regarded as imperious, he seemed content to have Marj direct and control the family's domestic and social agenda.

Without skipping a beat, DePuy made the transition from combat in dense jungles to policy formulation and interaction with senior national leaders in the bureaucratic thickets of Washington.

His Vietnam experience made him one of the better-known generals in the Army in 1967, and he had a reputation for being brainy. During the roles and missions debates of the Eisenhower-Dulles years he had weighed in with two articles published in *Army* magazine. In one he made the case for dual capability in the Army, that is, nuclear and conventional.[4] In the other he asked how much unification of the armed forces was enough, concluding that there was a need for the three Services, each driven by doctrines and cultures essential to their reasons for being.[5]

DePuy's incisive analysis and clear expression marked him as a fighting soldier who was also very articulate, someone who could speak for the Army among Service professionals, academics, and other departments of government. In the vernacular of the period, he was a soldier-scholar. While his letters, internal memoranda, public addresses, and instructions were numerous and well written, he didn't write much for publication until he retired. But leadership was aware that DePuy was a fighting general with brains.

In his first year as the SACSA, the year before the furor over Tet in 1968, he later observed, "It was rather shocking to return to Washington and see what the perceptions were. And there's no doubt that the perception in Washington was a gloomy one, one that pervaded all of the agencies of the government and the press." Given the mood in 1967, it is not surprising that when General Westmoreland later "tried to tell anyone who would listen that Tet was a victory, no one would listen to him."[6] American officials in Washington and Saigon would continue to see events in Vietnam differently, rather in the paradigm of the glass being half full or half empty.

The SACSA position had been created as the Kennedy Administration came to power and the Army was casting about for an alternative to the policy of massive retaliation. The job description was to monitor guerrilla warfare, psychological operations, escape and evasion, civic action, counterinsurgency, special operations, and unconventional warfare. Some of the classified organizations that reported to SACSA, and some of the special missions coordinated by this position, remained secret for years after DePuy's tenure. For example, Military Assistance Command, Vietnam—Studies and Observation Group (MACVSOG) conducted clandestine operations in Cambodia, Laos, and Vietnam and reported to SACSA. In addition, the exact role that the United States and SACSA played in running down Ernesto (Che) Guevara remains to be told in its entirety.

But the tasks given to DePuy's predecessors as SACSA weren't what his boss needed in 1967. Currency on Vietnam was what General Wheeler needed as Chairman of the Joint Chiefs of Staff. DePuy represented the Chairman as a member of an interdepartmental group that included Assistant Secretary of State for the Far East William Bundy's deputy, Phil Habib; George Carver of the CIA; International Security Affairs (ISA) member, and later ambassador, Dick Stedman; and White House member Bill Jordan. This group of deputies representing the civilian and military sides of the Pentagon plus State, CIA, and the White House met at least once a week regarding Vietnam. Their task was to be current and to prepare their principals for the Tuesday luncheons with the President. DePuy said, "They [the principals] were the equivalent of the War Cabinet." DePuy's job was to keep Wheeler up to speed so that the Chairman could advise LBJ regarding military aspects of the war in Vietnam.

DePuy served as SACSA from March 1967 to January 1969, when the war in Vietnam was the hot-button issue, particularly as the 1968 Tet offensive forced policy review. He was a very busy man in a high-pressure, high-visibility political-military job. His son said that DePuy resumed smoking about then, a habit he had stopped as a lieutenant colonel in the 1950s.[7]

DePuy had two major writing assignments while serving as SACSA, one for his old boss, Westmoreland, and one for his new boss, Wheeler. He supervised the writing of General Westmoreland's end-of-tour "Report on Operations in South Vietnam: January 1964–June 1968, as of 30 June 1968." It describes events in Vietnam following the classic arc of tragedy: introduction of the plot and dramatis personae, conflict, decision, and denouement. He had served Westmoreland as a staffer when the mission was advisory; during the buildup, tasking, and positioning of U.S. troop formations; and as staffer and commander in combat operations. Then he was immersed in the post-Tet policy review and change in Washington that brought General Westmoreland home. DePuy was at the center of what could be seen as the rise and fall of William Westmoreland, with the two men in almost daily contact in Vietnam from 1964 to 1966 and frequent contact when DePuy commanded his division from 1966 to 1967. Westmoreland recognized him as an excellent and terse writer, so it was DePuy who assembled the unclassified report. The handwritten inscription in DePuy's personal copy of the published report is about as warm as the formal Westmoreland allowed himself to be. It says, "To—Bill DePuy—With gratitude for your valued assistance and support. S/W. C. Westmoreland March 1969."[8]

DePuy was the only JCS staffer to accompany Wheeler on the Chairman's post-Tet 1968 visit to Vietnam, where the two generals from Washington met Westmoreland and his key people on 23 February. Their purpose was to get an estimate of the meaning of Tet from the perspective of the men on the scene so that Wheeler could formulate *his* net assessment for the President. The resulting "Report of the Chairman, JCS, on the Situation in Vietnam and MACV Requirements," dated 27 February 1968, was a classified military report signed by Wheeler. DePuy began his draft of the report aboard the aircraft as it departed Saigon for Hawaii on its way back to Washington. His military report was later summarized in a briefing DePuy gave to presidential advisers and then to the President. Others briefed the CIA and State Department portions of the comprehensive report. DePuy said of the military portion, "I wrote the report for General Wheeler."

The way Tet was seen in Saigon was very different from the way it was seen by the President's advisers in Washington. U.S. leadership in Saigon saw Tet as the destruction of the VC infrastructure that had taken Hanoi decades to build, which made it a victory. Washington saw it as armed enemy troops raising hell throughout Vietnam, including the halls and offices of the American Embassy in Saigon, which made it a defeat.

As he reflected on that post-Tet period a decade later, DePuy described how the meaning of Tet was briefed to the President's closest advisers and then to the President himself. DePuy believed in 1979 that he and his colleagues might have painted too dismal a picture of the situation in Vietnam in 1968, thus influencing those who had LBJ's ear to recommend that the United States cut its losses and get out of Vietnam. The feeling among American leadership in Saigon at the time, however, was that Wheeler's team and the President's advisers in Washington had already made up their minds to get out, even as they went through the motions of getting the view from the field. Westmoreland thought so. He said that Wheeler was "a tired man, seemingly near the point of exhaustion. He and his traveling companion, my old friend, Bill DePuy . . . mirrored the gloom that pervaded official circles in Washington, a reflection of the doomsday reporting by press and television" that made Tet "the worst calamity since Bull Run."[9] LBJ's decision in 1968 not to run for reelection was the culmination of a series of bad-news events, not least of which was the post-Tet Vietnam assessment delivered by Bill DePuy and his colleagues from the State Department and CIA.

A bipartisan group of elder statesmen had been brought to Washington several times from 1965 to 1968 to advise the President and his key people on courses of action in Vietnam. The veteran Cold Warriors of the eastern establishment old boys' net—men like Dean Acheson, George Kennan, Charles Bohlen, Averell Harriman, John McCloy, and Robert Lovett—had staffed big banks, law firms, and diplomatic corps, and had advised presidents since Franklin D. Roosevelt. They were supplemented by men like Omar Bradley, John Cowles, Arthur Dean, Ros Gilpatric, Paul Hoffman, George Kistiakowsky, Arthur Larson, Matthew Ridgway, James Gavin, and others and became known as the Wise Men.[10]

To illustrate what an abrupt about-face took place in March 1968, a quick recapitulation of events in Washington is useful.

On 7 June 1965, Westmoreland cabled Washington to say, essentially, either reinforce or watch South Vietnam go under. In July, the Wise Men advised LBJ that it was in the interest of the United States to fight in Vietnam. McNamara wrote, "McCloy, speaking for the group, told Dean Rusk and me: 'We are about to get our nose bloodied, but you've got to do it. You've got to go in.'"[11] By 1965 the military men on the spot, including DePuy, believed the choice was clear: build up or get out.

Their thinking was folded into the geopolitical Cold War truism that in a zero-sum game, any Communist gain was an American loss. Moreover, if Vietnam were to fall to Hanoi, other regimes in Asia would fall as well, like dominoes. The Democrats, who were in the White House from 1933 to 1953, had been accused of "selling out" China, mucking up the Korean War, and harboring Communists in the State Department, and they were sensitive to the charges in 1965. Hence, "You've got to go in."

The Wise Men were assembled again on 2 November 1967 as McNamara sought "an alternative program." As he later wrote, "The Wise Men had no clue that all this [debate in the government about alternative courses of action, including bombing, more troops, negotiating withdrawal, or a combination of all of the above] was going on. . . . with respect to how to unite the American people, they advised emphasizing 'light at the end of the tunnel' instead of battles, death, and danger."[12] In brief, they recommended that the President stick it out and put the best face on events. But pessimism about the war was in the air. Moreover, this meeting took place just before the Tet offensive. The contrast between the "light at the end of the tunnel"—which was identified with General Westmoreland just before Tet—and photos and film of an armed enemy team in the American Embassy during Tet, probably doomed General Westmoreland.

Four months later, on 29 February 1968, the day of his farewell ceremony as Secretary of Defense, McNamara wrote later that he was too emotional to say more than, "I cannot find words to express what lies in my heart today." That was very un-McNamara behavior. In his memoir published in 1995, he wrote that what he should have said as he left office was: neither the president nor his advisers, including McNamara himself, had managed the war wisely. It was said by others that he was close to a breakdown after a very tough slog of seven years of crises that included the building of the infamous Berlin Wall and American reaction in Europe; the Bay of Pigs misadventure; the missile crisis in Cuba, which brought the world close to nuclear war; the civil rights movement; assassinations at home and abroad; and the burning of American flags and cities. All of that had to be added to the highly contentious war that wore him down.[13]

Dean Acheson suspected that he and the other Wise Men were being used by Johnson as political cover for an unsound policy. After a sharp exchange of words with the President on 27 February, Acheson insisted on being fully briefed. No more "canned briefings." If his name and reputation were to be associated with the advice of the Wise Men, Acheson wanted "full run of the shop." He wanted to talk "to the engine room people."[14]

In early March, Phil Habib, George Carver, and DePuy, the "engine room people," appeared at Acheson's house on P Street one by one to respond in detail to Acheson's questioning. Fully briefed, Acheson concluded that the United States had to get out of Vietnam. "What really surprised me when we got into the whole question of Vietnam was that there was no political base on which to build."[15] That's what DePuy meant in his letters home in 1964 and 1965, when he described the Saigon political scene as "a comic opera."

McNamara, in his mea culpa, underlined two assumptions not sufficiently challenged by the decision makers from the beginning of American involvement in Vietnam: the domino theory and the capacity of leadership in South Vietnam to govern responsibly. McNamara was brutally frank in asking himself why he failed to address those two issues. He concludes about America in Vietnam: "We were wrong, terribly wrong."[16]

The Wise Men reassembled at the State Department for briefings on Vietnam on 25 March 1968. Cyrus Vance and General Matthew Ridgway joined them; McCloy and Lovett were absent. They read documents that had been assembled for them, dined, were briefed by Habib, Carver, and DePuy, and discussed how America's Vietnam commitment might be curtailed.

Habib believed that they had concluded the war could not be won. It was time to negotiate. Arthur Goldberg grilled DePuy sharply, especially regarding the claim that 80,000 of the enemy had been killed. What was the ratio of killed to wounded? Ten to one, was the reply; three to one conservatively. How many VC were in the field? Two hundred thirty thousand. Goldberg did some quick arithmetic and demanded, "Then who the hell are we fighting?"[17] More often than not it was DePuy who nailed briefers to the wall. This time he was on the receiving end of Goldberg's hammering.

The next day, after spending the early morning with General Wheeler and General Abrams, who was about to succeed Westmoreland in Vietnam, President Johnson met the Wise Men in the Cabinet Room at the White House. Their message to the President was clear: it was time to disengage. He asked who had "brainwashed" that group of "intelligent, experienced men," then insisted that the briefers—Habib, Carver, and DePuy—tell him exactly what they had told the group the previous day. DePuy recalled that the President's words were, who "poisoned the well"?[18]

Two days later Carver and DePuy gave the President the same briefing. "Habib had wisely left town," recalled DePuy. He added that the President was inattentive and distracted as he took the briefing in the White House, suggesting that he had already made his decision. According to DePuy,

> The President, it seemed to me, wasn't paying any attention to us; he was making and taking telephone calls. They were taking pictures. Patrick Nugent, who was President Johnson's grandson, was running around the room, and the President would pick him up from time to time and put him on his knee and give him a drink out of a Coke bottle from which the President was drinking. All in all it was a very disorderly, disconcerting episode—almost amusing in a comical sort of way. When we were finished, the President sort of waved us out of the room by saying, "Well, I don't see anything wrong with what you told them." . . . just two days later the President announced that he would not seek re-election. I guess he had made that decision *before* we briefed him, which may explain his relative lack of interest.[19]

A coda to the President's decision is provided by Anatoly Dobrynin, the Soviet Ambassador who served in Washington through several presidencies, from Kennedy to Reagan. On 31 March 1968, LBJ told Dobrynin in strict confidence "that at the end of his television address he intended to announce that he would not run for another term as president," in the hope that his decision might "help settle the entire Vietnam conflict." Dobrynin was the first foreigner informed, and only four or five Americans knew of Johnson's decision before his televised announcement. "It was a sensation," said Dobrynin.[20]

The surprise ending to the President's address to the nation was, "I shall not seek, and I will not accept, the nomination of my party for another term as your President."[21] The Vietnam War had driven LBJ from the White House.

DePuy's assessment of what had happened in the March 1968 briefings can be summed up in a word: perceptions. To the military in Vietnam, Tet was a victory. Washington interpreted the same events as a defeat. The Wise Men believed the war was lost. "They seized upon those parts of the briefing which supported their view and paid very little attention to the other parts. However, I must say that the briefings were not encouraging at that time. And perhaps those of us who gave the briefing were suffering a little bit from the Washington point of view, as opposed to the field point of view, despite the fact that some of us had just been out there."[22]

In March 1968 the policy of the United States became not to win the war in Vietnam but to get out. General Westmoreland would be brought back to Washington to become Army Chief of Staff.

General Wheeler telephoned from Washington on 23 March 1968 to inform General Westmoreland that President Johnson had just announced at a press conference that he, Westmoreland, was to be the new Army Chief of Staff. "The President was gracious," Westmoreland said later of a personal message to him from the President confirming the appointment. Wheeler met Westmoreland on his arrival at Clark Air Force Base in the Philippines to let Westy know what the President wanted conveyed to him. According to Westmoreland, "The President urged me to ignore the inevitable press speculation to the effect that I was being 'kicked upstairs.'" LBJ, McNamara, and Clark Clifford, McNamara's successor as Secretary of State, all agreed that he was their choice to be Chief.[23] But the fact is that Westy had failed to nail the coonskin to the barn door.

President Johnson treated his general with courtesy. Westmoreland was the President's guest in the White House as they consulted, and the general recommended Creighton Abrams as his successor. His account of that meeting ends with this wistful comment regarding the end of his tour in Vietnam. "I flew with the President in his helicopter over downtown Washington, where fires set in widespread rioting and looting were still burning. It looked considerably more distressing than Saigon during the Tet offensive."[24]

Westmoreland brought DePuy to the Army Staff from the JCS

on 2 January 1969 to be acting Assistant Vice Chief of Staff (AVICE). On 10 March 1969, Bill DePuy was promoted to lieutenant general and officially became the AVICE, a very influential position, and one that he would hold for the next four years. It was not a happy time for the U.S. Army.

14

To Fix a Broken Army

As the office gained stature and confidence, the Secretary was
willing to put back into the "green suit" part of the house,
through the AVICE and the Vice Chief, the authority and
responsibility which had been taken away from the Army staff
during the McNamara regime and for a long time thereafter.
                                        —William DePuy, 1979

The period 1969–1973 was a terrible time in the history of the U.S.
Army. The "raggedy-assed little bastards" in Vietnam were demonstrating a readiness to outlast the United States and win. They did
both. And while the U.S. Army was engaged in light infantry combat
in Asia for a decade, the Red Army had modernized its mechanized
and armored forces and massive mobile fire support in Europe. That
required the U.S. Army to refocus on the threat posed by the Soviet
Union in Europe, improve training, modernize weapons systems,
and rethink doctrine. Among the by-products of the unpopular war
in Asia were an end to conscription and the reliance upon volunteers to fill the Army's ranks. That was a sea change in personnel
policy and a plunge into the unknown. Along with these changes
was a reduction in the size of the Army, from 1.6 million to 800,000
people in the period from 1969 to 1973. Summing up the condition
of the Army in 1972, Major General Donn Starry unceremoniously
informed General Creighton Abrams, who was awaiting Senate
confirmation as Chief of Staff, "Your Army is on its ass."[1] Concur-
rent with other blows, the managerial revolution in the Department
of Defense had come as a culture shock to the Army, as the Army
was dragged into modern management.

When General Westmoreland was sworn in as Army Chief of
Staff on 3 July 1968, he set himself two tasks. One was to support
the soldiers who were fighting in Vietnam. The other was to revi-
talize the Army for future challenges. Consistent with his previous
practice, he assembled a gifted team for his Army staff. According to

one of them, "Westmoreland picked the best lieutenant generals in the Army, whether they agreed with him or not."[2] Two officers who worked with Westy on a daily basis as his assistants, one in Vietnam and the other in the Pentagon, emphasized his search for brains, not yes-men, to assist him. Lloyd Matthews said General Westmoreland hired the very best talent he could find, the implication being that he was a big enough man to surround himself with officers he knew to be smarter than he was. Paul Miles described instances in which the general sought his opinion as a young major, because he knew that his younger officers saw things from a different perspective. Both Miles and Matthews said the same of DePuy. When DePuy asked a junior officer a question, it was not pro forma or small talk. He listened intently to the answer to get a fresh perspective.[3]

The generals Westmoreland relied upon as his principal staff officers in the Pentagon came from the generation that had cut its teeth in battalion command in World War II, men like Bill DePuy, George Forsythe, and Dutch Kerwin. By the late 1960s, they had risen to the top of the Army hierarchy, where they found themselves the custodians of a broken institution that they were determined to fix. Revitalization would not be achieved during Westmoreland's tenure as Chief. Creighton Abrams, Fred Weyand, and others to whom the Army was a calling put their shoulders to the wheel, but the much maligned General Westmoreland had set that wheel in motion.

The sheer volume of work and the amount of time demanded from civilian and military senior leadership was staggering. One thinks of McNamara near nervous breakdown as he left the Department of Defense after seven pressure-filled years, and one recalls the "before and after" photos of Presidents as they age perceptibly in office. Westmoreland's executive officer, who was later a military assistant in the White House, recalled what was expected of his boss. Volney Warner (GEN, USA, Ret.) mentioned Westmoreland's 6 AM to 10 PM days in the Pentagon, the mass of details on his desk, the meetings, the decisions, the travel, and the JCS responsibilities, adding in 1983, "As I reflect on it now, being his age now myself, it was almost cruel and inhumane to send him home with bags and packages, and demand from him that he work through that until midnight or 1 o'clock, and . . . then Saturday and Sunday meetings."[4] Fortunately, the general had willing and talented help.

Some insiders believe that Westmoreland's staff was one of the best ever assembled by the Army. The Vice Chief of Staff was his

1936 classmate at West Point, Bruce Palmer. Joseph M. Heiser Jr. was DCSLOG (Logistics). Brilliant Dick Stilwell (he was called that so often by so many that "Brilliant" might have been his first name) was DCSOPS (Operations). Dutch Kerwin, an artilleryman by trade, had commanded an armored division in Europe and was DCSPER (Personnel). George Forsythe was SAMVA (Special Assistant for the Modern Volunteer Army). His charge was to take the Army from conscription to a 100 percent volunteer force at a time when the Army was an object of scorn to many Americans. American flags were burned by Americans, and men in uniform were shunned in public.

When General Westmoreland brought DePuy to the Army Staff to serve as AVICE, both DePuy and the office he assumed were controversial. His work in plans, programs, and budgets in 1962–1964 prepared him for his new job. The skills he demonstrated as AVICE and his cool, logical approach to problem solving conformed nicely to the management style and techniques that civilian leadership had earlier brought to the Department of Defense (DOD), through the work of such individuals as Robert S. McNamara, Alain C. Enthoven, Cyrus R. Vance, and Stanley R. Resor.[5]

The Army, like the Department of Defense, has both a civilian side and a uniformed side. The military provides war fighting expertise under the civilian control of an elected President and the secretaries he appoints. At times the military side is ascendant; President Roosevelt's confidence in General George C. Marshall in World War II comes to mind. In the Kennedy-LBJ years, the managerial methods of business executive Robert McNamara made the civilian side dominant in the DOD and in the Service staffs. DePuy, always a logical thinker, was pleased to learn the new game of operations research and systems analysis and to restore to "green suiters," the uniformed side, what he regarded as its proper respect and collaboration from the civilian side.

Some civilian leaders in the McNamara era regarded Army management as primitive and were unimpressed by generals (and admirals) as managers. But DePuy stood out as a general who "got it." His appreciation of facts and analytical intelligence, and his crisp presentation in speech and writing had won him the respect of both the civilian and the uniformed sides of Pentagon leadership. He was as bright as any of the Whiz Kids, the young civilian managers Robert McNamara brought to government.

As the commander of the Big Red One, DePuy became a public figure. Consistent with the maxim "If it bleeds, it leads," the press went to the sound of the guns. When they got there, they found a good story: a feisty division commander exercising personal leadership in combat. DePuy earned his reputation as a fighting general, but there was also an undercurrent of negative opinion about him. His disquieting intensity—one of his men called him a "banty rooster"—got mixed reviews: unreserved admiration from some, fear and suspicion from others. Rumors among soldiers in combat about their leaders abound. After sex, food, and home, criticism of leadership occupies a high priority in the GI rumor mill. Generals are fair game. When DePuy became AVICE, his admirers and boosters included William C. Westmoreland, but the hard decisions inherent in his new job would neither win him friends nor change the views of his detractors.

The Office of the AVICE was itself contentious from its inception in 1967 to its disestablishment in 1974. Harold K. Johnson, Dutch Kerwin, and others had reservations about its very existence. It came into being on General Johnson's watch as Chief, but it was forced on him and the Army from the Secretariat side of the Pentagon because of McNamara's managerial revolution. Johnson's personal view was that it was "dangerous but necessary."[6] It was dangerous because it could usurp the functions of the principal staff officers. It was necessary because the civilian masters wanted the Army to speak clearly with one voice. The existence of the office ruffled feathers among the deputy chiefs of staff. And not just because of the AVICE "decrement exercises." There was also a sense among the deputies for the functional areas—personnel, logistics, operations, and so on—that they could become less relevant by the decisions of the AVICE. Johnson felt so strongly about it that as he was handing the Chief's baton to Westmoreland, he warned him of the dangers of the office. Johnson said that that warning was the only written tip he passed on to the new Chief. "I was delighted when General Abrams [later] wiped out the position." When the AVICE ceased to exist, Program Analysis and Evaluation (PA&E), which DePuy considered vital, was pulled out as a separate function, reporting directly to the Chief of Staff and the Secretary of the Army.

Johnson's reservations about the AVICE office were exacerbated by his personal skepticism about DePuy's aggressive leadership style. Johnson knew of Westmoreland's very high opinion of DePuy and was not cheered by that knowledge.

DePuy later explained how the AVICE came to be and why something like it was needed. Appointed by President Kennedy, Secretary of Defense McNamara came to his Washington job with management credentials from the Harvard Business School, from strategic bombing analysis in World War II, and, most recently, from running the Ford Motor Company. Schooled in operations research, systems analysis, and quantification, he believed in them. None of the Services could provide him and his DOD team the kind of data required for his management style, least of all the Army Staff. "When McNamara came into the Pentagon," DePuy said, "he brought with him people like Charley Hitch from the University of California and Alain Enthoven of systems analysis fame. These people brought with them the McNamara Management System, which was the five-year defense program, and the system of making changes to that program, and studies as to what those changes should be, and whether or not the changes were going to be cost-effective. All of this caused a revolution in the Pentagon. All of the Services were found wanting by Mr. McNamara."[7]

Two civilians taught the Army how to work with McNamara: Cyrus R. Vance and Stanley R. Resor. Each served first in the Department of the Army and later in the Defense Department. They established a small group of people who became, in the words of Ferdinand Chesarek (General, USA, Ret.), "a special information channel through the Secretary of the Army to Mr. McNamara." Their coaching and arm-twisting produced the staff organization that DePuy inherited from his predecessor as AVICE, Chesarek, in 1969.

Chesarek said Vance "directed the Army to establish a Force Planning and Analysis Agency . . . because Mr. Vance did not trust the Army to do it themselves."[8] The directive resulted in the 21 February 1966 establishment of the office then called Force Planning and Analysis Office (FPAO) to "integrate Army requirement for force structure, manpower, materiel, and readiness." It was to be the Army's point of contact with the Office of the Secretary of Defense (OSD), especially in the Southeast Asia (SEA) programming system.[9]

As a further demonstration of the DOD's lack of confidence in Army uniformed management, Chesarek said that Vance prescribed that the FPAO would be dual-managed by a civilian appointee from the OSD and a general. As Secretary of the Army "Vance was loath to accept Army Staff positions and recommendations." And when Vance became Deputy Secretary of Defense, "he carried this uneasiness with him." As AVICE, Chesarek said he spent six to eight hours a day in Vance's office. "My office, the AVICE's office, became, in effect, a joint Army Staff/Secretariat Staff." Apparently the need to get the Army on track with McNamara's methods caused this violation of another management principle: fixing responsibility in a single person.

McNamara intended to get things done his way via the civilian side of the Defense and Service staffs, even if, in the process, generals were to be sent to the principal's office like schoolboys in need of correction. That is the significance of this observation of DePuy's:

> When I became the AVICE, I worked 80 percent of the time for the Secretary and 20 percent for the Vice Chief, General Palmer, and the Chief, General Westmoreland. Four years later, I was proud to be able to say that I worked 80 percent of the time for the Chief and the Vice Chief, mostly for the Vice Chief, and 20 percent for the Secretary. In other words, as the AVICE office gained stature and confidence, the Secretary was willing to put [trust back in] the "green suit" [uniformed people], through the AVICE and the Vice Chief, [restoring] authority and responsibility which had been taken away from the Army Staff during the McNamara regime and for a long time thereafter.

DePuy credits the office of the AVICE for the restoration of "authority and responsibility" to the Army, but the fact is that it was DePuy himself who made the system work. His was the "green suit" that won the confidence of the civilian masters. DePuy called his shop a "four-legged organization." Four Directorates made up AVICE: Force Planning Analysis; Weapons Systems Analysis; Management Information Systems; and Coordinator of Army Studies.

DePuy regarded the Force Planning Analysis Directorate as "the most important part." It later became the Planning and Programming Analysis Directorate, the integrating component Vance insisted upon from the beginning, which would allow the Army to speak with a single voice and do business the McNamara way.

The Weapons Systems Analysis Directorate "supported the Vice Chief in his role as the Army's System Acquisition Review Council."

DePuy said that by giving the Vice Chief advice independent of the staff, this Directorate "was thoroughly disliked." DePuy took positions regarding weapons systems acquisition after consideration of recommendations from this Directorate. His decisions were bound to disappoint advocates of systems that "didn't make the cut." Some that did make the cut remained with him through his years at TRADOC. They were the so-called "Big Five" weapons systems: a tank, two helicopters, an infantry fighting vehicle, and an air defense weapons system. The "Big Five" would survive scrupulous review in the 1970s, be fielded in the early 1980s, fight in the 1990s, and continue in the field well into the twenty-first century.

The Management Information Systems Directorate "tried to standardize and regulate both computer hardware and software for the Army's business systems." Notice the word "tried." This was early in the information revolution as the various Army and DOD organizations and agencies accommodated to change at varying rates. Some lagged, while others adapted quickly. In the process, often the parts did not add up to a coherent whole. Veterans of this era will recall that computers were incompatible. At early stages of the information revolution, some parts of the Army could not talk to other parts of the Army.

The fourth leg of AVICE, the Studies Directorate, was headed by a succession of very bright and energetic colonels who led bright and energetic lieutenant colonels, many of them former members of the Social Science Department at West Point. Teacher DePuy's pet at one time was Colonel John Seigle (MG, USA, Ret.). DePuy knew Seigle as a cavalryman from Vietnam, so he qualified as a real soldier in DePuy's eyes; and Seigle's raw intelligence, creativity, and iconoclasm attracted DePuy. A social relationship grew. Discretion and self-effacement were not John Seigle's style. In fact, some generals in the Pentagon may have enjoyed strangling him. He was charmingly and intelligently outrageous. Bill DePuy Jr. said his father loved John Seigle. "He could do no wrong in my father's book."

DePuy specifically credits his Studies Directorate with doing the groundwork leading to the Officer Personnel Management System (OPMS). This system introduced a centralized system of command selection at battalion and brigade levels. Commanders were selected by boards in a process similar to promotion boards. Previously command selection was dependent upon the "old boy network." Higher commanders selected their subordinate commanders and key staff officers and recommended promising younger men to their peers. OPMS also provided for a number of specialist programs. The officer corps reacted variously to OPMS, some preferring the centralized system and some not. DePuy liked OPMS. He preferred the objective screening for command to the old boys network within which he had personally prospered.[10]

The Studies bunch had fun. They were given a free hand; they were doing interesting and important work; and they had a sense of being protected by Seigle, their immediate boss, and DePuy as they exercised initiative. Many officers assigned to the Pentagon hate the place. They work as drones in an uncongenial and windowless workplace, sometimes performing dull tasks for unimaginative bosses. Their ideals of Service on the Field of Honor fade into the humdrum reality of in-box/out-box, suspense dates, and graceless snack bars in an ugly building. Moreover, Washington is an expensive place to live, and driving there is torture. Upon reassignment from the Pentagon, most officers rejoice like small boys beginning summer vacation or men released from prison. But the Studies bunch had fun.

Anthony G. (Tony) Pokorny (Colonel, USA, Ret.), then a major, was recruited by John Seigle to the Studies Directorate for his models and simulations skills. He recalled, "We were more or less the 'overwatch' group for DePuy." Pokorny had earlier met and admired Colonel DePuy, who was battle group commander of a sister unit in Germany. He admitted to being a bit nervous about DePuy's reputation in Vietnam when he reported for work in the Pentagon. However, like so many of the men who worked for DePuy, he came to know the charisma, intelligence, and professionalism of his boss. "He led by example, always wanted to hear more . . . he digested your comments and made you feel that you were giving him something important."[11]

DePuy's young men were comfortable with their boss. They admired his rational and rigorous decision-making, and they enjoyed his company. They wanted to please him, and they knew that the way to do that was by thinking through projects and presenting them clearly. Pokorny saw another quality. He said, "Westmoreland was stiff and formal, and so normally he would act that way. But with DePuy he relaxed. I think that was because of trust." Pokorny was pleased to serve later as DePuy's Executive Officer at TRADOC.

DePuy made it clear to his aides and executive officers that their role was to be a staff officer who dealt with matters of substance, not personal services. After a year or so, a new major from the Leavenworth course would be brought in as an aide as his predecessor moved on to a staff section. Despite his lack of enthusiasm for Army schools, DePuy was determined to get his fair share of Leavenworth graduates—as he had been determined to get at least his fair share of helicopter and artillery support in Vietnam. Leavenworth was, at a minimum, a quality check, since only the upper half of a year group attended, and staff procedures were taught.

Anthony A. (Tony) Smith (BG, USA, Ret.), another former member of the Social Science Department at West Point, was also recruited by John Seigle. Smith worked in partnership with Colin Powell on a project that put him in close contact with DePuy. Smith also accompanied DePuy to the United Kingdom for a ten-day period during which DePuy lectured at five military academies. He said DePuy was "clearly in charge, directive, and [he] communicated a firm grasp of what he expected . . . but he was at the same time open to suggestion, approachable, and reasonable . . . willing to debate the views of his subordinates." Smith heard DePuy discourse on his leadership style in Vietnam and concludes that DePuy recognized that he risked unfairly evaluating an officer in the fast-moving climate of war, but that "accomplishing the mission in combat would always have to trump any desire to be scrupulously fair in personnel judgments arrived at quite quickly."[12]

Thomas Edgar Carpenter III (BG, USA, Ret.), also recruited by Seigle, recalled the brilliance of both Seigle and DePuy, who, because they were so bright, could intimidate people. Carpenter confirmed that Seigle enjoyed DePuy's complete backing, and he made an interesting and relevant observation. Carpenter believes that DePuy had an innate sense of timing that told him when an issue was "ripe" for a decision. He characterized the DePuy style this way: "quick grasp of an important issue; go right to the heart of the matter; marshal his facts; take on/drive through obstacles."[13]

Others familiar with his style agree that DePuy knew the right time for decision, adding that "he prepared the battlefield." That is, while he certainly recognized when the timing was "ripe," he also created the conditions that made it easy for his bosses to make the decisions DePuy wanted. He didn't take "losers" to his bosses, meaning proposals that he had not carefully refined and vetted in open and honest discussions designed to find flaws before decision time. And he didn't surprise those whose support he required. He briefed them one-on-one, accepting changes and improvements so that they had a stake in the outcome as coauthor of the initiative.

About DePuy's later TRADOC command, Carpenter said that DePuy's "focus of Army doctrine and training on the *threat* was his key contribution." DePuy took his army from the distraction of Vietnam back to the center ring and the main prize: Europe. Some of the pieces he would assemble as TRADOC Commander were already on the table while he was AVICE.

As AVICE, DePuy often found himself in other people's business, whether he or they liked it or not. And there wasn't much to like, he admitted, as "we managed the Army down from 1.6 million men to 800,000 in four years—a traumatic period. . . . The Army was cut in half very rapidly, and yet somehow it survived—barely, but it survived." He said that it survived "physically" by 1973, "and I think has now [in 1979] demonstrated that it has rebounded intellectually and from a morale standpoint."

Literally thousands of program decisions had to be made. The process was roughly like this. DePuy's Force Planning major general chaired a screening called the Program Guidance and Review Committee. Then a Select Committee, consisting of the lieutenant generals of the Army Staff, chaired by DePuy as AVICE, made the tough decisions. Typically they confronted "decrement exercises." That meant, for example, the Army would get $23 billion for a $25 billion budget. In cutting the $2 billion, said DePuy, "Every decision was unpopular."

"There was a proponent for everything," he recalled, "and each proponent felt that the decisions taken [to chop his pet project] were a mistake." If he was unable to get consensus, DePuy would take the issue up to the Vice Chief of Staff for decision. In the "last hectic days" of the program or budget cycle, it was often necessary to call in the program and budget people from the Staff to sit up all night in DePuy's office to "take this out, subtract that, reduce this, scratch that out. It was very arbitrary, but it had to be!" As a result, he knew, he was regarded "as high handed by many people, which led to a certain dissatisfaction with the AVICE idea on the part of the regular staff agencies." Years later, he acknowledged the understandably resentful attitude among the staff that ultimately led to the demise of the Office. "Decrement exercises" were the skunk at the lawn party. To some at the party, DePuy was the skunk.

He was unapologetic in his admission of mistakes: "I think if your batting average is anywhere near 80 percent, then you're probably doing very, very well indeed." Late in his life he made a similar remark to his son. Reflecting on his leadership and decision-making over his whole military career, he said he was wrong 20 percent of the time, adding, "That made me right about 80 percent of the time." He could accept that, but obviously DePuy did not win popularity contests by taking an ax to proponents' pet projects.

As AVICE, DePuy had enormous clout. Paul Miles, Westmoreland's 1969–1972 aide and speechwriter in the Pentagon, and later confidant and friend right up to Westmoreland's death in 2005, said that DePuy could get to see the Chief whenever he wanted to. Miles described the two doors to Westmoreland's office, one through which visitors were ushered and another, a kind of back door used by DePuy and Westmoreland's personal staff. Miles noted that even now, after thirty-five years, while he has forgotten many names— even those of the generals and principals then in the Pentagon—he could still rattle off the names of DePuy's lieutenant colonels and majors of the Studies team, suggesting their high visibility at the time. DePuy's inclination was to trust his proven young men. They did a good job for him; he permitted them to shine brightly in the presence of the movers and shakers. The same young men were regarded by some in the Pentagon, however, as unguided missiles.[14]

General "Dutch" Kerwin didn't want meddlers in his domain, but he bore DePuy no personal malice. In fact, he said some years later that he liked Bill DePuy, not least because they worked hand in glove with efficiency and great mutual respect when DePuy was the first TRADOC Commander and Kerwin the first FORSCOM Commander after the big Army reorganization of 1973. Kerwin, however, had professional objections from his time spent as Army DCSPER when DePuy was AVICE. He said that some of his responses to the Vice or the Chief on matters of substance were so edited that they were barely recognizable to Kerwin, their author, when he saw them again. Kerwin would write a memo to respond to one of his bosses or to initiate an action. He believes that his DCSPER action officers were often so influenced by DePuy's young men that they modified his responses so greatly that they no longer reflected Kerwin's intent. The problem, as Kerwin saw it, was that his papers from DCSPER went to the Vice (Palmer) via the AVICE (DePuy), giving the latter's minions an opportunity to modify or edit the original.[15]

Kerwin knew this sort of thing was happening in other functional areas as well. He recalled how he and a couple of his fellow lieutenant generals confronted the Vice, Bruce Palmer, one day in the Pentagon's General Officers' Mess. Essentially Kerwin told the Vice to "trust the Deputies or relieve us." The Deputies proposed that the AVICE office be done away with, and in due course, that's what happened—after DePuy vacated the position.

Despite attending the Armed Forces Staff College in the same class back in 1953, Kerwin and DePuy did not really know each other then. DePuy commuted from Washington, while Kerwin lived in Norfolk. Later, General Abrams told Kerwin, then his Chief of Staff in MACV, about DePuy's relieving people in his 1st Infantry Division, but the first substantive conversations Kerwin recalls having with DePuy took place in Saigon in March 1968, when they were trying to assess the meaning of the Tet offensive. Kerwin said, "It was obvious that when he came over with [Earle] Wheeler that he was on the Pentagon side . . . I thought we [the leadership in Saigon] had lost the battle before it even started."

About DePuy's working style, Kerwin said, "I found that although I disagreed with him, sometimes almost vociferously, he was easy to work with if you got to know Bill DePuy. Bill DePuy was just great. . . . At times he was a little crusty, but if you sat down with Bill and held your own and knew what the hell you were talking about, it was no problem." And, referring to their later association, he said, "The two of us got along tremendously at CONARC, TRADOC, and Forces Command."

William G. T. (Bill) Tuttle (Gen. USA, Ret.) was one of DePuy's bright young men who went on to four stars and high command while preserving his natural, modest manner. His close association with DePuy at high staff levels in Washington and Fort Monroe blends nicely with George Joulwan's association with DePuy at the tactical level, revealing DePuy as a man of action in the field and a reflective staff officer in the Pentagon. Tuttle's observations while preparing the Army reorganization, called STEADFAST, are worth giving in some detail, because they provide insight into DePuy's leadership style and—perhaps surprisingly for those who saw DePuy from afar—his warm personality.[16]

Tuttle was recruited by then-BG Robert G. (Bobby) Gard (LTG,

USA, Ret.) to work in ACSFOR on the Army Staff. Gard knew from earlier associations that "Tuttle was good at numbers." In due course, John Seigle made a deal and "kidnapped" Tuttle to work in Seigle's Coordinator of Army Studies (CAS) shop. Tuttle said that Bill DePuy pretty much accepted Seigle's judgment regarding personnel recruitment. There were about a dozen people in the Studies group, among them Max Thurman, Jack Bradshaw, Tom Carpenter, and Tony Smith. Tuttle said that "three four-star generals, several three-star generals" came out of that office, and "just about everybody made general." DePuy was a magnet for talent.

"What struck me first when I came in there," said Tuttle, "is the informal way that he [DePuy] almost dealt with you as a colleague. . . . He [was] a brilliant decisive questioner, so for folks who weren't in the team that came in to brief him, he saw through BS very quickly. He was very kind to people. He did not beat them up, but he would shred people's lack of logic, and it was embarrassing to them, but not at all brutal."

Tuttle said that there were people on the AVICE team that DePuy "tolerated," people that Tuttle "would have fired within two weeks." But he learned something very important from DePuy that would serve Tuttle well later in his career. DePuy would "once in a while, on a Friday afternoon, stroll around to CAS, and we would all go into John [Seigle]'s office and sort of gather for a martini. This is like 5:30–6:00 PM on a Friday, and just talk. He would tell stories . . . he just wanted to chat . . . regarding his philosophy of leadership."

DePuy made a sharp distinction between combat leadership and Pentagon duties. Knowing that some people in his office were "not contributing," he said, "they won't go any further [presumably meaning that he knew who they were and they would not become generals]. I can accept that. They have done a lot for the Army, and we must recognize that." And then he said, "Be kind." Treat them with dignity.

DePuy expanded this point in detail, indicating to his team that the ordinary types, seen as plodders by his gifted young men, had served in World War II, Korea, and Vietnam. They were decent, loyal, and dedicated to Service—and they were the majority of the officer corps, mediocrities, just as mediocrities are the majority in any large organization. DePuy's words, plus his behavior, made his meaning clear. Bright, bold, and energetic men would be entrusted with important and complex issues. Those less talented did the routine tasks that will always need doing. But we should not in any way denigrate those who served in our wars and did their best. Treat them with dignity. "Be kind."

Tuttle recalled a very similar message from George A. Lincoln (BG, USA, Ret.), longtime head of the Social Science Department at West Point and a man known to cultivate intellectual talent for the Army. The message was that not everyone can keep up with men like DePuy and Tuttle, the brightest guys in the Social Science Department, and the men in CAS. Tuttle said he later had a sign made that said simply, "Be kind." As he served with three and then four stars on his collar, he would point to the sign when a particularly energetic officer was denigrating some fool or being hypercritical of a poor soul who just couldn't keep up. The point is that not all Army officers are front-runners; the Army also needs dedicated plodders who can be counted on to do their best at routine and ordinary tasks.

Tuttle said that DePuy "hated yes-men." He wanted thinkers who had the guts to take a minority position because it was right. In fact, DePuy said it was an officer's duty to fix problems where they were found. Tuttle reports that from time to time he was asked by DePuy to sit in and take notes at meetings DePuy had with senior people. Then, after the meeting, DePuy would ask Major Tuttle what he thought of various positions or statements and listen attentively to the young man's opinions. His majors and lieutenant colonels were not mere recorders. They were expected to think above their pay grade, to be objective in analysis, and to be honest in clearly laying out their views, even when they ran counter to those of the boss. He insisted that decisions be based on logic and evidence crisply presented, rather than on the status, position, or rank of his source. Those who worked closely with him describe an approach he took to problem-solving that one of them called his hypothetical method. DePuy would ask, Why shouldn't I . . . ? What if . . . ? If this, then what? and expect the junior man to take on DePuy or other generals at the table. This method, and DePuy's one-on-one briefings of peers, would smoke out the weaknesses of a proposition. He wanted to know the flaws, address them, and fix them before he asked his bosses to make a decision on something he recommended. That is a partial explanation of his high success rate in getting things done his way. He did not tolerate half measures. He did not take unchallenged propositions or "losers" to his bosses.

Tuttle recognized that AVICE staffers were routinely on the turf of powerful men, often in Kerwin's business as "the personnel guy." "Dutch would really get upset with us and with Bill DePuy," said Tuttle. Similarly, General Forsythe's men from SAMVA were routinely involved in personnel matters as they tried to figure out how to man the Army when conscription was phased out. That was the job Westmoreland gave to George Forsythe. Overlap and conflict among staff sections were inevitable. DePuy would conduct his one-on-ones with the other lieutenant generals, the barons of the Army Staff, to minimize friction, but the fact is that the very nature of AVICE and SAMVA put DePuy and Forsythe in the functional areas of their brother generals, particularly in Kerwin's business. Staff officers further down the pecking order saw the bright and energetic young men of AVICE and SAMVA as poachers.

DePuy's modus operandi was discernible in his AVICE years and later when he commanded TRADOC. Tuttle said, "We just formed little teams, two or three folks, to do a particular thing." For example, DePuy would tell a major or LTC to see if something was broken, or ask one of his young men if the Army should buy a certain weapons system or a piece of equipment. He'd say something like: Tell me by Christmas if I want to buy Patriot. Keep me posted each Friday for five minutes. Get a couple of smart guys to work with you on this. But Christmas is go/no-go decision time. You tell me.

What Tuttle saw as his personal major effort and accomplishment while working for DePuy came after he had spent a few months on various AVICE projects, among them a new Officer Efficiency Report, ROTC issues, and automation. Then Army reorganization became Bill Tuttle's baby.

In September 1971, Seigle told Tuttle that DePuy wanted to look at the organization of the Army and determine what changes might be needed. He felt that, as the Army left Vietnam and was facing major force reductions, it was a good time to take a hard look at the entire organization. DePuy told Tuttle to study CONARC (Continental Army Command) and CDC (Combat Developments Command). Figure it out, he said, and get back to me by such-and-such a date.

Tuttle did just that in a three-page paper that Seigle took to DePuy, asking, Is this what you mean? The paper, recalled Tuttle, stated that CONARC was "overwhelmed" by so many things, and "stuff just wasn't getting done well." DePuy responded, Yeah, that's the idea. Then DePuy directed that the paper be destroyed. There would be no more papers. Tuttle said, "That was DePuy's wisdom."

From then on, Tuttle was in "intimate contact with DePuy" as he worked on the details of what became STEADFAST, a part of a major reorganization of the Army. It would carve two big organizations, Training and Doctrine Command (TRADOC) and Forces Command (FORSCOM), from a cumbersome Continental Army Command (CONARC). James S. V. (Jim) Edgar (COL, USA, Ret.) was Tuttle's partner in the effort. They met frequently with DePuy, using butcher chart paper and felt-tip pens to draft, edit, and re-draft organizational schemes that would affect the entire Army. The charts were locked up and out of sight until needed and dragged out for skull sessions, briefings, and challenges to their validity. No papers were circulated. DePuy dealt one-on-one with key people, doing necessary missionary work.

Tuttle called Vice Chief Bruce Palmer and AVICE DePuy "the co-conspirators," and said that Westmoreland had given them the go-ahead for *planning*. The generals, and all thinking officers, were deeply concerned with the many problems the Army faced as it came out of Vietnam. DePuy's reorganization plans honored General Westmoreland's pledge to revivify the Army, but Westmoreland would leave *decision and implementation* to his successor, Creighton Abrams. He didn't want to saddle Abrams with a setup he couldn't live with.

Abrams was nominated as Chief of Staff, Army (CSA) on 20 June 1972, and Westmoreland left office on 1 July. Abrams was confirmed by the Senate on 12 October and sworn in as Chief on 16 October. The unusually long delay in confirmation was caused by an investigation of violations of the rules of engagement regarding bombing in Vietnam. In brief, General John D. Lavelle, Commander, 7th Air Force, was fired, and General Abrams was confirmed. An unintended—and positive—consequence of the delay was the opportunity it gave Abrams to relax a bit after a series of demanding jobs, culminating in overall command in Vietnam. The delay also gave him time to study the proposed reorganization of the Army and to put his personal stamp on it. He scrupulously stayed out of running the day-to-day business of the Army before he was confirmed, leaving that to the acting Chief, Bruce Palmer, from July until October. Interestingly Westmoreland, Palmer, and Abrams were all members of the West Point class of 1936.[17]

The Army was a shambles. Protests against the war, draft resistance, combat refusals, indiscipline, drug and race issues in the Army and in society, and a chastened President who had retreated to Texas, refusing to run again for the Presidency, were signs of a conflicted society and a demoralized Army. Disarray pervaded the Army, and frustrated soldiers blamed the press, the politicians, or the Zeitgeist. The 1970 Army War College Professionalism Study, was, to the great credit of Army leadership at the time, briefed around the Army by hand-picked teams. It was a very damning document—of Army leadership![18]

The generals and all who loved the Army were particularly attentive to the study and deeply shaken by the source of the findings, the winners in the system: the students at the Army War College. This carefully selected leadership pool, from which Army generals are selected, pulled no punches. Leadership had let the Army down, particularly in the realm of ethics. That went directly to the Army officer's sense of honor. The very essence of his profession and self-image was questioned.

Tuttle said that the study pointed to "absolutely recognizable" deficiencies in leadership. "I saw a lot of that [ethical lapses and self-seeking] in the 9th Division. I had almost gotten out of the Army when I came out of Vietnam. I was so disgusted, but I got persuaded to stay on and help fix it. . . . I am glad I made that decision." It took more than juggling line-and-block charts to "help fix it," but recognition of problems and the need for reorganization were important components in the Army's renaissance, a revival that did take place and was later demonstrated by success in battle.

In his initial three-page paper for DePuy, Tuttle pointed to the need for "major changes in training and education and a whole new focus to re-professionalize the Army." He found DePuy ready and able to do just that. The DePuy method is all there. Here was the bright young guy: Tuttle, a major. The three pages demonstrated that the young man had the right stuff, the brains to figure it out, and the guts to put it all on the line. The concept was born. DePuy gave it his imprimatur, with the admonition that his staff write no papers, that they keep their ideas from the turf-protectors, the nay-sayers, and the timid. Then they asked the hard questions: What exactly is the problem? What is broken? And then what? Then they began to articulate the solutions. They reworked the butcher-paper charts;

they challenged all assumptions. The boss brought key guys into the picture in private chats and briefings, one senior officer or civilian official at a time. The battlefield was prepared thoroughly before he asked for a decision.

The Army fraternity can't keep a secret. Tuttle said that the CONARC Commander, General Ralph E. Haines, got wind of what was happening and came to the Pentagon to protect his command. Tuttle believed that the general took the proposed reorganization as a personal attack. It was not. CONARC simply had too many activities, some fifty-four by Tuttle's count. It was a beached whale. General Haines departed the Pentagon an unhappy four-star general.

DePuy did his missionary work with the other three-stars, one by one. Palmer was already in his corner. He had Westmoreland's support and access. Tuttle said, "DePuy was sort of first among equals . . . the others respected his intellectual capacity . . . he was a hell of a commander." He was as good a tactician in "the building" as he was with squads and platoons in the field.

Tuttle said DePuy was in the middle of all of it: the thinking about feedback loops connecting doctrine, weapons, and training; nurturing the Big Five weapons systems to be fielded in the mid-term future; recognition that CONARC was too big. (A joke among middle-grade officers at the time was that Fort Monroe was "the largest bird sanctuary in America"—a play on the number of "bird-colonels" assigned there.) DePuy had his sleeves rolled up, his attention focused on the substance and logic of the matter at hand, thinking things through with the majors and colonels. Tuttle admired "the brilliant bureaucratic stroke of not putting it on paper, making a series of studies . . . it was just a masterful thing I learned from that approach."

DePuy refused to gloss over the weaknesses of his going-in positions. If there was a logical glitch or flaw, he would send his guys back to the drawing board. He was rigorous and intellectually honest. His engagement was not an ego trip, but incisive questioning and a cool style may have been taken as coldness by those who did not know him well. He may have appeared to be all brain and no heart.

He was less concerned than most of us with being liked. He didn't need stroking and approval. How much this is genetic, how much is the High Plainsman's stoic accommodation to harsh reality, how much the experienced professional soldier's acceptance of the situation of the moment is hard to know. Tuttle said, "Socially, he was a very private person. His social interaction in the office was quite good, but I think there was a line drawn [that separated his professional from his personal life.]" Perhaps that's as much as we can know.

General Paul Gorman, despite having a close professional relationship with DePuy, found it difficult to fathom DePuy's feelings. Asked if their professional relationship became friendship, Gorman paused for a long time before stating that he did not know. Gorman could express his own feelings, but he was never sure of DePuy's. George Joulwan, on the other hand, absolutely revered DePuy and without reservation or pause said, "He was my friend."

There were no doubts or reservations about DePuy's marching to the drum of duty he heard so clearly. James G. Kalergis (LTG, USA, Ret.) was asked regarding reorganization of the Army, "What was driving General DePuy? Were there signals coming from Congress or elsewhere that we had to do this?" His response: "Bill DePuy isn't driven by anything. He is driven only by his own insights, and as to those outside pressures, they are meaningless as far as he was concerned." He heard the drum and marched. The others could catch up.[19]

Kalergis, who spent hours daily with Abrams to brief the incoming Chief on the reorganization, confessed, "I had periods of depression. I would see the Chief was getting a little bit up tight. Bill DePuy would go in there and put things back in focus again."

Kalergis was asked if General Westmoreland initiated the reorganization. We know that Westmoreland wanted to revivify the Army, but Kalergis responded, "Bill DePuy initiated it. Let's keep the record straight. Bill DePuy was the guy that was able to conceptualize something like this. This is very important. The visualization just had to be done. And by God, if they do an oral history up here [at MHI or the Army War College at Carlisle Barracks], somebody better be doing one on Bill DePuy . . . because of the tremendous impact this man has had on the Army. He had the imagination, initiative and the vision to see where the Army should be going. He could lay it out." And he could instill confidence.

The way the reorganization was briefed to Secretary of Defense Elliot Lee Richardson by Secretary of the Army Robert Froelke had DePuy's stamp on it. Kalergis recalled, "The Secretary of the Army said, 'Here is what the Army is going to do.' You can bet your bottom dollar, they [DOD] didn't like that. They wanted to have a say in it."

Tuttle said that his ideas about logistics were completely compatible with DePuy's. He related a story DePuy had told him. In June 1944 in Normandy, DePuy needed to duck into a place to get some food and to spend the night. He found himself in an engineers' compound. DePuy asked what their mission was, and they said, "to support the Quartermaster depot." Later, at the QM depot, he asked what their mission was. They said, "to support the engineers." That made a deep impression on DePuy. Tuttle said of his own experience in Vietnam, "We didn't need all that stuff in Long Binh [a very large logistics compound near Saigon] and all that stuff coming down the road and getting ambushed." He was convinced that one or two C-5 aircraft plus petroleum, oil, and lubricants (POL) on the Mekong River could have kept the 9th Division supplied. In other words, a lot of the logistics troops in Vietnam were supporting logistics troops who were supporting more logistics troops. DePuy and Tuttle agreed that logistics should be a flexible hose to be aimed so that the business end supports the soldiers actually doing the fighting.

Under DePuy Tuttle also learned that a great idea would die on the bureaucratic vine if the change agent didn't think through the tactics of selling it. When Tuttle, as a four-star commander, considered the unthinkable—he wanted to reduce his large and complex Army Material Command (AMC) of some 111,000 by half—he recalled DePuy's techniques. What's the problem? Conceptualize. Refine. Study. Refine. Go one-on-one with key people. Learn the objections. Address them. Study. Refine. Do most of your missionary work behind the scenes. Then lay out your irrefutable plan to the approving authority.

Tuttle also learned that a sound idea in Washington—Base Realignment and Closure (BRAC) is a perfect example—looks different and less attractive to the congressional delegation from Maine, if closing a Kittery shipbuilding facility is the issue, or to the Michigan delegation, if reducing DOD facilities in Detroit is the issue. "I learned a lot from DePuy," said Tuttle. "I was willing to take it on [the issue of AMC reduction, jobs lost, congressional interest] because of the experience of STEADFAST. This is not going to sell, but it will be an idea that is planted for a generation . . . and has got to happen."

Tuttle learned some lessons in tactics and maneuver in bureaucracy, but he also learned from DePuy that some corrections that are doomed to short-term failure nevertheless must be attempted, because it is the right thing to do. That's why military officers take oaths. In the end, good senior officers are a composite, bits of Machiavelli and chunks of Don Quijote.

Tuttle was personally close to Max Thurman, another DePuy star pupil. "Max sort of inherited DePuy's leadership of a bunch of us," Tuttle recalled. Thurman also used DePuy techniques. He once called Tuttle and told him to fly with him on an executive aircraft to Alaska. Tuttle had no business in Alaska, but Max wanted to talk to him. "This is when he told me I am going to take AMC [a four-star billet]. So I went through another DePuy-type mentoring session." This story is a replica of an airborne session DePuy had with Thurman when Thurman was his resource person at TRA-DOC.[20] DePuy was keenly aware that the selection and grooming of talent for the successor generation of leaders was another duty of a general officer, and that it was essential to the future of his Army. The number of officers who once worked for DePuy and went to the top of the heap suggests he was successful as a tutor and mentor.

DePuy considered his AVICE years "an important period in the history of the General Staff. The Secretary [of the Army] was making the program decisions for the Army and was using the AVICE as his instrument and channel into the Army. . . . I came out of that assignment fairly well educated in the techniques of program management, and to this day [1979] I am an ardent and enthusiastic believer in program management as the way to go for any large organization." He called program management the antithesis of budget management and the opposite of General Staff management "of the old kind." Budget management for Army funding was rather like the allowance a parent gives to a child: here's your money; spend it as you wish. Sound management had to be far more interactive than that. General Staff management "of the old kind" tasked a staff officer to study a specific issue and come up with the optimal solution and recommendation for action *without careful analysis and due regard for how the part studied affected the system as a whole.* Sound management needed something better than tunnel vision.

DePuy was a firm believer in testing, measuring, and quantifying wherever possible. Working a solution to a specific problem, he never lost sight of the Army as an integrated system, a whole with many parts, a dynamic organization with feedback loops. Simple linear thinking, in which the analyst describes all processes as a simple one, two, three march to solution—without recognition that step three may affect steps one and two, even as it proceeds to step four—is much too simple. It does not show the world as it is. DePuy's belief in the utility of program management served him and the Army well.

Busy in his job as AVICE and in the final phase of the Army's 1973 major reorganization, DePuy was personally involved in the trial of Daniel Ellsberg, who leaked classified documents that led to the Watergate break-in and the resignation of President Richard M. Nixon. Ellsberg, a national security analyst and originally a strong supporter of the war in Vietnam, turned against the war and gave documents to the *New York Times* that became known as "the Pentagon Papers." Assembled on the order of Secretary of Defense Robert McNamara in 1967, the Pentagon Papers provided a detailed and massive record of the war. The *Times* published the papers beginning on 13 June 1971.

DePuy was involved because he was the primary author of Westmoreland's portion of the *Report on the War in Vietnam* (1964–1968) and of Wheeler's 1968 report to the president regarding the post-Tet situation in Vietnam, both of which were among the Pentagon Papers. In January 1973, DePuy was a witness for the prosecution in the trial of Daniel Ellsberg and his co-defendant, Anthony J. Russo, in Los Angeles. He testified regarding the defense allegation that what Ellsberg had revealed did not aid the enemy. The prosecution contended it did. Both DePuy and Paul Gorman testified that the information was useful to the enemy, but their testimony became moot when the case was dismissed because the government had tampered with evidence.

Of course the real issue at trial was the war in Vietnam itself. The papers exposed internal debates regarding policy that affected the reputations of the senior players in government. A thread ran from the Pentagon Papers to the "White House plumbers," who broke into the office of Ellsberg's psychiatrist in California to obtain information to discredit Ellsberg. They also broke into an office in a building in Washington called Watergate. The resulting investigations ultimately led to the resignation of President Richard M. Nixon on 9 August 1974. [21]

The establishment of TRADOC on 1 July 1973 was part of what has been called "one of the most sweeping reorganizations of the U.S. Army in the continental U.S. since the general reorganization of 1942 when the Army Ground Forces, Army Service Forces, and Army Air Forces were established."[22] DePuy was the major player in the creation of TRADOC and its first commander, appointed by General Abrams.

15

TRADOC Commander
The Army's Road Back

I am utterly convinced that the lesser man has been rewarded.
—DePuy, letter to Richard Stilwell as DePuy
was promoted and assumed command of TRADOC

You know, I consider this to be my life's work.
—DePuy, as TRADOC Commander, to Sam Wilder

On 7 June 1973, just three weeks before taking command of Training and Doctrine Command and four months before the Yom Kippur War, DePuy told a Fort Polk audience of infantry trainers that in World War II "we were an ill-trained rabble compared to what we have in the U.S. Army today." But now, he said, the training in the professional Army had to produce units five times as good as the enemy. Because U.S. and Red Army equipment was roughly equal, the key was training. Even as DePuy was about to pin on his fourth star, his message was that preparing for war is about producing "infantry squads and platoons to do the mission of the Army, to fight."[1]

The lethality of the Yom Kippur War convinced him that the next war would be a deadly come-as-you-are affair requiring the United States to win the first battle while fighting outnumbered. He would use the Yom Kippur War as leverage to get the resources he believed to be essential to the revitalization of the Army. When DePuy retired four years later, his Army was on its way to becoming a harmonized system of systems ready to fight.

Army Chief of Staff Creighton Abrams did not know DePuy before they began to have regular contact in 1972. He had reservations about DePuy, based upon hearsay, but it wasn't long before DePuy won his confidence. Abrams told Bruce Palmer that DePuy's papers were the best he had ever seen; that DePuy's anticipation of issues was unmatched; that in almost every case DePuy was way out ahead of everyone. So when it was time for Abrams to find the right men for big jobs at a critical time of need, he chose Bill DePuy for Training and Doctrine Command (TRADOC) and Dutch Kerwin for Forces Command (FORSCOM).[2]

Abrams made the assignments in his usual direct manner. He called Kerwin in and told him what he was going to do. Kerwin was going to CONARC as a "special assistant" to the incumbent, General Ralph E. Haines. Kerwin would then become CONARC Commander with DePuy as his Deputy. Next, CONARC would be disestablished, as Kerwin took FORSCOM and DePuy took TRA-DOC. Abrams looked at Kerwin and asked, Do you object to that? Kerwin did not. Abrams may have heard that DePuy was a difficult person or that there was bad blood between Kerwin and DePuy. Kerwin had made clear to Palmer his feelings about the AVICE office. But Kerwin was emphatic in dispelling any notion that he bore personal malice. He regarded DePuy as an exceptional professional and would later describe the 1973 transition "the best turnover."

Abrams knew Kerwin. Kerwin, an artilleryman, got command of the 3rd Armored Division in Europe because Abrams, when Vice, made it happen by talking to Harold K. Johnson, then Chief. Kerwin later said that giving that division to an artilleryman was a departure from previous practice. "It was the cause of great heartburn to all the armor officers who thought that the division belonged to them," he said. Kerwin did well in that command and was later Abrams' chief of staff in Vietnam.

Not all relations among the general officers were amicable. Kerwin believed that the reduction of the Army in the 1970s was badly done. About thirty-five or forty general officers were asked to leave as part of the drawdown, among them General Haines, the CONARC Commander, and his three-star deputy. Haines blamed Kerwin, the DCSPER, but Kerwin contended that his part of the action was "the pick and shovel work of managing general officers," not the decision of which generals had to go. Haines was sufficiently angry that he told Kerwin, who had been designated as his "special assistant" in November 1972 and had already been named as his successor, "not to come down" to Fort Monroe. So, when Kerwin left his DCSPER job, he spent his time visiting CONARC units in the field until Haines left Fort Monroe.[3]

For a very brief time, Kerwin was commander of three four-star organizations: CONARC, FORSCOM, and TRADOC. But, he says, "that was just a paper shuffle," an administrative oddity as the commands were legally sorted out.

When Donn A. Starry told Abrams that the Army was on its ass, Abrams responded, "OK. Where do we fix it?" Starry said, "We start with initial entry training [and then on] to recruiting and training individual soldiers and units, fixing the NCO corps, and training officers." Improved training was a top priority. Abrams told Starry to get to Fort Knox and start fixing armor. When Starry responded that someone else had been named to command Knox, adding that he'd rather command an armored division, Abrams said, "I know that. But I just told you that you're going to Knox."[4]

In Don Starry, DePuy would have an active subordinate commander at Knox who was intelligent and skilled. He was also independent, acerbic, and fully prepared to tell his boss when he disagreed. In DePuy's hierarchy of values, Starry's effectiveness trumped his inclination to stubborn independence. The U.S. Army would benefit enormously from their collaboration.

DePuy knew that CONARC had been a loose confederation inclined to pass problems from the field to the Pentagon. Bill Tuttle's initial three-page paper on reorganization had highlighted that defect. How could TRADOC headquarters at Fort Monroe, Virginia, control twenty major installations, among them sixteen branch schools, four specialist schools, and all of the ROTC detachments, and at the same time select among major weapons systems, comprehend hundreds of programs, and make thousands of decisions? DePuy's short answer was good people, sound management, and a method to control the installations and activities spread around the United States. Getting control of the floundering bureaucracy was one of the keys to TRADOC's success.

While planning and organizing the management of his far-flung empire, DePuy had three priority outcomes in mind: a revolution in training; clear expression of doctrine; and the integration and pacing of training and doctrine with combat developments. The organization he developed would manage a system of systems in which soldiers, tactics, and weapons were synchronized.

The human mind seeks a path from chaos to order. Perhaps that's why we so readily accept black/white distinctions, linear reasoning, and simple solutions, even when we know better. And we prefer to deal with problems one by one, even as the world comes at us in a rush of simultaneous events. DePuy thrived on complexity, simultaneity, and sorting things out. It was his habit of mind to seek the essence of an issue before chasing off to fix its parts, and he was unusually comfortable with indeterminacy even as he sought clarity.

When the Yom Kippur War broke out in October 1973, DePuy saw opportunity disguised as distraction. He said later that the war was "the most fortunate thing for us because it dramatized the difference between the wars that we might fight in the future and the wars we had fought in the past. And it drew our attention to those differences and to the current state of affairs in the U.S. Army. We became concerned first of all that we missed one generation of modernization during the Vietnam War, and the Russians were one to two generations of equipment ahead of us."[5]

The lethality of the 1973 war conjured images of a U.S. Army in Europe consumed in days of combat; DePuy was quick to realize that his nascent TRADOC plans could be brought to rapid fruition using the Yom Kippur War as leverage.

Concentrating on three big outcomes—a revolution in training, bringing combat developments back from the futuristic to the nearer term, and taking doctrine from the abstract to a "how to fight" series of notebooks—made DePuy's watch at TRADOC an extraordinarily busy time. DePuy founded and energized TRADOC as the Army became a volunteer force with the attendant issues of recruiting and retaining soldiers at the very time that the status and prestige of the Army, and morale in the Army, were at a low point. In addition, gender issues surfaced at this time, as women entered the military in career fields previously closed to them. That, in turn, opened the door to consideration of the Army as an instrument to cure the nation's social ills. In the 1950s the Army had led the way in racial integration. In the 1970s, gender issues moved front and center, as did the hope that the Army could transform the low performers among American youth into useful and productive American soldiers and citizens. All of these issues and more landed on DePuy's desk, since initial training, schools, ROTC, and skills courses all came under TRADOC.

DePuy had a friendly relationship with his Command Historian, Dr. Brooks Kleber. The gentle scholar and the general were on the beaches of Normandy as junior officers in the 90th Infantry Division in June 1944, although they did not know each other at the time. Kleber was captured and spent almost a year as a prisoner of war. He loved the Army and history, and DePuy knew it. On 23 May 1977, they sat for the last of several formal interviews as DePuy summed up his thoughts about TRADOC before he retired on 1 July 1977.[6]

Kleber began by saying he would like to hear about DePuy's four years at TRADOC. He mentioned such accomplishments as the development of Field Manual (FM) 100–5, the institution of total systems management, improvements in training, and liaison with the Germans. Finally, Kleber asked DePuy what he regarded as his greatest achievement as the first TRADOC Commander.

"Now that I am sort of at the end of the thing," said DePuy, "what I am impressed with is that it all seems to come together in a unified relationship, and I guess that the most illustrative aspect of that is the TRADOC systems manager system." But, he added, "We weren't really smart enough to see the end of the road when we started out. I would have to admit that the integration of all of this has only become apparent to us as we have gone along." The building blocks each seemed important in their own right at the time they were doing them. "But as time has gone on, they all seem to have begun to fit together, I think it's safe to say, in getting the Army ready to fight the next war."

It would have been easy in 1977, in what must have been a moment of enormous personal satisfaction as DePuy reviewed the considerable accomplishments of the previous four years, to say: Yes. It worked out just about the way I planned it in 1972–1973. But that would have been self-serving and untrue. It was only after the fact that the multitude of decisions and actions over four years took on the appearance of something designed whole from the beginning. DePuy was also quick to point out that "the combat development part of it," not included in Kleber's initial framing of his question, needed to be considered.

Before describing accomplishments affecting the entire Army, DePuy first turned to a process, a way of getting things done within TRADOC that was commonly called the "contract system." The acronym for its formal name was PRM, for Program Review Memorandum, and later it was more accurately, if more awkwardly, called Program Analysis and Resource Review. DePuy said that Max Thurman was his "guardian of program management," which is what the contract system was—program management. Before fixing the Army, DePuy had to fix his organization, which was scattered to hell and back. Failure at management had undone CONARC.

Maxwell Thurman's (GEN, USA, Ret.) professional life suggests a small boy taking tremendous pleasure in working a gift puzzle he got for Christmas. Thurman's gift puzzle was making the Army work. And he loved to stir the pot. In his Army War College presentations he delighted in calling the AWC "this hotbed of tranquillity," jabbing at students and faculty who were enjoying bucolic Carlisle, Pennsylvania, while he held the fort on the Potomac. Thurman graduated from the AWC in 1970 and then worked for DePuy for three years in the office of the AVICE, spending, he said, "the last five months in my tour working for DePuy in organizing what would become TRADOC." It was at that time that DePuy told him to get the twenty smartest colonels, the twenty smartest lieutenant colonels, and the twenty smartest majors in the Army. "DePuy's theory was, give me them and we can handle the work of the other 100,000 in TRADOC."[7]

After commanding the Division Artillery of the 82d Airborne Division, Thurman was made brigadier general. In March 1975 he was back with DePuy as TRADOC, DCS-RM (Deputy Chief of Staff–Resource Manager). Thurman called himself DePuy's "bag man" and enjoyed describing just how the contract system worked.

When the bag man made a resource pronouncement, everyone knew it had DePuy's blessing. Thurman declines taking credit for the creativity, innovations, and accomplishments of Paul Gorman and his "twenty or thirty really hot-shot guys" brought with him to TRADOC from the Combined Arms Training Board at Fort Benning. John Seigle, by then a BG, was one of them. "Paul Gorman was enormously gifted," said Thurman. So were many of the others who worked for DePuy. Thurman found the smartest guys in the Army when TRADOC existed only on paper. Then he had the pleasure of working with them and for a boss he revered.

Thurman said that DePuy would put several people on an aircraft to discuss bright ideas with him as he flew on TRADOC business. After hearing a Gorman scheme he liked, "He would turn to me and say, 'OK. Make it happen for Paul. Find the money.' I would find it and clean up the loose ends."

In one instance, General John H. Cushman, Commanding General at Fort Leavenworth, arrived three hours late for a meeting. "I was the guy doing the briefing," Thurman recalled,

> and I said, "Well sir, we just finished the school model. Leavenworth got 250 spaces, and you are a day late and a dollar short." For a brigadier general to talk to a [senior] general like that was uncommon. But it was the brashness of it all. I had the authority from the boss to go run the business. He told me to go get a bunch of spaces. We went out and carved it out. I was sort of the hatchet and bag man. DePuy told me to set [it] up. I set up a contract with each of the commanders of the TRADOC posts, camps, and stations. I said, "Look, we want you to do X number of SQTs [Skill Qualifying Tests], Y number of ARTEPs [Army Training and Evaluation Programs], and Z number of training manuals, and whatever else. Here is the money you will have to do it with. Sign the contract." Then DePuy went out and signed all those contracts. We had an adjudication session between the two-star commanders and the four-star commander . . . then DePuy got out of their way. He said, "I don't want to hear anything unless you have a major problem such as a hurricane or a tornado which comes along and takes the roofs off all your facilities."

Resources were matched to tasks. If tasks were added or deleted, resources increased or decreased. But responsibility was the installation or school commander's. Thurman explained in concrete terms what DePuy and he meant by centralized management and decentralized operations.

> I was treated very well by the post, camp, and station commanders because they knew if I said, "You don't get a dollar, you don't get it; and if you do get it, you do get it." We got a tremendous amount of leverage on the money in the command . . . it sounds pedestrian as hell. . . . Fort Benning was charging TRADOC about three million dollars annually for running the laundry. I looked at that and said, Listen, laundry is a reimbursable expense. They take it out of a soldier's pay to get his laundry done. So I go down there and talk to the post commander. I am a brigadier general and he is

a senior guy, [Major] General Tarpley. I say, "We are going to dock your accounts this year three million dollars for the post laundry." He said, "Like hell you are." So fisticuffs ensue; we took out the three million dollars at Fort Benning. That three million was keeping Benning in the manner to which it had become accustomed, which was to look spiffy. The resource manager down there never forgot my name.

Thurman manipulated the money within the command "to put it behind the training things that we were trying to do. But Paul Gorman was behind getting the systems approach to training organized. My task was finding the money. That was the division of labor between the two of us." Thurman literally robbed Peter to pay Paul. The management methods of the contract system, as executed by Thurman, can be paraphrased: Sir, your purse or your life.

As DePuy reconstructed for Kleber what had been accomplished in four years, he encountered the challenge of any narrative: simultaneity. He said that in explaining the accomplishments it is difficult to avoid giving the false impression that each "building block" was completed before the next was begun. That's not the way it happened. DePuy set out to address combat developments first, but Gorman arrived on the scene with training methods and the means to test and measure them that DePuy found absolutely fascinating and just what the doctor ordered—now! And the 1973 Israeli War underlined the need to provide doctrine for how to fight combined arms—now! The urgent need for each of the building blocks goes a long way in explaining how they overlapped and DePuy's impatience with delay anywhere in his command. A window of opportunity had opened, and he was prepared to drag his Army through it—now!

He said that it all "started out with the very simple process of putting the agencies [combat developments and doctrine] back into the schools . . . that was one of the main objectives of the STEADFAST reorganization." What followed in his summing up reveals an intelligence naturally inclined to integrate what lesser minds see as separate bits and pieces. "The second thing is that we had to establish, or at least rearrange and reinforce, the integrating centers at Leavenworth [combined combat arms], Lee [logistics], and Ben Harrison [administration] and establish the relationship of the integrating centers with the schools, and then we had to address the testing and analytical problems."

Testing and evaluation was applied to *systems:* command, control, communications, tactical systems, and integration of intelligence and electronic warfare (EW). Testing was also applied to *individual soldier skills* in all branches and at all levels, from incoming recruits through senior NCOs. An NCO educational system had to be designed and installed, something like the schools for officers at several levels. And officer training, particularly at the platoon level, had to *prepare tank and platoon leaders, not generic officers.* Testing and evaluation of combined arms systems presented challenges not found in solving, for example, outer space problems, many of which might be addressed mathematically. Infantry and armor soldiers operate in the "dirty environment" of terrain, smoke, night, and enemy, a combination of variables difficult to replicate with the precision possible in a laboratory. Close combat is messy. DePuy wished to bring order to chaos, to the extent that it was possible.

The "programs" approach DePuy had learned in 1962–1963 and mastered as AVICE in 1969–1973 was of use to him as he turned to major weapons development in the Army. As he put it, "we have got to show by the test evaluation and analysis, including cost analysis, that the new weapons systems are sufficiently better than the old weapons system to justify the differential in cost." To do that required a process DePuy described as an "inexorable, demanding, repeating, repetitious management problem."

The process began with working with engineers and scientists to arrive at technical opportunities for improvement. This was usually the first step. "Based on early promise," explained DePuy, "we proceed. As it takes shape, exactly what it looks like is less important than what it can do: how far, accurately, and with what effects at the other end. Then test and evaluation of technical results and reconsideration of cost effectiveness." If the system doesn't pass muster, "we are responsible for blowing the whistle on it and telling our masters in Department of Army that it either ought to be fixed, modified, or discontinued." Each system was tested at least "three times, analyzed three times, reviewed three times, and maybe modified many more times," and the larger systems were further reviewed later in the Pentagon, both at the Department of the Army (DA) and the Office of the Secretary of Defense (OSD). DePuy called it "a very big business and expensive business, bureaucratic, frustrating business, because there are so many levels of review. The congressional staffers, GAO [Government Accounting Office], OMB [Office of Management and Budget], the whole Washington gaggle of agencies become involved. . . . So it's just kind of a running gun fight to get any system developed and through the review process." By 1977 DePuy could say, "In all of that, of course, TRADOC and its combat development machinery play a very central role." Six thousand people were involved in the "bureaucratic, frustrating business," he said, "with thirty to forty major systems under development at all times and literally hundreds of little systems."

It became apparent to DePuy that to test and evaluate systems and equipment, realistic tactical scenarios were needed. The concept was to have a library of scenarios that would allow a soldier or engineer to pull out a scenario, and then explode or zoom in to test the idea or equipment, for example, using an old tank and the new tank. There were three or four NATO/Warsaw Pact scenarios, a couple for war in the Middle East, one for Korea, one for Southeast Asia, jungle scenarios, and plans for Panama and Alaska. They were constructed at the Combined Arms Center at Fort Leavenworth and supported by the integrated Logistics Center, the Administration Center, and relevant schools.

The scenarios, DePuy said, were "plausible, logical, accepted." They highlighted issues of tactics, doctrine, and the publication of the "how to fight" manuals. Equipment development, training, and doctrine were connected at every step of the way. Obviously, the projects briefly described here were enormously labor intensive. And combat developments was just one ring in the (at least) three-ring TRADOC circus of tasks—combat developments, training, and doctrine—that DePuy orchestrated. The internal management of the organization, via the contract system, was constantly used and improved.

The point was to get the Army ready to fight the next war. As TRADOC Commander, DePuy had an influence that pervaded the entire Army. And when General Abrams died in office as the Chief, Fred Weyand succeeded him. Thus, the men at the top of the Army were DePuy's peers. This increased his clout with men he knew and trusted as he pressed for objectives already clear to him.

In a conversation in Vietnam, Weyand and DePuy had noted a decline in the quality of NCO leadership from 1966 to 1967. Weyand said, "Out of that experience grew both Bill's and my determination that if we ever got in a position of authority back in the Pentagon, we would establish some sort of formal education system for NCOs."[8] They were not alone in this conviction, but by the 1970s they were in a position to address the issue as four-star generals. In January 1973 a design for the Enlisted Personnel Management System (EPMS) was agreed to, and by 1975 the NCO Educational System (NCOES) was in place.

DePuy's attention to NCO leadership was demonstrated throughout his career. In a 1976 interview he sketched the place of the NCO in his Army's history. "In 1939," he said, "the last professional Army we had, because it [the Army] was so tiny, the NCO ran the Army." In the late 1950s and early 1960s, "the NCO Corps was approaching the role it should play in a good Army," and it led well early in the Vietnam War. "We then consumed that NCO Corps in Vietnam. It was either wounded, killed, or exhausted." Because the Army of the late 1960s and early 1970s was on the defensive, officers attempting to put out the fires of protest dealt directly with young soldiers in various councils. "So this left the NCO out in left field. . . . Now [in 1976] we're trying to get it back."

DePuy believed that the Soldiers Manual and the Skill Qualification Test gave the NCO, the first-line supervisor, an essential tool. "You don't get anywhere until you have a clear, simple concept that can be explained and understood." Consistent with his view that "officers command units and NCOs command soldiers," the NCO had a tool analogous to what the architect and engineer on a construction project give the foreman: the blueprints. In 1976 he was optimistic that the Army NCO was on the right track.[9]

In Paul Gorman DePuy found an intellectual peer who shared his pragmatic approach to training and a determination to get things done. DePuy didn't need to convince Gorman of the need for training and leadership. Gorman (USMA 1950) shared with DePuy recollections of the truly bad leadership he experienced in his initial assignments, first in the 82d Airborne Division, an "elite" outfit, and then in a rifle company in the Korean War. And one needn't return to 1944 or 1950 to find poor leadership. His battalion in DePuy's division in Vietnam lacked professional leadership when Gorman took command in 1966. He found a dispirited and directionless shambles.[10] Of his many accomplishments in a distinguished career, the post-Vietnam revolution in training is Gorman's greatest legacy.

Bill DePuy gives Gorman credit for the vast improvement in

training from the middle 1970s. But Gorman says that neither the training revolution, nor the rationalization of combat developments, nor the swift production of the "how to fight" manuals spelling out revised doctrine would have happened as they did without DePuy. Gorman called DePuy the indispensable "enabler." He chose his words very carefully. Gorman believes that no other single person could have done what DePuy did. Gorman enhanced DePuy's teaching at the individual and small-unit levels with analytical tools and methods new to DePuy. The usually cool and seemingly detached DePuy embraced Gorman's methods with an enthusiasm approaching joy. They formed a team that accomplished in a few years what otherwise might have taken a generation, and they set the course for the Army that has been followed well into the twenty-first century.

CONARC had run the training centers with an iron hand from the center. There was no flexibility and no sense of responsibility for programs of instruction *expressed in numbers of hours* dictated from on high. In current management jargon, the school commanders had no stake in the process. Early on, DePuy sent a letter to his training center and school commanders describing how in a rustic French home a stew was always simmering on the stove. As family members passed the stove, each put something in the simmering pot, adding flavor and substance to improve the stew and feed the family. DePuy said that he expected the school commanders to put something in the TRADOC pot.[11]

When his generals were unresponsive to his broad invitation, DePuy was not shy about speaking in plain language. He said: Don't be dumb. Don't tolerate dumb answers. When a trainer is asked why something is being done, "because it is in the POI [program of instruction]" is the wrong answer. Don't do anything illogical, irrelevant, or stupid, and don't permit your sergeants to do anything dumb. Training must be purposeful. "Things that don't make sense should be quickly abandoned."

Nor did he hesitate to take pen in hand to scrawl biting critiques on the "homework" of his generals. In a letter to the Commander of the Infantry School, DePuy wrote these comments on a paper that DePuy had assigned him to write for an Anti-Armor Training Circular: "It is nowhere near ready for coordination, let alone publication. It is repetitious, discursive, hard to follow—in short, badly organized. . . . Nowhere do I find a clear simple concept of anti-armor tactics. It must *not* go out to FORSCOM or Europe. . . . It would be hard to imagine a worse way to start." There was a double underline under the word *not*. Instead of "Bill," which he used as a signature on communications to his generals, he signed this "D."[12]

These letters, the contract system as described by Max Thurman, and DePuy's body language communicated this message to his subordinate commanders, major generals: I will set the direction and provide resources commensurate to your mission and tasks. You will use initiative to get the job done in a decentralized fashion. Call me in the event that hurricanes and tornadoes rip off the roof of your headquarters. Get with it! Do it now!

DePuy and Gorman addressed the training deficiencies they had experienced in their respective careers. They called the 1942 or 1952 method "on the trail" training because, to them, it used methods akin to cowboys herding cattle by shouting and prodding. This was the method of mass mobilization training as civilians went through *time-oriented training* to ready them for war. The rookie soldier began from a zero base. He would have so many hours of instruction in various subjects—the M-1 rifle, first aid, gas chamber, and so on—whether he learned the lesson or not. The unit would do so many hours, or exercises, from squad through division before being stamped "ready," regardless of the likelihood that at the end of the prescribed hours the soldiers were at various levels of skills, and regardless of what they actually knew. It was time to change that. DePuy believed that by making the major generals who were running those schools and training centers responsible, and by providing them with the means to conduct *performance-oriented training,* "We turned the whole situation around."[13]

He praised "Gorman's apostles and disciples." Max Thurman called the same people "Gorman's little gang" brought from Fort Benning to TRADOC to teach the Army performance-oriented training. DePuy confessed that it took him time to digest the logic and benefit of what Paul Gorman was doing. Soldiers' Manuals and Skill Qualifier Tests (SQTs) were painstakingly thought through, identified, listed, and disseminated to the whole Army. The tasks an infantry soldier was expected to perform were spelled out in detail so that they could be taught and measured. The soldier moved to the next sequential task only after he had demonstrated competence at the basic level. The task was set to a standard to be achieved under varying conditions. The SQT of the fire team leader was established; then that of the squad leader's; then that of the platoon sergeant's.

Detailed SQTs were established for members of the tank crew, the maintenance people, the various artillery tasks, the switchboard operator, for all of the individual soldier skills in the Army. It was a mammoth job.

Essential to Gorman's teaching were demonstrations of improvements in ways that were clear and convincing to both soldiers and laymen. For example, DePuy applied Gorman's approach to tank crew training. "The tank is a good clean thing to look at because its output can be measured more easily than the output of other things because you either have crews that can hit the target under varying conditions or they can't." He went on to say that in Europe 2 percent of our soldiers are in tanks, but somewhere between one-quarter and one-third of our combat capability in Europe comes from tanks. Thus, if you can improve the 2 percent of your soldiers, he said, you are improving approximately 30 percent of your combat capability. That's called leverage! This was the kind of reasoning that characterized DePuy's TRADOC.

Gorman and DePuy found that the selection and retention of tank crewmen was badly done in the most fundamental ways. Some men could not see well. The promotion system provided no incentive. Personnel turbulence created instability in crews. Part of the reason for such obvious deficiencies was that during the war in Vietnam units in Europe were essentially a manpower pool, a holding station for replacements in Vietnam. Combat arms officers and NCOs would routinely spend a year in Europe before returning to Vietnam for another tour. Most regulars did two Vietnam tours.

Many tanks didn't have crews. They fired once a year. Crews were put together to fire for record and then were taken apart. DePuy concluded that something on the order of only 20 percent of the potential of the tank was being exploited. A well-trained crew could get 80 percent of the potential of the tank. "That's like multiplying all of our tank battalions by four or dividing by four, whichever way you look at it." Field testing showed that a very short and focused training program could get crews to that 80 percent of potential rather easily. "So training development is the effort to bring the individuals and the crews—and squads, platoons, and companies—up to that geometrically rising curve of capability which parallels the geometrically rising capability built into the weapons system." The challenge to DePuy was to synchronize the training package with the hardware and the logistics package in a doctrinal context—in other words, to put the building blocks in "a unified relationship."[14]

Upon first visiting the schools and training centers DePuy later recalled, "I was horrified by some of the things I found. For example, at the Engineer School I discovered that the engineer lieutenants were never given an opportunity to drive a bulldozer or run a road grader or a front-end loader. Yet they would eventually go to an engineer platoon having that type of equipment, and I couldn't understand how they would be able to supervise, or criticize, or train."

Similarly, at Fort Benning most of the training of lieutenants and captains took place in classrooms instead of out with troops. DePuy's conclusion was that Army schools had become too academic. He understood the debate contrasting education and training, and he came down strongly on the side of training at the lieutenant and captain levels. He believed that officers should be trained for their specific jobs, not to be generic officers. An armor lieutenant's training, for example, should be first as tank commander. After he mastered that, he could learn to be a tank platoon leader. Then he learned to be a tank company commander. Similarly, infantry officers should first be a private of infantry, then a corporal of infantry, then a sergeant of infantry, and finally a lieutenant of infantry. DePuy also believed in diagnostic testing for all soldiers so that time would be spent teaching what the soldier does not know instead of wasting time and boring him by telling him what he already knew.

Responding to Brooks Kleber's assertion that DePuy's emphasis on training had a cost in education, DePuy agreed. But, he said, the issue was where and when education should take place in an officer's career. DePuy didn't think that military history should be taught at Fort Knox or Fort Benning in the courses for company-grade officers; those, he felt, should be essentially trade courses in how to fight armor and infantry. But no one should attend the Command and General Staff College at Leavenworth without first passing a test that included military history learned on the officer's own time by reading recommended books or by taking correspondence courses. Half of the people attending the career courses as captains, in DePuy's words, "are going nowhere." The half that went on to staff college could do what he called "the whole man stuff" while there, or in graduate school, or on their own. "By the time you get to Leavenworth," he said, "you are dealing with the people who are going to run the Army." That's the place for "whole man stuff."

The lieutenants and captains should "shoot, fight, kill, lay mines, pick up mines, build a bridge, hands-on." He saw that in Israel, noting that there they taught tactical skills and the history of Israel. Period. They expected the tank company commander to be the best tank commander in the company. That was just what the U.S. Army needed. If the officer had the right stuff, he'd educate himself. If he didn't, well, he was "going nowhere" anyway.

DePuy said with satisfaction, "We are in fact now [1977] teaching soldiering . . . because of other constraints, until we get to Leavenworth we haven't expanded into the rest of the man, but before I leave I am going to have a letter to the Chief saying that I think we should go to testing. I am more than anxious to get some more intellectual content into the officer corps."[15]

General Donn Starry tells a story that provides insight into DePuy's desire to know exactly how things work and foreshadows an immeasurably valuable addition to hands-on training for large formations, the National Training Center (NTC).

DePuy said to Starry, "I want you to teach me how to fight tanks."

Starry said, "Why don't you come to Fort Knox?"

"I don't want anybody to know what we are doing."

Starry believed that the U.S. Army needed something like what the Germans had at Hohenfels and Grafenwoehr, places that allowed free maneuver and the firing of long-range weapons. He knew that the Israelis were good because they did a lot of live firing and free maneuver. Fort Irwin, California, had come to Starry's attention earlier when he had had a hand in turning it over to the California National Guard. So when it was agreed that DePuy would run through some crew drills with the two generals and their aides filling out the four-man crew, they did so at Fort Irwin. The aides were driver and loader; the generals swapped roles as tank commander and gunner. "We had a great time," Starry said. DePuy learned how to fight tanks, and the seed for a National Training Center (NTC) at Fort Irwin was planted. (It was established in October 1980.) Some officers found four-star generals teaching sergeants how to dig holes and crew tanks unseemly. DePuy didn't. He believed that generals pontificating about tank training should know what each member of a tank crew does when engaging the enemy.[16]

Establishing the NTC was a milestone in the Army's training

revolution. Battalion commanders tested their skills in free maneuver against an aggressor force using the doctrine and weapons systems of the Warsaw Pact. The outcome was carefully monitored by measuring devices and debriefed in detail to the commander.

One battalion commander who fought in the first Gulf War had the good fortune to go directly from his NTC rotation to ships that transported him and his battalion to the fight, before the Army had a chance to send his soldiers to the winds. His battalion (the "Bandits" of Task Force 4–67, 3d Armored Division) "killed over 30 tanks and BMPs [Soviet infantry fighting vehicles] and a number of trucks in a little over ten minutes." The final tally revealed that 77 tank rounds had killed 51 armored vehicles and an indeterminate number of trucks—without friendly losses. This commander gives full credit to field training at the NTC for his success.[17]

Historian and retired armor officer Stephen A. Bourque concurs on the value of the training. He wrote, "Multiple rotations at the National Training Center and Battle Command Training Program had created an almost veteran combat force."[18]

DePuy's reputation among Army officers—aside from his notoriety for relieving officers in Vietnam—is most closely linked to his role in training and Army doctrine, most particularly the 1976 version of FM 100–5. That manual stimulated thinking and lively debates in the officer corps in the decade that followed, but much of his creative energy was spent in the realm of combat developments. He was no stranger to American industry nor to the scientific and academic community, going back to his job in Chief's Office in the late 1950s. And he was accustomed to dealing with powerful men, such as Lyndon Johnson, Robert McNamara, and Dean Acheson. In 1973, Bill DePuy also brought his most recent four years of program management with him from the AVICE job, where he resolved fights among various staff proponents for declining resources as the Army was halved.

He favored integrating schools and combat developments. He also thought that projecting combat developments from 1960 to 1990 or the year 2000 was wrong. Such a focus, in his view, "never seemed to cause anything to happen." No one could "divine" a picture of the Army thirty years out. He preferred asking more specific, immediate questions: What don't we like about the current tank? Do we want a gun that shoots farther and more accurately, better armor, improved fuel consumption, enhanced maintenance, a capability to fight at night? What are the trade-offs? Could the Army Materiel Command (AMC) provide all or some improvements at costs justifying the project? If the developers assented, they were required to write it down, to certify that they could accomplish the task. These agreements were called Required Operations Capabilities (ROCs). DePuy said he got the reputation of being a "ROC-crusher" because "I wouldn't approve ROCs unless the developer certified that he could do it. I could hold his feet to the fire." He brought the process from some fuzzy futurism to the real world of hardware and practical steps. His technique seems to be a variation on the contract system Max Thurman described in dealing with schools and training centers. The intent was to give the user leverage with pauses in the form of tests and evaluation along the way, all of it by contract that fixed responsibility.

Nothing held still in DePuy's busy command. Training, doctrine, and combat developments were dynamic, interactive, and in flux. DePuy believed that the Yom Kippur War gave him the "springboard" he needed to get things done. It pitted Soviet weapons, equipment, and doctrine against U.S. weapons, equipment, and doctrine, making it a kind of NATO–Warsaw Pact war in microcosm. DePuy used it both to get the U.S. Army cracking and as leverage with civilian leadership to insure that resources—including his Big Five weapons systems—were provided to the Army.[19]

The advent of effective anti-tank guided missiles (ATGMs) and a quantum leap in artillery capability made combat far more lethal. It was at this time that the phrases "fighting outnumbered" and "win the first battle" became mantras in the U.S. Army. The Army's sense of urgency put it in step with DePuy's sense of time: doubletime. Although many major end items and hundreds of lesser items were nurtured during the DePuy era at TRADOC in the 1970s, the Big Five—the Abrams tank, the Bradley infantry fighting vehicle, the Patriot missile system, and the Blackhawk and Apache helicopters—are the systems associated with his name. They were fielded in the 1980s, proven in combat in the 1990s, and are in service in the twenty-first century.

DePuy's pragmatic side was evident in his direct methods as a troop leader. He reveled in face-to-face contact with soldiers and subordinate leaders as he taught tactics, techniques, and procedures and continually refined them. His management style in heading a large, complex organization exploited practical devices, such as the contract system and the ROCs. But he had another side that reveals a subtle intelligence and mastery of nuance that allowed him to be as comfortable with abstractions as he was with the concrete.

In 1985 the Director of the Military History Institute asked him to update his 1979 Oral History to insure that his observations would be available to an audience beyond scholars using the archives. He responded with ruminations on "the vast misunderstanding" regarding the impact of weapons technology on tactics and the widespread debate about doctrine. His remarks display a first-rate mind at work.[20]

In his "1985 Afterthoughts," DePuy charged the Congressional Reform Movement, a group of civilian intellectuals and congressional staffers concerned with military reform, with being "the source of nonstop rubbish on this subject [technology] . . . loose talk about an important subject."[21] He marveled that this movement had apparently convinced a number of usually sensible people that high technology is an enemy, distorting some facts into "the big lie." The worst examples of military weapons development, he said, have been ascribed to the honest and difficult effort to provide our military with excellent equipment, somehow making high technology synonymous with the reformers' bugaboo, "attrition warfare." DePuy was incredulous at the recommendation that we should return to yesteryear, when allegedly simple low-tech weapons systems like the P-51 fighter did the job, pointing out that in its time the P-51 was high-tech.

He took the "anti high-tech crowd" to task for advocating "maneuver warfare" (their antipode and straw man to "attrition warfare") while deprecating high-tech. He hammered home his point: maneuver warfare requires precisely the highest technology man can devise—and afford! The M-1 Abrams tank, the M-2 Bradley fighting vehicle, the A64 Attack helicopter, the UH60 Blackhawk utility helicopter (four of his Big Five), along with smart munitions, long-range delivery systems, airborne sensors, satellite communications, cellular radios—this, said DePuy, is "a fair inventory of the very highest technology" that makes maneuver warfare possible. He followed this statement with exquisite analysis.

The pertinent question is, said DePuy, How does the Army exploit American science and technology to support military efforts to do the nation's will? The uninitiated defense intelligentsia, quite logically, starts the process, with the military stating requirements derived from operational concepts coming out of history, out of soldierly experience. "This puts the conceptual people at the head of the line, that is, in the number one spot in a linear sequence." The "concept" folks look at Army missions, history, the threat, the state of technology, and then, using war games and studies, they say, I need a widget that does these things and fits my doctrine, organization, training, and other materiel considerations. That is logical. It seems to be a perfectly sound way of doing the nation's —the Army's—business.

But it doesn't work that way.

DePuy went on to describe a complicated process in lucid prose, his arguments made with flawless logic. Operational concepts, he contended, have never been able to "get out front." Instead, they describe the application of currently understood technology "within the mainstream of tactical evolution." For example, "ideas about air mobility *followed* the helicopter." Concepts like Deep Attack, Follow on Forces Attack, and Assault Breaker—the concepts *du jour* around 1985, when DePuy prepared his "Afterthoughts"—followed the discovery that we could make smart munitions. "There are virtually no exceptions to this sequence," he asserted. The technology comes first; then the applications follow, conditioned and constrained by tactical concepts.

The process is messy because it is circular. "As with all circles, there is no point of origin and no end point." Researchers are aware of potential applications, and those applications do not ignore employment. "Concepts of employment," said DePuy, "are a synthesis of tactical experience and new technical capabilities." The relationship between the research community, the developers, and the users is interactive and continuous—circular.

Alas, there's the rub! Human beings crave linearity. We like sequence, the notion that two follows one and three follows two, that B and C follow A in a chain. Our minds, organizations, and procedures are linear, none more so than the program and budget process. But it is naive to believe that the user states a military requirement and the research and development communities then salute, follow orders, and produce the desired result.

There is a feedback loop between the creator/researchers, the developer/applicators, and the exploiters/tactical users. "Linearity hates feedback loops," said DePuy. They interrupt the smooth flow of the program and funding process, embarrass the user who changes his performance specifications, and cause cost overruns. But there is no way out of the dilemma.

He offered examples of changes that were made in the course of developing the Bradley, despite the anger and frustration this caused, not least in the U.S. Congress, which had to pay the bill. One issue was the need to install a two-man turret instead of the programmed one-man turret. But, DePuy said, field tests and recent combat—the Yom Kippur War—made the change exactly the right thing to do. Human beings are just not smart enough to anticipate new information flowing in through feedback loops during the research, development, and tactical use. We seem to be incapable of building a fail-safe linear system. "Thank God we can't!" DePuy seemed to imply.

His enunciation of the complex process by which American soldiers are provided technology useful to them in winning wars is brief and lucid. It is a sophisticated expression of DePuy's oft-stated convictions: We are a rich country. Use technology. Spend firepower, not the lives of our soldiers. But don't believe for a moment that the process of putting the right systems in place is neat and linear.

Doctrine was high on the list of DePuy's priorities. He announced his intentions in a letter dated 10 October 1974 with the subtlety of a sledgehammer blow to the foreheads of the eight major generals who were commanding his schools. Subject: Field Manuals. His first sentence reads, "I intend that we write all the important field manuals in the United States Army and have them published by 30 June 1976." He provided guidance in the second paragraph. "All of you will meet with me at A. P. Hill. . . . At that time we will spend one-half day reviewing Field Manual 100–5 which is the capstone manual on the operations of the Army in the field. One week before our meeting, General Cushman will send a draft to each of you." Third paragraph: "General Maddox will send each of you a draft [of a manual on Army aviation] one week before our meeting." One-fourth of a day will be spent on that. Fourth paragraph: "General Tarpley [Commander, U.S. Army Infantry Center] will coordinate the anti-tank manual with Fort Knox [the Armor Center] and distribute the result to each of you one week before our meeting. One-fourth of a day will be spent on that."

In the unlikely event that someone failed to understand DePuy's sense of urgency, his fifth paragraph read:

> We have now participated in enough discussions, listened to enough briefings and seen enough demonstrations to have the best consensus on how to fight that has probably ever existed in the school system of the United States Army. It is now time to institutionalize and perpetuate this consensus through doctrinal publications. In this respect I look to each of you personally to bring this about. If necessary, you must write them yourselves, as I hold each of you personally responsible for achieving the objective I have set. I look forward to our meeting at A. P. Hill.
>
> Signed, Bill.[22]

The generals probably hadn't had the likes of DePuy's words directed at them since their first exercise of dismounted drill as privates or cadets.

Paul Herbert provides a succinct and very readable account of what followed in his Leavenworth Paper Number 16, published in 1988 as *Deciding What Has to Be Done: General William E. DePuy and the 1976 Edition of FM 100–5, Operations.* As Herbert tells the story, DePuy continued to apply the pressure necessary to get the task done by the deadline he set.

When DePuy took command of TRADOC, training and combat developments were probably uppermost in his mind. Training was his passion, and his four years as AVICE immersed him in sorting out and adjudicating internal fights for finite resources and competing new systems. But the intensity and lethality of the Arab-Israeli War of 1973 had foreboding implications for the U.S. Army and forced its leaders to think about how it would fight in Europe.

Herbert noted that FM 100–5 was the first doctrinal statement of the post-Vietnam years. "DePuy gave the Army a mighty shove" that took it from "its preoccupation with the war in Vietnam and on the road to the twenty-first century." In one sense FM 100–5 was a modest "how to" handbook, but it was also "an overarching concept of warfare that would rationalize everything the Army did, from training recruits to designing tanks." It would say "how the Army intended to fight." Herbert says it was at once "a fighting doctrine and a procurement strategy," because it so clearly linked training and hardware to doctrine.[23]

The "mighty shove" took the Army from wallowing in self-pity (not Herbert's words) about Vietnam and how to recruit an all-volunteer Army to the proper concerns of professional soldiers, including what to do about the increased lethality of advanced weapons systems, particularly the anti-tank missile systems and the development of smart long-range weapons as they applied to NATO Europe; and how to change the Army's focus from dismounted infantry to armored/mechanized infantry operations.

FM 100–5 was also an effort to demystify doctrine. Clausewitz, Jomini, Sun Tzu, and the Principles of War were deliberately left out of the "how to fight" 100–5 and derivative manuals. Ruminations by the philosophers of war were appropriate for learned journals, not for DePuy's concept of a slim handbook with a camouflaged cover for soldiers. In fact, there were some embarrassing moments when the generals were brought together to do their "homework" under Headmaster DePuy. One general carried golf clubs to a working session; he was told he wouldn't need them. Another general, who was engaging in erudite discourse about the number of angels on the head of a pin, was told to save that for another time; this was a working session. Another general's writing effort DePuy graded "sophomoric." DePuy tried to make his intent clear by comparing the "how to fight" manuals he wanted to the instructions that come with a Toro lawn mower, complete with diagrams and photographs. "Don't get too lofty or philosophical," he told the small group of selected officers (known as the "Boathouse Gang") who wrote the early drafts of the 1976 version of 100–5. This is what changed the relationship between Jack Cushman and his mentor and sponsor of the late 1950s in the Office of the Chief of Staff, Colonel Bill DePuy. General Cushman resisted General DePuy's concept of 100–5 and so fell out of DePuy's favor.[24]

Herbert emphasizes the degree to which the formulation of doctrine and the writing of the manuals, especially 100–5, were DePuy's babies, and how DePuy wanted his generals both to write the manuals and to buy into them. In the 10 October 1974 letter quoted above, he emphasized the generals' involvement by using the word "personally" twice in his last paragraph. He said, "I hold each of you personally responsible." No doubt DePuy's intensity in bringing the manual in on time, in accordance with the deadline he imposed, has contributed to his reputation as a tough guy and a taskmaster, but some amusing stories also came out of the experience.

After one session, Donn Starry noticed, as he passed a table at which some of DePuy's bright majors and lieutenant colonels were hard at work, that they had blue-penciled *his* work! Livid, he chewed out one unfortunate young man, who could only say that he was operating under General DePuy's instructions. Starry, still fuming when he got back to Fort Knox, sent a message to one of his fellow school commanders indicating that "the TRADOC staff assembled a group of wise majors and lieutenant colonels to grade our work." He said he would send a message to DePuy. DePuy probably smiled at Starry's indignation while acknowledging that he did indeed have an editorial staff that answered to him—personally.[25]

Donn Starry, Paul Gorman, and Bill DePuy were all independent thinkers and were never reluctant to express disagreement if the boss was on the wrong track. Reading their communications during this period is informative—and fun.

At one point Starry, the armor expert at Fort Knox, waxed indignant at something Gorman, the infantryman, had written regarding armor, and he charged in a message to DePuy that Gorman had all the smart armor guys at TRADOC headquarters. DePuy called Gorman in, showed him the message and said, in effect: fix this. Before the sun set on Fort Monroe, Gorman sent Starry a message, with a copy to DePuy, saying that effective that day all of Gorman's armor officers—two of them—were on orders to report to Fort Knox. Starry brooked no nonsense from staff officers; Gorman knew how to go for the throat; DePuy was blessed with bold and brainy helpers; the U.S. Army was the winner.

In a letter to Paul Herbert dated 27 April 1985, DePuy wrote that, in retrospect, "I think you gave me more credit for controlling events than I deserve. Remember that Starry and Gorman (both splendid men) were constantly in disagreement. Both were in complete disagreement with Cushman."[26]

Gorman tells a story on himself. At one point he recommended an action regarding training. DePuy said no. Gorman persisted, explaining how in the long run his recommended action would save money and get the job done. It was clearly the right way to go. DePuy said no. Gorman asked if that was final, and the interview ended with DePuy questioning Gorman's comprehension of the English language.

Some barbs hurt more than others. Sipping a drink that evening, Gorman intimated to his wife his unhappiness of the moment. She suggested it might be time to say good-bye to the Army. The next morning, Gorman took his letter of resignation with him to work. As he walked along generals' row from his quarters to his office, he was intercepted by a waiting Bill DePuy, whose quarters were along the way. "Good morning, Paul," he greeted Gorman. "About your recommendation. You're right. Do it."

When Gorman was asked if he revealed to his boss his near-resignation, Gorman raised his eyebrows, noting that while DePuy had a great sense of humor, it was best to allow him to initiate levity. The letter remained in Gorman's pocket until it was returned to a resting place in his quarters for possible use on some other bad day. Twenty years after the event, Gorman's facial expression said that even a teacher's pet didn't tweak DePuy.[27]

The 1976 version of FM 100–5 caused controversy in the Army. It was challenged, rewritten, and republished soon after its publication and DePuy's retirement in 1977, in part because it was too closely identified with its principal author. DePuy's observations about what influenced his sense of urgency in 1974 and his analysis of the doctrinal controversy that followed publication reflect his usual thoughtfulness and objectivity.

DePuy said that FM 100–5, "inaccurately but commonly known as the Active Defense," came from the following convergent influences: the lethality of modern precision weapons, especially the anti-tank guided missile; demonstration of that lethality in the 1973 Arab-Israeli War; the adverse correlation of forces in NATO and the effect of the lack of depth in the Federal Republic of Germany for defensive operations; the "tactical," as opposed to "operational," focus of its authors; and the German insistence on forward defense, as expressed in NATO and in German-American staff talks in 1975 and 1976.

DePuy stressed the importance of all five factors in the development of what was then called Active Defense. He then asserted that "Operational Art" was not in the lexicon of those who wrote FM 100–5, nor was the "operational level part of our consciousness. We were tactical guys by self definition and preference."

When DePuy commanded TRADOC, the U.S. Army taught and thought about war on two levels, tactics and strategy. Intelligence analysis revealed that the Red Army taught and thought about war at three levels: tactics, the operational level, and strategy. So did the Germans. DePuy was totally unpretentious in confirming that the idea of the operational level of war caught on with smart middle-grade officers before the senior leaders incorporated it into their thinking.[28]

In the 27 April 1985 letter to Herbert mentioned earlier, DePuy also wrote, "The greatest error we made was to focus [the 1976] 100–5 on the tactical level as opposed to the operational level. This was a major flaw and is leading to very dangerous misconceptions by the Army today [1985]. Because of this error we did not hold forth any real hope of victory in Europe—just one hell of a battle prior to going nuclear."

Of the senior leaders, DePuy went on to say that *they were*—the reader may safely infer he means *I was*—influenced by the Battle of the Bulge, the "pile-on" tactics of the Vietnam War, and the elasticity shown by the Germans in World War I, first in the east and then on the Western Front.

About the Bulge, he said it was "the only time in the history of the Army when we received a massive armored break-through attempt. The response was to slow the advance and attack the flanks of the penetration." Recall that he was a battalion commander at that time. His battalion, as a part of the 90th Division, slid left to join the force relieving the Allied defenders in December 1944. The perspicacious reader will see in this recollection aspects of what later evolved from the German-American staff talks in which DePuy spoke for the U.S. Army.

About "pile on," he wrote, "most battles [in Vietnam] started with a small American unit under attack by a large VC/NVA unit. The game was to reinforce quickly and massively by fire and maneuver." The specific reference is to Vietnam, but one recalls as well the breakout from Normandy and the part played by the 90th Division in the battle at Chambois that transformed the area into a killing ground of enemy as far as DePuy could see. Allied mobile forces plugged gaps to block German troops attempting to escape, while artillery and air forces did the killing.[29]

DePuy personally experienced and admired German elasticity in 1944 and 1945 and later rediscovered it in his reading of German military history and in his Imperial Defence College course. Both the Hutier tactics of World War I and the skill of the Wehrmacht, particularly on the Eastern Front against the vastly numerically superior Russian Army in World War II, demonstrated an elasticity in the German way of war that he felt was "never understood, mastered or accepted by the U.S. Army."

The Hutier tactics were used in the spring of 1918 on the Western Front in German General Erich Ludendorff's effort to win the war before American combat strength arrived in sufficient numbers to affect the outcome. These tactics were characterized by infiltration and the bypassing of enemy strong points. One war later, "haul ass and bypass" was the mantra of both German and American armored forces. That meant penetrate, bypass, and exploit. Don't worry about your flanks. Exploit enemy confusion.

As regimental S-3, 357th Infantry in September 1944, DePuy watched John Mason use infiltration by infantry squads, and he liked what he saw. Three months later, in the first forty-eight hours of his battalion command, DePuy infiltrated his battalion at night, in foul weather, across a river into a denied area. He used the methods of the Germans that he already admired from direct contact with them years before he studied what they had done in 1918. The British came close to defeat as a consequence of the Hutier tactics employed by German troops in the spring of 1918 and did not forget. It seems somehow poetic and fitting that the doctrine DePuy expressed in FM 100–5 would so harmonize with the Bundesheer (the post–World War II West German Army) doctrinal bible, HDv 100/100.

DePuy's generals, at his insistence, contributed to the writing of 100–5, but there is a lot of DePuy in that manual. The fact that DePuy demanded that it be written swiftly, his leading role in the German-American staff talks that took place to coordinate German and American doctrine, and later criticism of the 1976 manual require a short account of how U.S. doctrine figured in the planning for war in Europe on his watch.

In 1986 DePuy said he "applauded the work that has been done on 100–5 after my time," but, he said, he was "disappointed that the German influence on the '76 version has never been adequately described and Romjue ignored it."[30] He reviewed German attitudes that affected NATO and U.S. planning for war in Europe, pointing out that when he returned to Europe to command a battalion in the mid-1950s, the plan was to withdraw to the Pyrenees. There was no German Army from 1945 to 1955. When he returned to command a battle group in the early 1960s, the plan was to delay to the Rhine.

The Bundeswehr was at that point in the mix, but the Germans were understandably unenthusiastic about fighting in their cities as NATO conducted a mobile defense through Germany. The destruction of World War II was still fresh in the minds of Germans; they preferred forward defense to minimize destruction in Germany.

DePuy's job, assigned by Abrams and later Weyand, was to synchronize German and American doctrine. Typically, Abrams did not tell DePuy much more than "Get the Americans and Germans working together." The premise was that if the two biggest NATO armies got together, the others would go along. DePuy and German Lieutenant General Rudiger von Reichert agreed to focus on a general concept of operations. Details regarding weapons, tactics, and procedures would follow adoption of the common concept.

DePuy stressed that doctrine doesn't tell the commander what to do; it tells him how to do what he wants to do. Therefore, he said, when the 1976 version of 100–5 "acquired the reputation of being a defensive doctrine, it was not." There were chapters on offense and defense. It was up to the commander to pick his chapter. The doctrine for Europe, because of political constraints and force structure, was active defense. The doctrine could be applied to other wars, but the political circumstances—the unwillingness of NATO, particularly the Germans, to address offensive war in East Germany—left the initiative for choosing the time and place of the war in the hands of the enemy. However, from the division and brigade level down, "the Active Defense left a lot of tactical initiative to the defender as to where, how, and when he was going to channelize the attack, counter attack, and so on, to regain local initiative." The point is that tactics drove DePuy's thinking and the thinking of his peers.

Defensive operations in Europe had less to do with 100–5 than with a need to compromise with the Germans. As DePuy put it, "The German Army was formed to protect Germany not to destroy Germany." DePuy had to square a circle. The Germans wanted a forward defense, the Americans a mobile defense. What DePuy and his opposite number, von Reichert, Vice Chief of Staff of the German Army, came up with was a mobile defense that would be "compressed into the first 20 to 30 kilometers from the [inner-German and Czech] border. It would still be very mobile, a lot of movement," said DePuy, "but far forward." It was an accommodation to the Germans and to NATO's predicament. DePuy said, "It is not necessarily the best way to fight any war, but it may be the best way to fight *this* war." He was, he said, "responding to the political dimensions and objectives of the NATO mission and the German government and of the NATO alliance. We were also responding to the lessons we deduced from the lethality of modern weapons and their demonstration in the Arab-Israeli War of 1973."

DePuy said that he, Starry, Gorman, David Ewing Ott (Commander of the Field Artillery School and Fort Sill, 1 July 1973 to 13 October 1976, and GEN, USA, Ret.), "and the guys I had down in the boathouse, my own group of smart majors and lieutenant colonels," were preoccupied with "the fact that we had a light infantry Army because of Vietnam" and knew they needed armor and mechanized infantry for war in Europe.

Typical of his style in getting people aboard, DePuy conducted a series of training conferences at Fort Knox, Fort Hood, and Grafenwoehr, Germany, showing senior leaders precisely what he wanted done. After a demonstration at Grafenwoehr for American and NATO senior officers, he said, "These are the tactics we plan to teach: you slow them down, you finally get him stopped and trapped, then you counter attack and destroy him." Mulling over these words, and knowing what he saw at Chambois in August 1944, one comprehends DePuy's vision of forward defense in Germany as a series of battalion-size ambushes intended to channel the enemy into a killing ground where American and NATO firepower would finish him. General von Reichert said, "If this is what the American Army means, we, the German Army, buy it completely."[31] This statement crowned the close cooperation between the Bundeswehr and the U.S. Army.

Almost as a postscript to this explanation of what lay at the heart of the evolution of doctrine after 1976, DePuy said that the awareness of operational art came "at the lieutenant colonel level, not at the level of the generals. You know, the Wass de Czege, the Richard Sinnreichs and Don Holders, and so on."

Donn Starry names some of these same officers as ones to whom Leavenworth Commandant LTG William R. Richardson (TRADOC Commander, 1983–1986) assigned the task of writing what became AirLand Battle—at Leavenworth. After Starry succeeded DePuy as TRADOC Commander, he appointed BG Donald Morelli as Deputy Chief of Staff for Doctrine. His reason: to defuse criticism and "to change the perception that new doctrine could only come from the big leather chair in the front office." This is a clear reference to the impression among many in the Army that the 1976 doctrine was DePuy's project and was forced on the Army.[32]

But DePuy was insistent that the situation in Europe dictated defense, not FM 100–5. He defined operational art in 1987 this way: "You try to find middle ground, elbow room, to do something useful militarily that isn't in conflict with the political objective or is not excessive to the resources that you have. That is what operational art is."

He alluded to "Operations 404" in whimsical graduate school language: the Command and General Staff College at Fort Leavenworth brought the good student to the level of Tactics 101. Those selected for a second year of study at Leavenworth reached Operations 202. Field experience in a joint structure brought the student of war to Operations 303. Finally, as a CINC one gets to the level of Operations 404.

His remarks about what would be a "favorable outcome" of war in Europe defined DePuy as a realist: "Not to lose *and* not be destroyed by nuclear weapons. Those are my two definitions of favorable outcome." He played the game with the cards he was dealt, but he knew that American soldiers were grounded in an offensive spirit and can-do attitude. "They don't like to have a plan or a doctrine that doesn't win . . . they just couldn't be enthusiastic about a non-winner."[33]

In 1977, TRADOC was probably the best-managed organization in the Army. A revolution in training was under way; combat developments had been rationalized; a doctrine was in place; the creative energy of the Army was being tapped. There was a general sense that the Army had improved and was on a trend line to further improvement that just might make it five times as good as the enemy.[34]

DePuy's professional accomplishments are in the public record. His personal side is far less known, for several reasons. First, he was by nature a private person. His son called him "an autonomous man." Second, he believed that one's profession should not be the whole of his life. Third, his wife, Marj, insisted upon a private family sphere apart from the Army. Fourth, he exercised great power; his reputation evoked fear. As a consequence, he was generally regarded as a cold man, remote, ambitious, all head and no heart. But, as we have seen, throughout his life DePuy showed those who were close to him a charm, humor, and warmth that was not on public display.

Tony Pokorny (Col., USA, Ret.), who was DePuy's aide when Secretary of the Army Martin Hoffman was to visit TRADOC, recalled a story about his boss. "DePuy said, 'What are we going to do with him? Are the ducks running? Let's take him duck hunting.' But they [at Fort Eustis] said, 'The ducks aren't flying this year.' He says, 'Well, let's bring the ducks here.' So they brought ducks to Eustis. Marty Hoffman went to hunt. They had ducks in cages that they released, so that Marty would have something to shoot at. He got five or six ducks. DePuy thought that was a riot. He says, 'I can just see all the guys tossing ducks in the air just so the Secretary of the Army could have something to shoot at.' He got a big kick out of that."[35]

From time to time DePuy took a poke at pomposity. Jack Woodmansee (LTG, USA, Ret.) recalls being seated in the TRADOC auditorium when the sergeant major announced, "Ladies and gentlemen, the Commanding General!" All rose to attention in silence. "You could hear these little footsteps, and he [DePuy] hopped up on the stage. He said, 'Cripes, you'd think it was Julius Caesar.' . . . he would do little things to make himself human."

Woodmansee was the victim of DePuy's sense of humor on several occasions and one of the few to even the score, albeit briefly and inadvertently. Once, DePuy told Woodmansee to make a training film. Woodmansee hadn't the foggiest notion how films were made, and he was uncomfortably conscious of treading on Paul Gorman's training turf. But he proceeded with his assigned task. At one point, Woodmansee said to DePuy, "You know how Alfred Hitchcock always appears in his movies for just an instant? I want you in the training film." When DePuy dropped in to see how it was going, Woodmansee pounced. "This is the scene," said Woodmansee.

You are a Soviet tank commander and this is your hatch (a cardboard semicircle painted camouflage colors and mounted on a music stand). You have a Soviet uniform hat on. You look out, see Americans, raise the binoculars to your eyes, reach down to the radio, send a message, and then bring the binoculars back up. That's it. This will take about eight seconds.

So he puts his hat on and it swallows his head, but the film director was perfect. He grabs the hat in the back and puts a paper clip back there. So we run through this thing and he's a horrible actor. He fumbles around and can't find the microphone. I'm thinking this is a disaster, when the director says, "Perfect. That's wonderful. Cut. This time I want to try something a little different." He gets him corrected. We get the scene and put it in the can.

When we show the film at TRADOC headquarters, as soon as the scene comes on where DePuy is this wily looking Soviet tank commander, the entire staff erupts in a big guffaw. I'm sitting right behind DePuy and he turns and looks at me like he could kill me. "Do you think I ought to cut this out, sir?" He says, "Yeah. I think you should."

Woodmansee concludes his story. "Well," he says, "when I left TRADOC, this picture was his gift to me." A photo of DePuy as the Russian tank commander occupies a place of honor in Jack Woodmansee's study. Clearly, Bill DePuy could laugh at himself.

He could also express gratitude in a way that lasted a lifetime. Woodmansee describes a discussion in the TRADOC Headquarters in which he was the junior man and lone dissenter over what to tell the CSA Bernie Rogers about a specific issue. In effect, DePuy told him to pipe down, saying, "Goddamn it Jack, you're not listening," to which his immediate boss added, "Yeah, goddamn it, Jack, you're not listening!" Woodmansee, noting the echo in the room, piped down. After some continued discussion of the issue, he raised his hand, marched to the butcher pad next to DePuy, took DePuy's magic marker, and made his point—again. Then he returned to his seat.

"DePuy tapped his fingers while he was thinking," recalled Woodmansee. "Then he said, 'You know, Jack is right.' Then he looked at me and said, 'Goddamn it, Woodmansee!' And we all had a big laugh."

After the successful business with Rogers, DePuy sought out Woodmansee and said, "Jack, I want you to know that I appreciate what you did. After I chewed your ass out, you kept me from embarrassing the Chief. I want you to know that I appreciate that you didn't let me make that mistake."

Woodmansee concludes: "None of us knew how the affection came the other way, but all of us grew not only to respect Bill DePuy, but to love him greatly."

Woodmansee's wife, Patty, brings up Marj DePuy. "They had this relationship where she could say no, and he could make fun of it. He took her seriously and lightly at the same time. She had a great deal of influence over him in his personal life. She truly protected him." Patty adds, "Had they grown up together as an Army couple, I'm sure that there would have been more of a social relationship with other Army wives. But Marj was a very capable professional. She was not the officers' club wife. She did not do the programs that were typical of an Army community. She was detached somewhat in that way. I liked her. She was very direct. She didn't beat around the bush. You knew where she stood, what she liked and didn't like."

Paul Gorman suggests that at this stage of their lives Marj was focused on the next chapter. It was likely that Bill would retire soon, and Marj was ready for that. She certainly looked forward to getting away on Friday afternoons to spend the weekends at the recently purchased Highfield, which was in need of repair. Much DePuy family elbow grease went into preparing the retirement home. Jack Woodmansee adds, "It was hard to get to him personally if you were in TRADOC, because Marj defended his time when he wasn't at work. We all understood that."

Patty Woodmansee said, "I found him an absolutely delightful man to be with. He was funny. He had a marvelous wit, a great sense of humor. He was a wordsmith. Bill DePuy could edit. You would like to write like he spoke because he was such a wonderful self-editor. I found that it was wonderful being around him."

Then she recalled an incident that gave her pause. "When Jack was promoted to brigadier, I remember General DePuy put his star on him. He looked at Jack and said, 'Jack, you are a young man. You can be in the Army for a long time as a general officer, but I want to tell you something. When it is time for you to walk away from the Army, for whatever reason, don't expect them to thank you.' I was taken aback," she said, though she added, "He didn't sound bitter." The fact is, the last act of the Army in dealing with a general is rejection. When the Army has no "next assignment," the general is retired.

Summing up, Jack Woodmansee said, "DePuy did have his favorites. He was personally attracted to them and let you know. It didn't mean that you weren't going to get your ass chewed." Paul Gorman made a similar statement: those not among the "chosen" knew it and were probably demoralized and resentful. But there was enormous gratification among those chosen to do the important work.[36]

Sam Wilder (Col., USA, Ret.), who served with DePuy in Vietnam and later as his aide at TRADOC, was surprised by his wife's description of the boss. Wilder says, "He was not one of those warm, caring lovable Teddy bear types, as you have probably figured out. He was somewhat formal. To quote Marj DePuy, 'He wore a necktie to a picnic.' But he could be charming. He didn't go to many parties, but he went to one and danced with my wife. My wife thought he was a great dancer. She came back saying that he was cute and sweet. We looked at each other. That little guy is sweet? You've got to be kidding me!"

"Let me give you another personality trait people might not realize," continued Wilder. "He was humble. There was no braggadocio or showy style. He demanded that I [as aide] not allow any special favors for him or his quarters. Don't have the post engineer come in and do something, no matter how well meaning. One time I got in trouble with him. The mess sergeant thought he was doing something nice when he put a candelabra on the head table with DePuy and his commanders. After that he told me not to let that happen to him again. That was too showy. I have never seen him but with one row of ribbons. He never wore all of his ribbons. His bedroom in his [Fort Monroe] house . . . was simple, Spartan, an Army metal cot. It was like he was in troop barracks. I set up a reunion for him with his World War II friends at the Fort Knox Officers' Club, a dinner for five. I sent all of the details to him in another office. I heard him say, 'Forty dollars!' I knew what he was looking at, so I ran in there. He was a little bit frugal."

Sam Wilder warmed to his subject. "He was not a mentor in the sense of 'Come here, son, and I'll put my arm around you,' but he was a mentor to many people. He was a teacher of future leaders. As smart as Gorman was, he taught Gorman. He taught [future TRADOC Commanders] Starry [1 July 1977–30 June 1981]; Max Thurman [29 June 1987–1 August 1989]; John Foss [2 August 1989–22 August 1991]; and Jack Woodmansee. When they were with DePuy, he taught them. I was fortunate enough to spend four years with that guy. I learned more from him than I did from the War College, Leavenworth, and the Career Course combined. He didn't set out to say, 'Now I'm going to be a teacher,' but he was so knowledgeable and such a master of fact and logic that everyone thought he was correct. He was E. F. Hutton" (a reference to an advertisement in which everyone listens when unquestioned authority speaks.)[37]

Thomas Sweeney (Colonel, USA, Ret.) had an encounter with DePuy that highlights the utility of power and fear. He was a captain commanding a Terminal Service Company at Fort Eustice, Virginia, home of the Transportation Corps. The transportation industry was in the midst of a revolution: the conversion to containerization, in which a standard-size box is packed at source, moved by various modes of transportation, and unpacked at destination. Sweeney's company, a traditional stevedoring unit, had the lead in the Army's transition to containerization.

Major General Jack T. Fuson, Sweeney's commander, took advantage of a DePuy visit to Fort Eustis in December 1974, to show him the concept and to point out some impediments to the Army's ability to evolve with American industry. Fuson, who enjoyed an excellent reputation as the man who had cleared up the terrible congestion in the port of Saigon, had DePuy's ear.

Sweeney showed DePuy the old and the new systems. The old system required seventeen men in a slow process with some damage and waste. The container system required three men in a fast process that delivered 100 percent of the cargo intact. But the container system required a special crane. At this point, "General DePuy turned to a one-star who accompanied him, saying, 'I think we've been had,' sort of tongue-in-cheek." Further demonstrations of an over-the-beach operation and a big helicopter flying away a container concluded what Sweeney called "a great day. I was as high as a kite with the great success. Mission accomplished."

Sweeney said that the hearsay about DePuy "being tough as nails and all of that might be true, but he certainly came across as concerned, attentive, and understanding of the whole business. Just a little sidelight. The black overcoats and raincoats were just coming in, and he was the first person I had seen wear one. What struck me was what a little guy he was. His four stars barely fit on the shoulder straps on his raincoat, almost like one of them had to fit up under his collar. Nevertheless, they were all there, and they were all shiny."

As DePuy was about to depart in a car, Sweeney saluted, saying, "I sure would like to show you those cranes sometime." Sweeney recalled, "He looked me right in the eye and said, 'You mean you want me to buy those cranes for you. Right, captain?' And I said, 'Yes, sir. That's what I want.'"

A couple of weeks later, Sweeney was handed a copy of a "Dear Fred" letter to CSA Weyand signed "Bill." It said, "if we have to go to Israel [and places like that], it is imperative that we can handle containers." He recommended in the strongest terms that the cranes and required materiel handling equipment be procured—and soon. A copy of the letter was sent to General Fuson to let him know that DePuy was supporting him in the containerization matter. Fuson sent the letter to Sweeney. "So I read it to the troops," he said. "This was a great success for us, and it was a reward for their performance." Sweeney understood that DePuy was saying, "We are all in this together, and I want you to know that I haven't forgotten you guys. So he sends a letter to General Weyand."

The best was still to come.

Soon after, in the Pentagon, Sweeney took his place against the wall, the proper place for a junior officer, but he was directed to a seat at the end of the table. A major general was seated at the other end. The general told Captain Sweeney, "When you report back to General DePuy, be sure he knows that I am not the dead-ass in the Pentagon who is holding up this project." Then, Sweeney said, "he points to his name tag very clearly."

The acquisition people at St. Louis were equally clear. Tom Sweeney took this message from them: "You are here representing General DePuy. You are the TRADOC guy. The Army Materiel Command brings five guys who think they get five votes. The TRADOC guy gets the one vote that counts." Anyone who introduced impediments, recalled Sweeney, "got the evil eye" from the general, "and we were back on track. So it was just an amazing experience." Tom Sweeney ends his account by observing that DePuy "needed to be shown, he became convinced, and then he became an advocate." The "Dear Fred" letter from "Bill" that Sweeney read to his stevedores was a nice touch.[38]

DePuy's sense of whimsy emerges from time to time. As described earlier, he summoned his commanders to Camp A. P. Hill, where together they would write FM 100–5. Among the strong-willed men, there were sharp disagreements. DePuy was particularly amused by the reaction of Major General William J. Maddox Jr., his aviation commander at Fort Rucker, to the resistance he got from his peers. "There was a chapter in there somewhere on aviation," recalled DePuy. Maddox "was fighting for certain things and there were certain things we didn't want in there. Everybody gave him one hell of a time. He was a very nice guy. Everyone really liked him. But his colleagues, the other commandants, were really giving him a fit. When we were all done he turned to his colleagues and said, 'Thank you, you pricks!' I'll never forget that."[39]

Humility is not a word usually associated with DePuy, but it was a quality of his. DePuy's letter to Dick Stilwell upon the announcement of DePuy's promotion to four stars and his appointment to command TRADOC is a case in point. DePuy told Stilwill, "My good fortune has created a feeling of unease in my thoughts about you. I am utterly convinced that the lesser man has been rewarded. In those hectic early days in the 90th Division, you and your influence towered over all else. You and Bittman Barth persuaded me that the Army was the kind of organization to which I should belong. I did not feel that kind of reverence toward many others." In closing, he told Stilwell, "you are just one hell of a man."[40]

The centrality of World War II in DePuy's development as a leader in his Army is clear from his words and actions long after that war. In a letter he sent to Orwin C. Talbott (LTG, USA, Ret.), his deputy at TRADOC and comrade from 90th Division days, DePuy said that formal public remarks are not enough "to fully express my strong personal feelings on the occasion of your retirement. . . . You and I were fortunate in that we entered the Army just at the beginning of that great war and so, by accident of birth, our lives and fortunes have been coincident with that enormous experience which impacted upon us when we were most impressionable."[41] He had to have been fully aware of his own talents, but he believed that an accident of birth and circumstance, for which he could claim no credit, shaped him. Had he been born a decade earlier, he would not have been as "impressionable" during the war. And he would have been a thirty-five-year-old Reservist of little interest to the Regular Army at the end of the war.

Any assessment of DePuy's personality that assigns the primacy of either elitism or egalitarianism to him is a crude reckoning that misses the essence of this complex man. He was elitist in the realm of reason; he was egalitarian in normal social intercourse; he was popular with his soldiers and demanding of leaders. All of that is true. Two senior men, both of whom knew DePuy well, come to completely different conclusions when they compared the DePuy of 1966 to the man in a later decade. General Bruce Palmer believed that DePuy "mellowed" after division command, while Lieutenant

General Sid Berry says that the "supreme self-confidence" of the earlier DePuy became "border arrogance" in 1974–1977.[42] Despite these differing assessments, however, one thing is clear: throughout his life, DePuy's bedrock conviction was that merit is the currency of professionalism.

16

Retirement, Illness, Taps

I think I may have been able to propagate my ideas more
effectively if I had been a little more patient with people and
spent a little more time with them instead of being in such a
bloody hurry . . . that's the one great regret I have.
                                            —General William E. DePuy, 1979

Bill DePuy was a good soldier to the last.
                                            —Ambassador Harrison Symmes, 2005

He stood at attention on the green parade field at Fort Monroe, Virginia, in elegant summer whites as his former assistant division commander and current Army Chief of Staff General Bernard Rogers presided at his retirement ceremony on 30 June 1977. General William E. DePuy stepped into private life to meet another Rogers. Aide Tony Pokorny describes Bill DePuy's reintroduction to what his fellow Americans had been doing during his thirty-six-year absence from Main Street.

"The first thing he did on the day he retired," Pokorny recalled, "we went to Washington, and he says, 'I never had a Roy Rogers sandwich. Let's go get a Roy Rogers sandwich.' He had never been at a fast food place, so we had lunch at Roy Rogers and he enjoyed the heck out of that. He said, 'I've got to do this more often.'"

Pokorny recalled another incident soon after DePuy's retirement, when he had to buy lumber for Highfield. He told Pokorny, "You know, I asked for two-by-fours and they don't give me two-by-fours. Instead of two inches they gave me one and seven-eighths and three and a half inches." Pokorny went on, "Of course that's the regular size of a two-by-four, but he didn't know that. He thought he was being gypped."[1]

DePuy's daughter Joslin said her father would "discover" things in supermarkets and shops, buy them, and come home with "junk." She and the family were particularly amused by the cheap glass that so impressed him. "I don't think he had ever been in a store before, literally, besides the commissary," said Joslin. "He went into the place called the Pottery Factory in Williamsburg and bought cases and cases of wine glasses and glass bowls. Now why is a retired general doing that? Because he was a kid in a candy store. He bought that stuff for all of us for our new houses. We [the DePuy children, at that point in their twenties] were all sort of getting out in the world, and we would have these cheap wine glasses that were so thick you could put them in the dishwasher. And he was so proud of himself. 'Look what I did! Look what I found!' We'd say, 'Dad, it's just a store! They are just glasses!'"[2]

Those who were closest to DePuy have slightly varying memories of the earliest phase of his retirement, once he got beyond Roy Rogers sandwiches, shrunken two-by-fours, and bargain glass. Son Bill said, "There is no question that he derived enormous satisfaction from being both a good commander and staff officer." The last four years of his career as TRADOC Commander were the culmination of his long service, and he knew it. "He walked away, I think, with a sense of true, honest-to-God accomplishment." He was sufficiently perspicacious—one of his favorite words—to recognize that the proof of the pudding is in the tasting. It would take time for the training, doctrine, and weapons systems to percolate throughout the entire Army. But they did.

DePuy's son added, "He was around long enough to see the Gulf War that bore some things out. . . . By that time, we got the NTC [National Training Center] up and going and saw the effects of OPFOR [Opposing Forces, a generic name for an unidentified enemy that looked exactly like the Soviet Army]. I think he came out of all that with a profound sense that he had moved an institution" to where it would be able to fight effectively and to win the first battle without the stumbling he had experienced in his earliest days in uniform. "He was not a prideful or boastful man ever, but when they asked him to do the Oral History [in 1979] and the outcome of it was so spectacular in terms of who read it," said Bill Jr., he was very pleased and gratified. He added, "Even the title, *Changing an Army*, is a mouthful! To have that attributed to oneself is an accolade in and of itself."

The son believes that although his father must have been gratified by the feeling of a job well done, his departure from the Army was accompanied by a sadness and perhaps even disorientation.

"All of a sudden, it's all over. For a period of six or nine months, perhaps even a year or maybe a year and a half, he was sort of blue. He never talked to me about it, but I know that he talked to my sister Daphne about it, saying, 'You know, I'm really sort of depressed and not sure what to do about all of this.' He and she would go skiing [and talk]." Then he began consulting, and "he ended up doing the things he really wanted to do and became completely reenergized."

Daphne was interested to learn of her brother's remarks, but as she recalls it, her relationship with her father late in his life was just about what it had always been. "He was my wonderful friend," she said. "Throughout our whole adult lives I spent a lot of time coming home. I was more of a family-oriented child than Bill or Joslin." She did not discuss the military with her father. "I didn't understand the language and I wasn't really interested. I took after my mother in that regard. We talked about how things worked. That [philosophical excursions and tours of the horizon] was the relationship Bill had with him. Dad and I never had that conversation. It seemed [to me] like he transferred from his career to the next phase."

Joslin's recollections fall somewhere between Bill's analytical approach and Daphne's sweet memories. Joslin said of her father at that time, "I sort of felt he was at loose ends." But, she emphasized, "he was never bored." He became particularly interested in physics and theology and would discuss them with Joslin. Then, with his usual intensity and curiosity, he became captivated by wildflowers, a topic falling within Joslin's expertise as a professional landscaper and lecturer on the subject. Joslin observed that, while Daphne missed her father more than Joslin did when they were girls and he was in Vietnam, "Dad and I developed more of a relationship after he retired, a very close relationship." He bought a small house in Alexandria that was more convenient to National Airport than Highfield as he spent more time consulting, which required frequent travel. Joslin lived nearby. She would meet her father once or twice a week for dinner and conversation, often in "Saigon City," a section of Alexandria with many Vietnamese restaurants, including a favorite called The Queen Bee.

It wasn't long before Bill DePuy was comfortable in retirement. He loved to walk with his yapping dogs and visitors and family who cared to join him. He developed a close friendship with Eddie Strother, an elderly neighbor with deep roots in the area around

Highfield. Eddie was Bill's source of wisdom in local folklore, Fauquier County history, and horses. Tucked away in bucolic Virginia, Eddie was also Bill DePuy's unlikely coach regarding the stock market.

Another unlikely find for Bill DePuy was former Ambassador Harrison (Harry) Symmes, also retired in the area. Symmes recalled, "We were delighted to meet such a charming and urbane couple [Bill and Marj] in the midst of rural Fauquier County. Our friendship began at once." Symmes was a member of the Virginia Native Plant Society, the Audubon Society, and the Foundation of the State Arboretum, the latter located just down the road from Highfield. He persuaded Bill and Marj to join those organizations and said, "It was always a pleasure to be with him on these outings because he obviously enjoyed the learning experience and the companionship of other plant enthusiasts." Bill DePuy threw himself into the study of wildflowers with the same fire and intensity that he brought to whatever he did. Symmes saw something else he admired.

"As a citizen soldier of World War II, I could not help but be impressed by Bill's military record and attainments, his reputation for strict but always fair standards of performance, and the respect in which he was held by former colleagues whom I had met. I think what I admired most was his modesty. Bill needed no ego trips. He was a man who was happy with himself." Symmes saw in his friend "a successful military leader who had valued and felt responsible for those who served with him. As a graduate of the Infantry School OCS, I found Bill's obvious regard for the welfare of the common soldier deeply moving."[3]

DePuy blended his private joys with professional interests that were satisfied by consulting and writing. One sample of his work as a consultant illustrates his permanent interest in battle, his fascination with the German Army, and how useful his contributions to the U.S. Army continued to be. In May 1980 he served as catalyst and rapporteur for a four-day conference sponsored by the Department of Defense and the Defense Nuclear Agency. "The purpose of the conference," said DePuy in his report regarding the conference published later that year, "was to examine twentieth-century German military experience in battle against Russian forces with the intent of developing insights useful in aiding our understanding of the challenges NATO faces today [1980] in Europe as it prepares to confront the Soviets in any future conflict."[4]

German generals Hermann Balck and Friedrich von Mellenthin, who took part in the conference, had had numerous battlefield successes in World War II on the Eastern Front, despite being greatly outnumbered in men and materiel. They assumed the role of a U.S. division commander in a realistic operational 1980 context in U.S. V Corps. U.S. generals Glenn K. Otis and Paul Gorman did likewise in another iteration, after which analyses produced useful and interesting findings. In his report, DePuy identified several points of "enormous importance" that confirmed the validity of some of his personal convictions.

For one thing, small forces skillfully led can win battles against large forces if the small force is synchronized and the large force is disorganized. The Germans did just that repeatedly in World War II; NATO could do it against the same enemy, the Red Army. Nurturing an army's initiative and flexibility pays off. Most important, DePuy found, was the remarkable similarity in the tactics independently used by the German and American generals in exercises during the conference, indicating the compatibility of U.S. and German doctrine.

DePuy was pleased to learn that the German generals shared his convictions regarding the size of tactical units and the absolute need for close cooperation between air and ground forces. Balck and Mellenthin believed that seventy to eighty men was about the right strength for a rifle company, and three platoons of three tanks each, plus one tank for the commander, was about right for a tank company. Small size meant better control of weapons systems, and it also meant a higher proportion of leaders to led. That was gratifying to DePuy, since that had been his conviction since World War II.

Despite his extraordinary skill as a writer, Bill DePuy published only three articles during his thirty-six years on active duty (1941–1977), all for *Army* magazine.[5] He may simply have intended to help the newly founded Association of the United States Army, *Army*'s publisher, by providing them with good copy, but the subjects he addressed were clearly on his mind at the time. Coming out of his second battalion command experience, where his focus had been on training squads and platoons, he published "Eleven Men, One Mind" in 1958. As a by-product of his work for the Army Chief of Staff in the late 1950s, as the concepts of massive retaliation and flexible response were debated, DePuy's article on dual capability (meaning conventional and nuclear capabilities) appeared in 1960.

His article on the limits of "jointness" and the continuing need for the special skills and cultures of the Army, Navy, and Air Force ("Unification: How Much More?"), appeared in 1961. These three articles cover the A to Z of professional military concerns: from rifle squad to nuclear strategy.

The relative paucity of DePuy's publications over the years of his active duty conceals the fact that he was a prolific writer for his entire life. His letters, directives, lectures, and analyses on a multitude of subjects are voluminous, but they did not see the light of day until a compilation of some of DePuy's work was published in 1994.[6]

In the course of his retirement DePuy wrote twelve articles and six reviews that were published over twelve years (1978–1990), as well as much that was not published. The published articles are worth reviewing here because they reflect his mature thinking on issues of long-standing interest to him, and because they summarize the contribution he made to his profession in "retirement."[7]

In 1978 DePuy wrote an article entitled "Are We Ready for the Future?" and answered his own question: exploitation of high-technology weapons and equipment to attain maximum combat power requires better organization, doctrine, and training. He concluded pungently: "We cannot have the best man on a $200 typewriter while a less qualified soldier operates a million dollar tank." In "Technology and Tactics in Defense of Europe" (1979) he stressed the need for harmonization of tactics and modern weapons—and that it must be done with the Germans.

In "One-Up and Two-Back" (1980), DePuy returned to another lesson from World War II: how to penetrate enemy lines. "We have had it backward all along," he wrote. Bypassing and infiltration are the preferred methods. When frontal assault is necessary, heavy suppression is concentrated where a small assault force then penetrates and opens the gap for exploitation. Tests and the combat experience of the Israelis in 1973 and the Germans in World War II confirmed the wisdom of that approach. "Nine to one [suppression to assault] may be an extreme ratio," wrote DePuy, "but that seems clearly the way to lean."

In "FM 100–5 Revisited" (1980) DePuy rejected accusations that the 1976 Field Manual whose development he had spearheaded emphasized wars of defense and attrition. His remarks about "future war" were particularly prescient. "[It] will probably be fought under nonlinear circumstances which offensive action will dominate at the operational and tactical level no matter what the strategic mission may be . . . the Middle East presents the clearest example of that probability." And, he added, "The generation of officers now [1980] in command, seasoned in the airmobile environment of Vietnam, is especially suited for such operations. Accustomed to open flanks, to operating on the basis of ambiguous intelligence, seeking the enemy and not the terrain, concentrating rapidly, and adapting constantly to the flow of events—these leaders have maneuver in their bones. Let the critics relax."

His 1984 article, "Toward a Balanced Doctrine," addressed "the seductiveness of maneuver doctrine" and the understatement of synchronization. "Fast synchronization comes from good, simple procedures backed by reliable communication. Without synchronization, maneuver schemes can degenerate into indecisive minuets or end in disaster."

In "The Light Infantry: Indispensable Element of a Balanced Force" (1985), DePuy made the case that in "preferred terrain"—forests, mountains, urban congestion—light infantry is just the right tool. But it badly needed "an adequate shoulder-fired AT [anti-tank] capability. It must be light, short-ranged, and effective against the latest armor." His memories of fighting German armor and stories of Task Force Smith in Korea bouncing AT rounds harmlessly off T-34 tanks were much on his mind as he contemplated fighting the Red Army in the 1980s.

He turned his attention to Vietnam in three articles written in 1986 and 1987. In "Vietnam: What We Might Have Done and Why We Didn't Do It" (1986), he maintained that the United States drifted through its longest war without a concept of operations that would have aligned strategy with the political goal. Not cutting the Ho Chi Minh Trail by extending a line through the panhandle of Laos, generally along the 17th parallel, when the North Vietnamese Army (NVA) escalated combat in 1964, restricted U.S. activity to South Vietnam, while the enemy used Indochina—Vietnam, Laos, and Cambodia—as a theater of operations. The American concept was, DePuy said, like "setting the dinner table while the kitchen was on fire." It permitted the enemy to set the tempo of the war by fighting when conditions were favorable and withdrawing to sanctuaries when conditions were unfavorable.

"Troop A at Ap Tau O" (1986) is a combat story that demonstrates DePuy's excellent narrative skills, his admiration for the soldiers at the cutting edge of combat, and his lifelong concern for synchronizing the intelligent massing of fire with adroit maneuver. His recreation of the 1966 combat actions of A Troop, 1st Squadron, 4th Cavalry Regiment is inspirational.

In "Our Experience in Vietnam: Will We Be Beneficiaries or Victims?" (1987), DePuy dubbed television "the final sanction" and warned that since in our system of government the "out" party offers "clear alternatives," policy direction can be expected to change with a change of administrations. He also wrote that long and inconclusive operations like those in Vietnam were doomed. "Regular forces are generally ineffective against embedded forces because they lack local sources of information" he said. "The heart of prudence and cold realism suggest that U.S. combat forces stay away from embedded forces. Any violation of this advice is almost certain to be militarily futile and politically ruinous."

In "Concept of Operations: The Heart of Command, the Tool of Doctrine" (1988), DePuy asserted that the concept of operations is the sine qua non that unifies military effort in the midst of ever-increasing complexity. It is the commander's "supreme contribution to the prospect of victory" at the tactical or operational level. He refers with contempt to what he called the Tyranny of Boundaries and to "corridor commanders," those who merely divide missions and tasks uniformly among subordinate units and commanders—and wait for the bad news.

Emphasizing the concept of operations as the heart of command—and Erwin Rommel and Matthew Ridgway as exemplars of leadership in combat because they were creative and forceful—DePuy provided a command, communications, and control matrix to illustrate the synchronization of "battlefield functions/agencies" from company level to echelons above corps. Functions—which grew from eleven in the days of Clausewitz to twenty in the days of Patton to thirty in the days of AirLand Battle—were listed on a horizontal line across the top of the matrix. Levels of command, from company to echelons above corps, were stacked on the vertical to the left. DePuy called it the "C³ Matrix." The outcome of integrating some thirty functions with units at some eight levels is synchronization.

The road to hell is paved with good intentions. DePuy's matrix is a useful reference for a commander. It is also a means of evaluating performance, with the matrix used as a checklist in writing a commander's report card. Similarly, the National Training Center (NTC), designed for realistic training, including free maneuver and live firing, could become a tool to measure performance in order to write the Efficiency Report of the exercising commander. Commanders going through an NTC rotation could become more concerned with covering their asses—by not making mistakes—than with demonstrating the creativity DePuy personified.

Soldiers have a joke about the Army, saying: If a thing is worth doing, it's worth overdoing. This could be applied to DePuy's matrix. Richard Swain (Colonel, USA, Ret.), who compiled DePuy's papers and wrote a history of the first Gulf War, says that the matrix grew in complexity and became a part of doctrine via the NTC because it was an easy way to grade and critique personnel. He writes that in the first Gulf War "it became the molasses in the system," calling it "the culmination of DePuy's obsession with control over chance." Swain believes that in the hands of a master, synchronization is a force multiplier; but in the hands of "mere mortals," it can delay action as commanders are forced to go through a cumbersome checklist. He says, "DePuy's last legacy was the synchronization matrix which in time became a drag on opportunism."[8]

Thirteen of DePuy's fifteen published articles appeared in *Army*, with just one each in *Infantry* and *Parameters*, despite the prodding of the latter's editor, Lloyd Matthews, who was DePuy's briefing officer at MACV in 1964–1965. In the *Parameters* article, "For the Joint Specialist: Five Hills to Climb" (1989), DePuy set out the tasks that he felt needed to be addressed by the emerging Joint Specialists created by the Goldwater-Nichols DOD Reorganization Act of 1986. He cautioned that "there is the unmistakable presumption of a zero-sum game" in which "Congress seemed to believe that strengthening the joint establishment required the weakening of the services. This is both unfortunate and unnecessary. . . . What is required is a strengthening of both." Here DePuy was reiterating ideas he had expressed in his 1961 article, "Unification: How Much More?" where he emphasized the importance of the distinct cultures and unique capabilities of the land, sea, and air services and the expertise of their personnel and leaders, particularly in tactics. The new Joint Specialists, wrote DePuy in 1989, must figure out the limits of tactical jointness.

It is fitting that the last article DePuy published before his fatal illness rendered him incapable of professional writing was entitled

"Infantry Combat." It appeared in *Infantry,* the professional journal of infantrymen, in 1990. The linear tactics of the two world wars and Korea, wrote DePuy, were a thing of the past. Increased free maneuver is the future. Directed at junior infantry officers, the article is pure DePuy. His advice: Read Rommel. Where junior infantry leaders do their work, successful methods of close combat—reconnaissance, assault, and exploitation—will remain constant. This was something DePuy learned in 1944 and taught to the U.S. Army for his entire life.

In retrospect, the two earliest indications that DePuy had a serious health problem appeared at about the same time in the late 1980s, one on the back roads of rural Virginia and the other in the bosom of the Army at Fort Leavenworth, Kansas.

Bill, Marj, and Daphne, with gardening tools, set out in two cars, headed for the Brown-Walker family burial site in Brown's Cove, not far from Charlottesville. Daphne followed her parents for the trip from Highfield in her own car, because after their maintenance work on the graves she planned to continue on to her home. As she observed her father's erratic and dangerous driving, she became very upset. He passed on curves and while ascending hills, where he couldn't possibly observe oncoming traffic. Attributing the problem to simple inattention, when they arrived at Brown's Cove she accosted her father, accusing him of endangering Marj, himself, and anyone else on the road. He was repentant, apologized profusely to Marj and Daphne, and promised to "sit up" and be attentive to his driving. Later, as his health deteriorated, Daphne realized that what she had observed on that day was the first sign of the illness that would kill him.

Daphne recalls another incident that took on significance only later. Sometime in the late 1980s she asked her father about a skin rash that had been bothering him. He said, "That's the least of my problems." When Daphne asked what he meant by that, he responded by repeating, "That's the least of my problems." Daphne suspects that either he had gotten a medical opinion that he did not share with the family or he had engaged in some self-diagnosis and concluded that "something was very wrong."

Barrie Zais (Colonel, USA, Ret.) was an eyewitness to DePuy's first slip-up in public. By this time it seems that DePuy was aware that something was wrong, but he apparently believed that he could conceal it and handle it. He intended to go about his business.

In 1987 DePuy addressed the students at the Command and General Staff College in a plenary session before joining Barrie Zais and his seminar, which was made up of advanced students studying at Leavenworth for a second year. Zais had first met DePuy briefly in 1966, when Barrie's father, Melvin Zais (General, USA, Ret.), who was at the time DePuy's Assistant Division Commander in 1966, returned with his son to the United States to be with Barrie's mother, who was fatally ill. Two decades later LTC Zais encountered DePuy again at his seminar.

At the end of the seminar session, Barrie explained to DePuy that Barrie's brother Mitch Zais (BG, USA, Ret.), also stationed at Leavenworth, would drive him to lunch. After lunch they would continue on the planned itinerary for the day. DePuy acknowledged the plan and got in the car. As the car began to move, DePuy asked, "Where are we going?" Mitch had heard his brother brief DePuy, and he heard DePuy's acknowledgment. Something was indeed amiss.

Mitch deliberately drove on a route that would pass the post hospital. Approaching the hospital, Mitch asked DePuy if he'd like to stop at the hospital for a quick check-up. DePuy declined. Mitch slowed, approaching the entrance to the hospital while repeating the invitation/suggestion/recommendation to enter. DePuy acquiesced.[9]

A coda to this incident is provided by Richard Hart Sinnreich (Colonel, USA, Ret.). Sinnreich and DePuy had met in 1980 and become friends based upon their shared passion for the U.S. Army and the meeting of two fine minds. DePuy was at Leavenworth that day at the invitation of Sinnreich, who was at the time Director, School of Advanced Military Studies (SAMS), the second-year program for selected students. After DePuy received a diagnosis at the Leavenworth hospital, Sinnreich escorted him from Kansas to Walter Reed Army Hospital in Washington, D.C., where "a slight stroke" was diagnosed.[10]

Another faculty member describes his discovery of a DePuy he did not know, perhaps during this DePuy visit. "Rick Sinnreich used to have him out to SAMS, and one year he came to the dining in. We were in Blues, he in a Tux, quite dapper and quite relaxed. He was easy to talk to and at the end of the dinner he set to teaching us British dining-in games of the less raucous sort. . . . That he was perfectly at home with a bunch of majors and lieutenant colonels blew my mind. It was a new look at the ogre of Fort Monroe, which he had seemed to be to Leavenworth when he was TRADOC CG. It was then I started reading what he had written, and I pursued that later when I had the time and resources. Later, I also discovered some of the reasons he treated Leavenworth like he did. I always think of him lying on the floor in the Leavenworth Club in his Tux with a rolled up newspaper in his hand playing a kind of horizontal blindman's bluff."[11]

DePuy's daughter Joslin, looking back to the time before her father's illness was evident, said that her father was so smart that she's quite sure that he concealed it from everyone for some time as he tried to solve this problem as he had solved so many others. Whining was not his style.

Paul Gorman recalls a visit to DePuy at Highfield during which Bill misplaced his keys. Marj, showing some impatience, admonished him to keep track of things. Gorman joined DePuy in the hunt for the keys, which were eventually found on the roof of Bill's car. Of course, DePuy was neither the first nor the last to misplace keys or glasses, perhaps while fumbling and juggling an armload of bundles or distracted by conversation. But Marj's reaction suggested to Gorman that forgetting and misplacing were becoming annoyingly frequent. What appeared to be carelessness was in fact the early stage of a fatal illness.[12]

Another misplaced key caused William F. Burns (MG, USA, Ret.) to discover an interesting point regarding Bill DePuy and religion. Burns knew DePuy from Vietnam, and as a colonel had served as DePuy's TRADOC Liaison Officer to the Heeresamt (the German Army Office) in Cologne. In 1989 or 1990 the two retired generals were at Leavenworth to speak to the class. Burns hosted DePuy in his VIP suite there because DePuy had lost the key to his. Over a drink, while waiting for a key, the old comrades discussed a wide range of subjects, including religion. Knowing that Burns was a devout Catholic, DePuy announced that he was "rethinking religion." Wes Geary (Colonel, Chaplain, USA, Ret.) made a similar remark about DePuy's interest in religion in his later years. However, DePuy's son said that his father toward the end of his life was inclined to think that electro-chemistry was at the core of man's complex of mind and body. DePuy was serious, well-read, and informed about religion as an intellectual pursuit, just as he was curious about science and human nature. But it is unlikely that he "got religion" at the end of his life.[13]

DePuy's children, in separate interviews, described how their father's absorption in the details of daily rural life would have made it possible for him to conceal his problem. They knew that while digging post holes, mending fences, and cutting and splitting firewood he had always simultaneously puzzled through complex issues about which he was consulting, writing, or testifying before committees of Congress. It was not at all unusual that in retirement, as before, he went about his chores like a farm laborer while contemplating tactics, doctrine, training, leadership, weapons systems, and other esoterica of the military art. As one of his children put it, while he was doing his heavy-duty thinking, listeners would hear "chop, chop, chop" as he split wood. These routine activities might have concealed his progressive deterioration of mind. They took him off by himself, as before; they kept him physically fit, as always. His intention to build a barn for what was becoming a mountain of wood—it was still being burned at Highfield in 2006—could be seen in the late 1980s as dad's intensity and prudence. And it kept him from prying eyes. In retrospect his repetitive behavior can be seen as obsessive behavior consistent with the onset of a kind of dementia.

Asked how his mother held up as his father's illness rapidly progressed, Bill said that the usually self-reliant and in-control Marj was devastated for about two years. She had been content with her quiet life in her native Virginia. The kids had matured and grown into adults. She was unprepared for what was happening to her husband.

He alternated his wood chopping with the drafting of ideas for articles and speeches. He continued to noodle and doodle on legal tablets as he had for his entire life, most recently at the round kitchen table at Highfield. Distraught at what she saw, Marj saved samples of his work to show to the children. His handwriting became an increasingly undisciplined scrawl. The legal pad eventually revealed a single black line on which he had written sentence after sentence in the same space, one on top of the next. He would be in the bathroom for a long time, brushing his teeth three and four times. He had trouble tying his shoelaces. Marj felt helpless.

Harry Symmes and his wife were also "sad witnesses to the relentless effects" of disease. "We had noticed the early stages and had seen and been told about some of its odd effects on him," he wrote. "When we went out to dinner or to a nearby summer stock theater in his last months at home, I would sometimes help him to tie his tie or to cut his meat at the table."[14]

Generally his "old boys" learned of DePuy's illness via the Army grapevine, but some of them stumbled into it. Romie L. Brownlee (Colonel, USA, Ret.) had served as aide to LTG Orwin Talbott, DePuy's wartime comrade in the 90th Division and his Deputy Commander at TRADOC from July 1973 until August 1975. As students at the Army War College, Brownlee and William J. Mullen III had interviewed DePuy for his 1979 Oral History, "Changing an Army." Brownlee was later a Senate staffer and still later Acting Secretary of the Army. Right after the Gulf War, he said, he got several calls from media representatives asking "how in the world did this Army that was on its ass after Vietnam" succeed so brilliantly in the Gulf War? Who did that?

Brownlee recalled, "I said a lot of people contributed to that, but most would agree that if you identified a single leader who caused it to happen, it would be General DePuy." The journalists asked to be put in contact with DePuy. Brownlee said he'd call DePuy to ask him if he wanted to be interviewed. "Well, I called him. That was the first indication I had of what was wrong with him."

Bill DePuy said to Brownlee, "Well Les, I don't want to do it right now. I'm having some problems." When Brownlee asked, "Sir, are you OK?" he said, "Yeah, yeah, I think I'm OK. But Les, you know I was always able to think of two or three things at once. I could be setting post holes and I could compute how many chopper lifts it takes to move a division, and at the same time I was thinking of a strategy for how we might approach the next NATO meeting. I could do all that at once. Les, I can't even load the dishwasher anymore. I put all the dirty stuff in the cabinet and all the clean stuff in the dishwasher."

DePuy told Brownlee to call Paul Gorman; he said that Gorman could talk to the press. Brownlee got in touch with Gorman, and Gorman expressed worry. When Brownlee suggested Alzheimer's, Gorman said, "It sounds to me like it's worse."[15]

Gorman, who visited his old boss at Highfield from time to time, had seen a rapid deterioration. He also noticed that Marj was showing signs of wearing down. The inexorable slide into dementia was causing DePuy, once a paragon of responsibility and propriety, to regress to childish behavior, pettiness, sometimes meanness. One can hardly imagine Marj's reaction as she was confronted daily by Bill's slide from brilliance to infantile behavior. Episodes of lucidity punctuated longer periods of blankness and confusion; the man who had been known for logic, crispness of decision, and clarity of expression was generally muddled.

Jack Woodmansee, one of DePuy's favorite "old boys," was warned by his comrades in 1990 or 1991 that there was no point in visiting DePuy. He only recognizes Max Thurman, they said. William B. Burdeshaw (BG, USA, Ret.), another veteran of those heady days of the mid-1970s at TRADOC when they were transforming the Army, said, "Jack, he doesn't know who most of us are anymore." But, said Woodmansee, "I just need to go say good-bye," and he went to visit his old commander in an institutionalized setting.

He found General DePuy sitting in a walker propped up with pillows, making clicking sounds. Jack could see that he had lost weight. An attendant said, "General, you have a visitor here to see you." Woodmansee recalled, "So he turned around and saw me. 'Well, well! Jack Woodmansee is here.' He got that gleam in his eye. He would start a sentence just as clearly as ever, but after getting out a sentence, he just drifted off. We carried on about a five-minute conversation. Then I said good-bye. I caught him in one of his lucid times."[16]

Others remarked on this pattern of DePuy's beginning a statement clearly and then drifting off into incoherence, often with signs of exasperation at not being able to say what he wanted to say. At one point he rarely spoke, though he could show people he recognized them. George Joulwan (GEN, USA, Ret.), DePuy's 1961 lieutenant in Schweinfurt, 1966 captain in Vietnam, and lifelong student and friend, visited him toward the end. DePuy could not speak, so he put his hands on Joulwan's face, indicating with his eyes and body language, "I know who you are." Joulwan, a tough old soldier, teared up at the telling of this story a dozen years after the event described. He always thought of Bill DePuy as the fit and energetic colonel, impeccably turned out even in fatigues, jumping into the foxhole while asking, Who's on your right? Who's on your left? Where's the dead space? Show me your FPL (Final Protective Line).[17]

Tony Pokorny, who said of DePuy, "After Vietnam he took the Army and stood it back up on its feet again," probably expresses the feeling of those who knew him best. "He had the worst of all possible deaths, because the first thing that went was his mind, which was his strongest point."[18]

DePuy's son provides the most comprehensive recollection of

the course of his father's fatal illness from its onset until it killed him. After the 1987 episode of temporary disorientation at Fort Leavenworth, to the best of Bill's knowledge, his father seemed to be generally well until about 1990. Then, "all of a sudden he began to lose first his fine motor coordination and then his gross motor coordination. Originally they thought it might be Alzheimer's, but he was knifing through the levels of what is usually experienced in Alzheimer's as a step-by-step progression. He was dropping down through levels of capability at an exponential rate. Finally, when they got him to the National Institutes of Health (NIH) in Bethesda, because Walter Reed couldn't figure it out, the NIH guy said the best we can tell, it's the Creutzfeldt-Jacob disease (CJD). That conclusion was drawn from a brain scan revealing a 'spongified' brain [a characteristic of CJD]." (An electroencephalogram, or EEG, can indicate CJD, but it is not diagnostic. A variant of the disease is known as "mad cow disease.")

CJD is an extremely rare disease, and the NIH pronouncement caused speculation about how DePuy came down with an illness that is literally a million-to-one shot. He had contact with Montagnards in Vietnam back in 1962; since dignitaries are honored by the Montagnards with a ceremony including food and drink, and since one of the foods is monkey meat, and since monkeys are carriers of CJD, it is possible that he contracted the disease in the 1960s. It is an interesting possibility, but because the expiration of the incubation period for CJD is about twenty years, DePuy's son is inclined to discount this possibility in favor of another, which is also pure speculation. Bill and Marj made two trips to England in the mid-1980s. By eating beef while they were there, they could have been exposed to mad cow disease. This possibility has to be filed with the Montagnard story in the "could be" box. There was an autopsy. The cause of death was indeed CJD. What is not known is how DePuy got the disease.

There is no known cure for CJD. Complete dementia commonly occurs within six months of the onset of symptoms. Some survive for a year or two. Eventually care of the patient requires "a safe environment," control of aggressive or agitated behavior, close supervision in home care, and then an "institutionalized setting," precisely the course DePuy's family took in caring for him.[19] When his illness required care beyond management at home, he was placed with a couple to care for the general in their home, but, said young

Bill, "that didn't work out." With profound regret, the family agreed that he required the constant care that only a specialized institution could provide.

Harry Symmes, in the graceful prose of the career diplomat, provides a fitting last glimpse of Bill DePuy. "When I visited Bill at Walter Reed and at the nursing home in which he spent his last days, I always marveled at his good humor. He seemed oblivious to the disease that was destroying his life. I never heard a word of self-pity or despair. Bill was a good soldier to the last."

At 11:00 PM on 9 September 1992, William E. DePuy died in Arlington, Virginia. He would have been seventy-three on 1 October. He was buried in Marj's family plot in Brown's Cove, Virginia. Marj joined him there ten years later, after her death on 15 March 2002. She was eighty-seven.

17

Legacy

An Army Ready to Fight the Next War

> We dedicated the book to your father because he was the
> person most responsible for GETTING IT RIGHT.
> > —Letter from Ray Macedonia, coauthor of
> > *Getting It Right,* to Bill DePuy Jr., 22 October 1993

> These years were some of the richest for professional dialogue
> in the U.S. Army's history.
> > —Historian Richard Swain, on the doctrinal debate
> > from 1976 to 1986

American boys know that the simplest way to terminate a school-yard fight is to whip the other fellow and make him say "uncle." When General Norman H. Schwarzkopf forced Iraq to say "uncle" to end the Gulf War in 1991, it had been almost half a century since America experienced such an apparently simple termination of hostilities. Since the German and Japanese unconditional surrenders in 1945, fog pervaded the commencement and termination of American wars as much as it pervaded the conduct of war. The war in Korea, for example, was never declared and didn't officially end.

Americans understand the ideas of "win" and "loss" very well, but they are confused and frustrated by indeterminacy, particularly when it takes the form of what they see as third-rate powers thumbing their noses at the United States. American forces left Vietnam in 1973 and watched it fall to the enemy in 1975. Vietnam, Mayagüez, Pueblo, Desert One, and Beirut became code words for ineptness, incompetence, lack of will, a drift from the greatness and promise of 1945. The U.S. Army looked like the gang that couldn't shoot straight. To fully comprehend the elation of professional soldiers after Desert Storm, one needs to know their despair in the post-Vietnam era and the disrepair and demoralization of the Army in the 1970s. It felt good to see the buildup of force, the air campaign, and the competent ground combat that culminated quickly in victory in 1991. There was a sense that the country was back on track. Americans prefer their wars to be short, decisive, and—of course—victorious. The Gulf War was all of that. When it was over, President George H. W. Bush exulted boyishly, "By God, we've licked the Vietnam syndrome once and for all."[1]

Savoring the victory, the natural questions from the public and the media were: How did it happen? How was the ragged post-Vietnam Army transformed into the capable force that won the Gulf War? And who deserved credit for this transformation and for the gratitude of the nation?

The short answer is that American soldiers fixed the Army. It was widely believed that the U.S. Army, indeed all U.S. forces, were the best ever committed to battle. Military analysts put Bill DePuy in the first rank of the soldiers who fixed the broken Army in the 1970s and 1980s. Many of the most knowledgeable single him out as the central figure of the reform movement. Bill Tuttle called DePuy the "change agent," making the point that few human beings have all of the parts—mental, physical, emotional, experiential, and creative—required to turn around a large and complex organization. (Add to this the confidence and impatience required to make it happen quickly.) Others, particularly those closest to DePuy, often his acolytes, described him as the greatest soldier of his generation, the most influential officer since World War II. Some of that assessment may be discounted as the enthusiasm of the star-struck so common in our age of hyperbole, when even the ordinary is called "awesome"; but attention should be paid when the discerning Paul Gorman assigns DePuy to a trinity with George C. Marshall and Lesley J. McNair as "past trainers of the Army" to whom much is owed. "In 1973," Gorman wrote, "William E. DePuy's TRADOC undertook to insure that the Army could train not only leaders at the strategic and operational levels who could draw arrows on the map to discomfit any enemy, but also units capable of advancing those arrows." Gorman knew from experience that moving the arrows on the ground was a trickier and dirtier proposition than drawing them on maps. He believes the Army's reform would not have gone so deep or so fast without DePuy. Nor, he implied, would it have taken root. DePuy enabled the fixing; the roots are his legacy.[2]

Donn Starry was asked directly if saying that "DePuy fixed the broken Army" gave one man too much credit, since other first-rate people were involved, not least among them Gorman and Starry himself. Starry, who chooses his words with care and courts no man, didn't pause long before responding, "I accept that statement."[3]

Other professional soldiers and analysts with insight into the post-Vietnam Army assign DePuy first place in the transformation. "Spark plug" and "point man" are words they use to describe how DePuy cranked up the Army and led to get it right. Harry Summers (COL, USA, Ret.), who served as an operations officer in one of DePuy's battalions in Vietnam and covered the Gulf War as military analyst, reflected on military affairs for his entire life. Summers held DePuy in the highest possible regard as a commander, thinker, and reformer. He inscribed a copy of his book, *On Strategy II: A Critical Analysis of the Gulf War*, "[To] Gen. DePuy, With great respect for an outstanding soldier who put the Army on track to victory."[4]

DePuy's influence went well beyond tending to business on his watch. It extended into the future with the confluence of his doctrine, training, and weapons systems on the battlefield. The Army he had prepared to fight the Soviet Army in Europe became the perfect instrument for swift victory in the next war, the first Gulf War. As one scholar noted, "Gen. William DePuy had always said that it took roughly ten years to develop a new weapons system or doctrine, and another five to get them comfortably out into the hands of soldiers in the field. As in so many other things, the tough old general, whom Starry considered perhaps the greatest soldier of his time, was close to the mark."[5]

Insuring the health of the Army in the future required identifying, nurturing, and advancing the best, to develop successor generations of leaders who would put it all together. Professional soldiers stuck it out in the bad times of the 1970s and 1980s. The Army was at its nadir at about the time that DePuy took command of TRADOC in 1973. Bill Tuttle came close to giving up on the Army after Vietnam, and he was not alone. It was that bad. But he didn't. DePuy found peers, near-peers, and acolytes who loved their Army yet saw its defects and were prepared to join him in fixing it.

A sense of continuity, a passing of the baton, is suggested in the recital of just some of the names of men who came in waves. They ranged in age and rank from seniors, beginning with William Westmoreland, Bruce Palmer, and Creighton Abrams, to DePuy's peers such as Fred Weyand, George Forsythe, Bill Rosson, Melvin

Zais, and Walter Kerwin, to the next crop, among them Donn Starry, Paul Gorman, and Glenn Otis. Then came the bright young men, the aides and young tigers who were DePuy's majors and lieutenant colonels when he was AVICE and TRADOC Commander. Max Thurman commanded TRADOC from 1987 to 1989, ten to twelve years after DePuy retired. He was succeeded in that job from 1989 to 1991 by another DePuy protégé, John W. Foss, as the Gulf War was fought and DePuy was in his decline.

Jack Woodmansee and Sid Berry got three stars, and Berry became the Superintendent at West Point. Les Brownlee served as Acting Secretary of the Army. Bill Tuttle got four stars and command of the Army Materiel Command. Colin Powell became Chairman of the Joint Chiefs of Staff and Secretary of State. DePuy acolytes from the days of Schweinfurt and Vietnam were also successful. George Joulwan became Supreme Allied Commander, Europe (SACEUR), and got four stars, Bernie Rogers became Army Chief of Staff and was SACEUR, and the charismatic Richard Cavazos got four stars. Alexander Haig was SACEUR and then Secretary of State.

Bill DePuy found the men who would help him in what he called "my life's work": a thorough reform of the Army, a task he set for himself. And he seeded the system with talented people who would directly succeed him and others who would succeed them to direct the Army a dozen years and even two decades after his retirement.[6]

Bill Jr. is convinced that his father left active duty deeply gratified in the conviction that he had done his best, that what he had done mattered, and that the best was still to come. The son's words bear repeating: "He walked away with a sense of true, honest-to-God accomplishment." General DePuy knew that it would take time for what he had begun to percolate through the system. His regular meetings with his command historians, particularly with Brooks Kleber, indicate that he had a sense of history and a consciousness of continuity. He wanted successor generations to understand why they were where they were and how they got there.

Sound management, training, doctrine, and combat developments—and, most significantly, their integration—were seeds planted during DePuy's active duty. They took root in the following decade, as he nurtured them by consulting, writing, and testifying as an expert witness before congressional committees. As a retired officer he was asked to testify because Army leadership recognized both his skill in explaining complex issues and his gift of persuasion. The Gulf War, a stunning revelation to those unfamiliar with what the Army had been doing since the war in Vietnam, may be seen as the fruition of DePuy's efforts. Fortunately, he was able to see the results of his labor before illness robbed him of his intelligence, focus, and lucidity.

The doctrine that DePuy literally forced through a cumbersome Army bureaucracy with the 1976 version of FM 100–5 was followed by the publication of the more specific "how to fight" manuals to guide commanders, particularly those of tank and mechanized infantry companies and those of battalion task forces of tanks and infantry fighting vehicles. His 1976 initiative stimulated the thinking of the best of the bright young men and touched off passionate debate that, in turn, produced ever more sophisticated tactical and operational concepts, progressing from mobile defense to AirLand Battle and deep strike. The 1986 version of FM 100–5 codified the doctrine the Army took to the Persian Gulf in 1990. It welded into a focused and harmonious whole the human efforts and material investments that became an Army qualitatively unmatched anywhere in the world.[7]

As a consequence of Gorman's creativity and DePuy's forceful leadership, measurement of training effectiveness became performance based, and continues to be so well into the twenty-first century. Individual soldiers were tested by performing tasks in conditions and by standards that guided and measured the process. Units were similarly measured by performance, using technical devices during realistic training. All training culminated at the National Training Center, where free maneuver and the firing of all weapons were possible; soldiers and leaders practiced in the California desert precisely what they would do in combat in another desert. And the opposing force in California was a mirror image of the Soviet-armed and -equipped force defeated in 1991. That's why American soldiers said after the Gulf War that they had fought the war the way they trained to fight it for fifteen years.[8]

From his AVICE job in 1969 through his TRADOC years, Bill DePuy was personally and deeply involved in combat developments. He knew about the almost endless changes and modifications inherent to the process as systems evolved, and he knew the tedious labor required in deciding which weapons were to be developed and nursed from concept until they were in the hands of troops in the field. The Big Five—a tank, an infantry fighting vehicle, an air defense missile system, and two helicopters—were a part of his life for many years before the sophisticated systems were crewed by soldiers skilled in their use in combat. Doctrine, training, and combat developments came together at the right time.

DePuy's vision of a resurrected Army was fulfilled just as his mind began to cloud and his body failed him. In the Gulf War there was no Kasserine Pass, no wasted American life as in June and July of 1944, no Task Force Smith as in Korea in 1950, no stumbling as amateur American leaders killed American soldiers.[9]

Some of his admirers, convinced of his indispensability in transforming the post-Vietnam Army, might turn to Shakespeare to describe DePuy, as in these lines from *Richard II:*

> As in a theater, the eyes of men,
> After a well-graced actor leaves the stage,
> Are idly bent on him that enters next,
> Thinking his prattle will be tedious.

One suspects that Bill DePuy the realist would smile in the knowledge that the U.S. Army is more important than one man's reputation. It really does just keep rolling along. He would have warned against excessive glee or resting on oars. He would have insisted on getting ready for the next war.

General William E. DePuy's career was a calling; considered experience was his foundation. His intelligence, energy, dedication, and powers of persuasion moved his Army toward his vision. It was ready to fight the next war and to win the first battle. His was an "honest-to-God accomplishment." That was enough for him.

Notes

Preface

1. Adolf von Schell, *Battle Leadership* (Fort Benning, Ga.: The Benning Herald, 1933). Freud cited in Tim O'Brien, *In the Lake of the Woods* (New York: Penguin, 2005), 291.

2. Foreword to Henry G. Gole, *Soldiering: Observations from Korea, Vietnam, and Safe Places* (Dulles, Va.: Potomac Books, 2005), xiv.

1. Dakota Days

1. See Marvin A. Kreidberg and Merton G. Henry, *History of Military Mobilization in the United States Army, 1775–1945,* Department of the Army Pamphlet no. 20-212 (Washington, D.C.: Department of the Army, 1955), 379, and Russell F. Weigley, *History of the United States Army* (New York: Macmillan Co., 1967), 568, for manpower and expenditures. See Henry G. Gole, *The Road to Rainbow: Army Planning for Global War, 1934–1940* (Annapolis, Md.: Naval Institute Press, 2003), for planning for World War II. For public opinion in the United States, see George H. Gallup, *The Gallup Poll: Public Opinion,1935–1971,* 3 vols. (New York: Random House, 1972). See also Hadley Cantril, *Public Opinion, 1935–1946* (Princeton: Princeton University Press, 1951). "Impotent": Peyton C. Marsh, *The Nation at War* (Garden City, N.Y.: Doubleday, 1932), 341; "pitiable": Richard M. Ketchum, *The Borrowed Years, 1938–1941: America on the Way to War* (New York: Random House, 1989), 537; "ineffective": *Annual Reports, War Department, Fiscal Year Ended June 30, 1941* (Washington, D.C.: U.S. Government Printing Office, 1941), 48.

2. Oral History, William E. DePuy, *Changing an Army* (henceforth OH, DePuy), U.S. Army Military History Institute (henceforth MHI). Unless otherwise indicated, the DePuy quotations in this chapter are from OH, DePuy. Note that three different sources used throughout this book may be confused: the DePuy Oral History at MHI just cited (OH, DePuy, MHI is identified in the bibliography by title, *Changing an Army*); the DePuy Papers, also found at MHI; and the DePuy Family Papers, currently held by the DePuy family.

3. Joslin DePuy Gallatin, interview with Gole, 25 January 2005.

4. Waltz, interview with Gole, 2 March 2005. DePuy's son, William E. DePuy Jr., told me that his paternal grandmother once remarked to

him that the general grew up largely unsupervised by his parents. The general adored his grandfather and always loved dogs. One gets the picture of a content and self-contained little boy. Interview with Gole, 12 September 2007.

5. Jeannie Mattison Rotz, letter to Gole postmarked 17 March 2005. She died on 12 July 2005. In a letter to the author dated 4 March 2006, Jeannie's daughter, Jeanne Bertacchi, says, "My mother had a special smile and tone in her voice when she told the stories of Bill DePuy. She was no more proud of his accomplishments in the military than his abilities on the dance floor! He was a true friend to her—that speaks volumes of the man."

6. The transcripts are in DePuy Papers, MHI.

7. Western Union Telegram dated 26 August 1941 to PMS&T, South Dakota State College, Brookings, S.D., file marked "Career Management Files," DePuy Family Papers.

8. DA Form 66, DePuy Family Papers. DA 66 is a standard form with information regarding the subject soldier, including education, appointments (promotions), foreign service, duty assignments, awards and decorations, campaigns, and skills.

9. Murphy letter dated 26 August 1941 to Headquarters, U.S. Marine Corps, DePuy Family Papers.

10. See, for example, Murphy letter dated 20 November 1945, DePuy Family Papers.

11. Stofft to Gole, e-mail, 14 March 2005. Garrison Keillor's radio program, *A Prairie Home Companion*, pokes fun at the Upper Midwest.

12. Tom Brokaw, *A Long Way from Home: Growing Up in the American Heartland in the Forties and Fifties* (New York: Random House, 2002), 22. See also Brokaw's *The Greatest Generation* (New York: Random House, 1998).

13. Stofft to Gole, e-mail, 14 March 2005.

14. This apt formulation, fitting in while standing out, is gratefully borrowed from sociologist Anna Simons, *The Company They Keep* (New York: Free Press, 1998). She used it to describe the characteristics of the Special Forces soldier.

2. Apprentice to Journeyman

1. A note about military designations: 20th Infantry means 20th Infantry Regiment; 1/20 is the First Battalion of the 20th, 2/20 is the Second Battalion of the 20th, and so on.

2. All quotations and paraphrasing of DePuy in this chapter, unless noted otherwise, are from OH, DePuy, MHI.

3. Roster dated 3 April 1942, Officers' Communications Course no. 16, Fort Benning, Georgia, DePuy Family Papers.

4. See tables of War Department expenditures and strength of the active army in Russell F. Weigley, *History of the United States Army* (New York: Macmillan Co., 1967), pp. 560–561, 566–569.

5. Ely Jacques Kahn, *McNair, Educator of an Army* (Washington, D.C.: Infantry Journal, 1945), 23–24. See Edward M. Coffman, *The Regulars: The American Army* (Cambridge, Mass.: The Belknap Press of Harvard University Press, 2004), for a masterful portrayal of the American enlisted soldiers in the four decades before World War II.

6. Peter R. Mansoor, *The GI Offensive in Europe* (Lawrence: University Press of Kansas, 1999), 19. See also Kent Roberts Greenfield, Robert R. Palmer, and Bell I. Wiley, *The Organization of Ground Combat Troops* (Washington, D.C.: Historical Division, Department of the Army, 1947), especially the table "Ground Forces in the Army, December 1941–April 1945," 161, and the notes, analysis, and sources that follow. See also Russell F. Weigley, *Eisenhower's Lieutenants* (Bloomington: Indiana University Press, 1981), 12–14, for how thinking about the eventual strength of the U.S. Army at 89 divisions evolved from earlier estimates of 334 and 200. Considering that the Soviet Army had 400 divisions, the German Army 300, and the Japanese Army 100, even allowing for differences in size and composition, Weigley concludes, "mobilizing a ninety division army for the Second World War was not an altogether impressive performance for a super-power." See also John Colby, *War from the Ground Up: The 90th Division in World War II* (Austin, Tex.: Nortex Press, 1991), for first-person accounts on activation from 25 March 1942 to the war's end. June–July 1944 was particularly bloody for the 90th, as was November 1944 to February 1945.

7. Robert R. Palmer, Bell I. Wiley, and William R. Keast, *The Procurement and Training of Ground Combat Troops* (Washington, D.C.: Historical Division, Department of the Army, 1948), 472. See table, "U.S. Army Divisions in World War II: Number, Classification, and Dates of Activation and Movement to Port of Embarkation," 489–492.

8. Monsoor, *GI Offensive*, 29.

9. Quoted in ibid., 218.

10. Ibid., 73–76.

11. Michael D. Doubler, *Closing with the Enemy: How GIs Fought the War in Europe, 1944–1945* (Lawrence: University Press of Kansas, 1994), Table 9.1, 236.

12. Ibid., 240.

3. The 90th Division Goes to School

1. John Colby, *War from the Ground Up: The 90th Division in World War II* (Austin, Tex.: Nortex Press, 1991), 2 (italics added). Description

of the precombat training is brief, but it includes this (probably accurate) self-appraisal by a lieutenant: "I was not qualified to lead a Boy Scout troop, let alone a platoon of men in combat." Hanson Baldwin, the *New York Times* military correspondent, wrote the following after visiting the war zone: "The greatest American problem is leadership: the Army so far has failed to produce a fraction of the adequate officer leadership needed." *New York Times*, 11 May 1943, cited in Rick Atkinson, *Day of Battle* (New York: Henry Holt and Co., 2007), 8.

2. Unless otherwise noted, quotations and paraphrasing of DePuy in this chapter are from OH, DePuy, MHI.

3. Colby, *War from the Ground Up*, 6.

4. Talbott, interview with John Votaw, 17 September 1994.

5. DePuy, OH, and Colby, *War from the Ground Up* describe the fighting in Normandy in similar terms.

6. Edward Smith Hamilton, interview with Gole, 18 February 2005. (I was saddened to learn of Ed Hamilton's death in July 2006. He was Old Army, and hard core.) DePuy, OH, MHI, and Bealke Papers (Barth file) tell this story in a similar manner, as does Colby.

7. Barth's recommendation for DePuy's integration into the Regular Army lavishes praise on DePuy. DePuy Family Papers.

8. Barth's narrative of the July 1944 events and DePuy's attached Training Memorandum no. 1 were found in the DePuy Family Papers. The training memo is remarkably similar to DePuy's training directive for the 1st Infantry Division some twenty-two years later, described by Richard Cavazos (General, USA, Ret.) in Chapter 12 of this book.

9. Uhlig was later captured by the Americans. He was interviewed in 1979. Colby, *War from the Ground Up*, 144. Colby discusses the Normandy Campaign in his chapter with that title. He includes a section by DePuy called "Learning How to Fight in the 357th Infantry," ibid., 159–162.

10. Colby, ibid., 116–117.

11. Russell F.Weigley, *Eisenhower's Lieutenants* (Bloomington: Indiana University Press, 1981), 125.

12. DePuy quoted in Peter R. Mansoor, *The GI Offensive in Europe* (Lawrence: University Press of Kansas, 1999), 147.

13. Omar Bradley, *A General's Life: An Autobiography* (New York: Simon and Schuster, 1983), 262, 269, 337; see also Bradley, *A Soldier's Story* (New York: Henry Holt and Co., 1951), 298.

14. Colby, *War from the Ground Up*, 159, citing David Eisenhower, *Eisenhower at War, 1943–45* (New York: Random House, 1986).

15. Colby, *War from the Ground Up*, 159, and George S. Patton Jr., *War As I Knew It* (Boston: Houghton Mifflin, 1947), 164.

16. The Barth quotes here and following are from Jacob W. Bealke Papers, MHI. See the first file, Barth, 1–15.

17. Ibid.

18. Michael D. Doubler, *Closing with the Enemy: How GIs Fought the War in Europe, 1944–1945* (Lawrence: University Press of Kansas, 1994), 248.

19. Barth quoted in Colby, *War from the Ground Up*, 176. See also Barth file, Bealke Papers, MHI. See Martin Blumenson, *The European Theater of Operations: Breakout and Pursuit* (Washington, D.C.: Office of the Chief of Military History, Department of the Army, 1961), for a detailed narrative from the breakout to 11 September 1944. See Hugh M. Cole, *The European Theater of Operations: The Lorraine Campaign* (Washington, D.C.: United States Army Historical Division, 1950, reprinted 1981), for the period 1 September–18 December 1944.

20. Russell A. Hart, *Clash of Arms: How the Allies Won in Normandy* (Boulder, Colo.: Lynne Rienner Publishers, 2001), 8. See also Mansoor, *GI Offensive in Europe;* Doubler, *Closing with the Enemy;* and John Sloan Brown, *Draftee Division: The 88th Infantry Division in World War II* (Lexington: University Press of Kentucky, 1986), who challenge the thesis that material superiority explains U.S. military success. Rather, initial poor performance was followed by skill in combat as leaders learned and adapted, particularly in employing combined arms and air support.

4. The 90th Breaks Out

1. Bradley quoted in Russell F. Weigley, *Eisenhower's Lieutenants* (Bloomington: Indiana University Press, 1981), 98.

2. Dwight D. Eisenhower, *Crusade in Europe* (Garden City, N.Y.: Doubleday, 1948), 279.

3. See John Whiteclay Chambers, ed., *The Oxford Companion to American Military History* (New York: Oxford University Press, 1999), 632 and 284 for succinct accounts of COBRA and the breakout. See Martin Blumenson, *The Battle of the Generals* (New York: Morrow, 1993), for a full treatment of Falaise Gap. The subtitle of Blumenson's book reveals the author's opinion: "The Untold Story of the Falaise Pocket—the Campaign that Should Have Won World War II." A complete account of the entire campaign in Europe is found in the famous "Green Books" series The U.S. Army in World War II: The European Theater of Operations, produced by the Office of the Chief of Military History, Department of the Army. To put the 90th Division's combat from Normandy to Czechoslovakia in perspective, see the following entries in that series: Gordon A. Harrison, *Cross-Channel Attack* (1951); Martin Blumenson, *Breakout and Pursuit* (1961), for the period 1 July–11 September 1944; Hugh M. Cole, *The Lorraine Campaign* (1950, reprinted 1981), for the

period 1 September–18 December 1944; Charles B. MacDonald, *The Siegfried Line Campaign* (1963), 11 September–16 December 1944; H. M. Cole, *The Ardennes: Battle of the Bulge* (1965), 16 December 1944–3 January 1945; and Charles MacDonald, *The Last Offensive* (1973).

4. Blumenson, *Battle of the Generals.*

5. The Hamilton quotes here and following are from Hamilton, interview with Gole, 18 February 2005. See also Frank Holober, *Raiders of the China Coast* (Annapolis, Md.: Naval Institute Press, 1999).

6. Unless otherwise noted, all direct quotations of DePuy in this chapter are from DePuy, OH, MHI.

7. William E. DePuy Jr. said that his father told him this story of Hamilton's courage several times. E-mail, DePuy Jr. to Gole, 21 August 2006.

8. DePuy, OH.

9. 90th Infantry Division Report of Operations, Northwest France, August 1944, Signed Stilwell for McLain, DePuy Family Papers. See especially Part 2, LeMans to Chambois, 10–22 August 1944, Battle of the Pocket. See also *Upstarts,* a self-published manuscript by Robert E. Moore, World War II Veterans Survey, 90th Infantry Division, Moore folder, MHI. Moore commanded the 915th Field Artillery Battalion, which was usually in direct support of the 359th Infantry. An appendix to *Upstarts,* Part 4, "The Falaise Gap," contains seven eyewitness accounts of what happened in the vicinity of Chambois, confirming both DePuy's recollections and the official 90th Infantry Division Report of Operations. The 915th, just one of many artillery battalions engaged, expended 7,963 rounds from 16 to 21 August 1944; the organic Cannon Company of the 359th fired 1,341 rounds in the same period.

10. Blumenson, *Breakout and Pursuit,* 557.

11. Freeman Dyson, "The Bitter End," *New York Review of Books,* 28 April 2005, 4–6.

12. Tacitus, *"The Agricola" and "The Germania,"* trans. H. Mattingly, rev. S. A. Handford (Baltimore, Md.: Penguin Books, 1975), 113.

13. Blumenson, *Breakout and Pursuit,* 696.

14. Weigley, *Eisenhower's Lieutenants,* 107, 38.

15. Blumenson, *Battle of the Generals,* 272. See also Steve R. Waddell, *United States Army Logistics: The Normandy Campaign, 1944* (Westport, Conn.: Greenwood Press, 1994), especially 163–165. Waddell says that despite two years to plan, "the logistical system sputtered across France" (163). He contends that the need for detailed planning for the landing phase at Normandy wrongly carried over to later operations, making them inflexible.

16. John Colby, *War from the Ground Up: The 90th Division in World War II* (Austin, Tex.: Nortex Press, 1991), 486–487; DePuy, OH, 52.

17. Reimers quoted in Colby, *War from the Ground Up*, 323.

18. 90th Division, Histories, World War II Questionnaires, MHI. The survey was begun in 1988.

19. Quoted in Colby, *War from the Ground Up*, 331.

20. Quoted in ibid., 335.

21. Michael D. Doubler, *Closing with the Enemy: How GIs Fought the War in Europe, 1944–1945* (Lawrence: University Press of Kansas, 1994): Patton memo, 241; cold weather, 240; combat exhaustion, 242. See also Leon Crenshaw (Colonel, USA, Ret.), interview with Gole, 5 April 2007. Crenshaw commanded C Btry 345 FA Bn in the ETO campaign. He shared a unit history, 345th (printed by F. Bruckmann KG, Munich, Germany, n.d.) with me. "Wear anything" is on p. 37. New shoe packs and new sleeping bags arrived in December 1944 and January 1945. Crenshaw also showed me *The 90th, a History of the 90th Division in World War II, 6 June 1944 to 9 May 1945* (published by the 90th Infantry Division, 1946), which was apparently the main source for Colby, *War from the Ground Up*.

22. Roy Gordon quoted in Peter R. Mansoor, *The GI Offensive in Europe* (Lawrence: University Press of Kansas, 1999), 191.

23. Ibid., 191, 205. See also Paul Fussell, *The Boys' Crusade* (New York: Modern Library, 2003), for a rifle platoon leader's passionate account of what sustained infantry combat does to young men.

24. Richard Stilwell, on behalf of Colby and the editors of *War from the Ground Up*, asked DePuy to describe his Berle attack. DePuy did so in a letter to Stilwell. The letter was published as an appendix in Colby, *War from the Ground Up*, 456.

25. See Weigley, *Eisenhower's Lieutenants*; Martin Van Creveld, *Fighting Power* (London: Arms and Armour Press, 1983) and T. N. Dupuy, *A Genius for War* (Englewood Cliffs, N.J.: Prentice-Hall, 1977) for earlier, generally accepted interpretations of American combat skill. See Mansoor, *GI Offensive in Europe*; Doubler, *Closing with the Enemy*; Russell A. Hart, *Clash of Arms: How the Allies Won in Normandy* (Boulder, Colo.: Lynne Rienner Publishers, 2001); and John Sloan Brown, *Draftee Division: The 88th Infantry Division in World War II* (Lexington: University Press of Kentucky, 1986) for more recent scholarship.

26. Seven soldiers of the 357th were killed on 5 May. Colby, *War from the Ground Up*, 456.

27. Moore, *Upstarts*.

28. Handwritten letter, 25 January 1946, DePuy Family Papers.

29. Handwritten letter, 17 October 1945, DePuy Family Papers.

30. Letter, 9 October 1945, DePuy Family Papers.

31. The letter is undated; the return address given is Strategy Branch, G-3 Division, Theater General Board, APO 408. DePuy Family Papers.

32. Letter, 28 August 1945, DePuy Family Papers.
33. DePuy Family Papers.

5. Regular Army

1. Unless otherwise noted, direct quotations of DePuy in this chapter are from DePuy, OH, MHI.

2. His application is dated 31 December 1941. Receipt was noted by HQ Second Army in a letter to DePuy dated 12 January 1942. He was turned down, "not recommended for this appointment," in a letter from HQ Third Army to DePuy dated 11 July 1942. Career Management File, DePuy Family Papers.

3. DePuy's standard DA Form 66.

4. Harry P. Ball, *Of Responsible Command: A History of the U.S. Army War College*, rev. ed. (Carlisle Barracks, Pa.: Alumni Association of the United States Army War College, 1994), 158.

5. DePuy Family Papers. Murphy to DePuy dated 20 November 1945.

6. DePuy Family Papers. The application to language school dated 24 September 1947 is in the file marked "Career Management File." Barbara was on Bill's orders to Budapest dated May 1949, and Bill's effective date as Assistant Military Attaché was 11 July 1949. The divorce date is 7 October 1949. As the state of Nevada required six weeks' residence prior to granting a divorce decree, apparently she did not accompany him overseas.

7. William E. DePuy Jr., interview with Gole, 21 October 2004.

8. Wayne Waltz, telephone conversation with Gole, 2 March 2005.

9. Undated Officers Academic Efficiency Report, DePuy Family Papers.

10. According to his DA Form 66, he was in Washington in 1952.

6. CIA Detail

The chapter epigraphs are drawn from Frank Holober, *Raiders of the China Coast: CIA Covert Operations during the Korean War* (Annapolis, Md.: Naval Institute Press, 1999), 1, and Alfred W. McCoy, *The Politics of Heroin: CIA Complicity in the Global Drug Trade* (Brooklyn, N.Y.: Lawrence Hill Books, 1991), 166. The McCoy book is a revision of a 1972 edition, *The Politics of Heroin in Southeast Asia*, coauthored with Cathleen B. Read.

1. DePuy, OH. MHI. Quotations and paraphrasing of DePuy in this chapter, unless otherwise noted, are from this source.

2. DePuy's DA Form 66. DePuy Family Papers.

3. The Dulles letter, dated 27 February 1953, DePuy Family Papers. It was, in fact, a performance evaluation that was routed through Army Chief of Staff J. Lawton Collins, the Adjutant General, and the Commandant of the Armed Forces Staff College, where DePuy was a student after his CIA detail.

4. Stilwell, Oral History, MHI.

5. Hamilton, interview with Gole, 18 February 2005. See also Holober, *Raiders of the China Coast*, for numerous references to Hamilton.

6. The DePuy Family Papers include DePuy's travel orders to Burma, Thailand, Indochina, Formosa, Hong Kong, Korea, Japan, and the Philippine Islands.

7. McCoy, *Politics of Heroin*, 57.

8. Ibid., 57–58.

9. Michael Warner, ed., *The CIA under Harry Truman* (Washington, D.C.: History Staff, Center for the Study of Intelligence, Central Intelligence Agency, 1994), 287–294. See especially Appropriations, Sec. 10b. A glossary of abbreviations and acronyms, identification of some key players, a chronology, and key declassified documents make this a very useful source. Some of the documents published openly in the book were later reclassified. See note 20 below.

10. McCoy, *Politics of Heroin*, 166. Some things never change. According to *The Economist*, 13–19 January 2007, being the director of national intelligence is the worst job in Washington, "an impossibly sticky wicket" (29).

11. John Prados, *Safe for Democracy: The Secret Wars of the CIA* (Chicago: Ivan R. Dee, 2006), 127. The CIA has on occasion been self-critical. See, for example, Warner, *CIA Cold War Records*, 385, for a memo of 8 June 1951 from Lyman B. Kirkpatrick to Deputy Director of Central Intelligence regarding "bureaucratic controls." My own attempts to get information about the OSS and CIA service of William and Marjory Walker DePuy were met with unfailing courtesy and no substance, despite my scrupulous adherence to Freedom of Information Act (FOIA) rules. In a letter from the CIA dated 12 October 2007, I was thanked for my patience in awaiting response to my request for information dated 10 December 2004. The information the CIA then gave me was edited so that what remained was mostly administratvie: promotions and evaluations of Marjory DePuy; clearances of both Marjory and Bill. Any information regarding the substance of their work was deleted. The Agency regards this information as still classified. "Bureaucratic controls" persist.

12. McCoy, *Politics of Heroin*, 165, quoting from The Pentagon Papers.

13. Ibid., 165–173.

14. Ibid., 166.

15. The career information for Marjory DePuy that follows is found in the DePuy Family Papers.

16. William E. DePuy Jr., interview with Gole, 21 October 2004.

17. Frank Holober's *Raiders of the China Coast* is much more forthcoming, as are the Prados, McCoy, and Warner books cited above.

18. Warner, note 9, above.

19. See *New York Times,* 3 March 2006, p. 1, regarding reclassification of once declassified documents. No one knows how many documents were copied, by whom, or where they now are held.

20. Warner, *CIA under Harry Truman,* 369.

21. Ibid., 373–381, especially 378.

22. Foreword by Barrow in Holober, *Raiders of the China Coast.*

23. Holober, *Raiders of the China Coast,* 1.

24. D. H. Berger, "The Use of Covert Paramilitary Activity as a Policy Tool: An Analysis of Operations Conducted by the United States Central Intelligence Agency, 1949–51," written in fulfillment of a requirement for the Marine Corps Command and General Staff College, www.fas.org/irp/eprint/berger.htm.

25. Quoted in Prados, *Safe for Democracy,* 137.

26. Ibid., 138.

27. Dulles letter, 27 February 1953. See note 5 above.

7. Armed Forces Staff College and a Second Battalion Command

1. All quotations and paraphrases of DePuy in this chapter, unless otherwise noted, are from DePuy, OH, MHI.

2. Barrie Zais, interview with Gole, 15 December 2004. Barrie, a USMA graduate, said that his father, Melvin, and other ROTC men among his peers, including DePuy, wondered if they could go "all the way" to four-star generals. They did.

3. The similarity of DePuy's and Gorman's views is striking. See Paul Gorman, *The Secret of Future Victories* (Fort Leavenworth, Kans.: Combat Studies Institute, U.S. Army Command and Staff College, 1992). Gorman puts DePuy, George C. Marshall, and Lesley J. McNair at the top of his list of great Army trainers.

4. The original brochures are in the DePuy Family Papers. They are reproduced in Richard M. Swain, comp., *Selected Papers of General William E. DePuy: First Commander, U.S. Army Training and Doctrine Command* (Fort Leavenworth, Kans.: U.S. Army Command and General Staff College, Combat Studies Institute, 1994), 1 and 9.

5. George P. Psihas, letter to Gole, 26 August 2006. Psihas maintained contact with DePuy after leaving the Regular Army for the

Reserves and a career in industry that directly involved him in the development of the Abrams tank.

6. DePuy's DA Form 66 has the pertinent dates.

8. Clever Chaps

1. Lloyd Matthews, interview with Gole, 21 September 2004.

2. All quotations and paraphrases from DePuy in this chapter, unless otherwise noted, are from DePuy, OH, MHI.

3. Hollingsworth quotes here and below from Hollingsworth, interview with Gole, 18 January 2005.

4. E-mail, William E. DePuy Jr. to Gole, 21 August 2006. The tall one and his father were later prolific publishers of military books.

5. Matthew B. Ridgway, as told to Harold H. Martin, *Soldier: The Memoir of Matthew B. Ridgway* (New York: Harper and Brothers, 1956); James M. Gavin, *War and Peace in the Space Age* (New York: Harper and Brothers, 1958); and Maxwell D. Taylor, *The Uncertain Trumpet* (New York: Harper and Brothers, 1959).

6. See Ridgway, *Soldier,* especially 293, 312, 323–332.

7. Gavin, *War and Peace,* 288–289.

8. George Kennan, *The Realities of American Foreign Policy* (Princeton, N.J.: Princeton University Press, 1954).

9. Taylor, *Uncertain Trumpet,* 158.

10. DePuy-Stilwell letter, 2 October 1956; Stilwell-Depuy, 25 October 1956; DePuy-Stilwell, 16 November 1956; all in DePuy Papers, MHI.

11. Kissinger to DePuy, 31 July 1958, DePuy Papers, MHI.

12. Huntington-DePuy, 23 August 1957; DePuy-Huntington, 26 August 1957. See also Huntington's observations regarding "American liberal values" and "security" in the introduction and conclusion of *The Soldier and the State.* They remain pertinent to policy debates today.

13. DePuy-Atkinson letter, 20 January 1958, DePuy Papers, MHI.

14. The memo written by DePuy was from the Coordination Group to Westmoreland, Box 3, DePuy Papers, MHI, along with DePuy's correspondence with the people mentioned in notes 10 through 13 above.

15. *Army,* no. 8 (March 1958): 22–24, 54–60. The article is reprinted in Richard M. Swain, comp., *Selected Papers of General William E. DePuy: First Commander, U.S. Army Training and Doctrine Command, 1 July 1973* (Fort Leavenworth, Kans.: U.S. Army Command and General Staff College, Combat Studies Institute, 1994), 17–24.

16. For example, see the exchange of letters Col. Willard Pearson–DePuy, 1 May 1958, and DePuy-Pearson, 13 May 1958, DePuy Papers, MHI, in which they discuss "11 Men 1 Mind." "Bonding" has been refined since DePuy wrote of it in 1958. Currently one speaks of organi-

zational bonding; vertical bonding, as in the chain of command; and horizontal bonding, as among buddies in a squad.

17. Matthews, interview with Gole, 21 September 2004. Lloyd Matthews was editor of *Parameters* for a number of years and had worked for DePuy in Vietnam. Nevertheless, DePuy declined frequent invitations by Matthews to publish in *Parameters,* saying that the *Army* audience was right for his purposes. See also Chapter 16 in this book regarding DePuy's articles written for *Army* and other publications.

18. See DePuy Papers, MHI, for Stilwell, Forsythe, and Cushman letters to and from DePuy.

19. Cushman-DePuy, 23 August 1957; Cushman-DePuy, 11 December 1957, DePuy Papers, MHI. See Chapter 15 in this book for discussion of the 1976 version of FM 100–5.

20. National strategy debates in the late 1950s found the Services in competition for resources; as AVICE (1969–1973) DePuy was again in the middle of resource allocation. In 2007, resource allocation forces competition between funding Army and USMC "boots on the ground" and investment in future carrier battle groups and advanced aircraft systems of the USN and USAF.

9. School in London; Command in Schweinfurt

1. Colin L. Powell, with Joseph E. Persico, *My American Journey* (New York: Random House, 1995), 158. In a 28 May 2006 e-mail to Gole, General Powell said, "We all admired Bill as an icon of integrity, brilliance, steadfastness, and honesty. He only cared about getting it right and rebuilding the Army."

2. Separate interviews with all three DePuy children regarding their year in England and their recollections of their father and family life attest to this.

3. Unless otherwise indicated, all quotations and paraphrasing of DePuy in this chapter are from DePuy, OH, MHI.

4. Daphne DePuy, interview with Gole, 16 January 2005.

5. Joslin DePuy Gallatin, interview with Gole, 25 January 2005.

6. William E. DePuy Jr., interview with Gole, 21 October 2004.

7. DePuy Family Papers; interviews with the three DePuy children.

8. William E. DePuy Jr., interview with Gole, 21 October 2004.

9. Paul Gorman, interview with Gole, 8 October 2004. General Gorman and Bill DePuy Jr. in separate interviews indicated that Marj's "high church" affiliation was more social than spiritual. Joslin told me that her mother was not religious.

10. George Joulwan, interview with Gole, 10 November 2005.

11. Tony Pokorny, interview with Gole, 22 February 2005. Pokorny observed DePuy from another battle group in Schweinfurt, more closely while working for him in the Pentagon when DePuy was AVICE, and even more closely as DePuy's XO in TRADOC.

12. The Goodpaster evaluation is in the DePuy Family Papers.

13. Charles Kriete, interview with Gole, 28 August 2004. Chaplain (Colonel) Kriete was in the sister battle group in Schweinfurt as a captain. He later commanded the Chaplains' School and taught at the Army War College.

14. E-mail, Jim Holland to Gole, 2 February 2005.

15. E-mail, William Mullen to Gole, 29 March 2005. Mullen was a general's aide in 1961 and later served as a company commander under DePuy in Vietnam. He also interviewed DePuy for his Oral History in 1979 and maintained contact with him until DePuy's death.

16. Letter to DePuy and his negative response are in DePuy Family Papers.

10. Back to Washington

1. Robert S. McNamara, *In Retrospect: The Tragedy and Lessons of Vietnam* (New York: Vintage Books, 1996), 35.

2. Ibid., 29.

3. Ibid., 333.

4. William DePuy Jr., interview with Gole, 21 October 2004. Highfield is twelve miles southeast of Winchester, Virginia, an hour by car to Washington, and two to three hours from Fort Monroe.

5. Daphne DePuy, interview with Gole, 16 January 2005.

6. Joslin DePuy Gallatin, interview with Gole, 25 January 2005.

7. Joslin DePuy Gallatin and Daphne DePuy, interviews with Gole.

8. E-mail, William DePuy Jr. to Gole, 21 August 2006.

9. Colonel (USA, Chaplain, Ret.) Wes Geary, interview with Gole, 10 January 2005.

10. David Halberstam, *The Best and the Brightest* (New York: Random House, 1972), 541–542.

11. The DePuy Family Papers are the basis of the facts; some speculation by her children is contained here as well. Marj attended Girls Latin School in Boston 1929–1932 and Western High School in Washington 1932–1933.

12. DePuy's picture was on the cover of *Newsweek* (5 December 1966); Joseph Alsop called him "an old friend" and the 1st Division "The new Model Army" (1 May 1966, *Washington Post*); Peter Arnett praised DePuy as "a genius. . . . He will kill all the Viet Cong in his division area north of Saigon, or they'll kill him" (31 August 1966, AP).

13. Unless otherwise indicated, DePuy citations and attributions are from DePuy, OH, MHI.

14. In addition to DePuy, OH, MHI, see Louis Menand, book review, "Fat Man, Herman Kahn, and the Nuclear Age," *The New Yorker,* 27 June 2005, 92–98 for more recent commentary on the roles and missions of the Services and the place of nuclear weapons in military planning. For the Cuban battalion, see National Archives and Records Administration, Lyndon Baines Johnson Library, General William E. DePuy interview with Ted Gittinger, 28 October 1985.

11. Vietnam

1. DePuy Family Papers. The DePuy family made the letters quoted here available to me, as well as twenty more from 1965, eleven from 1966, and four from 1967.

2. Lloyd Matthews, interview with Gole, 21 September 2004. Matthews later edited *Parameters,* the U.S. Army War College Quarterly, edited books, and wrote articles, many focused on officership.

3. Charles F. Kriete, interview with Gole, 28 August 2004.

4. Henrik O. Lunde, interviews with Gole, 16 September 2004 and 17 November 2005.

5. Max Thurman, OH, MHI.

6. Later, a group known as the Boathouse Gang, a cell of bright young officers, was used as "an extension of his [DePuy's] own mind" to write doctrine that captured the consensus among the German Army, the USAF, and TRADOC after the 1973 Yom Kippur War. See Paul H. Herbert, *Deciding What Has to Be Done: General William E. DePuy and the 1976 Edition of FM 100–5, Operations* (Fort Leavenworth, Kans.: U.S. Army Command and General Staff College, Combat Studies Institute, 1988), 85–88.

7. Barrie Zais, interview with Gole, 15 December 2004. Having a West Point pedigree became less important in the course of DePuy's career. DePuy, Melvin Zais, and other non–West Pointers wondered if they could go all the way to four stars without having gone to West Point. They did.

8. David Halberstam, *The Best and the Brightest* (New York: Random House, 1972), 541–543.

9. Neil Sheehan, *A Bright Shining Lie: John Paul Vann and America in Vietnam* (New York: Vintage Books, 1969), 619.

10. Ibid., 203–265.

11. Unless otherwise indicated, DePuy's remarks in this section are from DePuy, OH, MHI.

12. Robert S. McNamara, *In Retrospect: The Tragedy and Lessons of Viet-*

nam (New York: Vintage Books, 1996), xi. See also Peter Arnett, *Live from the Battlefield* (New York: Simon and Schuster, 1964), especially 200–205 for the press and senior leadership in Vietnam, including DePuy.

13. See, for example, Walter Isaacson and Evan Thomas, *The Wise Men: Six Friends and the World They Made: Acheson, Bohlen, Harriman, Kennan, Lovett, McCloy* (New York: Simon and Schuster, 1986); Phillip B. Davidson, *Vietnam at War: The History, 1946–1975* (Novato, Calif.: Presidio, 1988); William C. Westmoreland, *A Soldier Reports* (Garden City, N.Y.: Doubleday and Co., 1976); Halberstam, *The Best and the Brightest;* H. R. McMaster, *Dereliction of Duty: Lyndon Johnson, Robert McNamara, the Joint Chief of Staff, and the Lies that Led to Vietnam* (New York: HarperCollins, 1997); Harry Maurer, *Strange Ground: An Oral History of Americans in Vietnam, 1945–1975* (New York: Avon Books, 1990); Andrew Preston, *The War Council: McGeorge Bundy, the NSC, and Vietnam* (Cambridge, Mass.: Harvard University Press, 2006).

14. McNamara, *In Retrospect,* xi.

15. Matthews, interview with Gole, 21 September 2004.

16. Maurer, *Strange Ground,* 449, 450.

17. Ibid., 451, 453.

18. Ibid., 451. Henrik Lunde was the 101st Division liaison officer awaiting the decision to locate his brigade when it arrived in Vietnam. There were frequent changes as the staff decided where to put the arriving U.S. combat formations. Lunde said he had the feeling that the staff "didn't know what it was doing." Lunde, interview with Gole, 3 September 2007.

19. E-mail, Richard Hooker to Gole, 19 December 2004.

12. The Big Red One

1. James Scott Wheeler permitted me to read from his history of the 1st Infantry Division manuscript, since published as *The Big Red One* (Lawrence: University Press of Kansas, 2007); see 425–456. For combat operations of the U.S. Army in Vietnam, see also John M. Carland, *Combat Operations: Stemming the Tide, May 1965 to October 1966* (Washington, D.C.: Center of Military History, United States Army, 2000); and George L. MacGarrigle, *Combat Operations: Taking the Offensive, October 1966 to October 1997* (Washington, D.C.: Center of Military History, United States Army, 1998).

2. Quotations and paraphrasing of DePuy in this chapter, unless otherwise specified, are from DePuy, OH, MHI. See also Harry Maurer, *Strange Ground: An Oral History of Americans in Vietnam, 1945–1975* (New York: Avon Books, 1990), 447–455, for an interview with DePuy that confirms what he said in the MHI account some ten years earlier.

Historian Richard M. Swain observes that Weyand "had a remarkable capability to engender affection from other officers." E-mail, Swain to Gole, 31 August 2006 (after reading a draft of this manuscript).

3. MacGarrigle, *Taking the Offensive,* xi.

4. See Carland, *Stemming the Tide,* 305–336.

5. Ibid., 306.

6. George C. Wilson, *Mud Soldiers* (New York: Charles Scribner's Sons, 1989), 7–42.

7. The Seaman quotes here and following are from Seaman, interview with Patterson, 18 March 1971, OH, MHI; also available in Center for Military History, Historians' Files. See also the *Study on Military Professionalism* (Carlisle Barracks, Pa.: U.S. Army War College, 30 June 1970). Peter Arnett called Seaman "an admirable officer who encouraged us in our news coverage," suggesting that Seaman tended to his public relations image. Peter Arnett, *Live from the Battlefield* (New York: Simon and Schuster, 1964), 227.

8. E-mail, Richard Hooker to Gole, 19 December 2004.

9. E-mail, James Holland to Gole, 2 February 2005.

10. "Company Commander in Vietnam," MHI. See also Weyand, OH, MHI.

11. Alexander M. Haig Jr., *Inner Circles: How America Changed the World: A Memoir* (New York: Warner Books, 1992), 159. Haig was later Supreme Allied Commander, Europe (SACEUR) and Secretary of State under President Ronald Reagan. See also note 33 below, and the Richard Cavazos remarks on DePuy's methods discussed later in this chapter.

12. E-mail, William J. Mullen III to Gole, 29 March 2005.

13. E-mail, Holland to Gole, 2 February 2005.

14. Gorman, interview with Gole, 8 October 2004. Joulwan, Madden, and Cundiff, DePuy's lieutenants in Schweinfurt, did "exceptionally well" as company commanders in Vietnam, said Gorman.

15. Haig, *Inner Circles,* esp. chapter 12. In an e-mail, Haig to Gole, 10 September 2006, Haig credits DePuy with "reducing each battlefield skill to the rote or habit level starting especially with the squad and platoon."

16. Burns, interview with Gole, 25 October 2004. Interviews with Hendrik Lunde, John Stewart, Paul Gorman, Sidney Berry, and Robert Gerard interviews cited elsewhere in these notes attested to DePuy's imposing presence and the feeling of fear in DePuy's headquarters.

17. Paul D. Walker, *Jungle Dragoon: The Memoir of an Armored Cav Platoon Leader in Vietnam* (Novato, Calif.: Presidio, 1999), 13. Walker also provides a clear picture of how the armored cavalry operated in Vietnam while confirming DePuy's firm control of his division.

18. For artillery commentary, see Carland, *Stemming the Tide,* 359–

361; John M. Hawkins, "The Costs of Artillery: Eliminating Harassment and Interdiction Fires during the Vietnam War," *Journal of Military History* 70, no. 1 (January 2006): 91–122; Robert H. Scales Jr., *Firepower in Limited War,* rev. ed. (Novato, Calif.: Presidio, 1995), chapter 3.

19. Gorman, interview with Gole, 8 October 2004. See also Sidney B. Berry Jr., interview with Robert Broyles, 1984 (edited version by Douglas Johnson, 2006), OH, MHI. John Stewart and Robert Gerard join Lunde, Gorman, Berry, and others in describing the "unpleasant atmosphere" when the division staff briefed DePuy and Hollingsworth.

20. A letter from Richard Nunez to DePuy (28 July 1966), asking how his brother, Sgt. Rudolph Nunez, was killed on 13 June 1966, and DePuy's response (10 August 1966) are in DePuy Family Papers. In his letter, DePuy informed Mr. Nunez of scholarships for the sons of soldiers killed in Vietnam, a program inspired by Sgt. Nunez's pride in the 1st Infantry Division, which he had expressed to his wife. See also DePuy, OH, MHI, and Mullen, e-mail to Gole, 29 March 2005, regarding the first money for the scholarships coming from a poker game.

21. The four-page, neatly handwritten letter from Richard M. Davis is answered by DePuy in a letter dated 6 October 1966. A flurry of DePuy stories appeared in the *New York Times,* the *Washington Post,* and wire services while he commanded his division. Joseph Alsop wrote several pieces featuring DePuy. "Dear Bill" and "Dear Joe" letters exchanged between Alsop and DePuy on 15 March, 10 June, 8 July, and 16 October 1966 are in the DePuy Family Papers. The tone indicates that they knew each other well. DePuy's new fame was noted by many men who had served with him. They wrote, and he responded with modesty and good humor.

22. Stewart, interview with Gole, 3 January 2005. Regarding the boundaries issue and Gorman's conversation with Weyand in Paris, see e-mail, Gorman to Gole, 22 February 2006, a follow-up to the Gorman interview with Gole on 8 October 2004. See also *Blue Spaders: The 26th Infantry Regiment, 1917–1967* (Wheaton, Ill.: Cantigny First Division Foundation, 1996), 150–151.

23. Waltz, interview with Gole, 2 March 2005.

24. Weyand interview with Lewis Sorley, 9–15 November 1999, OH, MHI. See also DePuy, OH, MHI, and Carland, *Stemming the Tide,* maps on pp. 26, 74, and 167 for an appreciation of how the missions of the 1st and 25th Infantry Divisions differed.

25. Robert J. Gerard, interview with Gole, 20 December 2004. Gerard allowed me to see portions of his memoir before it was published in 2006 as *The Road to Catoctin Mountain: A Twentieth-Century Journey* (Xlibris, 2006), 168, 169, 178–181. Gerard muses about Seaman's unwill-

ingness to confront DePuy, but Seaman and insiders knew of Westmoreland's high opinion of DePuy. In a message to the personnel people in Washington, Westmoreland wrote, "With respect to DePuy, it is my earnest hope he will be promoted and that it will be possible to reward him with divisional command in country." CMH WP Box 25: WCW Message Files 1 October–31 December 1965; Message WCW to Woolnough (DCSPER DA), MAC 5015, 080450Z October 1965.

26. Cavazos, interview with Gole, 11 January 2005.

27. Bruce Palmer, interview in The Abrams Story, MHI. DePuy's response to Johnson's back-channel is a letter in which he explains why he fired eleven people.

28. Quoted in Lewis Sorley, *Honorable Warrior: General Harold K. Johnson and the Ethics of Command* (Lawrence: University Press of Kansas, 1998), 256–257.

29. Hollingsworth, interview with Gole, 18 January 2005. DePuy refers to Johnson's Christmas 1966 visit, as does Sorley.

30. As stated earlier (Chapter 11, note 1), the letters from DePuy quoted here were made available to me by the DePuy family; DePuy Family Papers.

31. Haig, *Inner Circles*, 161–162.

32. E-mail, Haig to Gole, 7 September 2006. See also e-mail from Frederic J. Brown III (LTG, USA, Ret.) to Gole, 16 October 2007. Brown was Executive Officer to DePuy later, when DePuy was a major general and lieutenant general, and admired him as a brilliant mentor and friend. However, as a staff officer in DePuy's division in Vietnam, Brown said, "I about turned him into DAIG [Department of Army, Inspector General] for inappropriate baiting of commanders about to be relieved." DePuy, Brown said, was "cruel when he did not need to be."

33. The letter naming those relieved is in both DePuy Papers, MHI, and in DePuy Family Papers.

34. Harold K. Johnson with Rupert F. Glover and James B. Agnew, 23 April 1973, OH, MHI.

35. Student paper, Richard Cavazos et al., "Analysis of Fire and Maneuver in Vietnam, June 1966–June 1968," Army War College, 1969. See also Orwin C. Talbott, interview with John Votaw, 17 September 1994, Cantigny 1st Division Foundation, in which Talbott compared use of artillery in World War II and Vietnam. The Germans, he said, "with so few people, did so very, very well under brutal circumstances. . . . But we crushed them. Bill DePuy was adamant on the desirability of using overwhelming firepower in Vietnam and refused to take any restrictions." The implication is that DePuy's use of artillery was questioned in Vietnam, but the use of American firepower had not been questioned in World War II.

36. Berry, interview with Broyles, 1984, edited by Douglas Johnson, 2006.

37. Maj. Gen. George P. Seneff Jr., CG 1st Aviation Brigade, interview, 12 September 1967, U.S. Army Center for Military, History, Unit 50. Seneff is as frank in criticizing some generals in Vietnam as he is in praising DePuy. The debriefing was by a History Team member and was initially classified Secret. Perhaps the classification allowed for Seneff's unusually frank assessment of fellow generals.

38. Paul Miles, interview with Gole, 18 September 2004.

13. SACSA, Tet, and Policy Review

1. William E. DePuy Jr., interview with Gole, 21 October 2004.

2. Colin L. Powell, with Joseph E. Persico, *My American Journey* (New York: Random House, 1995), 158.

3. The direct quotations and paraphrasing of Bill, Joslin, and Daphne in this chapter are from William DePuy Jr., interview with Gole, 21 October 2004; Joslin DePuy Gallatin, interview with Gole, 25 January 2005; and Daphne DePuy, interview with Gole, 16 January 2005.

4. "The Case for Dual Capability," *Army,* January 1960.

5. "Unification: How Much More?" *Army,* April 1961.

6. Unless indicated otherwise, quotations and paraphrasing of DePuy in this chapter are from DePuy, OH, MHI.

7. Bill DePuy Jr., interview with Gole, 21 October 2004. That's the way young Bill remembers his father's smoking habit, but the *Newsweek* cover of 5 December 1966 shows General DePuy with a cigarette in his hand.

8. DePuy's copy of the report, inscribed by General Westmoreland and dated March 1969, is in the DePuy Family Papers.

9. William C. Westmoreland, *A Soldier Reports* (Garden City, N.Y.: Doubleday and Co., 1976), 354. Generals Bruce Palmer and Walter T. "Dutch" Kerwin, among others, concur with Westmoreland that the feeling in Saigon was that leadership in Washington saw Tet as a disaster. See Palmer's OH in The Abrams Story and Kerwin's 3 February 2005 interview with Gole.

10. For a sense of the high-powered advice at this time, see, among others, Robert S. McNamara, *In Retrospect: The Tragedy and Lessons of Vietnam* (New York: Vintage Books, 1996); Walter Isaacson and Evan Thomas, *The Wise Men: Six Friends and the World They Made: Acheson, Bohlen, Harriman, Kennan, Lovett, McCloy* (New York: Simon and Schuster, 1986); Phillip B. Davidson, *Vietnam at War: The History, 1946–1975* (Novato, Calif.: Presidio, 1988); Westmoreland, *A Soldier Reports;* David Halberstam, *The Best and the Brightest* (New York: Random House, 1972); H. R. McMaster, *Dereliction of Duty: Lyndon Johnson, Robert McNa-*

mara, the Joint Chiefs of Staff, and the Lies that Led to Vietnam (New York: HarperCollins, 1997).

11. McNamara, *In Retrospect*, 197.

12. Ibid., 309.

13. Ibid., 317.

14. Isaacson and Thomas, *Wise Men*, 687. The sharp exchange caused Walt Rostow to call Acheson to ask why he had walked out on the President. Acheson, believing that Rostow was in the presence of LBJ, said, "You tell the President—and you tell him in precisely these words, that he can take Vietnam and stick it up his ass" (ibid.).

15. Acheson quoted in ibid., 697.

16. McNamara, *In Retrospect*, xx.

17. Isaacson and Thomas, *Wise Men*, 700.

18. Ibid., 703; DePuy, OH, MHI.

19. DePuy, OH, MHI.

20. Anatoly Dobrynin, *In Confidence* (New York: Times Books, 1995), 171–173.

21. The full text is found in *Public Papers of the Presidents of the United States: Lyndon B. Johnson, 1968–69*, Book 1, 469–476.

22. DePuy, OH, MHI. See also U.S. Department of State, *Foreign Relations, 1964–1968*, vol. 6, *Vietnam, January–August 1968*, Document 67. In a 7 February 1968 memo to Rostow, DePuy describes the short-term impact of Tet on pacification as "very bad" and the long-term impact as "unclear" (Doc. 56).

23. Westmoreland, *A Soldier Reports*, 361.

24. Ibid., 362.

14. To Fix a Broken Army

1. Donn Starry, OH, MHI. The figures on reduction of Army strength are from DePuy, OH, MHI.

2. Volney F. Warner with Dean M. Owen, OH, MHI. Warner was grateful that Westmoreland "put up with me even though I had so many radical and different views from him on Vietnam." Warner was Westmoreland's executive officer, later a four-star general.

3. Lloyd Matthews, interview with Gole, 21 September, 2004; Paul Miles, interview with Gole, 18 September 2004.

4. Serving near the top of government can be disillusioning. Warner said, "When I got into the White House, it destroyed all the illusions that somebody up there knew what he was doing." Warner, OH, MHI. Fred Weyand, while Chief of Legislative Liaison, watched the Secretary of Defense in action. "McNamara made up the numbers he rattled off to Congress [in hearings], knowing that he would get the raw transcript

of the testimony to edit. Sometimes not one fact was right, but he got away with it." Weyand, OH, MHI, 91.

5. Enthoven was Assistant Secretary of Defense (Systems Analysis) in 1965–1969. Vance was Secretary of the Army and Deputy Secretary of Defense before serving as Secretary of State, 1977–1980. Resor was Under Secretary and Secretary of the Army and had a personal relationship with Robert S. McNamara. See McNamara, *In Retrospect: The Tragedy and Lessons of Vietnam* (New York: Vintage Books, 1996), 297.

6. Unless otherwise indicated, Johnson's views cited or paraphrased are from Johnson, OH, MHI. General Heiser used the word "dictatorial" to describe DePuy's style. See Joseph M. Heiser Jr., *A Soldier Supporting Soldiers* (Washington, D.C.: United States Army Center of Military History, 1991), 201.

7. Unless otherwise indicated, all paraphrasing and citations of DePuy in this chapter are from DePuy, OH, MHI. See also John R. Martin, "The Role and Progress of the Office, Assistant Vice Chief of Staff in the Management of Army Resources," U.S. Army War College Research Element (Case Study), 8 March 1971.

8. Unless cited otherwise, quotations and paraphrasing of Chesarek in this chapter are from Chesarek, OH, MHI.

9. See Raymond Maladowitz, "Office of the Assistant Vice Chief of Staff: Parkinson's Law or Progress?" U.S. Army War College Research Element (Case Study), 9 March 1970, for rationale and steps leading to the establishment of AVICE on 16 February 1967.

10. Thomas E. Carpenter III (BG, USA, Ret.) had reservations about OPMS. He called DePuy "the father of the Officer Personnel Management System" and acknowledged the importance of specialties in the Officer Corps. But, he said, "in my opinion [OPMS] contributed to the erosion of the preeminence of the Combat Arms at West Point and throughout the Army." He opined that Abrams, had he been Chief at the time, would not have approved OPMS. Carpenter, e-mails to Gole, 1 and 4 November 2004.

11. Pokorny, interview with Gole, 22 February 2005.

12. Tony Smith, e-mail to Gole, 1 November 2004.

13. Carpenter, e-mails to Gole, 1 and 4 November 2004.

14. Miles, interview with Gole, 18 September 2004. General Abrams once remarked, "You know these lieutenant colonels and majors up here are very smart. If one doesn't give one something to do, he will find something to do. What bothers me is, if you don't watch him, he will get somebody to fund it as well." Lewis Sorley, *Thunderbolt: General Creighton Abrams and the Army of His Times* (New York: Simon and Schuster, 1992), 349. Abrams probably had DePuy's "unguided missiles" in mind, the same men Miles remembered.

15. Unless otherwise indicated, paraphrasing and quotations of Kerwin in this chapter are from Kerwin, interview with Gole, 3 February 2005. See also Walter Kerwin, OH, MHI, 1980.

16. Unless otherwise indicated, paraphrasing and quotations of Tuttle in this chapter are from Tuttle, interview with Gole, 23 November 2004.

17. See The Abrams Story, MHI, particularly the interviews with Generals Palmer and Kalergis regarding the transition from Westmoreland to Abrams.

18. *Study on Military Professionalism* (Carlisle Barracks, Pa.: U.S. Army War College), 30 June 1970.

19. The Kalergis quotes here and following are from The Abrams Story, MHI. Kalergis confirmed Palmer's observation that Abrams was at first skeptical of DePuy, probably due to Harold K. Johnson's opinion of DePuy. But Abrams came to admire DePuy, who seemed always to be "a step ahead of everyone else" and so lucid in oral briefings and in writing. Kalergis would have been pleased to know that there is now an Oral History of DePuy at MHI.

20. Maxwell Thurman, OH, MHI.

21. There is a vast literature on the Watergate break-in, the Pentagon Papers, and Nixon's resignation. The Ellsberg trial in Los Angeles, at which DePuy and Gorman testified, was widely covered in the press. See the *New York Times* from 13 June 1971 for the publication of the Pentagon Papers. See the *Washington Post,* among other newspapers, for coverage of the trial on 19, 20, 23, and 24 January 1973.

22. Jean R. Moenk, *Operation Steadfast Historical Summary: A History of the Reorganization of the U.S. Continental Army Command (1972–1973)* (Fort McPherson, Ga., and Fort Monroe, Va.: Headquarters U.S. Army Forces Command and Headquarters, U.S. Army TRADOC, 1974), 290.

15. TRADOC Commander

1. *Selected Papers of General William E. DePuy: First Commander, U.S. Army Training and Doctrine Command, 1 July 1973,* Richard M. Swain, comp. (Fort Leavenworth, Kans.: U.S. Army Command and General Staff College, Combat Studies Institute, 1994), 60, 63.

2. Bruce Palmer, Walter Kerwin, James G. Kalergis, OH, MHI.

3. Kerwin, interview with Gole, 3 February 2005.

4. Donn Starry, interview with Gole, 10 February 2005.

5. Unless otherwise indicated, the DePuy quotations and paraphrasing in this chapter are taken from DePuy's forty-three-page "Final Interview" with Dr. Brooks Kleber, TRADOC Historian, 23 May 1977, found in the DePuy Family Papers.

6. In a memo dated 5 November 1974, Kleber describes a 4 November 1974 meeting with DePuy and his chief of staff at which "General DePuy wanted to make sure that we [the Office of the Command Historian] were getting access to the information we needed" about the command. DePuy set up the meeting because his son, who was working at the AMC Histories Office, told his father on a weekend visit that the main problem of Army historians was getting access to information. Periodic office calls by historians with DePuy resulted, right up to the exit interview of 23 May 1977.

7. Quotations and paraphrasing of Max Thurman come from Thurman, OH, MHI. In DePuy's order to Thurman to get the smartest officers in the Army for TRADOC we hear an echo of what DePuy told Lloyd Matthews in Saigon about how he would use the "smartest majors in the Army."

8. The Abrams Story, MHI. Weyand, OH, MHI.

9. DePuy, interview with Ernest F. Fisher, "Role of the NCO," 22-page typescript, 8 October 1976, DePuy Family Papers. See also Ernest F. Fisher Jr., *Guardians of the Republic: A History of the Noncommissioned Officer Corps of the U.S. Army* (New York: Ballantine Books, 1994); and William G. Bainbridge and Dan Cragg, *Top Sergeant: The Life and Times of Sergeant Major of the Army William G. Bainbridge* (New York: Ivy Books, 1995).

10. Gorman, interview with Gole, 8 October 2004.

11. The letter is dated 23 July 1974. It can be found most conveniently in Swain, *Selected Papers of General William E. DePuy*, 60. It is also in DePuy Papers, MHI.

12. "Stupid" MFR, Subject: CG's Comments on Training at Fort Ord, 4 March 1975, 6 March 1975; "Things that don't make sense," letter to Training Center Commanders, Subject: Basic Combat Training, 24 March 1975; Dear Tom, letter with handwritten note, 3 June 1974. All in DePuy Family Papers.

13. DePuy, OH, MHI.

14. DePuy with Kleber, Final Interview. See also DePuy, OH, MHI.

15. DePuy with Kleber, Final Interview. The Leavenworth program was enriched later.

16. Starry, interview with Gole, 10 February 2005.

17. Timothy J. Reischl, "A Few Hours in My Twenty Years: Reflections on Combat Operations in the Gulf War," 26 February 1993. Reischl permitted the author to cite from this U.S. Army War College student paper.

18. Bourque's excellent essay, "The Hundred-Hour Thunderbolt: Armor in the Gulf War," can be found in George F. Hofmann and Donn A. Starry, eds., *Camp Colt to Desert Storm: The History of U.S. Armored*

Forces (Lexington: University Press of Kentucky, 1999), 497. *Camp Colt* is a superb and tightly written history whose chapters, written by experts, can nonetheless stand alone. Chapters 11 to 16 are particularly useful in describing DePuy's emphasis as TRADOC Commander on training, doctrine, and combat developments and how that emphasis paid off in the Persian Gulf War of 1991.

19. Thanks to Saul Bronfeld for allowing me to consult his manuscript "Fighting Outnumbered: The Impact of the Yom Kippur War on the U.S. Army," later published in *Journal of Military History* 71, no. 2 (April 2007): 465–498. He stresses the use of that war by DePuy and other American generals as leverage to get resources for the U.S. Army.

20. DePuy, OH, MHI, "1985 Afterthoughts." In a personal correspondence to Gole dated 4 December 2006, Israeli scholar Saul Bronfeld compares Moshe Dayan's efforts after the 1948 Israeli War of Independence to DePuy's post–Vietnam War efforts. He says that an army's rehabilitation—getting it out of a moral and professional funk—can begin even with an imperfect doctrine (Active Defense for the Americans and relying too heavily upon infantry for the Israelis).

21. The quotations here and in the following paragraphs are from DePuy, OH, MHI, "1985 Afterthoughts."

22. DePuy Papers, MHI; DePuy Family Papers.

23 Paul H. Herbert, *Deciding What Has to Be Done: General William E. DePuy and the 1976 Edition of FM 100–5: Operations,* Leavenworth Papers no. 16 (Fort Leavenworth, Kans.: U.S. Army Command and General Staff College, Combat Studies Institute, 1988), 1.

24. In addition to Paul Herbert's account of the writing of the 1976 version of FM 100–5, see also Max Thurman's OH, MHI, and several interviews: Paul F. Gorman with Gole, 8 October 2004; Donn A. Starry with Gole, 10 February 2005; David Meade with Gole, 28 January 2005; Samuel D. Wilder Jr. with Gole, 13 April 2005; Tony Pokorny with Gole, 2 February 2005; Romie L. (Les) Brownlee with Gole, 3 March 2005; and DePuy, interview with Michael Pearlman, 23 September 1986. For Cushman's account of his differences with DePuy, see John H. Cushman, *Fort Leavenworth: A Memoir, September 2001,* 2 vols., MHI. He sums up, "We never quite connected" (47).

25. TWX Starry to MG Latham, Cmdt U.S.AIS Ft Benning, Subject: 71–1, dtg 241400Z Nov 75, DePuy Family Papers.

26. Thanks to Paul Herbert for showing me this letter, in which DePuy offered his initial response to what became Herbert's Leavenworth Paper Number 16.

27. See Gorman, interview with Gole, 8 October 2004, for both stories.

28. DePuy with Michael Pearlman, three interviews: 23 September

1986, 15 January 1987, and 16 May 1987. DePuy Papers, MHI. Important to any discussion of doctrine is the introduction of the operational level of war to the U.S. Army in the 1970s and 1980s. See Robert A. Doughty, *The Evolution of U.S. Army Tactical Doctrine, 1946–76*, Leavenworth Papers (Fort Leavenworth, Kans.: U.S. Army Command and General Staff College, August 1979). See also Clayton R. Newell and Michael D. Krause, general eds., *On Operational Art* (Washington, D.C.: Center of Military History, United States Army, 1994).

29. Handwritten note by DePuy on the reverse of the typed "Introductory Statement of General DePuy" and on an added sheet to the 23 September 1986 interview with Michael Pearlman. DePuy Papers, MHI.

30. The Romjue mentioned is TRADOC historian John L. Romjue.

31. DePuy, interview with Pearlman, 23 September 1986. See also both DePuy Papers, MHI, and DePuy Family Papers for DA Form 1614, a consolidated list of twenty-two letters exchanged between TRADOC (DePuy) and the senior officers of the German Army in 1976. See also, in the same sources, DA Form 1614, listing nine letters exchanged by DePuy and the Israeli military in 1976. The point is that DePuy was personally and deeply involved in the cooperation with the Germans and Israelis after the Yom Kippur War of 1973.

32. See Starry, "Reflections," in Hofmann and Starry, eds., *Camp Colt*, 552.

33. DePuy, interview with Pearlman, 23 September 1986.

34. See Huba Wass de Czege, "Lessons from the Past: Making the Army's Doctrine 'Right Enough' Today." Landpower Essay No. 06–2, an Institute of Land Warfare Publication (Association of the United States Army, September 2006). De Czega traces the evolution of doctrine from the 1976 version of FM 100–5 through the 1982 and 1986 versions, noting that the 1976 version "provoked rigorous thinking," which prompted the next revisions. He says that Generals DePuy and Starry were "sufficiently blessed with military genius" to recruit, educate, and harness minds they respected "and were willing to immerse themselves in the work."

35. Quotations and paraphrasing of Pokorny are from Tony Pokorny, interview with Gole, 22 February 2005.

36. Jack and Patty Woodmansee, interview with Gole, 9 January 2005.

37. Samuel D. Wilder Jr., interview with Gole, 13 April 2005. Wilder was DePuy's aide in his first year at TRADOC, served in Gorman's Concepts Branch, and then headed up the Tactical Doctrine Office, also known as the "Boathouse Gang," whose mission was to review the "How to Fight" manuals.

38. Thomas W. Sweeney, interview with Gole, 29 April 2005.

39. DePuy, interview with Paul Herbert, June 1984. For samples of DePuy's own directness, see a DePuy letter of 24 March 1975 to his Training Center Commanders, in which he wrote, "You must insure that nothing which is silly, ridiculous, illogical, superfluous, or otherwise unproductive takes place during training." A 4 October 1976 letter from DePuy to LTG Camm sent Camm to Fort Benning to investigate management and leadership, saying of Fort Benning, "it is my opinion that it's the most bureaucratic and rigidly run of all the TRADOC schools." His correspondence with his commandants is replete with such directness. See DePuy Papers, MHI.

40. DePuy, letter to Stilwell, 10 May 1973, DePuy Papers, MHI. See also DePuy's emotionally powerful tribute to George Bittman Barth (MG, USA, Ret.), his World War II regimental commander, in *Assembly,* Summer 1970: 121–122.

41. DePuy, letter to LTG Orwin C. Talbott, 29 August 1975, DePuy Papers, MHI.

42. Sidney B. Berry Jr., interview with Gole, 8 April 2005.

16. Retirement, Illness, Taps

1. Tony Pokorny, interview with Gole, 22 February 2005.

2. Quotations and paraphrasing of the DePuy children in this chapter are from interviews with Gole as follows: Joslin DePuy Gallatin, 25 January 2005; Bill DePuy Jr., 21 October 2004 and 12 September 2007; and Daphne DePuy, 16 January 2005.

3. Harrison Symmes, e-mail to Gole, 11 February 2005, with attached "Recollections of Bill DePuy."

4. William E. DePuy, "Generals Balck and von Mellenthin on Tactics: Implications for NATO Military Doctrine," BDM/W-81–077-TR. Contract No. DNA001–78-C-0114. (McLean, Va.: BDM Corp., 1980).

5. The three articles in *Army:* "Eleven Men, One Mind," March 1958; "The Case for a Dual Capability," January 1960; "Unification: How Much More?" April 1961. They are reprinted in *Selected Papers of General William E. DePuy: First Commander, U.S. Army Training and Doctrine Command, 1 July 1973,* Richard M. Swain, comp. (Fort Leavenworth, Kans.: U.S. Army Command and General Staff College, Combat Studies Institute, 1994).

6. *Selected Papers of General William E. DePuy,* comp. Swain.

7. Details of publication for the published articles are found in the body of this chapter; all twelve articles are reprinted in the Swain compilation, *Selected Papers.*

8. E-mail, Swain to Gole, 23 August 2006 for "legacy"; Swain to Gole, 24 August 2006, for "control over chance." See also Richard Swain,

"Lucky War": Third Army in Desert Storm (Fort Leavenworth, Kans.: U.S. Army CGSC Press, 1994). In an exchange with the author regarding DePuy as an elitist, Swain wrote: "He was a great man and he acted great—and overbearing. Those who knew him well in the Army were a small circle of the favored, selected on the basis of performance, but something of a court, nevertheless. So, in my view, calling him an elitist does not miss the essential DePuy. It captures him." E-mail, Swain to Gole, 1 September 2006.

9. Barrie Zais, interview with Gole, 15 December 2004.

10. E-mail, Sinnreich to Gole, 20 December 2004.

11. E-mail, Richard Swain to Gole, 20 August 2006.

12. Gorman, interview with Gole, 8 October 2004.

13. Burns, interview with Gole, 25 October 2004; Geary, interview with Gole, 10 January 2005.

14. Symmes, e-mail to Gole, 11 February 2005.

15. Brownlee, interview with Gole, 3 March 2005.

16. Woodmansee, interview with Gole, 9 January 2005.

17. Joulwan, interview with Gole, 10 November 2004.

18. Pokorny, interview with Gole, 22 February 2005.

19. See MedlinePlus Medical Encyclopedia, Creutzfeldt-Jacob disease, www.nlm.nih.gov/medlineplus/ency/article/000788.htm.

17. Legacy

The letter quoted in the epigraph is found in the DePuy Family Papers. The book dedication reads: "To the Memory of GENERAL WILLIAM E. DEPUY, U.S. ARMY. 'He led the way in breaking the mold by creating an Army trained and ready to win its first battles quickly, decisively, and with minimum casualties.'" See James F. Dunnigan and Raymond M. Macedonia, *GETTING IT RIGHT: American Military Reforms after Vietnam to the Gulf War and Beyond* (New York: William Morrow and Co., 1993). The epigraph by Richard Swain is from Swain, "AirLand Battle," in George F. Hofmann and Donn A. Starry, eds., *Camp Colt to Desert Storm: The History of U.S. Armored Forces* (Lexington: University Press of Kentucky, 1999), 377. Swain says that the doctrinal debate can be seen as DePuy's thesis in the 1976 doctrine, the antithesis of his critics, and the synthesis: the 1986 version of FM 100–5.

1. President George H. W. Bush, 1 March 1991, cited in Harry G. Summers Jr., *On Strategy II: A Critical Analysis of the Gulf War* (New York: Bantam Books, 1995), 7. Summers gives full credit to political authority for assigning the military a clear mission, for allowing the soldiers to do the job, and for terminating hostilities when the political purpose was achieved.

2. Paul Gorman, *The Secret of Future Victories* (Fort Leavenworth, Kans.: United States Army Command and General Staff College, Combat Studies Institute, 1972), Abstract. Richard Swain would reduce Gorman's troika of master trainers to a pair, Marshall and DePuy, saying, "I think he was a great man. I'd put him and Marshall side by side and leave out McNair." E-mail, Swain to Gole, 1 September 2006.

3. Donn A. Starry, interview with Gole, 10 February 2005.

4. The inscribed book is in the DePuy Family Papers. Summers, a professional soldier, became famous for *On Strategy,* his analysis of the U.S. war in Vietnam, published in 1982.

5. James Kitfield, *Prodigal Soldiers: How the Generation of Officers Born of Vietnam Revolutionized the American Style of War* (New York: Simon and Schuster, 1995), 317.

6. To this discussion of protégés must be added that many of the people associated with DePuy—as with any senior officer—were serving on high-level staffs or in command when he found them, so they had already been identified as candidates for high positions in the Army. His "young tigers" at the Pentagon and the "Boathouse Gang" at TRADOC had shown promise before DePuy "discovered" them. They all had high praise for him, including three who were SACEUR and two who were Secretary of State. It should also be noted that the list of leaders provided here is not intended to be comprehensive.

7. For a concise discussion of the evolution of a doctrine of war on land from 1973, the year TRADOC was established and the year of the Yom Kippur War, to 1986, the year doctrine was codified, see Hofmann and Starry, *Camp Colt,* especially the essay by Swain. See also Huba Wass de Czege's essay "Lesson from the Past: Making the Army's Doctrine 'Right Enough' Today," Landpower Essay No. 06–2 (Association of the United States Army, Institute of Land Warfare, September 2006). Tracing the post-Vietnam evolution of doctrine, Wass de Czege says, "The genius of DePuy was to recognize that if the Army failed to get the tactics of the First Battle right, then all else was secondary" (5). He adds, "Generals DePuy and Starry . . . were sufficiently blessed with military genius, recruited, educated and harnessed the minds they respected, considered doctrinal reforms of paramount importance and were willing to immerse themselves in the work" (15).

8. Sam Wilder, who served as DePuy's aide at TRADOC, then in Gorman's Concepts Branch, and then as a member of the "Boathouse Gang," pointed out that in testimony at a congressional hearing after Desert Storm, Barry McCaffrey (GEN, USA, Ret.) said that we didn't win the Gulf War in fifteen days; it took fifteen years. Those fifteen years began with General Bill DePuy. Wilder, interview with Gole, 13 April 2005.

9. See Neal Creighton, "The Legacy of a Leader," *Chicago Tribune*, 5 October 1992. Creighton, a retired major general and president of the Robert R. McCormick Trust and Foundation at the time, asked, "What was it about Bill DePuy that allowed him to lead the Army out of its worst days?" His answer: DePuy's quick mind and self-confidence stand out; but, added Creighton, "he had an amazing ability to get things done," to make the Pentagon bureaucracy work. "He could charm congressional committees or visiting politicians. Other generals were reluctant to oppose him, for they knew the power of his intellect. He developed a cadre of talented officers."

Selected Bibliography

Books, Documents, and Pamphlets

Abrami, Joe I. *A History of the 90th Division in World War II, 6 June 1944 to 9 May 1945*. Baton Rouge: Army Navy Publishing Co., 1946.

Aldrich, Richard J. *The Hidden Hand: Britain, America, and Cold War Secret Intelligence*. Woodstock, N.Y.: Overlook Press, 2001.

Ambrose, Stephen E. *Citizen Soldiers: The U.S. Army from the Normandy Beaches to the Bulge to the Surrender of Germany, June 7, 1944–May 7, 1945*. New York: Simon and Schuster, 1997.

———. *D-Day, June 6, 1944: The Climactic Battle of World War II*. New York: Simon and Schuster, 1995.

———. *Eisenhower*. 2 v. New York: Simon and Schuster, 1983.

Anderson, David L. *Facing Mylai: Moving beyond the Massacre*. Lawrence: University Press of Kansas, 1998.

Atkinson, Rick. *An Army at Dawn: The War in North Africa, 1942–1943*. New York: Henry Holt and Co., 2002.

Bacevich, A. J. *The Pentomic Era: The U.S. Army between Korea and Vietnam*. Washington, D.C.: National Defense University Press, 1986.

Badsey, Stephen. *Utah Beach*. Battle Zone Normandy Series. Phoenix Mill, U.K.: Sutton Publishing, 2004.

Bainbridge, William G., and Dan Cragg. *Top Sergeant: The Life and Times of Sergeant Major of the Army William G. Bainbridge*. New York: Ballantine Books, 1995.

Beckwith, Charlie A., and Donald Knox. *Delta Force*. San Diego: Harcourt Brace Jovanovich, 1983.

Bellamy, Chris. *The Future of Land Warfare*. London: Croom Helm, 1987.

Bergen, John D. *Military Communications: A Test for Technology*. United States Army in Vietnam Series. Washington, D.C.: United States Army Center of Military History, 1985.

Blair, Anne. *There to the Bitter End: Ted Serong in Vietnam*. Crows Nest, Australia: Allen and Unwin, 2001.

Blue Spaders: The 26th Infantry Regiment, 1917–1967. Cantigny Military History Series. Wheaton, Ill.: Cantigny First Division Foundation, 1996.

Blumenson, Martin. *The Battle of the Generals: The Untold Story of the Falaise Pocket: The Campaign That Should Have Won World War II*. New York: Morrow, 1993.

————. *Breakout and Pursuit*. United States Army in World War II: The European Theater of Operations. Washington, D.C.: Office of the Chief of Military History, Department of the Army, 1961.

Bolger, Daniel P. *Death Ground: Today's American Infantry in Battle*. Novato, Calif.: Presidio Press, 2000.

Bradford, Zeb B., Jr., and Frederic J. Brown. *The United States Army in Transition*. Beverly Hills, Calif.: Sage Publications, 1973.

Bradley, Omar. *A General's Life: An Autobiography*. New York: Simon and Schuster, 1983.

————. *A Soldier's Story*. New York: Henry Holt and Co., 1951.

Brokaw, Tom. *A Long Way from Home: Growing Up in the American Heartland in the Forties and Fifties*. New York: Random House, 2002.

Brown, James, and Michael J. Collins, eds. *Military Ethics and Professionalism: A Collection of Essays*. Washington, D.C.: National Defense University Press, 1981.

Brown, John Sloan. *Draftee Division: The 88th Infantry Division in World War II*. Lexington: University Press of Kentucky, 1986.

Buzzanco, Robert. *Masters of War: Military Dissent and Politics in the Vietnam Era*. Cambridge, U.K.: Cambridge University Press, 1997.

Carland, John M. *Combat Operations: Stemming the Tide, May 1965 to October 1966*. United States Army in Vietnam Series. Washington, D.C.: Center of Military History, United States Army, 1988.

Chapman, Anne W. *The Army's Training Revolution, 1973–1990: An Overview*. Fort Monroe, Va.: TRADOC Historical Studies Series. Office of the Command Historian. United States Army Training and Doctrine Command, 1991.

————. *The National Training Center Matures, 1985–1993*. Fort Monroe, Va.: Military History Office, United States Army Training and Doctrine Command, 1997.

————. *The Origins and Development of the National Training Center, 1976–1984*. Fort Monroe, Va.: TRADOC Historical Monograph Series. Office of the Command Historian. United States Army Training and Doctrine Command, 1992.

Citino, Robert M. *Blitzkrieg to Desert Storm: The Evolution of Operational Warfare*. Lawrence: University Press of Kansas, 2004.

Clarke, Jeffrey J. *Advice and Support: The Final Years, 1965–1973*. United States Army in Vietnam Series. Washington, D.C.: United States Army Center of Military History, 1988.

Coffman, Edward M. *The Regulars: The American Army*. Cambridge, Mass.: The Belknap Press of Harvard University Press, 2004.

Colby, John. *War from the Ground Up: The 90th Division in World War II*. Austin, Tex.: Nortex Press, 1991.

Cole, Hugh M. *The Ardennes: Battle of the Bulge*. United States Army in

World War II: The European Theater of Operations Series. Washington, D.C.: Center of Military History, United States Army, 1993 (first printed 1965).

———. *The Lorraine Campaign.* United States Army in World War II: The European Theater of Operations Series. Washington, D.C.: United States Army Historical Division, 1950 (reprinted 1981).

Conboy, Kenneth, and Dale Andradé. *Spies and Commandos: How America Lost the Secret War in North Vietnam.* Lawrence: University Press of Kansas, 2000.

Cronkite, Walter. *A Reporter's Life.* New York: Alfred A. Knopf, 1996.

Davidson, Philip B. *Vietnam at War: The History, 1946–1975.* Novato, Calif.: Presidio Press, 1988.

DePuy, William E. *Changing an Army: An Oral History of General W. E. DePuy, USA Retired* by Romie L. Brownlee and William J. Mullen III. Carlisle Barracks, Pa.: U.S. Army Military History Institute [1979].

———. "Generals Balck and von Mellenthin on Tactics: Implications for NATO Military Doctrine." McLean, Va.: BDM Corp., 1980.

———. *Selected Papers of General William E. DePuy: First Commander, U.S. Army Training and Doctrine Command, 1 July 1973.* Richard M. Swain, comp. Fort Leavenworth, Kans.: U.S. Army Command and General Staff College, Combat Studies Institute, 1994.

Diem, Bui. *In the Jaws of History.* Bloomington: Indiana University Press, 1999.

Dobrynin, Anatoly. *In Confidence.* New York: Times Books, 1995.

Doubler, Michael D. *Closing with the Enemy: How GIs Fought the War in Europe, 1944–1945.* Lawrence: University Press of Kansas, 1994.

Doughty, Robert A. *The Evolution of U.S. Army Tactical Doctrine, 1946–76.* Leavenworth Papers. Fort Leavenworth, Kans.: U.S. Army Command and General Staff College, 1979.

Dunnigan, James F., and Raymond M. Macedonia. *Getting It Right: American Reforms after Vietnam to the Persian Gulf and Beyond.* New York: William Morrow and Co., 1993.

Ebert, James R. *A Life in a Year: The American Infantryman in Vietnam, 1965–1972.* New York: Ballantine Books, 2004.

Fisher, Ernest F., Jr. *Guardians of the Republic: A History of the Noncommissioned Officer Corps of the U.S. Army.* New York: Ballantine Books, 1994.

Fulton, William B. *Riverine Operations, 1966–1969.* Vietnam Studies Series. Washington, D.C.: Department of the Army, 1973.

Fussell, Paul. *The Boys' Crusade: The American Infantry in Northwestern Europe, 1944–1945.* New York: Modern Library, 2003.

Gavin, James M. *War and Peace in the Space Age.* New York: Harper, 1958.

Gibbons, William Conrad. *The U.S. Government and the Vietnam War: Executive and Legislative Roles and Relationships, Part III, January–July 1965*. Prepared for the Committee on Foreign Relations, United States Senate, by the Congressional Research Service, Library of Congress. Washington, D.C.: U.S. Government Printing Office, December 1988.

———. *The U.S. Government and the Vietnam War: Executive and Legislative Roles and Relationships, Part IV, July 1965–January 1968*. Princeton, N.J.: Princeton University Press, 1995.

Gordon, Don E. *Electronic Warfare: Element of Strategy and Multiplier of Combat Power*. New York: Pergamon Press, 1981.

Gorman, Paul. *The Secret of Future Victories*. Fort Leavenworth, Kans.: United States Army Command and General Staff College, Combat Studies Institute, 1992.

Greenfield, Kent Roberts, Robert R. Palmer, and Bell I. Wiley. *The Organization of Ground Combat Troops*. Washington, D.C.: Historical Division, Department of the Army, 1947.

Hackworth, David H., and Julie Sherman. *About Face*. New York: Simon and Schuster, 1989.

Hadley, Arthur T. *The Straw Hat: Triumph and Failure: America's Armed Forces: A Report from the Field*. New York: Random House, 1986.

Haig, Alexander, M., Jr. *Inner Circles: How America Changed the World: A Memoir*. New York: Warner Books, 1992.

Halberstam, David. *The Best and the Brightest*. New York: Random House, 1972.

Hammond, William H. *Public Affairs: The Military and the Media, 1962–1968*. United States Army in Vietnam Series. Washington, D.C.: United States Army Center of Military History, 1988.

Hart, Russell A. *Clash of Arms: How the Allies Won in Normandy*. Boulder, Colo.: Lynne Rienner Publishers, 2001.

Heiser, Joseph M., Jr. *A Soldier Supporting Soldiers*. Washington, D.C.: United States Army Center of Military History, 1991.

Herbert, Paul H. *Deciding What Has to Be Done: General William E. DePuy and the 1976 Edition of FM 100–5: Operations*. Leavenworth Papers No. 16. Fort Leavenworth, Kans.: U.S. Army Command and General Staff College, Combat Studies Institute, 1988.

Hickey, Gerald C. *Window on a War: An Anthropologist in the Vietnam Conflict*. Lubbock: Texas Tech University Press, 2002.

Hofmann, George F., and Donn A. Starry, eds. *Camp Colt to Desert Storm: The History of U.S. Armored Forces*. Lexington: University Press of Kentucky, 1999.

Holober, Frank. *Raiders of the China Coast: CIA Covert Operations during the Korean War*. Annapolis, Md.: Naval Institute Press, 1999.

Huntington, Samuel P. *The Soldier and the State.* New York: Vantage Books, a division of Random House, 1957.

In Tribute to General William E. DePuy: Remarks by General Maxwell R. Thurman, Lieutenant General Orwin C. Talbott, General Paul F. Gorman. Remarks read at General DePuy's memorial service at Fort McNair, Washington, D.C., 16 September 1992. Fort Leavenworth, Kans.: United States Army Command and General Staff College, Combat Studies Institute, 1992.

Isaacson, Walter, and Evan Thomas. *The Wise Men: Six Friends and the World They Made: Acheson, Bohlen, Harriman, Kennan, Lovett, McCloy.* New York: Simon and Schuster, 1986.

Johnson, Haynes, George C. Wilson, Peter A. Jay, and Peter Osnos. *Army in Anguish.* Washington Post National Report. New York: Pocket Books, 1972.

Just, Ward. *To What End.* New York: Public Affairs, 2000.

Kahn, Ely Jacques. *McNair, Educator of an Army.* Washington, D.C.: Infantry Journal, 1945.

Kelly, Orr. *King of the Killing Zone.* New York: W. W. Norton, 1989.

King, Edward L. *The Death of the Army: A Pre-Mortem.* New York: Saturday Review Press, 1972.

Kinnard, Douglas. *The War Managers.* Hanover, N.H.: University Press of New England, 1977.

Kitfield, James. *Prodigal Soldiers.* New York: Simon and Schuster, 1995.

Kreidberg, Marvin A., and Merton G. Henry. *History of Military Mobilization in the United States Army, 1775–1945.* Department of the Army Pamphlet No. 20-212. Washington, D.C.: Department of the Army, 1955.

Krepinevich, Andrew F., Jr. *The Army and Vietnam.* Baltimore: Johns Hopkins University Press, 1986.

Lanning, Michael Lee, and Dan Cragg. *Inside the VC and the NVA: The Real Story of North Vietnam's Armed Forces.* New York: Ballantine Books, 1992.

Leinbaugh, Harold P., and John D. Campbell. *The Men of Company K: The Autobiography of a World War II Rifle Company.* New York: William Morrow and Co., 1985.

Leonhard, Robert R. *The Art of Maneuver: Maneuver-Warfare Theory and Airland Battle.* Novato, Calif.: Presidio Press, 1994.

London, Herbert I. *Military Doctrine and the American Character: Reflections on Airland Battle.* New York: National Strategy Information Center, 1984.

MacDonald, Charles B. *Company Commander.* New York: Bantam Books, 1982.

———. *The Last Offensive.* United States Army in World War II: The European Theater of Operations Series. Washington, D.C.: Office of the Chief of Military History, 1973.

———. *The Siegfried Line Campaign*. United States Army in World War II: The European Theater of Operations Series. Washington, D.C.: Office of the Chief of Military History, 1963.

MacGarrigle, George L. *Combat Operations: Taking the Offensive, October 1966 to October 1967*. United States Army in Vietnam Series. Washington, D.C.: Center of Military History, United States Army, 1998.

Maclear, Michael. *The Ten Thousand Day War: Vietnam: 1945–1975*. New York: St. Martin's Press, 1981.

Manchester, William. *American Caesar: Douglas MacArthur, 1880–1964*. Boston: Little, Brown and Co., 1978.

Mangold, Tom, and John Penycate. *The Tunnels of Cuchi*. New York: Random House, 1985.

Mansoor, Peter R. *The GI Offensive in Europe*. Lawrence: University Press of Kansas, 1999.

Marshall, S. L. A. *Men against Fire: The Problem of Battle Command in Future War*. Gloucester, Mass.: Peter Smith, 1978.

Maurer, Harry. *Strange Ground: An Oral History of Americans in Vietnam, 1945–1975*. New York: Avon Books, 1990.

McCoy, Alfred W. *The Politics of Heroin: CIA Complicity in the Global Drug Trade*. Brooklyn, N.Y.: Lawrence Hill Books, 1991.

McMaster, H. R. *Dereliction of Duty: Lyndon Johnson, Robert McNamara, the Joint Chiefs of Staff, and the Lies that Led to Vietnam*. New York: HarperCollins, 1997.

McNamara, Robert S. *In Retrospect: The Tragedy and Lessons of Vietnam*. New York: Vintage Books, 1996.

Merry, Robert W. *Taking on the World: Joseph and Stewart Alsop, Guardians of the American Century*. New York: Penguin Books, 1996.

Moïse, Edwin. *Tonkin Gulf and the Escalation of the Vietnam War*. Chapel Hill: University of North Carolina Press, 1996.

Moore, Robert E. *Upstarts*. Self-published, 1995.

Moyar, Mark. *Triumph Forsaken: The Vietnam War, 1954–1965*. New York: Cambridge University Press, 2006.

Newell, Clayton R., and Michael D. Krause, general eds. *On Operational Art*. Washington, D.C.: Center of Military History, United States Army, 1994.

Oberdorfer, Don. *Tet! The Turning Point in the Vietnam War*. Baltimore: Johns Hopkins University Press, 2001.

O'Brien, Tim. *In the Lake of the Woods*. New York: Penguin Books, 1995.

O'Toole, G. J. A. *Honorable Treachery: A History of U.S. Intelligence, Espionage, and Covert Action from the American Revolution to the CIA*. New York: Atlantic Monthly Press, 1991.

Palmer, Bruce, Jr. *The Twenty-Five-Year War: America's Military Role in Vietnam.* Lexington: University Press of Kentucky, 1984.

Palmer, Robert R., Wiley I. Bell, and William R. Keast. *The Procurement and Training of Ground Combat Troops.* Washington, D.C.: Historical Division, Department of the Army, 1948.

Perry, Mark. *Four Stars.* Boston: Houghton Mifflin Co., 1989.

Powell, Colin L., with Joseph E. Persico. *My American Journey.* New York: Random House, 1995.

Prados, John. *Presidents' Secret Wars: CIA and Pentagon Covert Operations from World War II through the Persian Gulf.* Rev. and expanded ed. Chicago: Ivan R. Dee, 1996.

———. *Safe for Democracy: The Secret Wars of the CIA.* Chicago: Ivan R. Dee, 2006.

Puckett, David H. *Memories.* New York: Vantage Press, 1987.

Rickard, John Nelson. *Patton at Bay: The Lorraine Campaign, 1944.* Washington, D.C.: Brassey's, 2004.

Ridgway, Matthew B., as told to Harold H. Martin. *Soldier: The Memoir of Matthew B. Ridgway.* New York: Harper and Brothers, 1956.

Rogers, Bernard William. *Cedar Falls–Junction City: A Turning Point.* Vietnam Studies Series. Washington, D.C.: Department of the Army, 1989.

Rölvaag, O. E. *Giants in the Earth.* New York: Harper and Brothers, 1929.

Romjue, John L. *The Army of Excellence: The Development of the 1980s Army.* TRADOC Historical Monograph Series. Fort Monroe, Va.: United States Army Training and Doctrine Command, Office of the Command Historian, 1993.

Romjue, John L., Susan Canedy, and Anne W. Chapman. *Prepare the Army for War: A Historical Overview of the Army Training and Doctrine Command, 1973–1993.* TRADOC Historical Study Series. Fort Monroe, Va.: United States Army Training and Doctrine Command, Office of the Command Historian, 1993.

Romjue, John L., Anne W. Chapman, Carol J. Lilly, and Susan Canedy. *Prepare the Army for War: A Historical Overview of the Army Training and Doctrine Command, 1973–1998.* TRADOC Historical Study Series. Fort Monroe, Va.: United States Army Training and Doctrine Command, 1998.

Rose, John P. *The Evolution of U.S. Army Nuclear Doctrine, 1945–1980.* Westview Replica ed. Boulder, Colo.: Westview Press, 1980.

Scales, Robert, Jr. *Certain Victory: The U.S. Army in the Gulf War: The Desert Storm Study Project.* Washington, D.C.: Brassey's, 1997.

———. *Firepower in Limited War.* Rev. ed. Novato, Calif.: Presidio Press, 1995.

———— *Yellow Smoke: The Future of Land Warfare for America's Military.* Lanham, Md.: Rowman and Littlefield, 2003.

Sharp, U. S. G., and William C. Westmoreland. *Report on the War in Vietnam (as of 30 June 1968).* Washington, D.C.: U.S. Government Printing Office, 1968.

Sheehan, Neil. *A Bright Shining Lie: John Paul Vann and America in Vietnam.* New York: Vintage Books, 1969.

Shelton, James. *The Beast Was Out There: The 28th Infantry Black Lions and the Battle of Ông Thanh Vietnam, October 1967.* Cantigny Military History Series. Chicago: Cantigny First Division Foundation, 2002.

Shultz, Richard H., Jr. *The Secret War against Hanoi: Kennedy's and Johnson's Use of Spies, Saboteurs, and Covert Warriors in North Vietnam.* New York: HarperCollins, 1999.

Singlaub, John K. *Hazardous Duty: An American Soldier in the Twentieth Century.* New York: Summit Books, 1991.

Sorley, Lewis. *A Better War: The Unexamined Victories and Final Tragedy of America's Last Year in Vietnam.* New York: Harcourt Brace and Co., 1999.

————. *Honorable Warrior: General Harold K. Johnson and the Ethics of Command.* Lawrence: University Press of Kansas, 1998.

————. *Thunderbolt: General Creighton Abrams and the Army of His Times.* New York: Simon and Schuster, 1992.

South Dakota State University. *Ninety-first Annual Commencement [Program], May 7, 1977.* Brookings: South Dakota State University, 1977.

Spiller, J., ed. *Combined Army in Battle since 1939.* Fort Leavenworth, Kans.: U.S. Army Command and General Staff College Press, 1992.

Stanton, Shelby L. *The Rise and Fall of an American Army: U.S. Ground Forces in Vietnam, 1965–1973.* Novato, Calif.: Presidio Press, 1985.

Starry, Donn A. *Mounted Combat in Vietnam.* Vietnam Series. Washington, D.C.: Department of the Army, 1978.

Stroud, Carsten, *Iron Bravo: Hearts, Minds, and Sergeants in the U.S. Army.* New York: Bantam Books, 1978.

Study on Military Professionalism. Carlisle Barracks, Pa.: United States Army War College, 30 June 1970.

Sullivan, Gordon R., and Michael V. Harper. *Hope Is Not a Method: What Business Leaders Can Learn from America's Army.* New York: Times Books, 1996.

Summers, Harry G., Jr. *On Strategy II: A Critical Analysis of the Gulf War.* New York: Bantam Books, 1995.

Taylor, Maxwell D. *The Uncertain Trumpet.* New York: Harper and Brothers, 1959.

Tolson, John J. *Airmobility, 1961–1971.* Vietnam Studies. Washington, D.C.: Department of the Army, 1973.

United States Army Training and Doctrine Command. *Twentieth Anniversary Ceremony: Where Tomorrow's Victories Begin: TRADOC, 1973–1993.* Fort Monroe, Va.: United States Army Training and Doctrine Command, 1993.

United States Army, 1st Infantry Division. *DePuy Hall: Dedicated to the Memory of William E. DePuy, General, United States Army, 1919–1992: Battle Simulation Center, 26 September, 1997.* Fort Riley, Kans.: [United States Army, 1st Infantry Division], 1997.

United States. Congressional Record. *"The Death of General William E. DePuy."* 102nd Cong., 2nd sess., S13640-S13644. 16 September 1992. Washington, D.C.: U.S. Government Printing Office, 1992.

United States. House of Representatives. Committee on Armed Services. *Crisis in the Persian Gulf: Sanctions, Diplomacy, and War: Hearings before the Committee on Armed Services, House of Representatives, 101st Congress, 2nd sess.* Hearings held December 4, 5, 12, 13, 14, 17, 19, and 20, 1990. Washington, D.C.: U.S. Government Printing Office, 1990.

Van Creveld, Martin. *Fighting Power.* London: Arms and Armour Press, 1983.

Volkman, Ernest, and Blaine Baggett. *Secret Intelligence.* New York: Doubleday, 1989.

Von Schell, Adolf. *Battle Leadership.* Fort Benning, Ga.: The Benning Herald, 1933.

Wadell, Steve R. *United States Army Logistics: The Normandy Campaign, 1944.* Westport, Conn.: Greenwood Press, 1994.

Walker, Paul D. *Jungle Dragoon: The Memoir of an Armored Cav Platoon Leader in Vietnam.* Novato, Calif.: Presidio Press, 1999.

Weigley, Russell F. *Eisenhower's Lieutenants.* Bloomington: Indiana University Press, 1981.

Westmoreland, William C. *A Soldier Reports.* Garden City, N.Y.: Doubleday and Co., 1976.

Wheeler, James Scott. *The Big Red One.* Lawrence: University Press of Kansas, 2007.

Whiting, Charles. *Siegfried: The Nazis' Last Stand.* New York: Stein and Day, 1982.

Wiley, Bell Irvin. *Training in the Ground Army, 1942–1945.* Washington, D.C.: Historical Section, Army Ground Forces, 1948.

Willenson, Kim. *The Bad War: An Oral History of the Vietnam War.* New York: New American Library, 1987.

Williams, F. D. G. *Slam: The Influence of S. L. A. Marshall on the United States Army.* Edited and introduced by Susan Canedy. TRADOC

Historical Monograph Series. Fort Monroe, Va.: United States Army Training and Doctrine Command, Office of the Command Historian, 1990.

Wilson, George C. *Mud Soldiers: Life inside the New American Army.* New York: Charles Scribner's Sons, 1989.

Woodward, Bob. *The Commanders.* New York: Simon and Schuster, 1991.

Articles

Creighton, Neal. "The Legacy of a Leader." *Chicago Tribune.* 5 October 1992.

DePuy, William E. "Are We Ready for the Future?" *Army* 28 (September 1978): 22–29.

DePuy, William E. "Armor Conference [1977]: Keynote Address." *Armor* 86 (July–August 1977): 31–35.

———. "Battle Participation and Leadership." *Military Review* 69 (July 1989): 96–98.

———. "The Case for a Dual Capability." *Army* 10 (January 1960): 32–40.

———. "Concept of Operation: The Heart of Command, the Tool of Doctrine." *Army* 38 (August 1988): 26–40.

———. "Eleven Men, One Mind." *Army* 8 (March 1958): 22–24, 54–60.

———. "FM 100–5 Revisited." *Army* 30 (November 1980): 12–17.

———. "For the Joint Specialist: Five Steep Hills to Climb." *Parameters* 19 (Fall 1989): 2–12.

———. "Infantry Combat." *Infantry* 80 (March–April): 8–13.

———. "The Light Infantry: Indispensable Element of a Balanced Force." *Army* 35 (June 1985): 26–41.

———. "One-Up and Two-Back?" *Army* 30 (January 1980): 20–25.

———. "Our Experience in Vietnam: Will We Be Beneficiaries or Victims?" *Army* 37 (June 1987): 28–41.

———. "Technology and Tactics in Defense of Europe." *Army* 29 (April 1979): 14–23.

———. "Toward a Balanced Doctrine." *Army* 34 (November 1984): 18–25.

———. "Troop A at ApTau O." *Army* (November 1986): 50–60.

———. "Unification: How Much More?" *Army* 11 (April 1961): 30–38.

———. "Vietnam: What We Might Have Done and Why We Didn't Do It." *Army* 36 (February 1986): 22–40.

Doerfel, John S. "The Operational Art of the Airland Battle." *Military Review* 62 (May 1982): 3–10.

Dubik, James M. "FM 100–5: Comparing the Operational Concept and the Defense." *Military Review* 62 (December 1982): 13–19.

Goldich, Robert L. "The Siren Song of Mobile Warfare." *Army* 34 (May 1984): 22–29.

Jones, Archer. "FM 100–5: A View from the Ivory Tower." *Military Review* 64 (May 1984): 17–22.

———. "The New FM 100–5: A View from the Ivory Tower." *Military Review* 63 (February 1978): 27–36.

Ledbetter, Homer M. "Armored Assault across Europe." *Armor* 83 (September–October 1974): 12–15.

Lind, William S. "Some Doctrinal Questions for the United States Army," *Military Review* 57 (March 1977): 54–65.

Loomis, Dan G. "FM 100–5 Operations: A Review." *Military Review* 57 (March 1977): 66–69.

Oseth, John M. "FM 100–5 Revisited: A Need for Better 'Foundation Concepts'?" *Military Review* 60 (March 1980): 13–19.

Smoler, Fredric. "The Secret of the Soldiers Who Didn't Shoot." *Military Review* 69 (July 1989): 100–101. (Reprinted from *American Heritage*, March 1989.)

Spiller, Roger J. "S. L. A. Marshall and the Ratio of Fire." *Military Review* 69 (July 1989): 99–100. (Reprinted from *RUSI Journal*, Winter 1988.)

Starry, Donn A. "Extending the Battlefield." *Military Review* 61 (March 1981): 31–50.

———. "Portrait of a Contemporary Soldier." [Highlights General William E. DePuy's contributions to the Army.] *Military Review* 72 (August 1992): 11–13.

———. "The Principles of War." *Military Review* 61 (September 1981): 2–12.

———. "A Tactical Evolution: FM 100–5." *Military Review* 58 (August 1978): 2–11.

Tamminen, David L. "How to Defend Outnumbered and Win." *Armor* 86 (November–December 1975): 39–44.

Tate, Clyde J., and L. D. Holder. "New Doctrine for the Defense." *Military Review* 61 (March 1981): 2–9.

Wass de Czege, Huba. "Lessons from the Past: Making the Army's Doctrine 'Right Enough' Today." An Association of the United States Army Institute of Land Warfare Publication. Landpower Essay No. 06–2 (September 2006).

Wass de Czege, Huba, and L. D. Holder. "The New FM 100–5." *Military Review* 62 (July 1982): 53–70.

Weller, Jac. "Infantry and the October War: Foot Soldiers in the Desert." *Army* 24 (August 1974): 21–26.

Winton, Harold R. "Partnership and Tension: The Army and the Air Force between Vietnam and Desert Shield." *Parameters* 26 (Spring 1996): 100–119.

Case Studies

U.S. Army War College
Maladowitz, Raymond. "Office of the AVICE: Parkinson's Law or Progress?" 9 March 1970.
Martin, John R. "The Role and Progress of the Office, Assistant Vice Chief of Staff in the Management of Army Resources." 8 March 1971.

Unpublished Papers

"After Action Report: Operations 90th Infantry Division, 6 June 1944–8 May 1945." Headquarters 90th Infantry Division.
"A History of the 90th Division in World War II." Copyright 1964 by the 90th Infantry Division.
Barth, George Bittman. "Narrative: Operations of the 357th Infantry in the Vicinity of Beau Coudray and Le Plessis, France, July 5–13 1944."
"Company Commander in Vietnam."
Reischl, Timothy J. "A Few Hours in my Twenty Years: Reflections on Combat Operations in the Gulf War." 26 February 1993.
345th Field Artillery Battalion, 90th Infantry Division, Third U.S. Army. Printed by F. Bruckmann KG, Munich, Germany, 1946.

Other Sources

Interviews Conducted

Sidney B. Berry, Jr.; Frederic J. Brown III; Romie L. Brownlee; William B. Burdeshaw; William F. Burns; Richard G. Cavazos; Leon Crenshaw; Daphne DePuy; William E. DePuy, Jr.; John W. Foss; Joslin DePuy Gallatin; Wesley V. Geary; Robert J. Gerard; Paul F. Gorman; Edward Smith Hamilton; Paul H. Herbert; Betsy Holdhusen; James F. Hollingsworth; George Joulwan; Walter T. Kerwin; Charles F. Kriete; Frederick J. Kroesen; Hendrik Lunde; Lloyd J. Matthews; David Meade; Carroll S. Meek; Paul L. Miles; William J. Mullen III; Tony Pokorny; George P. Psihas; William R. Richardson; Richard Hart Sinnreich; Donn A. Starry; John P. Stewart; Thomas W. Sweeney; William G. T. Tuttle; Wayne M. Waltz; Samuel D. Wilder, Jr.; Jack Woodmansee; Patty Woodmansee; and Barrie E. Zais.
Letters and e-mail: Thomas E. Carpenter III; Woodbury Carter; Alexander M. Haig; James Holland; Richard Hooker; Colin Powell; George P. Psihas; Jeanne M. Rotz; Anthony Smith; William A. Stofft; and Harrison Symmes.

Interviews Consulted

Cantigny 1st Division Foundation
Rudy Egersdorfer, Paul F. Gorman, James F. Hollingsworth, Jim Madden, Orwin C. Talbott with John Votaw
Paul F. Gorman with Scott Wheeler

National Archives and Records Administration, Lyndon Baines Johnson Library
William E. DePuy with Ted Gittinger
William E. DePuy with Paul Herbert

U.S. Army Center for Military History, Unit 50
George P. Seneff, Jr.

U.S. Army Military History Institute
Oral Histories
Ferdinand J. Chesarek; Walter T. Kerwin; David E. Ott; Jonathan O. Seaman; Richard G. Stilwell; Maxwell R. Thurman; Volney F. Warner; William Childs Westmoreland; Frederick C. Weyand
The Abrams Story: James G. Kalergis; Bruce Palmer, Jr.; Donn A. Starry
DePuy Papers
William E. DePuy with Michael Pearlman

U.S. Army Training and Doctrine Command
William E. DePuy with Brooks Kleber, John L. Romjue, and Richard P. Weinert

Papers Consulted

Virginia Military Institute, George C. Marshall Foundation, George C. Marshall Library
James Alward Van Fleet Papers

U.S. Army Military History Institute
Jacob W. Bealke Papers
Frederic J. Brown III Papers
John H. Cushman. *Fort Leavenworth: A Memoir.* 2 vols. September 2001.
William E. DePuy Papers
William R. Richardson Papers
Donn A. Starry Papers
Maxwell R. Thurman Papers

Index

Military units are indexed as if spelled out; for example, *357th Infantry Regiment* is alphabetized as if printed as *Three Hundred Fifty-Seventh Infantry Regiment*.